Where are we Going and are we Nearly There Yet?

WHERE ARE WE GOING

AND ARE WE NEARLY THERE YET?

Global Dialogue and a New Enlightenment

Paul Hodson

Copyright © Paul Hodson 2024

The right of Paul Hodson to be identified as the author of this work has been asserted in accordance with the Copyright, Design and Patents Act 1988. All rights reserved. Except for the quotation of short passages for the purposes of criticism and review, no part of this publication may be reproduced, stored in a retrieval system, or transmitted, in any form or by any means, electronic, mechanical, photocopying, or recording or otherwise, without prior permission of the publisher.

First published by Arena Books in 2024
www.arenabooks.co.uk

Paul Hodson
Where are we Going and are we Nearly There Yet?

ISBN 978-1-914390-36-4 Paperback
ISBN 978-1-914390-37-1 Ebook

A CIP catalogue record for this book is available from the British Library.

Thema: NHB; JB; GTQ; KCY; GTM; JBCC9; JP; JPS; JPSL; QRAM2; RNT.

Cover design by Jelena Mirkovic

Contents

INTRODUCTION	1
I HUMAN NATURE, VIRTUES AND VICES	9
II INDIVIDUALISM, SOCIETY, CITIZENSHIP	21
Individualism and Civic Society	22
Western Secular Attitudes Now	23
A Global Perspective	28
Current Non-Secular Contributions	32
A Future for the Ancient Greeks or for Modern Liberalism?	36
Individual Morality	38
Real Life	42
Childhood and Education	43
Generational Divide	47
Partnership/Marriage, and Family	52
Parenting	58
Retirement and Old Age	61
Thinking	65
Understanding Thinking	66
Thinking About Ourselves	69
Citizenship	75
A Good Citizen	75
Global Citizenship	80

    Daily, and Democratic, Citizenship   83

III GOVERNMENT AND LEADERSHIP   91

Government We Recognise   92
    Government, and Human Nature, Nurture, and Character   92
    The Path to Modern Government in the West   98
    The Journeys to 'Democratic' Government Across the World   101

Contemporary Democracy   107
    The Challenges to Democracy: Interests   108
    Specific Challenges to Nations Around the World   114
    The Challenges to Democracy: Science and Technology   116
    Democratic Recovery   121

The Alternatives to Democracy   123
    Acquiescent 'Democracy'   124
    Nationalist, Conservative, and Economic Anti-Democracy   127
    The People's Republic of China   130

Leadership   138
    The Leaders We Have   139
    The Corruption of Power   143
    Democratic Maintenance and Improvement: Systems, Hierarchies, and Leadership   147

IV THE ECONOMY   153

Systems   156
    The Theory   156

The Practice	160
The Social Contract: Is It Working?	**162**
Work	163
Health	166
The Economic Generational Divide	169
The Morality and Future of Taxes	173
Changes	**178**
Automation	180
Openness and Innovation	183
A Four-Day Week	188
Universal Basic Income (UBI)	192
Saving Capitalism for the Capitalists	198

V CONFLICT — 205

Crime, Punishment, and Justice	**209**
Punishment and Justice	210
Evidence: The Bystander, Golem and Pygmalion, and Pluralistic Ignorance	214
Domestic Abuse and Violence Against Girls and Women	219
Addiction	221
Capital Punishment	223
Discrimination	**225**
The Reach of Discrimination	226
Addressing Gender, Race, and Class	231
The Politics and Morality of Changing Discrimination	240
War	**242**
Our Current Warrior Virtues	242
Causes of War and Dealing with Them	246

The United Nations	254
The Hardest Example: The Israeli-Palestinian Conflict	257
Science and Technology	259
Freedom Fighting and Terrorism	262
The Future of Conflict	265

VI GLOBALISATION — 269

Climate Change — 274
The Beef	275
Nuclear Energy	278
Population Control or Family Planning	280

Economic Inter-Dependence — 285
Inequality Between Nations	286
Multinational Business	295
Aid and Trade	299

Nationality — 303
Nationalism: Ghost of the Past and the Future	304
The Misuse of Citizenship	309
Migration	311
A New Culturalism through Global Dialogue	316
Frameworks for Progress	322

VII RELIGION — 325

The Religion We Have — 327
What Do We Mean By Religion?	327
Where Does Our Religion Come From?	330

Adapt, Be Marginalised, or Perish? — 339
The Adaptability of Religion	340
Hard Issues	344

Soft Influence	351
Government and the Power of Religion	353
The Long-Term Choices for the Future that are Beginning Now	**360**

VIII SCIENCE AND TECHNOLOGY — 367

Origins and Nature — 369
- A Reassessment of the Natural World — 371
- Homo sapiens, Then and Now — 374
- Our Planet and its Place, Now and into the Past — 376

Opportunities and Threats — 379
- Bioscience and Biotechnology — 379
- New Material: Nanotechnology — 386
- Internet and Digital Access — 387
- Algorithms, Machine Learning, and Artificial Intelligence — 390
- Virtual Reality — 397

The Scope and Importance of Science and Technology — 400
- The People Factor — 401
- Human Rights — 404
- Our Place in a Scientific Age — 407

IX UNTHINKABLE — 413

Speciesism — 414

Eliminating Suffering, Illness, and Disease — 419

Lunar Exploration, Deep Space, and Aliens — 422

CONCLUSION — 429

Human Nature — 429
- Character and Change — 430
- Maturity — 432

The Challenges We Must Face — 434
- A Global Perspective — 434
- How We Measure Ourselves: The Economy into Government — 435
- The Future of Democracy and Non-Democracy — 439
- The Equality of Women — 441
- How We Measure Ourselves: Philosophically, Psychologically, Emotionally — 443
- The New Enlightenment — 444
- Science and Technology: Its Range — 447
- Changing Ourselves — 449

To Be More Specific... — 451
- Urban Living — 451
- Religion — 452
- Science and Technology: Its Development — 454
- International Relations — 457
- Future Government — 460
- Future Citizen — 462

Bibliography — 467

Index — 473

Acknowledgements

I would like to thank Arena Books for their belief in this work, and their unstinting help throughout the publication process, and my family of supporters, and ad hoc advisers, including Hannah and Hattie.

INTRODUCTION

All the world's a stage, And all the men and women merely players
William Shakespeare.*

*No culture is self-authenticating and above criticism... No culture
represents the last word in human wisdom.
Bhikkhu Parekh. Indian-born British political scientist.*
Bhikhu Parekh.†

*...authentic political life, built upon respect for law and frank dialogue
between individuals, is constantly renewed whenever there is a realisation
that every woman and man, and every new generation, brings the promise
of new intellectual, cultural and spiritual energies.*
Pope Francis.‡

The seeds that have come together in this book include experience of the religious sites of Jerusalem/Al-Quds, walking the Statue of Liberty in New York, witnessing the final year of the Berlin Wall, and being immersed in the organised chaos of New Delhi. Listening to a woman talk about her childhood experience of the Cultural Revolution in China and what the country means to her now, and a Turk in Istanbul who simply wanted to practise his English; seeing huddled homeless people stretch along one of central Vancouver's better-known streets, and listening to racist and disparaging comments about 'Gravesindia'

---
* William Shakespeare. *As You Like It.*
† Bhikhu Parekh. "Multiculturalism is a civilised dialogue," *The Guardian*, 21 Jan 2005.
‡ Pope Francis, Chapter 5, *Encyclical Letter Fratelli Tutti.*

instead of Gravesend in the UK, makes one wonder how far, or not, we have come as a species. Together these are a testament to the diverse human experience of our world today and inspired this reflection of where we might be going.

As a teacher, listening to school children living in situations of domestic abuse or neglect, seeing a young girl trance-like on her ADHD medication, admiring the courage of a Muslim sixth former in a Kuwaiti school reading the banned *Satanic Verses*, makes one wonder what our future generations would think of us. I have also seen the uplifting ambition of girls in a largely Sikh school in Southall in London, heard a seventeen-year-old school-leaver working two jobs cheerfully express that 'achieving something in life shouldn't be easy,' and listened to a robot playing the piano in Shanghai's Museum of Science and Technology. I wonder what the future holds for our younger generations, and how they can shape that future themselves.

Having seen the UK's NHS and social care in practice, migrant labour at work in the UK and elsewhere, taught Religious Education to a class in a London school that could represent every major religion, and visited middle-class homes of various cultures across the world, it is clear that people can have very different experiences of what the world is like now. Being guided along the hallowed halls of Westminster's Houses of Parliament, the White House of America's Presidents, and The Great Hall of the People in Beijing, our confusion, or different perspectives, over how the world can be changed is also clear.

This book is a reflection of, and on, those experiences, and many more, with a little research, nods to philosophy, and hopefully some common sense. It reflects an increasingly global understanding of our current circumstances and our future, and how we might make life better for some of those I have met, and those still to come. The world is full of the good, the bad, the ugly, and the misunderstood. Change outside realism is utopian and is to be avoided as much as the naturally dystopian futures it is too easy to imagine. There is ample evidence that we can improve our own lives, the lives of others, and what we can all do together. We must recognise achievements but still face up to our failures. We should be asking ourselves – individually and together – what sort of people are we, what more are we trying to achieve, and who

INTRODUCTION

do we want to be? We should, and can, do better.

In my generation, there have been dizzying changes. Humanity has landed on the Moon and seen Earth as a single entity. Attitudes towards gender have undergone a revolution. Animals and plants have been cloned and re-engineered. We can sell and buy necessity and luxury from across the world at the press of a few buttons. We can physically replace someone's heart. We have accepted many life-changing developments without necessarily understanding them or how they work.

We can destroy the world we live in many times over in a variety of ways. We know more about people but continue to discriminate against, or conflict with, or simply under-value, people we do know and people we don't know, both near and far. We are increasingly understanding how emotions and the brain work, and our ability to manipulate people's opinions and identities, but with no real understanding of consciousness. We still do not agree on the importance of 'nature' or 'nurture' in developing personality and character. In a sort of split personality, for many people, humans are emotional and psychological beings, but society is increasingly impersonal. We know that our own species of *Homo sapiens* was not the first on this planet, although knowing the fragility of previous groups does not yet translate into learning lessons for our own future. We know that we need to live in a more sustainable way without yet understanding how the planet's eco-system works. We do not yet seem to have a fully evolved sense of a common purpose for humanity, yet we are exploring other planets and learning from beyond our solar system.

In parts of the world small tribes live as they did many hundreds of years ago without ever having experienced tractors or telephones. In large parts of the world, people accept specific laws about what to wear or eat, and answers to the 'big questions' like 'Where do we come from?' in religions formed centuries ago. Global media shows us that conflict in all its many guises is persistent and deep-rooted. For many people, recent 'progress' has meant a more difficult life, not an easier one, and yet hundreds of millions have been taken out of absolute poverty in historically quick time. People's expectations are certainly not what they once were.

The need to address these inconsistencies seems more important than ever. How to change them – indeed, the need to do so or not – is framed in a different context than previous generations. We think we know more about how we work. We know that we are more dependent on, and inter-dependent with, a vaster range of people and places than we ever knew about before. We have multiple identities that shape who we are, and multiple 'stories,' some of which clash. We may feel that innovation is stretching beyond our understanding, while some form of these feelings may be as old as humanity, there having always been change, whether in our beliefs, innovation, landscape, or hierarchy. These changes go to the heart of what we are as people – how we think of ourselves, what our relationships with others are, and our place and uniqueness on the planet or among the stars.

Our global perspective is a new one. In the past, we have tended to look to the heavens rather than across the globe. People are familiar with the idea of 'chaos theory'; the ripples of a butterfly's wings can trigger huge end results and big change. For many people, this is a nightmarish loss of control. It indicates billions of influences from anywhere and everywhere. Even our responsibility for the Earth has been thrown into a more urgent reassessment in recent years. The Covid-19 pandemic, economic inter-dependence, climate and biodiversity changes, migration flows, varied ideas of identity, nationalism, geo-political co-operation or conflict, and worldwide campaigns to address gender and racial discrimination, have produced a combination of issues that highlight our turning point, and perhaps crisis point. These are not the ripples of butterfly wings as much as cross-currents from the expansive wings of an eagle. They may add up to a 'threshold' experience that divides one generation, or era, from another. Peter Singer has written about what he calls an 'expanding circle of humanity.' In our changing world, how do we meet our challenges, and more to the point, what answers might we come up with? What sort of life do we really want to lead and what do we want society to be like? Humanity knows that it is not at the end of its journey, but what comes next? This is the work of this book. If you believe that humanity has stopped changing and cannot improve any further, then this book may be of little interest and you could stop reading now. If you believe that 'all the world's a stage, and all the people players,' then continue.

INTRODUCTION

Time and wisdom are humanity's most precious resources. The ability to think for oneself – free will – with a sense of perspective, exists either within very broad parameters of fate or divine providence, or exists because those things do not. The most well-known phrase in modern Western philosophy may be Descartes' *'cogito ergo sum'* or 'I think, therefore I am.' Furthermore, we can choose how we think, and the modern Western creed is to think through Reason. This is the creed of the Enlightenment that has come to dominate Western thought over the last three centuries and has been exported to the rest of the world. The acceptance of Reason as a basis for understanding is to acknowledge that it will not succeed in explaining everything, but that in our search for Truth through Reason, we have a hope of moving towards wisdom. Immanuel Kant, one of the key philosophers of the Enlightenment, would then say that wisdom informs duty. Not understanding or knowing everything is therefore not a reason for inaction.

As Shakespeare would appreciate, some parts are bigger than others, but the whole is better when everyone plays their role. A Head of State may have unique power, a devoted activist outsize impact, but if individuals choose to buy or not buy a brand, to recycle, or to vote, they have an influence. Every single day millions of people make choices and changes that have an influence. They rarely assume that they are in full control of their circumstances. They reassess what can be achieved on a regular basis, whether intuitively or through writing lists. People frequently decide that they can and should use their freedom whatever the authority, circumstance, fear, and temptation they face, and however imperfectly. They understand that they won't make 'progress' without application. People also know that impressions and assumptions can hold them back, but that they can learn even when things go wrong, and that it is what they do that matters more. People from a Brazilian favela to a Silicon Valley millionaire understand that the more they know about themselves then the more they know of their qualities and understand their weaknesses and can make the most of their talents. They share a common understanding that living in fear is not being free. This may include, but goes well beyond, a Western idea of 'liberty' and 'freedom.' It is a practical, perhaps intuitive, attempt at the 'considered life' that the Ancient Greek Socrates challenged people to lead. In less philosophical language, we might say that people try to live 'useful' lives. It applies whether one believes in a greater divine providence or not.

We must also believe that things *can* change. In the 19th century, John Stuart Mill wrote that opinions need to be challenged even if they have been generally accepted. Through experience and debate – not experience alone – each generation understands the house in which it lives. Humanity accepts that it is not infallible; and Mill effectively writes that it should continually be tested. This may be disconcerting, or exhausting, but this is how society's norms have changed throughout human history, from pastoralism to the development of agriculture, from strict hierarchical governance to an acceptance of universal rights.

If we believe that the inconsistences of the current world *need* to change, that we *can* change them, and that we *should*, then what *sort* of change do we need? Our challenges are internal and global. Globally, they involve the way we live in relation to others, the use of the resources that we have at our disposal, our idea of economic progress – including progress being economic – and our ideas of governance and conflict. One argument against the dominance of the Enlightenment is that it has simply furnished 'us' in 'the West' with the ability to justify and find logic for our own convictions that have entrenched our own interests. That form of 'superior,' European, 'old,' Enlightenment ignored gender and racial inequality and is not good enough for the global challenges we face now. It ignores cultural diversity and dismisses religious faith. There is still, however, a place for a 'purer' Enlightenment of real universal rights, liberties, and freedoms, as part of an emerging philosophy with a global perspective. The latter requires both an institutional and personal, or internal, re-think. As we learn more about global inequality and prospective change, especially through scientific innovations, we may now be at the point where we realise that more fundamental change is necessary. Such change requires philosophical accommodation with people who have a different history, different politics, different beliefs, different experiences, and approaches, with people whose own philosophy of life is not the same as yours, wherever or whomever you may be. The depth of change being experienced requires us to go back to understanding our human nature, what gives us purpose and satisfaction, what we want our lives to be like, and how we engage with

INTRODUCTION

and treat others.

This book is organised using thematic chapters. It begins by looking at what we think of ourselves and how that works in our societies and governments, before then looking at specific areas in which the world is changing and in which we might apply a new-found reflection. These chapters can stand alone, but the links between them are undeniable and as an interlocking jigsaw they create a bigger picture. I hope they generate reflections and questions in your mind, as they do in mine.

I
HUMAN NATURE, VIRTUES AND VICES

… you find sometimes that a Thing which seemed very Thingish inside you is quite different when it gets out into the open and has other people looking at it. A. A. Milne.*

[It was]… the last of the human freedoms to choose one's own attitude in any given set of circumstances.
Viktor E. Frankl (holocaust survivor).†

Julian Baggini, in his study of philosophy, identifies three distinctive core traditions – those from Ancient Greece, the teachings of Buddhism, and Confucianism.‡ All three attempt to enlighten us about the big questions of who we are, where we are from, and our purpose. These core traditions are the foundations of all the major cultural and religious traditions that we more commonly think of – Judeo-Christian, Islam, and what might be termed the Hindu-Buddhist traditions. In the West, 'will it make me happier?' has become a more central question, reflecting that we are individually unique, physically, emotionally, psychologically,

---

* A. A. Milne, The House at Pooh Corner, Methuen, 1928.
† Viktor E. Frankl, *Man's Search for Meaning*, Beacon Press, 1946.
‡ Julian Baggini, *How the World Thinks*, 2018. Baggini then adds Islam as a fourth, as those with ancient, written, recognisable, texts.

and intellectually. Economist Douglass North writes, 'an overwhelming feature of the last 10 millennia is that we have evolved into radically different religious, ethnic, cultural, political and economic societies.'* However, it has always been thought that humanity has its own common 'human nature'; with unique virtues to employ in life, and its vices to resist. Human nature may be unchanging and fundamental, but the specific virtues and vices and the character traits they form have changed through the ages. Writing in the 16th-century state of Florence, Machiavelli wrote that if people want to be successful, they should change as circumstances change. Although he was writing political strategy rather than philosophy, this may encapsulate the nature and purpose of virtue (and vice). If we believe, as many do, that the course of humanity is now changing whether we like it or not, we should surely reassess the virtues we require, and the vices that we should resist, to steer us to the next part of our journey. Perhaps we even need to reassess the role, and nature, of human nature itself.

There are some questions that it seems we can never quite answer definitively. How does nature relate to nurture in how we mature? What is a good balance between self- and community interest? And between rights and responsibilities? How much of our individual identities, beliefs, and instincts come from community memory that has been psychologically or biologically established over generations? In our search for happiness and fulfilment, what motivates us, the carrot, or the stick? Are we co-operative and social beings or competitive and mired in conflict? How do we justify the means when we want serious change? Do we enact change from the point of being an optimistic or pessimistic species? Are we risk-taking or inherently cautious? With 8 billion people on the planet, are we all of these things? Can the contradictions live side by side? Are successful leaders one sort of person, or are there multiple ways of being in leadership? Unless we understand the part that these questions play in our human nature, and in our strategies for survival and success, it is doubtful that we can reassess the lives we lead and the progress we want to make as individuals, in communities, or as humanity. We may literally behave like animals, or at least mammals or apes, but our ability to think individually and collectively in these

---

*North, 1990, 6; Yueh, 2018, 240.

ways is likely to be the one determining factor that makes us uniquely human. Using this intellect is part of the challenge set by Socrates to lead a 'considered life.'

Our natural personal characteristics are shaped by outside influences and by our perceived experiences. A child who experiences manipulation and abuse may well become manipulative and abusive – unless other experiences give them a different perspective. This is a simplistic example of the essence of what has been called 'cultural evolution' and the beginnings of 'multi-level selection.'* Darwin's Theory of Evolution is 'survival of the fittest,' but is frequently or wilfully misunderstood as survival of the strongest. Survival of the fittest means being able to adapt to one's changing circumstances. It is not all about 'being stronger.' The 'fittest' includes those that find more benefit in co-operation. Multi-level selection enhances this to understand how different or opposing forces can find evolutionary accommodation. If the permanent mindset was conflict, then who would survive? Society has needed 'non-fighters' as well as warriors. This is the group dynamics of evolution. This is cultural multi-level selection. Both survive.

The size of the *Homo sapien* brain has not changed, but how we talk to, co-operate with, and defend ourselves from a changing list of friends and foes has vastly changed our identity from the Stone Age. Written and fixed laws have also changed our identity and our view of ourselves – and this applies whatever form governmental, religious, or societal structure we find ourselves with. In relatively recent times, more education, extensive migration (internal and external), and more individualism, even rootlessness, have made the nature of the identities we feel more fluid. Add concepts such as human rights, and the practical ability to meet or even marry someone from a different class, caste, faith, and colour whose heritage is from an entirely different part of the globe, and our identity becomes less fixed than ever before. If identity is not fixed, then how can the virtues that people seek to live by be fixed? In the context of writing about different forms of authority and government, Thomas Paine (of American Independence fame) wrote that (good) virtue is not hereditary, and neither is it perpetual. It therefore follows that progress, too, is neither inevitable nor permanent. So, have the

---
* Peter Turchin, 2015.

virtues of humanity changed over time?

The Ancient Roman Seneca (from Cordoba, writing in the first century CE, or traditional AD) wrote that two things are unchanging – the universal nature of man and individual virtue. He wrote that goods, fortune, and even friends were all less necessary for individual happiness than what was inside of oneself. Earthly goods get in the way of genuine ones. Marcus Aurelius, writing from the unique perspective of being a Roman Emperor in the second century CE, wrote that ignorance of good and evil was as crippling as ignorance of black and white. This is also to be found within oneself. Furthermore, we have the power to stand on our own two feet, independent of others, even if circumstances change, as they inevitably will, and even if we are not in control of the Gods' will. This 'stoic' approach was to accept, adapt, and 'reason,' in order to be true to oneself. He believed that as things change, then changing one's mind is natural and does not signify either weakness or a sacrifice of independence. His stoicism was not an attempt to control fate or to accept the temporariness of life in a defeatist way, but rather it was a call for individual action based on an inner sense of right and wrong. Aurelius' stoic philosophy was to live one's life by being generous to others, and about others, through reason, truthfulness, and conformity with nature – the latter of which is neither good nor bad. Seneca's philosophy was more specific but of the same flavour; it focussed on temperance, wisdom, piety, a system of fair duties, and knowledge of man and God. Seneca believed that nothing satisfies greed, that understanding misfortune such as grief and poverty can build character, and that to feel 'poor' is an attitude of the mind. A modern Buddhist, and probably many others, would recognise these ideas. These are fundamentals when considering 'virtue.' Virtue is within us. Misfortune can be character-building – if it doesn't kill us first. A person should learn to stand on their own two feet by being true to themselves first, and then to others. With confidence, a person can recognise change and adapt accordingly. Although Roman philosophy envisioned overall control by the Gods, it also encouraged knowing oneself, individual responsibility and action, the application of reason, and the importance of community.

Going back in time, these philosophies built upon those of Socrates who emphasised the importance of civic virtues such as justice and temperance over warrior attributes. He believed that these virtues were to be found and developed through earthly action rather than via cosmology or academic or philosophical theories. For Socrates, virtues could be 'known,' knowledge was to be sought through reason, and together, these would lead to truth. His view was that no-one did wrong deliberately, for why would they damage their own soul? Reason and debate, which would lead towards truth, would help to prevent moral weakness and enable humanity to make progress. Aristotle, who was a student of Plato from whom we know about Socrates, wrote of the idea of 'full virtue' or moral excellence being evident through actions as well as principles. His *Nicomachean Ethics* argued that habitual actions, 'good habits,' would lead to a good, stable character. Leaders would need honour and modesty, justice and fairness, practical judgement, and to be a good friend. These, in turn, would need courage, self-control, and generosity. This effort at 'contemplative wisdom' would lead to the highest 'good' of happiness or wellbeing. He also wrote of virtue being a balance within and between individuals. Therefore, the search for truth and progress, through excellence in virtue, is both practical and theoretical. It is individual in the sense that it essentially arises from within, but it is not divorced from the reality of life or relationships with others. Ancient Greek and Roman and other belief systems the world over all included the setting of humanity inside a natural world of spirits or Gods that humanity needed to accept. However, unlike other belief systems, the Ancient Greek and Roman view was that being able to consider these virtues (and the higher Gods) was itself confirmation that humanity was superior to the natural world around it.

This view or philosophy of life was to find further expression in the 'free will' within divine providence; and the search within oneself is echoed in individual enlightenment. At the same time, the search for virtue through action in the real world was to be echoed in the establishment of virtuous religious communities. Post-Roman religions went on to define these virtues, or philosophical principles, further and in a more specific way, a more regulated way, without the freedom of individuals to pick and choose which specific God's orbit they would appeal to or find comfort within.

WHERE ARE WE GOING?

Different belief systems around the world since ancient times have given us a high degree of global commonality in the virtues that people should pursue. Some form of temperance, modesty, and humility recognises that a person is not always right and must be moderate in nature and action. We often say today that there is always someone who knows better – whether a person, a computer, or a God – and that excess is to be frowned upon. Some form of generosity, charity, or compassion, and justice and honesty or both, recognises that each person has a relationship with their community. These qualities also infer some level of worth, respect, or equality in or for other people and find an echo in the commonly known 'Golden Rule' of established religions, that is, 'do to others what you would have them do to you.'[*] Notably, this does not, in common, stretch to mercy. There is also a recognition that God may move in mysterious ways that we do not or cannot always understand. Hence, resilience, or faith, denotes strength of character being tested. Chinese *Te* or *De* also specifically refers to the creative power of the 'natural way,' an active and compelling impulse to pursue a virtuous life, just as Aristotle, Christianity, and other religions expect an 'active' and 'exemplary' virtue.

There are some differences in what virtues are considered inherently important. For example, one virtue considered essential in Islam and East Asian philosophies is respect for one's elders. This is echoed in the Jewish and Christian Ten Commandments but does not remain at the forefront of Christian teaching, while in Chinese and Japanese philosophies, it refers not only to one's living relatives but to ancestors as well. The virtues of Taoism (or Daoism) also include the concept of 'harmony' as a separate concept to 'peace.' While peace may have something in common with 'love,' harmony is the specific importance of community wellbeing, and reflects the equal importance of family and societal order alongside individual virtue. This reveals a fundamental difference with Western Enlightenment's emphasis on secular individual liberty and goes some way to explaining the different views of society that exist globally in the world today.

As expected, vices are generally the opposite, and have much in

---

[*] Matthew 7:12, *New International Version*, Biblica. Baggini notes more neutral, restrictive, and specific, versions in other religions, 264.

common. Pride, in religious terms, means a lack of humility in the face of God, which today we may equate with selfishness or a sense of superiority. Greed denotes wanting too much, addiction, or obsession, and can be applied to desiring anything beyond either moderation or reason. Envy and anger remain self-explanatory. Sloth, thought of nowadays as laziness, is also to be avoided, but its origin may be more like 'non-engagement' in life and virtue, and may be seen as having a half-sibling in one of Buddhism's Three Poisons, of Ignorance, the others being Greed and Hatred. Ravan (or Ravana, or Dashmukh), with ten heads, is the major antagonist of the Ramayana Hindu epic, who rejects the expected notion that the head of intellect should predominate over the others: lust, anger, delusion, greed, pride, envy, mind, will, and ego. He is characterised as a villain who attempted to balance good and evil but whose embracing of these emotions, or vices, results in his defeat. Naturally, these are summaries. Islam has ninety-nine names for Allah that portray his virtues – the merciful, etc.

All these virtues and vices have been 'translated' over time within religions and by others. Only in 590 CE did Pope Gregory I standardise the list of seven 'cardinal' or 'deadly' sins. They may all be seen as mechanisms of religious practice to define a community and to build a belief system as a distinctive way of life, originating in a specific historical era. All were interpreted within the context of power hierarchies societally and in religious authority, often permitting slavery or other discriminatory separation. In all these virtues, respect may be implied, but there is no clear mention of equality. All the major religions, except perhaps Sikhism, have practical fundamental issues with gender equality.

Given that different belief systems across the world do have key concepts such as justice, compassion, and humility in common, it is reasonable to expect that they relate to a more fundamental human nature. While a sense of justice may be changed over time, its bedrock of fairness may be said to be less changeable, and therefore part of human nature. On this basis, compassion and charity may therefore be said to originate in empathy and co-operation. The latter two, and fairness, are attitudinal. Honesty, trustworthiness, duty, love, and peace might be considered behavioural aspects of human nature that we struggle to put into practice or find a comfortable or practical or effective balance of. This approach links human nature and the active pursuit of virtue in search of another commonality – happiness, or wellbeing.

Let us go back to the questions that we find it so difficult to answer definitively, such as, are we co-operative or competitive? The human nature and virtues we have identified may illuminate some answers, as well as highlight why we struggle with others. Fairness and empathy point to a co-operative social being. The active nature of the virtues shows why we struggle with others. For example, justice and harmony, duty and loyalty, are subjective. They subjectively influence and are influenced by our idea of self- or community interest, optimism and pessimism, carrot, or stick. Most of all, they are subjective in relation to who we identify with, know, and understand, and how we think. More on this after a significant detour to the Enlightenment.

Building upon the Renaissance that had re-discovered the Ancient Greek and Roman writings – importantly, from Arabic translations and critiques – and promoted experimentation and questioning, the Enlightenment gave humanity a renewed purpose: the pursuit of Liberty through an empirical 'Truth' found through 'Reason.' We think of the Enlightenment as rationalist and progressive. Through experimental science and the social sciences over the last 300 years, it has become a, or the, accepted Western creed. Yet it is also a product of its time, and originally there was a mainstream Enlightenment and a more radical one. The criticism of the mainstream Enlightenment that became predominant is that it allowed moral, scientific, and economic practices that entrenched the European and moneyed or establishment interests and prejudices of the time. It advanced the Hobbesian idea of brutal humanity, at least in others, that needed to be civilised. The accompanying conversion of others to Christianity was an allied strand of attack in the assumption of superiority and that civilising mission. The mainstream, or what we might now call the old European Enlightenment, may be seen as giving people the language and justification to continue to support slavery, colonialism, religious and cultural intolerance, and keep women in their place, out of the public discourse. We clearly still struggle with this legacy, but it should have no place in any modern consideration of the nature or virtues of humanity. The Enlightenment remains a work in progress. Its critics still see in it the religious wish for salvation. Others accuse it, and Christianity, of making progress seem inevitable and ongoing, because their sense of time is linear, not cyclical like most other philosophies around the world. Others see an extreme individualism. Others, like Edmund Burke at the time of the American and French Revolutions, criticised the idea that all people are equal, and instead wrote of difference, and preferred talents that raise some above what was once called 'the mob,' which then became the 'great unwashed' (by knowledge), and now we call 'the public.' He was more afraid of the vices and excesses of ignorance and pride. He lost faith in the idealistic virtues of revolutionaries whom he saw destroy in order to build anew for a different set of 'interests.' Burke's ideas are a common conservative view of change and people's motives that still exist today.

Only in recent years have Enlightenment followers faced up to the global nature of its application. There remains resistance to the fair consideration of other beliefs or practical ideas. The original practice still sullies its reputation for belief in reason, liberty, and tolerance. However, what was once seen as radical Enlightenment is now more prominent in the West and elsewhere. A non-discriminatory form of individual liberty and freedom is considered a fundamental value, even though imperfectly expressed in gender and race, and in the promotion of questioning and reason in education, objectivity in science, and in the pursuit of democratic governance. Even Pope Francis' 2020 Encyclical *Fratelli Tutti* stated that 'God has created all human beings equal in rights, duties and dignity, and has called them to live together as brothers and sisters.' He emphasised the importance of compassion, empathy, and solidarity as responsibilities contributing towards the rights of all. He professed an ultimate optimism, or faith, in the co-operative nature of humanity and reaffirmed the positive virtues required of individuals to enable it.

The Enlightenment strand of science – biological, physiological, psychological, and sociological – continues to debate and redefine what is meant by human nature and the virtues pursued by humanity. Neuroscientists are beginning to identify areas of the brain that are highlighted, strengthened, or neglected when people exercise certain virtues or vices. We are on the verge of being able to recognise, exercise, and strengthen different emotions neurologically and of being able to manipulate them. Given the pace of physical evolution, this points to a human nature that changes over time rather than remains static. It links physical and cultural evolution. One landmark experiment recently given a renewed profile is one that allowed only co-operative rather than competitive Silver Foxes to breed together, which created, over several generations, a physically changed and more psychologically domesticated Silver Fox.* *If* our world is becoming more peaceful, then perhaps humanity is undergoing something similar.

Social science experiments demonstrate that the youngest children recognise and sympathise with fairness and co-operation. They also showed recognition of people as similar or as different from themselves. This recognition alone can have major implications in areas such as individual personal humility, and policy areas such as discrimination.† It encourages debate about the origins of our character, what is most fundamental or natural to us, how much is learnt behaviour, and how much changes through nurture. We also believe we understand more about the difference between automatic or intuitive thinking and reflective thinking. If we know that the former is the product of repetition and familiarity, then we can change people's 'intuitive' reaction by changing the inputs that make up their surroundings. If we continually tell students that they will be great at something, do success rates rise? Most teachers would tell you that not only is the answer yes but that the opposite is also true both of individual students and institutionally of groups (whether based on colour or class or culture or gender). This is the whole point of engaging role models. However, one group's good practice can become another group's propaganda or dogma; manipulation, either benign or deliberately self-serving, is also an issue here. Starting with the young is hardly new. There are enormous policy implications for this science. There are enormous implications for how we think about the virtues and vices we employ.

Many of these ideas are not new. The attempted moral conditioning

---

* Rutger Bregman, 2020, 66–68.
† Bregman, 2020, 211–214. Bregman uses Yale University 'Baby Lab' Studies (from 2007, using studies by J. Kiley Hamlin, Karen Wynn, and Paul Bloom, see Notes, 431) showing that eighteen-month-old toddlers have a natural affinity to help each other; although they also preferred familiar over stranger contemporaries, even if familiar were meaner.

of people has always been part of governance, propaganda, and advertising. However, the science we are developing is defining them and raising their profile. Acknowledging and being wary that sometimes poor science has derailed us – such as the application of social Darwinism and eugenics which dismissed whole races and cultures as inferior – we can begin to envisage how we can take more control of our brains to shape human nature, emotions, and habits. Human nature and virtues may not be as fixed and elusive as we have thought them during most of our human existence. Having the chance to shape ourselves can be disturbing or an opportunity; it can be seen as either dangerous or benignly idealistic. This will be considered again in other chapters. Fundamentally, the new sciences are showing that we can change our decision-making. Even more fundamentally, this may, or should, make us think again about the purpose and practical pursuit of a 'considered life,' and of humanity itself.

As we learn about individual and community, government, science, etc, we must remember that the foundation of virtues, their surrounding contexts and what they are interpreted for, have produced different belief systems, cultures, and philosophies. These have different ideas of time, of self, of universality, of relationships to nature, and to an internal or external essence of energy or power or God or soul. Although the Western world needs to earmark its own distinctive contribution to the whole and to any emerging global philosophy, it needs to understand that it is in a minority in this regard. It needs to recognise its own foundations, contexts, and interpretations in order to understand itself, and its relationships to others, better. Ironically, its universalist idea of rights, as applied to all individually and equally, is not the universally accepted modus operandi of life elsewhere. New Zealand's Wanganui River was declared a legal person in 2017, in recognition of Maori indivisibility of land and people (not ownership or coexistence or interdependence), and with it the Maori idea of identity and cycles of time. The individual decision-making of Western democracy is a different approach to the individuality of East Asian philosophies, which must more obviously exist within, and for, the collective good. In the Islamic world, one's virtues cannot and should not exist outside the theological framework of Islam; religion cannot be separated from the individual.

WHERE ARE WE GOING?

Virtues may appear similar in different places, but they cannot, like elements of philosophical thought, be stolen wholesale and expected to survive in a different context, though they may be grafted to another stem and then change in the process. This is not a philosophy book, but clearly values, expressed through belief, culture, and philosophy, are an important thread within it.

II

INDIVIDUALISM, SOCIETY, AND CITIZENSHIP

Any masterpiece just becomes noise disturbance when emanating from earphones. Julian Baggini.*

According to Thomas More, writing in the 16th century, people are naturally virtuous whether it be for themselves or the common good. He thought it illogical to help others without helping oneself – an early dig at the Puritans. He believed that leading a virtuous and balanced life would lead to 'happiness' and that this would naturally contribute to the common good. 'Pleasure' meant good health and the contemplation of truth and understanding through a clear conscience and good behaviour. In his *Utopia*, a lack of private property meant that the public interest would be taken more seriously, and a lack of personal selfishness would promote personal happiness. Utopia envisioned a society built upon a Christian ethos and upon laws that were not a pretext for power and wealth. He believed, or hoped, that such a society would lack crime and poverty. In his eyes, money embodied pride, jealousy, difference, and division, and these traits were deeply ingrained in human nature. He saw these traits as the reason for Tudor materialism and a period of history that included the beginning of the enclosure Acts, the development of

---

* Quote taken from a public info message on the Tokyo underground, Julian Baggini, *How the World Thinks*, 2018. 191.

Contract Law, and the ongoing conflicts between the guilds (who held the most power) and the 'free' merchants that would ultimately lead to the entrepreneurial industrialisation of commerce. He argued for social order and harmony based upon respect, individual freedom to banish inferiority, and a shared philosophical education for security and wellbeing. Now, we would view this idealism somewhere between social democracy and communism, hence our understanding of the name of his book.

In contrast, Hobbes focussed on the 'brutal' nature of humanity. Individuals, and perhaps 'humanity,' have 'character,' but personality may be different; a 'persona' is an actor's mask which may disguise our real intentions. Hence, mankind can seem 'good' but can nevertheless commit all sorts of atrocities individually and collectively. It is to their destructive inner self that people will remain true. Any good morality, in this approach, is not natural or of the real world, and is not based on knowledge or education. It is the brutal experiences of life that shape us.

Between these two fundamentally different interpretations of humanity – More's individual action for the common good, and Hobbes' brutal Man – can be found the contrasting but overlapping realms of individualism and civic action, of rights and responsibilities. The balance between these still eludes us and is argued about today.

Individualism and Civic Society

The common ground between individualism and civic society is infused by the factors of duty, relationships, and identity. One owes a duty to oneself, to support oneself and be true to oneself, and a duty to family, and the community and environment in which we live. We do not and cannot live in isolation. Our relationship with others includes a respect for tradition and for earlier generations. It also involves the sense of a 'fair share' and 'sharing the burden' and a recognition of others 'less fortunate' to whom we owe some duty of care, or of those more 'naturally privileged' to whom we may feel we owe deference. Duty and relationships play upon our individual characteristics to create our multiple identities. We offer a persona – sincere or not – that may appear different depending on who we are with. We buy into different narratives and find a way to compartmentalise or harmonise them. Indeed, one person may virtuously encourage some and 'corrupt' others, be welcoming and sharing as well as suspicious and distant. The mafia boss can be both a calculated murderer and a family man or woman. The strength of our 'true character' – our honesty, etc – will determine if we are true to ourselves or if we are of very different personas in different circumstances. It is here that we struggle with those balances and dilemmas of rights and responsibilities, and of individualism or civic action. The consequences include our varied attitudes to others, to justice, tolerance, materialism, progress, conflict, religion, change, and continuity. There is also the impact of our past experiences. Some of these experiences are individual, while others are more collective and cultural, such as the influence of a predominant religious belief or historic events like industrialisation or equality under the law. Some experiences may be both – the individual and collective experience of war or famine. All these can be very different across the world, and this helps to explain why there are such different attitudes to individualism and to society from community to community.

Western Secular Attitudes Now

In the West, the idea of 'progress' has come to be contingent upon the idea that economic wealth and materialism is necessary in order to be 'happy.' This differs, for example, from Rabindranath Tagore's idea of the importance of human connection over materialism, and the importance of dignity, education, and creativity for all. Although this view of Western society could be viewed as an over-simplification, the result is clearly in evidence: societies in which working, social, and family life are often an enterprise of worry, stressful competition, or survival. The skilled middle classes have become 'squeezed.' The next generation may be worse off than the last. This is not true for everyone and is belied by the historic rise in life expectancy, but even more common is a sense of powerlessness and political marginalisation. The future is apparently both here and now, but also continually changing, with changing expectations. This applies socially and culturally as well as economically and politically. People complain about the outside world without feeling as if they are affecting it or recognising that they are part of it for other people, and they demand leadership from others without the ability or inclination or time to feel like leaders themselves. Thomas More's utopia is further away than ever.

This was not the promise of the Enlightenment. The American Declaration of Independence promised 'the right to life, liberty, and the pursuit of happiness.' The French Revolution promised Liberty, Fraternity, Equality. Free trade promised affordable goods to buy and markets to make money. People's living standards would be raised, trade would mean peace, people would be able to raise themselves to positions of power on merit. Mass education would produce engagement and flowering democracies. Compared to the historical record, serious progress was made in the secularising West in the 19th and 20th centuries. Yet we are where we are now. Enlightenment became restrictive in terms of who it was applied to and how it was to come about. It became more important to make money. People lost sight of the connection between their everyday real-world actions and the principles of their respective religious faiths. Slavery, child industrial labour, colonialism, unplanned and polluted urban sprawl, disconnection from nature, and a permanent struggle to be healthy and safe, or a constant pursuit of more middle-class comfort, became predominant.

Governments trying to be responsive adopted Jeremy Bentham's utilitarian philosophy, seeking 'the greatest happiness of the greatest number.' It has lasted 200 years, and people's social, economic, and cultural lives and opportunities have been immeasurably improved – but only within the context of materialism and consumerism. The common refrain is that the spiritual has been neglected in favour of the material, and community has been ignored in favour of the individual. Somehow the material system has improved, and the individual has been prized, but the community in which the individual and the system are set has been battered and neglected. Some might even say that it has been discredited or broken. Is this where we are now?

It may not quite be so. The 'rights revolutions' that began in the 1950s – civil/racial rights, feminism, attempts to improve social mobility – undoubtedly produced benefits. These changes have themselves altered challenges and expectations. The internationalisation of everything from crime to climate, decolonisation, and the Apollo photograph of the Earth have all encouraged greater co-operation and a sense of global community. The rights revolutions redefined the Enlightenment principles of freedom and equality to make them more genuinely individual and more comprehensive across the globe, while reassessing the balance between the individual and the community. This is leading us to re-evaluate what sort of people we are, and how we can, and may need to, change. It is a debate that is being influenced by the traditions and ideologies of others too, as we enter a period of greater global understanding and dialogue.

In October 2019, the American city of Chicago abolished library fines for overdue books. The 20th-century view of Western humanity is that naturally people would take advantage and choose not to return books, or be careless about returning them, with more books lost. Yet, after the fines were abolished, more books were returned, and 7% more books were borrowed in the first year. There were more borrowers, including younger and poorer borrowers. Trust was reflected in people's actions.* What Chicago libraries did was the embodiment of More's idea that humanity is a trust to or with itself. Their libraries became more welcoming and more effective. The Chicago library mentality is a 21st-century view of co-operative humanity. It is a re-balance of individualism predominating over civic responsibility.

This rebalancing is not always clear-cut. The rights revolutions are ongoing and drive deeper into individual rights than ever before. Privacy and individualised protections are key features of the early 21st century in the secular West and will continue to be so for the foreseeable future. These include issues relating to personal data, image, and action, and individual protections to not be physically or emotionally harmed, from a distance or digitally, and the protection of individual opinions. In practice, these include whether someone has the right to take your photograph when you are in private or public mode, has the right to 'out' you in public for behaviour or opinions, has the right to say

---

* Rica Bouso, "Chicago Public Library officially goes fine-free," Blog, *Chicago Public Library Foundation* (website), 5 October 2019. Mitch Dudek, "Chicago Public Library says eliminating fines has paid off," *Chicago Sun Times*, 11 November 2020.

things which you find offensive, or publish your address. There are also issues of personal liberty versus public protection, such as compulsory vaccinations, social media-banning, or anonymous slander and libel. The issue of free speech has become deeply connected to the issue of the rights and responsibilities of individualism and civic action – both in the real and digital realms. There is probably a balance of honesty and diplomacy that must be struck to protect oneself and different groups in speaking out against one group's rights in favour of another. Can someone burn a book or a flag? However much that may infuriate others? How much civil disobedience can be tolerated by the courts? Who has the right to 'cancel' an opinion in an era and society that believes in free speech? Should the insulting nature of a comedian's political or social commentary be viewed as educational and campaigning, or abusive and inciting? Should speech at a private function be considered exempt from offence, or should offence not be considered private? Personal expression of opinions that go against the prevailing culture can be inappropriate or insulting or dangerous, but they may also be the origin of new thinking. The argument about 'wokeism' centres around the question of whether or not such expressions are necessary for change and progress. Hisorically in the West, progress has been viewed as occurring when individuals and ideas have challenged a communal conservatism.

Our current limits are both legal and social. We can be limited by slander and libel laws, laws relating to evidence and incitement, the extent of media outcry, 'likes,' or ticket sales. In most current Western secular societies, these boundaries are democratised, however imperfectly. People elect politicians to enact their laws, choose to buy one campaigning newspaper or another, or none. Or they write their own letters or banners of complaint. It is within the power of the public to make or break a populist or an offender. This has the advantage of being able to move with the times. Few comedians do mother-in-law jokes these days, and people know their brand will be damaged if they were to use the racial descriptions of fifty years ago. Fixed constitutions may set broad parameters, and laws may set minimum expectations. The interpretations of judges act on the margins. Democratic nations, for whom thriving civic society is part of the definition, have addressed these issues in ways that are flexible. Autocratic regimes demand control and obedience and are not inclined to allow such institutional trust, adaptability, or resilience. The natural ebb and flow of changing public opinion, influenced by people's real personal and community experiences as lives change over time, has no safety valve in an autocratic state. This is one of the weaknesses of autocracy. In Western societies, the mechanisms we have for change are allowing a re-thinking of the balance between individualism and civic responsibility. Hence, the Chicago libraries opting to do something different.

The Covid-19 response in Europe shows that allegedly secular society in the West can still find a sense of community above individualism. An estimated 12.4 million people volunteered in the UK during the pandemic for health and social projects, one-third for the first time. Volunteers encompassed all ages, faiths, social groups, and geography.[*] As a consequence, many volunteers reported a greater sense of connection with family and friends, increased general political trust, and a greater sense of neighbourliness. They followed the Olympic volunteers and others before them. Aside from raising the possibilities of the potential benefits of a four-day working week, this showed that many people wanted to be engaged in the community. It also showed that people were encouraged by other people, and were able to overcome hesitancy and cynicism about the world they live in.

Ronald Dworkin questions whether liberalism requires roots in a society to thrive or whether it is a natural behavioural instinct.[†] He notes 'minimal liberalism' where ultimate power rests with the people with no constraints, which is not practised anywhere. He notes that 'classical liberalism' – where there are rights of free trade, privacy, the rule of law, etc – is either interpreted in policy terms as an empowering liberalism or a conservative one. This can be seen as a glass half full or half empty. In mainland Europe, this liberalism is historically conservative, and in the USA and UK increasingly so. There is also 'egalitarian liberalism' which adds government intervention through rights and constraints to promote equality and justice, in many places given a 'social democracy'

---

[*] Harriet Sherwood, "Our chances to connect," *The Observer*, 28 February 2021, based on a study by the charity 'Belong' and the University of Kent.
[†] Ronald Dworkin, "How universal is liberalism," *Ralf Dahrendorf Memorial Lecture*, 2012.

label, and more left of centre. Liberalism can, therefore, be applied across a relatively wide political and social spectrum. For Dworkin there are two fundamental principles for government action to be illegitimate: the first is if there is no consensus to act, and the second is if the rights of individuals to decide for themselves what constitutes a 'good life' are not respected. Classical and Egalitarian liberalism both involve a balance between individual rights and civic, and governmental, action and a democratised consensus forms from the sum of these parts. The application of liberal rights is therefore also dependent on the acceptance of responsibilities, and free and informed individual opinion, requiring free speech and a level of education, rule of law, accountability, and respect for others. Another principle of consensus will therefore be required – the allowance for individual expression and personality. Societies in which the consensus does not freely emerge from informed individuals are therefore illiberal, and government action is coercive. This does not resolve the issue about whether liberal instincts are natural or artificially man-made and require specific circumstances – other than the need for the development of civic society – but it does clarify which governments and societies may be seen as liberal or illiberal, or in practice where on that spectrum they may be.

A Global Perspective

The social and cultural globalisation of the last few years – or since at least the Silk Road, depending on your historical perspective – has begun to erode the globe's divisions. In the West, the social upheavals that have flowered since the 1960s have been judged by some to be 'as significant as the Protestant Reformation' and have been seen as the tipping points for global change as well as for global crisis (and the backlash against these changes).* The UN Declaration of Human Rights states in Article 19: 'Everyone has the right to freedom of expression and opinion.' In the West, this is thought of as the new global orthodoxy. However, even if this is true, they are subject to change and to interpretation. Freedom of expression does not mean shouting *Fire!* in a crowded theatre or inciting

---

* Esther Adley, "A very dangerous epoch: historians try to make sense of Covid," *The Guardian*, 13 February 2021.

racial hatred. Freedom of action does not mean the right to buy and sell slaves in the interests of a free market. It is only our own certainties that make our interpretations seem so self-evident to us.

A global dialogue of ideas also includes views that have a different starting point. To be consistent with our beliefs, we must recognise the competition of other ideas, and we fail to do so at our own peril. These may be historical, cultural, religious, or political in origin. They have a different balance between individual rights and civic responsibilities, and different interpretations of duty, relationships, and identity. One example of this would be that religious influence is seen in the past to have restricted freedom and liberty in the West. Yet today more of the world retains its religious faith, and moreover often sees in it freedom from a dominant, imported, perhaps colonial, lifestyle. This is an idea that is not only in evidence in places such as Asia but also in evangelical circles in the USA. In many places, the Russian invasion of Ukraine is seen as a European war about power and influence, not something principled, for if that is so, how does one explain other wars and 'interventions' led by Western powers? The new global dialogue may be a dialogue without end, itself reaffirming the individualistic nature of interpretation, but it may be a dialogue that results in a new consensus or new consistency on the balance between individualism and community, to take effective action on international issues like climate change. J.S. Mill wrote that we should periodically debate even the most fundamental of our beliefs. He believed we should do this in order to educate new generations and to reaffirm these ideas and their importance, but we should also debate them to make necessary adaptations in changing circumstances and in recognition of new influences. This helps to ensure that our sense of self-evident righteousness does not become a fixed idea of superiority that loses its resilience in the face of inevitable change.

The question therefore arises of whether Western secular liberal values are applicable to a global audience and global circumstances. There are philosophical and practical aspects to this. Care, empathy, and inter-dependence for community self-preservation and for social order, including the sharing of skills and responsibilities, are applicable the world over, in any benign governmental system, including Western liberalism, and are as old as the idea of community. Other liberal ideas may be less globally accepted. These may include individual privacy, competition, free speech and individual expression, self-regulation of action, religious tolerance, and a liberal idea of free contact between a community of nations. These ideals are also central to the Western ideas of progress, lifestyle, and philosophy. It is these ideals that President Putin of Russia and Xi Jinping of China reject in their repudiation of 'Western world dominance' and 'Western values.' They also often interpret or replace 'civic' rights and responsibilities with governmental rights and (their version of) responsibilities. Other nations have different religious-based determinations of what these rights and responsibilities should be. Furthermore, we must admit that these Western liberal values have not been and are not now perfectly enacted within Western societies nor always exhibited by liberal nations towards others. Nor are they always clearly definable in real-life situations, like wearing masks or ratios of executive and worker pay. Furthermore, liberalism must take account of the dignity of those that feel coerced by the decided governmental action. This is the warning against a tyranny of the majority or persecution of minorities, and the taking of utilitarianism too far. Despite its past and current imperfections, however, it remains true that in Western democracies liberal values are the publicly strived-for ideals.

Dworkin's liberalism is therefore a bottom-up development which shapes the top end of action. The conclusion must be that whether liberalism is natural or not, it can nevertheless only survive or flourish where there is a free civic society, where people can develop their own personalities and opinions, where the minority view is not squashed, and where those in power are continually subject to the consensus of the sum of the individuals, which usually means through elections. Whether this is exportable to other nations and peoples depends on whether it is seen to work and is therefore aspirational, and whether people are free enough to develop their own personalities. This is why it cannot simply be transplanted into areas with no liberal or civic tradition or individualised education, and why liberal governments see an economically entrepreneurial spirit as essential for a liberal society. It is the infrastructure of civic society that must be encouraged for a bespoke liberalism to emerge through consensus. The very words of that sentence imply the passing of time, that it cannot be imposed, and that there will be different versions. Iran is a case in point. What if the free consensus of the people is for a theocracy, or some form of discriminatory government and society? Dworkin's liberalism accepts the 'new' Enlightenment of people being free to make bad, or non-Western, or even anti-Western, decisions. Their individual morality is their own; their public morality is the public consensus. Is this so dissimilar to a liberal democracy through consensus accepting the continuation of monarchy? When there is a deeply polarised society such as Northern Ireland in the 1970s then some form of stronger government may appear permissible, but this needs to be temporary, and meanwhile a consensus needs to be sought to achieve the 'common good' understanding of a civic society – a consensus that both unifies opinion and protects its minorities. Holocaust denial may be odious and un-historic but making it illegal is illiberal – the answer to any influence or spread it may achieve is education, and while that may seem idealistic it is the only solidly foundational principle of a society that seeks to be free. The 'oxygen of publicity' is countered by the purifying and clarifying glare of sunlight. A popular theocracy may thrive, therefore, but the consensus of a free and informed people is paramount, and if it is, then that form of government is accountable, and can be changed if the people change their view.

We can say that rarely in human history has a society instantly transformed from deeply traditional autocracy into civic society-based liberalism. Possibly after the Second World War when the governments and power structures of Nazi Germany and Imperial Japan were swept away and 'modern' democracies imposed we might look for evidence, but there were germs of civic society before authoritarianism or militarism took hold, and that were struggling to be heard even at the height of those regimes. The inter-war Weimar Republic of Germany seems to show that while an abrupt change from autocracy to liberalism cannot be achieved, it can nevertheless plant roots for change. There are many more examples of the slower development of liberal democracy, from Iraq post-Saddam Hussein to Chile post-Pinochet.

Globally, we know that the original Enlightenment and Western liberalism that allowed for slavery and colonialism in its we-are-superior version is baggage that needs to be ditched. We must also be prepared to work through the fundamental questions that manifested in those actions: the balance of individual rights and civic responsibility, legitimacy of spirituality and belief as central to happiness and fulfilment; and the resource-driven nature of 'progress.' Western liberals must be prepared for genuine debate to learn, and be open to change as a result, not just to win the debate with a preconceived stance. The values of the real or new Enlightenment, like genuine empathy and respect for others, are probably universal, perhaps natural and can be role modelled. They need to be part of the global dialogue taking shape. They can form the developmental bedrock of the civic societies that the West should be trying to encourage, and should be confident can be developed, that would over time lead to some form of 'liberal democracy' in the classical or egalitarian sense, and, fundamentally, with government by informed consensus.

Current Non-Secular Contributions

It is too easy to forget that Western secular societies are still based to a large extent on Christian fundamentals, and that many people in the West retain a basic Christian approach. Religion may even be undergoing a revival, as it has done at various times since the Enlightenment appeared.

The concern that Pope Francis has shown for civic solidarity, for tolerance of others, concern for the poor domestically and internationally, and concern for the environment has translated into comments on inequality, discrimination, the treatment of migrants, and climate change. He has also sought to establish stronger relations with other Christian churches and other religions. In doing so, he has sought to promote a better balance of individualism and civic responsibility in Western society. Three specific writings have outlined his spiritual and intellectual tradition and coherence – *Let Us Dream* (December 2020), a short book of reflections on the Covid-19 pandemic, and two encyclicals, *Fratelli Tutti* about society and social relationships, and *Laudato Si* about 'caring for our common home.' To a secular Westerner, these may reflect a tacit admission that the papacy is now an Enlightenment institution, accepting the inviolability of individual liberty and freedom. To the papacy, these are set within the most basic Christian doctrine of love of others, the common good, helping those in need, and stewardship of the planet. There is a recognition of the individualism of faith, but also an encouragement to put faith into action in the real world. It matters less whether religious belief or the Enlightenment are predominant. The point is that the Christian message is still finding a voice. Pope Francis is not lauded by traditionalists, but he is speaking for, and popular among, a more globally aware congregation. It is not just the papacy which is (re-)addressing this fundamental question of individual rights and civic responsibilities. The Orthodox (Christian) Church in *Towards a Social Ethos of the Orthodox Church* has called upon followers to engage with inequality, and to confront the wealthier with moral obligations towards refugees. It includes the line, 'Our spiritual lives cannot fail to be social lives,' and notes that the early Byzantine Church had 'a bold voice on social justice.' In *Morality*, the Chief Rabbi in the UK, Jonathan Sacks, criticises the apparent current preponderance of 'I' over 'We.' With the Grand Imam Ahmad Al-Tayyeb in Abu Dhabi, Pope Francis issued a statement that 'God has created all human beings equal in rights, duties and dignities, and has called them to live together as brothers and sisters.' As 'institutions' themselves which are battling to keep members there is some self-interest here, but part of the strength of these statements is that they are part of the tradition of each of these religions, from Christ's Sermon on the Mount to Islamic Zakat/Charity and Judaism's good deeds of Mitzvah; and these find echoes in other faiths around the world.

In *Fratelli Tutti*, Pope Francis writes, 'we can contribute to the rebirth of a *universal* aspiration to fraternity' (my italics). In this encyclical, he writes that globalisation has become economic and financial and that it imposes a single cultural model of the influential without bringing people together. He argues that it has promoted individual competition, benefitted the already powerful and weakened communities. He – a Pope from Argentina – decries the creeping in of cultural colonisation that denies the social and co-operative nature of history in favour of an emphasis on individual freedom. The promotion of separate interests has resulted in moral inconsistencies and the idea that some people are 'not useful.' Discrimination and personal isolation therefore continue, and social media/technology encourages confrontation. He worries that the 'idea of a single human family' has started to fade. The Parable of the Good Samaritan is used in a cross-cultural appeal, supporting the idea that people must think more of doing 'unto others as you would have done unto you.' In *Laudato Si*, there is a warning that there is such a thing as 'ecological sin.' Environmental destruction and climate change, and their human consequences, are placed within the greater concern of continuing, if not deepening, inequality. He calls for a 'new network of international relations,' and 'fundamental reform and major renewal' on a global scale. He argues that 'private life cannot exist unless it is protected by public order,' which means an infrastructure of law and justice, and an economic morality.

The attitudes and commonalities of Pope Francis and other faiths represent religious input into the debate about the balance between individual rights and civic responsibility. Whether Christianity or religion in general becomes more popular or not in Europe through such leadership and engagement is a moot point here; the key is that there is a religious influence presented through religious faith, tradition, and logic that continues to shape our ever-developing attitudes. It is an influence that is more related to the global dialogue, more related to pre-industrial ideas of individual responsibility and community, and more obviously centred on the most fundamental Christian tenets. In the West, 'self' is defined by individual experience. In other cultures, 'self' is defined in relation to others. In genuine Confucianism, there is a real alternative to Western individual freedom and liberty as the driving force of progress, or social stability. Confucius struggled to align cosmic and governmental order with the inequality of real Chinese society. His answer was to concentrate on the relationships between the living through duty and honour in shaping their lives. He emphasised the importance of ritual in all aspects of life. He saw the benefits of ritual as being psychological as well as physical, with the repetition of action becoming muscle memory, and inducing calm in the individual and harmony and order in society. Warmth and respect would show care and affection, and in return, engender loyalty and obedience. It includes a version of 'what you don't wish for yourself, do not do to others,' and, like Ancient Greek philosophy, it required active and daily practice. Baggini has argued that Confucian 'harmony' is not the same as acceptance of the status quo: 'It is not bland uniformity but balanced diversity.'* Confucianism is a way of improving the world, not just living in it as it is. Confucius also lived in an innovative period of Chinese history. He believed that relationships with government, or leadership of any kind, should work on the principles of loyalty and obedience on the part of subjects and a duty of care and affection on the part of those in authority. This is the Confucian idea of social or governmental 'contract' rather than mere deference. Elements of this are faintly democratic and individualist. In resurrecting Confucianism for its own reasons, the Chinese Communist Party may find that it cannot contain the original ideas. Confucianism, pre-industrial, and non-divine, may still have something to contribute to Chinese, East Asian, and global dialogue in shaping the future of the debate between individual rights and civic responsibility.

Like Confucianism, South Asia also has a pre-modern philosophy. There is a saying that whoever invades India gets swallowed up by its ancient philosophy, or philosophies. The conglomeration of gods and ideas within the overall idea of Brahma, which Westerners call the belief system of Hinduism, also has a reverence for the past, ancestors, divinity, fate, nature, and the cosmos. Within this, there are the ideas of Karma and reincarnation. In the pre-Buddhist era and 'classical' Hinduism this was fixated primarily on actions to improve the next life. Hinduism has also, however, developed a practical hierarchy that is not in tune with modern global sentiment; a caste system more fixed and central to life than any Western system of class. The caste system is weakening in India, under the pressure of urbanisation, uniformity, communication, and Western values of individual liberty and freedom. It is nevertheless clearly still a formidable force in Indian/Hindu society. In assessing Western colonialism and immorality, Tagore also wrote, just over 100 years ago, of India's 'race problem.' Just as Confucianism can seem as though it fixes a status quo of social order, so the caste system is a fixed blight on India's race towards 'modernity,' and there would seem little room for compromise with the idea of individual non-discriminatory freedom. Yet in its ancient history, the subcontinent also found a new way, that is now about two and a half thousand years old, in the

---

* Baggini, 2018, 224.

teachings of Buddha. Buddha reimagined Karma. It was reformulated to concentrate on the intent of actions in the present life. People do not just have responsibility for themselves but have a relationship with, and responsibility for, others in the present. It is a stretch to write that this represents a 'democratisation' of Karma, but there is an application here, even at the time a revolutionary one, like Confucianism, to the two-way responsibility between governed and governing. The multi-religious 'do unto others as you would do unto yourself' therefore has a contemporary similarity to it in Buddhism. A 'middle way' of moderation with the Four Noble Truths, Eightfold Path, and various 'right' attitudes and actions is not just individually centred, it is a moderate and unharming relationship with others too. Again, these are simple statements of a complex philosophy, but they show a balance between individual rights and civic responsibility which is not alien to Enlightenment, liberal, Western, secular thought, or Christianity. Buddhism too can contribute to a global dialogue of how we should interact with each other and the responsibilities we have to society in general, even though it is also 'pre-modern,' non-divine, and can seem at its core quite individualistic.

A Future for the Ancient Greeks or for Modern Liberalism?

In the Ancient Roman Empire, Seneca wrote that 'it is better to understand the balance sheet of one's own life than that of the corn trade.' Seneca emphasised the 'thoughtful life' over preoccupation with earthly goods. Like Confucianism and Buddhism, Ancient Greek thinking takes us back to the fundamentals of our human nature, and perhaps of universal human nature, and to before the time of our dominating modern narratives of money, industrialisation, competitive 'capitalism' for materialist and resource-driven 'progress,' the measurement of everything, the construction of borders, and the separation of our identities into cultural, religious, and social groups. Is it possible that in order to move beyond the current imbalance between individual rights and civic responsibility we need to go back to pre-modern ideas?

This approach gives us an alternative that is applicable outside the narratives of modern life that are now being called into question, and one that could exist beyond them. Yet, to fall back onto the wisdom of the

Ancient Greeks, or Confucius or Buddha, is to fall back into an ancient time so different from our own, and with their own contradictions or omissions. We need to be more global-minded and all-inclusive, and remain realistic too about how we get there, and maintain an option to change the very nature of who we are, if we decide that we need to. Our global dialogue on the question of the emerging struggles between individual rights and civic responsibility therefore needs to go beyond ancient wisdom.

John Rawls is often seen as one of the most celebrated modern philosophers of the basic principles of Anglo-American liberalism. In his 1971 *A Theory of Justice* Rawls made it clear that political rights and economic and social justice and equality must be achieved in parallel. He asked people to think of the decisions that would be made if they started with a 'veil of ignorance' – that is, an original starting point of not knowing how their life would turn out, including how their identity, born or otherwise, would shape their life. From that perspective, he had faith that people would adapt extensive and equal basic liberties, and that social and economic inequalities would and could be managed for the greatest benefit of the disadvantaged. His ideas are compatible with the classic and egalitarian liberalism of Dworkin, and have had a significant influence on Western democracy and the development of liberal policies. Choosing an inclusive path seemed natural to Rawls after the horrors of war and the Holocaust that he had seen, but the choices of individuals cannot be guaranteed. Most people would say that some will always be more successful than others, and that those who are able to influence the rules will inevitably allow hierarchy, the development of 'interests,' assumptions of 'better' character, and judgement, and development of privileged position. Rawls was revolutionary in his time in his explanation of how inequality and a lack of social justice undermined democratic institutions and society. However, the weakness of the argument, as evidenced by real-world experience and the lack of such a system of governance anywhere at any time, would seem to highlight that the virtues that we may have may not be wholly shared. It seems that within the fundamental character of different people are quite different ideas of what the balance should be between individual rights and civic responsibility. In practice, Rawls' liberalism can only go partway towards satisfying our need for a more effective balance between individual and society. This is one reason why we need a more modern, progressive, inclusive, and global philosophy. Neither Rawls' liberalism nor ancient wisdom gives us a good enough path forward.

Individual Morality

None of the debates about individual rights and civic responsibility pronounce on the private, internal morality of an individual. If people can think for themselves, if this is 'natural' or thought of as 'free will,' then even if we completely define and control the public face of individualism, there may still be 8 billion different private moralities in the world. It will be helpful, however, to understand the red lines between internal individual morality and the expressed public 'morality' that develops or is reflected in the individual rights we claim.

How private should our private individual morality be? This is relevant if we take the view, like Hegel, that history since the Reformation has been about how societies' individual freedoms are finding expression. J.S. Mill believed that the only allowable reason for interference in an individual's liberty in mind or body, either by law or social compulsion, was if they do harm to others. Persuasion was allowed otherwise, but not compulsion – except in certain limited cases of mutual beneficial action, such as jury service or contribution to national defence, but these would be uncommon. This was his working support for how Bentham's Utilitarianism – working for the good of the majority – could avoid a tyranny of that majority over others.

However, 'harming others' clearly needs more definition to be effective. For example, what about smoking? One harms oneself, and inside one's own house it might be considered acceptable, but standing outside might now be considered harmful to others due to passive smoking. What about its potential effects on (health) services and resources that others might be deprived of? Or the harming effect on relationships with others if those others decide that it is harmful to them? Denying healthcare or banning the selling of tobacco might be considered attacks on people's personal freedom and their personal morality. Another level would be the question of how much interference is allowable if the choice is to remain ignorant of consequences, to oneself as well as to others, and what if that is the majority stance, and what if a destructive action produces pleasure and happiness; a majority or minority might enjoy smoking, whether or not they know that it will cut short their life. What would be the balance of persuasion and compulsion in those cases? More up-to-date thinking must also consider the movement in modern times, from trying to influence physical action directly to trying to influence what people think. This is why mental harm is still very much debated. This is partly a politicisation, and partly a reflection and use of the greater knowledge we have about how the brain works and how people think. Some people will think that they can, and should, influence the core inner personal morality of others.

Maintaining individual morality is not just about keeping freedom of thought, it is also about maintaining individual power and development. From this comes the originality of humanity. Only by being able to think freely, by questioning the taboos of the status quo, and by thinking beyond what is established does humanity make progress. This mirrors the five-year-old always asking, Why? and the rebelliousness but developing maturity of an adolescent. Humanity is not a machine that should be programmed. Furthermore, it is arguably one's hopes and fears, ambitions, and impulses, which create the unique character of each member of humanity, even if that is then shaped by experience and regulation. This is why the holy grail of authoritarian regimes is the search for any form of mind control, to control originality and character. When that is accomplished then there is no need for punishment and surveillance, for the required actions will follow. The way to stop people smoking is to use persuasion to develop an alternative judgement within smokers. If there was a switch to flick, then free will would be lost, and the only originality would be what is programmed, which is a contradiction. The reality of what we can influence is reflected in the division between the personal choice of being drunk which may be frowned upon, and being drunk in the driver's seat of a car which has formal and legal consequences because of the potential of harm to others.

WHERE ARE WE GOING?

This is why education is the central battlefield in the political culture wars. Persuasion and compulsion meet in education. Physical coercion is not acceptable. Coercion, like torture, produces distorted results, not long-term compliance. Coercion through law is also unacceptable without any form of informed consensus, whether it applies to a majority or a minority. It is social pressure that largely determines people's individual morality and their behaviour. This may itself be the ultimate proof that at least most of us are social beings. The withdrawal of social acceptance forces most people to review what they are saying or doing and then also what they are thinking. Social pressure may be seen along a timeline as well as a spectrum. It may be the personal process of learning acceptable language. It may be well established, such as a religious tolerance or intolerance. It may originate in the depths of time, such as in protective parenting. These determine the success of the narratives we accept in our lives. Social pressure being reinforced sufficiently to become custom is not necessarily based on reason. It is reinforced simply by the prevailing acts and words of others. Indeed, it may be reinforced more by emotion than reason. It could be argued that loyalty to one's nation is based more upon emotion than upon reason; it is martyrs for a nation's cause that lead others to invest in the narrative. Faith is the key component in accepted custom, whether religious or secular. It may have common sense or reason attached – if going around killing people was a workable way for society to survive or make progress then there would be no Christian Commandment not to kill – but with reason we could get around that, which of course we do through the idea of 'just war' or 'an eye for an eye.' Hence, we use reason to make our faith workable. However, if we used only reason, then many of our narratives, and personal moralities and behaviours, would not be as they are.

To modernise how we live therefore requires both new reasoning and faith in that reasoning, and the investment of emotion in the change. This has the potential to change our individual morality. People believe the emperor even though he has no clothes, until a tipping point of a lack of faith is reached, and people are prepared to think the unthinkable, and then it becomes obvious, their faith in the original narrative crumbles, and what one day was established is the following day dismissed. We can produce the originality that can question the prevailing faith. Social pressure will decide its expression. Obvious coercion is a sign of weakness, presenting the idea that a narrative cannot stand on its own merits, and provoking someone to ask why coercion is needed.

When social pressure is acceptable, it is known as the consensus. When the consensus is firmly established, it becomes education. That may be ongoing societal education or formal, social, and academic education of the young in a 'system' of education or schooling. Deliberately promoted values and actions can ensure their longevity. At its worst, this becomes propaganda, based not on reason but on emotions like loyalty. With propaganda-based education, a society may demonise others to legitimate itself. Nazi Germany and Cambodia's Khmer Rouge swept away what had gone before to promote entirely different values and behaviours. Some can be more subtle than others. The CCP determines a tightly controlled education system that supports its values and follows its political trends. Liberal democracies promote liberal values, not just in clearly political topics, but more deeply in encouraging the individual freedoms and liberties of the Enlightenment, hence open scientific exploration and contemporary debate. Debate is both a strength and a weakness of liberal democracy; open debate within a determined framework that allows questioning of the system. All these education systems recognise the importance of training people how to think. It would be easy to say, as some libertarians might do, that all state education is propaganda, but remember that propaganda is false or misleading information even with an element of truth, and when students are taught to think for themselves, allowed to debate and research without predetermined ends, then that education system is not propaganda. It may have limits on what is allowed – establishing red lines for tolerance/racism, for free speech/incitement to violence – but it is not propaganda. Social pressure in a liberal democracy can be huge, but authoritarian regimes attempt to alter the process of people's thinking for its own ends. This is most obvious in the way that a liberal democracy loosens the shackles of thought and debate when children become adults. An authoritarian regime does not do that. Individual morality is not allowed to blossom on its own after the guardrails of learning through maturity have been removed. Authoritarian regimes risk too much in doing so. Original ideas are what produce questioning, reform, and a new consensus that allows a liberal democracy to renew itself more peacefully. Established centres of power may have a major influence on the narratives and social pressures within a liberal democracy, but they can always be questioned. This is why we must have confidence that we can change our communities for the better, and even question, re-work, or dispense with, some of our most established narratives. The possibility of overthrowing an authoritarian regime will remain for as long as people have their own individual morality.

Jean-Paul Sartre wrote that people are free but impose limits on themselves by the constructed interpretation of their circumstances and experience – for example by deciding that success is making money, or by defining what good parenting is based on their own experiences in childhood of being punished when questioning authority. Although these personal constructs may be a core, everyday part of their lives, they are still constructs that can be changed. Social pressure, self-enforced or not, can be resisted. Originality can bloom. Many people may feel that they are not in control of their lives, but the person they can be is shaped by their own constructs as much as anyone else's. Their individual morality is their own.

Real Life

Most people spend their energy living their lives as best as they can, buffeted by all sorts of pressures they feel they have no control over. Their lives are broadly predictable. But this does not apply to everyone. Some people have different perspectives and opportunities through wealth, ill-health or disability, or particular life-changing experiences. Most people in the Western world have what we recognise as a childhood, and develop into maturity, work, family life and parenting, retirement and older age. These stages themselves may play out with a sense of empowerment or powerlessness. Values and behaviours may not be the same from one generation to the next – the place that women hold in society is clearly the most obvious. The pressures are multi-dimensional:

social, political, cultural, economic, technological, even climatic, as well as specific peer, family and local community pressures, and physical and mental changes of a life being lived. In these areas is experienced the reality of individual rights and civic responsibility, and the development of individual personal morality. Change may be regressive. Across the generations and in each stage of life, expectations may change. Some of the worries, hopes, and ambitions may be the same, but the context, challenges, and outcomes may be different. The experience of change itself is different and often unpredictable for different people within and across generations.

Childhood and Education

Children are different. They are children. As daft as it may be to write that, we often seem to not know what it means. Most people recognise when they see a dependent child, and when they see someone in transition to maturity who is trialling and developing their opinions and behaviours. Equally, people recognise a young adult, someone able to argue their opinions, who has an informed opinion themselves, and whose actions recognise a balance of rights and responsibilities that includes some empathy towards others, although they don't necessarily have great experience of 'adult' relationships or events. This is not necessarily identifiable or determined by age, but there is, of course, a physical development aspect of this. We can recognise, sometimes understand, and judge, adults whose mental development does not quite fit into this journey to maturity, and we label them in particular ways, perhaps with some form of medical-social diagnosis, and give them varied amounts of help and empathy, or adopt a negative judgemental attitude.

Childhood and education in terms of rights and responsibilities are defined inconsistently both within nations and between different nations. Many of the differences in attitude to education are historical and determined by factors such as different cultural practices in relation to class, wealth, expected occupation, marriageable or working ages, and the farming calendar. Much of the education of the upper classes has been about being schooled in control, so instilling attributes such as confidence, or even a sense of superiority, has been considered crucial.

WHERE ARE WE GOING?

Middle-class education developed to be managerial, and order- and responsibility-based. Working-class education often developed from religious observance to avoid sin and to be productive and deferential, and was focussed on the technical and vocational, based on instruction. Girls' education historically was about motherhood and the home, when it existed. Rural education concentrated on rural skills.

The world we live in now is quite different. To some degree, virtually everywhere has mass education based as much on rights as need. It aims to give equality of opportunity. The right to education, free at least in 'elementary' stages, is number 26 in the UN Universal Declaration of Human Rights. The Taliban Afghan government is the only one in the world formally preventing girls' secondary education, although in other places it is hindered by payment costs and other social pressures. Societies can still be divided over the necessity of, and resource allocation for, educational opportunities. Some allocate opportunity via testing and division, while others organise on individual choice. Formal schooling now is a dominant aspect of childhood almost everywhere. It has also become a necessity for many working parents. It has become 'professionalised' and uses measurement, curricula, timetables, targets, comparisons, reports, and an overall judgement of academic and social performance, at the expense of an open learning process. It is high stakes and mentally draining for many children. At its core is supporting the commercialised world that adults have created. To some extent, success or failure is always personal, but this is reinforcing itself in the education systems that we are promoting. Students take those lessons into their working and adult lives in the form of accepting pressurised working environments, testing, competition, and an emphasis on knowledge. Some people dispute this view and claim that there exists a strong emphasis on learning personal, social, life, and communal skills in education. However, although these skills are often spoken of as though they are valued, they are overwhelmingly considered as secondary in the final measurement. Naturally, good education values these skills for their input into effective learning, but childhood gets very mixed messages: academic or vocational, individual or collective, knowledge or understanding, schooling or lifelong, life-determining or not. It does a lot right, but so much is expected of it, and adults often seem to expect a finished article rather than investing in that training themselves. This is a harsh judgement on both sides, but we have not embraced continual and lifelong education in both soft and hard skills in the way that we should.

We have gone through phases of letting children be seen but not heard, of being 'family friendly,' of dressing them differently, and of dressing them as small adults, of encouraging adventure and being risk-averse. The circumstances in which we bring up our children have changed dramatically. They used to work in the fields with us, or in cottage industries at our feet. Now we outsource much of their education and skills to others in a way that goes far beyond traditional communal upbringing. We used to keep them close, and may still try to do so, but now at least digitally they can scan the world without us knowing. We understand that the sum of knowledge to be learnt is far greater than ever before. It is continuing to increase and changes rapidly beyond our own educational experience or skills. Parents have surely always wanted their children to be happy, safe, and confident in themselves, but it is interesting to wonder how much we are now more ambitious for them, how much we want them to have a better life than ourselves, how much we expect progress, in comparison to previous eras. All of this requires different and difficult judgements of experience and development: how to balance the development of individual personality and instruction, or when to let children be free and when to ensure safe controls are in place. We do understand the need for individualism in our children and know their paths to maturity will be different. This is Enlightenment in action and in its weakness. Freedom allowing varied parenting and education is what allows the development of individualism and originality, including different perspectives, within the guardrails of a liberal democracy. The comprehensive psychology of education, and the whole child development not just the schooling, surely requires more investigation in terms of the exploration of balance between confident individual rights, personality, the collective relationships and responsibilities that need nurturing, and the knowledge, skills, and understanding required for an active and positive economic and social contribution as an adult. When we have a better understanding of these balances then we can fulfil individual and societal potential.

Nor, however, must we lose the learning of the parent in parenting that clarifies their own values, honesty with themselves, tolerance, resilience, humility, and adaptability. Learning with children or young adults is and should be a two-way process, with gains on each side.

We are also beginning to understand that experiences such as stress affect brain function. We already know that adolescent brains function differently to fully adult ones. Furthermore, early studies show that young children of higher socio-economic and health backgrounds have, in general, a greater surface area of the brain, making higher cognitive function possible. This still requires far more study, and a correlation between high socio-economic-health-rich brains and high-achieving students is not inevitable. As we learn more about the brain, it may be that educational and social interventions can originate from studying the brains of individuals, and enable individualised education that mirrors individualised medicine. This might be alarming to many people.

All this means we must address the glaring inadequacies in childhood. Creativity needs to flourish, as well as skills investment. Open routes to, and less separation philosophically and practically, between academic and vocational education are needed. Childhood needs to have some of its mental pressure alleviated (and physical activity enhanced). What we decide are the legalities, and legal boundaries, need enforcing – social media age limits, working hours of children, etc. We need to do much more to address inequalities of opportunity within education, within nations, and across nations. We need to reinforce not just the education of, but also the understanding of and reasoning behind, our key values. We must teach much more about mental health for life. We need to teach thinking and co-operative skills, including different perspective and judgement, and how to self-educate and how to be informed, and what all that really means. We need to do this in a context of an increasingly global and digital, technological, and bio-scientific world. We need to measure our success as well as allow variety and originality and not treat all children the same. Most of all, we need to be clearer when we are working with children, or with adults, about, for example, the messages we are sending on nutrition, equality, violence, and freedom of expression. We need to ensure that we are giving young developing adults a taste of adult rights and responsibilities and a chance to learn for themselves. Education, health, and safety are the greatest things we can bestow on our societies, and our future societies are our children. We must take greater care of them.

If an authority's relationship with society is one of control, then education cannot nurture creativity or interpretation except in a purely technical and economic context. It cannot abide variety, for that recognises difference, and difference breeds alternatives, empathy, individuality, and originality. It will not loosen the shackles of control from child to mature adult. To some extent, all education of childhood is propaganda if a society has any confidence that it is doing the right thing, and liberal democracies should acknowledge that too, and be prepared to reflect. They should trumpet that they build in the originality and individualism that allows accountability, change, and resilience within an inclusive democratic framework, that allows everyone the opportunity to flourish, even if this is an ideal to be constantly perfected.

Generational Divide

The existence of a generational gap, or change, is not new. Everyone is of 'their' generation, and that gives each generation a unique perspective and starting point for comment and interpretation. It also gives each person an element of their own identity, which they will want to be proud of and defend, or rebel against and denounce.

When there are changing circumstances or new challenges, there will be new ideas. There are tipping points in history and while these are rarer than the emergence of each generation, they are nevertheless the cause and effect of generational, or multi-generational, changes. They stretch and break social norms and values, producing different behaviours and different 'politics,' perhaps even different languages, by changing priorities as well as ways of doing things. The 1960s in the Western world is seen clearly as beginning a generational change socially, and the same period could also be such a turning point for many others around the world through decolonisation. If links are maintained between generations, then there is no dislocation, and the parents' wish for a better life for their children is itself a strong incentivising link.

'Link,' though, is not quite the right word. 'Trust' would be better.

WHERE ARE WE GOING?

Older generations must be able to trust that younger generations will carry on the baton of the society as they broadly know it. They may have their own generational failures to acknowledge, a recognition of changing circumstances, even a 'tiredness' or resignation to effect change that makes handing over that baton easier to do. They will want to see a younger generation succeed and carry on their family stories and societal narratives. They must trust that it will do so, not change everything in a 'year zero' destruction of all that they valued. With such trust, society remains cohesive, and the younger generation will be allowed and supported to find its new ideas and new ways in its new solutions. However, it works both ways. The younger generation must see value for themselves and the future in at least some of what has gone before. They need to be prepared to build on it. The past forms part of their own identity and to simply condemn it and wish it away is a revolutionary thought leading to rare revolutionary action and unpredictable consequences. A lack of leadership or resilience of new ideas when they come into collision with real life can derail change, sometimes inspiring a more successful next-generation attempt. People have a natural desire to express curiosity, to seek their own originality. This may not at that time or in future years be judged as progressive, it may be regressive or result in failed change, but stagnation is a rare human characteristic.

Allied to the rights revolutions, global demographic change and scientific and technological development may make the generational differences playing out today more of a tipping point than many generations experience. Whether we want it or not, whether it is beneficial or divisive, with or without economic integration, globalisation is affecting our identity. We are more knowledgeable of each other across the globe than ever before, on individual, societal, and governmental scales, in beliefs, philosophies, histories, and contemporary lifestyle. We may misunderstand, we may not like all we perceive, we may pick and choose and make poor judgements, but the dialogue is happening between peoples, not just between elites as in earlier times. Older generations – and of course this is a stereotype – have much less experience of completely different global perspectives, and the changes that globalisation brings may seem disruptive or destructive to their own lives and values. We should not underestimate their ability to adapt, from the acceptance of 'foreign' food to internet use, to mixed racial marriage. But change can be unsettling and require more explanation, understanding and patience, and personal good experience. Change needs to be 'sold' to an older generation in a way that it does not need to be to a younger one who may already be looking for something different – whether due to rebelliousness or to solve perceived societal problems. For many, global change is making the link with the younger generations weaker. The speed of this change can be head-spinning. If parents have some understanding of the change, then the break is less fundamental. This is one difference between revolution and reform. One example of this is the extension of the rights revolutions to the redefinition of gender itself. This is a profound change, affecting the security of identity, of marriage and relationships, of language, of tradition and history, and of the meaning of religious faith and belief. It elicits a need for changed values and behaviour. Where such a change of perspective is suddenly imposed without empathy, it produces anxiety or may seem alien, and may therefore be rejected. Clearly, not everyone in any generation thinks the same way, either young or old, but this is how an older generation comes to be seen as ignorant, intolerant, or Luddite. In the face of such accusations, they may, in turn, feel isolated and powerless. Sometimes the logicality and practice of a change simply needs time to be processed. This is a clash of time and numbers with youthful impatience and idealism.

Demographic changes are not the same across the world but in general, populations are getting older. Where a younger population is in the ascendant in terms of numbers, more substantial change is likely to be called for. How successful it is may then depend upon how they can influence the levers of economic and political power. Where they do not do so, physical action for change becomes more likely – the Arab Spring, the anti-hijab protests in Iran, anti-corruption – though not necessarily more certain of success in the short or medium term. They may be resisted by an older generation exercising political power but feeling no association with the change others want. They may be resisted by a governing class that becomes more isolated and depends more on surveillance and the willingness to use force. This creates a class that becomes more fortified by the belief in their own superiority and more intolerant of the global dialogue being carried out by those 'below' them.

Let us be clear that older people are interested in the life chances of their children and grandchildren, and frequently sacrifice their time, interests, and money for them when they can. They are also not immune to being sold novelty or new ideas and are not without courage to try new things. Self-interest, though, is also self-preservation and they will vote and protest from the perspective of their own instilled opinions and ideas and their own life experiences. Older people will demand health and social care and say that they have 'paid their taxes' and struggled for their rights. They may have also benefitted from the circumstances of their own youthful generation and from policies such as welfare development, widening access to free education, and locks ensuring pension value, etc. In Western nations these did not happen without a struggle, but the result has been a considerable build-up of wealth for many, although not all, of those who are older, more relative value in wealth than income, and the growing importance of inheritance. A younger generation can look at these as in-built advantages that they have not shared. They have lost free higher education, for many house prices and rents have risen beyond affordability, and saving has become impossible. Younger people report a greater sense of powerlessness, less political influence, more awareness of discrimination and lack of social mobility, more pressure for qualifications, more external issues that they see as affecting their future (most notably but not only environment- and climate-related), more personal freedoms but without the wherewithal to enjoy them, and a sense of fewer of them paying more tax for people who already have, or have had, advantages. The idea of a younger generation being poorer and living shorter lives than their parents has taken hold in the Western world even though many things have undoubtedly improved. The political aspect of this is very important. Younger generations are political in terms of issues, but untethered in terms of party politics. Party politics has encouraged competition between the interests of generations, rather than balance and responsibility for each other. The generational divide we have now is at least partly of our own making, but it is not broken and can be shrunk with the skills and commitment required in solving any division, that is, dialogue and a willingness to compromise. Policies are available such as paid intern work rather than being unpaid, rent controls that can re-balance and re-create stability and increase fairness in the tenant-landlord relationship, and addressing zero-hour contract work instability. These would help younger workers struggling to save and start families. This is aside from more radical solutions like Universal Basic Income. Without change generational division will grow, and simply entrench those social, cultural, and economic divisions that we already have. These are divisions of hope and ambition, expectations and possibilities, outlook and power, quality of life and life expectancy. The gaps in society are not just or even primarily generational, but like in education, these are entrenched the earlier they start.

Someone now sixty years old has experienced the sort of economic shocks that have moved them on from the post-war regeneration era. It is quite possible that their own struggles will make them more sympathetic to the next or youngest generation, for they have experienced some or similar issues themselves and at times in their life felt equally powerless. Traditionally people get more socially and economically conservative as they grow older – more to defend, less comfortable with change – but that is not inevitable. While this description of the generation divide is focussed on the UK so much of it is also true across the Western world.

In places like China and Iran one sees a maturing of the larger younger generation, and a distancing from them of older elites, complicated by politically fixed ideology that does not bridge the generational divide. It was always the hope of the West that economic liberalism would produce social and then political change, but older and distinct groups have solidly entrenched themselves in power. They have the leadership and mechanics of the surveillance or military state so invested in their success that a younger generation's access to the levers of power seems a very distant prospect. In India there are more underlying social trends for change that can find public, commercial, and private expression, but also a cumbersome state-federal system of government and a distractive or fundamental – depending on your view – movement of politics towards a more conservative and expressive Hindu majority view. The maintenance of representative Western-style Indian democracy may depend on the religious-secular-economic balance that the younger generation want.

As rapid as scientific discovery and technological innovation often seems to be it may still take a generation or more to move from discovery to general application. Some of this is forgotten when we think in retrospect. The denial of the secondary nature of Earth in relation to the universe must have taken generations to reach general acceptance. Biotechnology and machine learning may be equally profound, or disruptive. The question is whether development remains recognised across generations. Some changes may be so dramatic when unleashed on society that they do not seem recognisably moored to what came before. The names and language may also seem alien. This is not inevitably a fracturing point in society. For example, germs were once unheard of, but soap quickly became understood; social sciences were once derided as irrelevant and unreal, but now we understand at least the presence and usefulness of psychology. Nevertheless, the fracturing of society when big changes occur is always a danger.

Aside from the dislocation of understanding between generations are the difficulties of learning. If there is a valid point to learning something new, then this can be done until physical abilities prevent it, but access, quality, and availability of explanation, and practice, are the stumbling blocks. We do not currently appreciate and plan enough for older people, with or without physical impairment or mental decline. Is remote or non-human-contact good enough to establish success, integrity, and trust? How much will both sides lose from the lack of real human contact? How can mental health be maintained and isolation reduced? Even with remote access, many are barred from this due to logistical and financial restraints, and deliberate intervention would therefore be necessary. Scientific and technological development need not be a sign of, or a cause and consequence of, generational division, but we must actively make sure it is not, otherwise it will be.

Partnership/Marriage, and Family

'Marriage' comes in three main forms: love marriages that are freely entered into; 'arranged' (or 'assisted') marriages that occur in perhaps the majority of places around the world; and forced, which must become unacceptable. Arranged marriages do come with some expectation and real pressure but can nevertheless usually be refused. Often, they originate from a matchmaker who has chosen a match based on 'suitability' and factors such as class/caste, geographical heritage, education, character, the reputation of the family. Or they may be chosen for the benefit or advancement in some way of both families. In 2018 in a main Shanghai park, I saw hundreds of profiles of people written out like CVs, with photos, looking for partnerships and marriages. Social media dating sites are modern tech versions of this. Such ways of meeting increasingly narrow our possibilities as we, or an algorithm, delve into family background, education, career prospects, political association, and other factors. A YouGov Economist poll in the USA in 2020 stated that '86% think it has grown more difficult to date someone who supports the opposing political party…'[*] To some extent marrying outside one's known group has always been radical.

Around the world marriage echoes family values and represents 'normalcy.' It represents societal pressure that associates marriage and having children as a cultural duty and expectation. Indeed, the issue of marriage is a key point of disagreement in minority communities where there is a deliberate parental effort to keep the family's cultural identity. Living together as a large extended family is a common factor in many parts of the world from traditional southern European cultures to African, to South and East Asia. However, living in smaller nuclear family units is also on the increase around the world, due to adult children living further afield, having more social freedom, and the availability of contraception. Historically, urbanisation has enabled individuals to live more independently. The stigma of single parenthood and of staying single itself is also weakening. For some, due to cultural and social norms, marriage is still only legitimate between a man and a woman. For others, the institution of marriage itself, even without the religious aspect, is a valuable contribution to a partnership and should be available to anyone whatever their sexuality and however they

---

[*] Alejandra O'Connell-Domenech, "Politics are increasingly a dating dealbreaker – especially for women," *The Hill* (an American politics-based media group), 25 March 2023.

view their gender. Practicality and ideologically the freedom to cohabit without marriage is also increasing. In other places, cohabitation is accepted but socially frowned upon. In most places legality does still favour a formally married couple, in financial, child, and other rights.

The ease of divorce varies greatly from place to place, and cultural and religious acceptance of it also varies. Divorce is one of those issues related to women's rights, independence, and equality. In a number of countries the practicality and social isolation resulting from it continue to make it a predominantly male option. In many countries the fate of children and assets after divorce continues to favour men.

Arranged marriages vary according to cultural regions and national customs.* In India 90% of all marriages are still arranged. These marriages have a traditional reputation of being more stable and long-lasting than 'own choice' or 'love' marriages, but in many nations, and minority communities, ending such a marriage is still heavily discouraged by family and community pressure, pride, and practicality. Divorce rates per thousand in the UK, Germany, France, and Japan range between 1.5 and 1.9, in the USA it is 2.3. Yet, in Islamic Saudi Arabia and Iran divorce rates are 2.1 and 2.2 respectively. In strongly Catholic Mexico it is 0.7 per thousand and in 'non-religious' China it is 3.2.† In the UK, reasonably typical of most Western nations, divorce rates seem to have reached a plateau.‡ In the UK of those who married in 1995, 25% did not reach their tenth anniversary, whereas of those who married in 2011, it is 18%. Over a long period of time women and men have been getting married later in life, and according to the 2021 census, 37.9% of UK adults have never been wed. Globally, women have always been the younger partner. The reasons for not marrying, or for delaying marriage, seem to be the same, or similar, globally and the most prominent reasons are lack of housing, low wages, and cost-of-living pressures. In the UK, it is now more likely for motherhood

---

* Raksha Pande, "Young British Indians are embracing arranged marriage – just not in the traditional sense," *The Conversation*, 29 April 2021.
† "Divorce rates by country," *Wisevoter*, an independent American organisation set up in 2019 to provide information globally 'to citizens, voters, and elected officials.' www.wisevoter.com.
‡ Figures in this section for England and Wales, or the UK, are from the Office for National Statistics, including the 2021 Census.

to happen before marriage (whatever the age), but around the world, this is still unusual. Later marriage is a global trend. In the UK about 15% of families are single-parent families, and this is a number that has levelled out over the last ten years. In the USA 23% of under 18s are raised by a single parent (of whom 80% are mothers), but this compares globally with 7% of all families, with, for example, the figures in India being at just 5% of all families. In the USA about 10% of children are raised in extended families (whose definition can vary), whereas globally this would be 38%.* Single figures do not always measure the same things and interpretation can be different. Figures are further complicated by the increasing multi-cultural nature of societies globally, making national figures and traditions sometimes very unrepresentative of specific groups. Ideas of moral decline and increased freedom remain standard bearers of debates about partnership, marriage, divorce, and family life.

Individualism is also changing the nature of family life. Real female equality is part of this, altering the nature of legal, financial, child, and separation rights, and expectations of child-rearing, paid work, housework, and general decision-making in partnerships and family. The changing role of women is also making society think about the changing role of men – changes that encompass both emotional and intellectual factors. To some, this is seen as the 'feminisation' of men. To others, it is more about seeing men in the round and about a maturing of societal views around discrimination, conflict, and how people work together, the priorities of government, and religious practice. For some, these changing roles are seen as lessening the place of women as life-givers through childbearing. Sometimes, these objections are by women themselves, at other times, these objections separate and 'protect' women in ways determined by men. The right of same-sex couples to marry has caused a re-focus on the institution of marriage itself. Increasing same-sex couples having children has produced a parallel re-focus on the institution of 'family.' These gender role changes are having a revisionist effect on some basic beliefs and interpretations of religion, including the nature of love in Christianity. Multiple wives remain legally possible in

---

* US Census Bureau, www.census.gov; Stephanie Kramer, "US has world's highest rate of children living in single parent households," *Pew Research Center*, 12 December 2019.

the Middle East and West and Central Africa, by virtue of treating wives 'equally.' An estimated 11% of sub-Saharan Africans live in polygamous households.* A woman with multiple husbands is known in some tribal communities around the world but is far rarer. In the 1990s I met an Egyptian man whose father had two wives, but as a more formally educated urban thirty-something he could not conceive of doing so himself. Traditions and practices do change.

The nature of family, and the power dynamics within family, are important parts of how we identify 'family values.' These have importance in political, community, religious, and legal systems, in the distribution of the world's wealth, and in mechanisms of conflict resolution. To some extent these family values can be controlled or influenced by existing controlling interests in society. However, they are also the cause and consequence of social trends under the surface, practised and changed on an individual and family basis, with everyday decisions and repercussions, taken intuitively, emotionally, or deeply thought out, which cannot be checked by the powerful institutions of societies. The women-led demonstrations that erupted after the death of Mahsa Amini in September 2022 after her detention for not wearing a hijab 'properly' are a serious part of the social and increasingly political dynamic in theological Iran that has since the 2000s seen increasing demonstrations in favour of female equality, accompanied by the willingness of many young men to see that as acceptable and normal, and beneficial. There are now more women than men in Saudi universities – although in 2016 according to the World Bank only 22% of Saudi women worked outside the home compared to 78% of men.† No-one knows how sustainably acceptable that disparity will be for Saudi women. In many black communities around the world, from the United States to West Africa, women are notably on the rise as small-scale entrepreneurs, and are unlikely to give up that individual independence and power when they marry. Indeed they are likely to only marry someone who accepts them not just for who they are but who they could be.

---

* "Religion and living arrangements around the world," *Pew Research Center*, 12 December, 2019.
† Al Arabiya News (English), from Saudi Ministry of Education, published 28 May 2015, updated 20 May 2020; Alainna Liloia, "Saudi women are going to college, running for office and changing the conservative country," *The Conversation*, 25 March 2019.

INDIVIDUALISM, SOCIETY, AND CITIZENSHIP

Fundamental change, of course, is not easy. This is illustrated by the continuing struggle to legally and socially even out the responsibilities of child-rearing between women and men. In China, for the first time, in February 2021 a man was ordered by the court acting under a new civil code to pay for housework done over the course of the marriage when he filed for divorce.* It indicated the global reach and recognition of the changing dynamics of family, how family is valued, and the influence of individual rights. Multiple wives, or husbands, cannot have a future in a world of equality. Matchmakers may become more common, whether the matchmaker is a personal specialist or a technology platform. The institution of marriage is still strong but entering it as a religious commitment much less so. As partnerships become more varied, and more freely and equally entered into, religious and legal authorities will have to reassess their acceptability, as well as reassess the idea of divorce and re-marriage. They will need to address fundamental questions of what marriage is for and what it should reflect. The values inherent in a serious partnership, of love, mutual respect, honesty, etc, should be echoed in religious-based or supported values. The institution of marriage as a formal statement of partnership would seem to have just as much of a future as it has always had, and will be more equal in the future. If formalised marriage does not adapt, then partnership rather than formal marriage will replace it rather than coexist alongside it. Therefore, divorce is not necessarily the enemy of marriage. Maintaining a lifelong permanent 'bad' marriage with no way out does the institution a disfavour and will discredit it. Divorce is therefore to be welcomed in principle. It can save the institution, although it must also be fairly applied.

This is not to say that the greater picture of individualism, of which women's rights are just one part, does not present some danger. Whether informal partnership or formal marriage, civic or religious, no relationship must become simply materialistic or transactional, subject to individual whim. Marriage is not to be dismissed easily when voluntarily begun just because it has become difficult for the individual, that is also part of the respect of the institution. Care, mutual respect,

---

* Helen Davidson, "Woman awarded $7,700 for five years of housework in China divorce ruling," *The Guardian*, 24 February 2021.

to begin with and fight for a commitment to last, and to avoid harm to any resulting children, should be universal values in marriage. They may echo the politicised 'family values' but the philosophy is quite different. There is similarity in a wish for continuity, certainty, and tradition. However, politicised family values have become a culture war issue linked subjectively to others such as state intervention, support for different types of families, of provision for separation and divorce, and the idea of state promotion of specific meanings of family. The state has almost as much to do to accept the 'freedom' of family and adapt to its changing nature as religion does. This is true across the globe where the journey of 'family' as an institution mirrors not just the journeys across the globe of women's, LGBTQ, and disability rights, but also the balance of individual or societal predominance, and government accountability, responsibility, or control.

Parenting

Giving children rights, rather than viewing them as just being the property of parents, may have been the greatest state intervention in family life that there has ever been. But there is still a balance being sought between the triangular points of excessive child individualism, parental responsibilities, and the rights of the carers/parents themselves. The change from dependent child to young maturing adult can be fraught for everyone concerned, with missteps along the way that are part of the learning process, and which should not be subject to moral judgement on an individual level. Just as the institution of the family is constantly changing, so are the dynamics within individual families, and this is not automatically 'a bad thing.' This allows adaptability and development in the politicised public 'family values' too. Religious, cultural, or social constraints will mean that there are limits to the pace of change.

These are also changing the nature of parenting. It is and always has been a pressurised job, not least because it revolves around individuals who change. What worked in one generation may not work in another – lifestyle and standard of living are different. The historic trend towards individual educative parenting should be welcomed. Treating children as learning youngsters, understanding their own character, relationships, and navigating the guardrails of their freedoms and responsibilities within the society in which they live, is difficult. This has replaced the Victorian-style parenting, which was based on the idea that children should be 'seen but not heard.' In the pre-industrial era, children would become part of the working family much earlier than they do today, but in general there was more freedom, space, and community – depending upon the circumstances of status, working life, feudal restrictions, and the various levels of criminal violence, war, or ill-health. Since that time, formal education, industrialisation, and urbanisation have given children knowledge and skills, but have also hemmed them in. Our more recent developments in modern education and parenting should therefore be welcomed. They are good not only for children's development but also for nations. Informed by psychology, imparted with empathy, and provoking emotional intelligence, these result in more tolerant, resilient, mentally healthier, and creative individuals, better able to manage risk, and make positive contributions to society, and workers who are more adaptable. These are not the only skills necessary in the modern world, but they are needed alongside the specific knowledge, skills, and understanding that formal education imparts. Overall, our modern approach to parenting is one of our most substantial applications of individualism, and one of the most revolutionary changes in how we choose to live.

Within this general approach, there are subtleties and pressures. Choosing whether to perform or conform is also part of a child's learning process. Performing educationally has become a valuable commodity, where a good job is so important for personal progress. In some developing nations, only one child may be afforded schooling. Parents can be so acutely conscious of this that they place tremendous pressure on their children and the educational experience can become suffocating. This 'tiger parent' strategy in upper- or middle-income nations, a phrase coined in the USA from a more commonly East Asian approach, is understandable and can clearly be taken too far. It is promoted by the idea of progress through individualism and is often the cause of stress for individuals and societies. It is often intertwined with a sense of national duty. It is difficult not to imagine that this is an approach that will be changed by future generations as they match mental health, freedom, creativity, happiness, and, yes, individuality, with duty to nation and family. Globally, suicide is the fourth leading cause of death for fifteen to twenty-nine-year-olds.* Around the world, online-expressed mental health issues are a symptom of the stress experienced by today's youth. In more liberal nations, there are some people who feel that children are not put under enough pressure to build resilience and fulfil potential, and they contrast the academic educational achievement of various East Asian nations, often from a perspective of 'national progress.' However, the national and cultural contexts are quite different and should be taken into account.

In a West with less connection between national duty and individual success, a stronger welfare safety net, and less individual and family conformity, there is generally a more liberal approach. This is the education of a fairer, emotionally intelligent, more citizen-based society, rather than one led more by government. Class or status, financial stability, and discriminatory division still matter in Western societies, but these issues stand out because the principles of society in the long term are more clearly than ever tilting towards equality of opportunity and respect, and individual freedoms. Clearly, not all parents can afford, in time, money, or patience, an idealistic liberal form of parenting, and most still see the need for their children to have a better life than they have had in a world where not everything is improving. But the individual character of their children is still their core parenting approach.

Many parents hear about lower life expectancy than themselves, mental health pressures, a daunting array of choices and influences, and insecurity. It is easy in such a scenario to be too risk-averse online or in the real world. This is an approach which produces more nervous and less healthy, and less entrepreneurial or creative, adults. With such an education, individuality has less expression, but the conformity achieved is also more fragile. This is also a parenting that stores up trouble for the future of the child and the nation.

Single parents have been a source of politicisation for a long time. They are variously accused of destroying the family, of being welfare

---

* "Suicide, Key Facts," *World Health Organization,* 17 June 2021. https://www.who.int/news-room/fact-sheets/detail/suicide.

dependents, and of depriving their child of an essential parent, usually the father. These attitudes are tied to traditional ideas of family and motherhood, and indeed an ideal of fatherhood. This is particularly applied to single women choosing to have a child when not in a relationship. Alternatively, choosing to be a single parent is one of the most important and difficult decisions of their lives, both for themselves and for their child. Single parents become so for many different reasons and, as in other spheres of life, we need to look more carefully at the details of why. Often, the alternative to single parenthood is a dysfunctional family that harms a child's emotional development and its notion of healthy relationships. In this context, single parenting should be viewed as a selfless route to take. We must neither blame nor seek to put the challenges of family, fatherhood, motherhood, or society's general ills at the doorstep of single parents. Single parents need the support of society, both morally and practically; they should be supported whether they choose to take part in a functioning economy or alternatively decide that being a stay-at-home parent is the best thing for themselves and their child. These are important points to consider in the necessary continuing improvement of equality between the genders.

Progressive and individualised education (despite being an anathema to an authoritarian-minded government) continues to become more widespread, and is the key reason why so many trends in global life will continue to improve; this includes the realisation that single mothers and fathers need to be supported while the rights of non-parent adults are also protected.

Retirement and Old Age

Historically, people did not retire at a specific age. They worked until they were no longer able to. This was partly due to a lack of welfare, and they were instead taken care of by family. Official retirement is a modern construct. However, Dr Lochana Shrestha, chairperson of Health Home Care Nepal, says: 'Nowadays most families are nuclear… they have no time to spend with the elderly or care for them… the children have to earn money for their medical treatment.'* Historically, army

---

* Nunuta Rai, "The growing popularity of elderly care homes in urban Nepal," *Online*

pensions were the first pensions in existence. In industrial and urbanised economies from around the 1800s, governments gradually extended tax rates, insurance schemes, and their own welfare programmes in order to match expectations and increase democratic accountability. The increasing wealth of nations made this possible in the context of a growing working-age age population and relatively small number of 'old people,' with many living only a few years into their formal retirement age.

However, these circumstances are changing. Over 100 countries currently have pension schemes for the elderly, but in 2000, the International Labour Organization (ILO) estimated that 90% of the world's working-age population was not covered by a scheme capable of providing adequate retirement income.* Since 2000, any improvements in the amounts provided have occurred against a tide of worsening worker-pensionable ratios. Using Thailand as an example, it estimated that in 1970, the worker/over-65 ratio was 17:1, but by 2030, this ratio is likely to be 13:1. A smaller number of people are therefore paying a greater share of the tax burden for an increasing number of retirees. This has become a generational issue, and a financially unsustainable one. We are now seeing how different governments are trying to cope. Approaches include getting older people to work longer, getting more women into work, developing new technologies, or using immigration. In turn, many of these approaches have created their own complications, including social and political consequences that have impacted issues as far-reaching as national identity.

The formalisation of retirement, even its acceptance as an idea, has contributed to other serious consequences. As older people have become separated from society and treated differently, their status has changed and diminished. In the past, when older generations were rooted in community, their identity as a source of experience and wisdom meant that they were treated with respect. Generational division has occurred as generations have become more defined, and this applies to the 'old' as well as to the young.

Khabar (English), 9 February, 2022. Also see, Sharad Shrestha, Arja R. Aro, Bipna Shrestha, and Subash Thapa, "Elderly care in Nepal: Are existing health and community support systems enough?" *SAGE Open Medicine*, Vol 9:1–5, 2021.

* "Ninety per cent of world excluded from old age pension schemes," *ILO*, 28 April, 2000.

INDIVIDUALISM, SOCIETY, AND CITIZENSHIP

There are also more generations, and life has become more fluid. Partnership and parenting are starting later and, therefore, lasting to a later age. This also means more independent youthful years beforehand and more time spent as a single adult. Life has become distinctly longer than in historic times too, so whereas once 'the old' was a single generation, now it is not. Even as pension age increases, a new retired but active generation is being created. Then, there is the post-active generation from the age of eighty or so, who are living longer with an onset of multiple health conditions that can be survived but require support. There are older people who have not been able to save, can give nothing in inheritance, depend on rent or state support, while others own property and wealth, maintain health and opportunity, and can afford insurance. So, there are more generations, more defined, who all exist within the greater context of wealth inequality. Despite the often diminished status of older generations, they nevertheless hold political influence, which is something that politicians choose to manage or to exploit with deliberate, or perhaps careless, policy. The older generations tend to vote more than younger generations. Some older people, therefore, may feel that they have greater influence, and as numbers increase, a greater right. Just as it is incumbent upon the young to understand their elders, so it is also therefore incumbent on the older to balance their rights with those of the younger – especially the wealthier older to contribute to the care of the poorer. There are many advantages for individuals and nations in the continued participation of older generations but in this context, none has yet found a good or settled balance between the rights and responsibilities of older individuals and groups, and the rights and responsibilities afforded to and by the nation as a whole.

In searching for a more up-to-date balance, the idea of retirement is being called into question. This is almost certainly a good thing as long as the individualism and individual circumstances of people can be accommodated. If more older people work, then there will also be more older people who are able to pay tax. Some will be able to put off state pensions, while others will need more support due to ill-health. Currently, these are specifically Western trends, but they are becoming global issues. For those who wish to work, they should be allowed to do so. Charitable work, helping with grandchildren, pursuing individual creativity and entrepreneurial ambitions, are not just worthwhile but personally and economically productive activities. For those who wish to make an active contribution without the pressure or formality and structure of paid work, that should be supported. Those able to depend on work-based pensions should be encouraged to do so. Pension ages are on the increase. For the oldest generation there is not yet a fair balance between how much free social care individuals receive and their inheritance wealth and savings. Ever-increasing property values might be seen as a deliberate electoral and economic tool, while passing on what one can, and has been earned, may itself be a moral right. For this more fluid life, things will have to change. These would include not just ditching a fixed pension age but also making education and training more available for older generations, ensuring that wages are in line with living expenses, and providing effective support for carers. We need a recognition too that there will be many more single older people in both the active retired and in the post-eighty groups who require some form of care.

Just as important as these practical changes, and crucial to their success, are attitudinal changes that in some ways take us back to pre-industrial times. Changes are needed that erode the separation of the 'old' from younger and 'working' generations, and that recognise the wisdom of experience. As we are making our economies and climate more sustainable so we must pay more attention to making our people more sustainable. This is not simply expecting people to carry on working for ever and ever, to in effect bypass the benefits that have been fought for over modern generations, for these must be maintained; and nor is it a blind acceptance of the correctness of an older point of view. This is a new path. We must achieve new levels of maturity that allow for the individuality that we say we prize – in all generations that are physically and mentally capable. There must equally be a willingness among older people to accept that some will wish to be productive formally, and 'earn money' in conventional work, at the same time as others claim a pension (or perhaps a universal basic income). Perhaps some older people in the wealthier middle classes are ready to delay, or not claim at all, a state pension because they already have enough. Government itself promotes workplace and private pensions but is not ready for that yet. How common are support and advice groups for active retirees to support each other or link up with others in creative, charitable, or entrepreneurial activity? There are already some foundations for these ideas in what happens now. The changes needed are not completely new but do require a stronger moral stance on behalf of individuals and government, and practical flexibility. They require that age itself is seen as less important than maturity and capability. They are part of a necessary re-commitment to equality of opportunity and to fairness, and most of all to a sense of mutually beneficial community action. Ageism needs to be consigned to history as much as other limiting and destructive 'isms.' The individualism of opportunity through genuine options in the context of communal benefits is one way in which individual rights and civic contribution can be combined. Such an approach could combine health-giving personal fulfilment with national benefit.

Thinking

We also have a responsibility to think for ourselves, and to understand how we do so. The latter has changed considerably in recent times and the former seems under increasing threat, although there is much we still do not know. We often inflate 'the human mind' with both intellect and consciousness. We often hear it said that we use a small proportion of our brain power, but without really knowing what that means, or it giving us the potential to do more.

Understanding how we think, and how we contextualise, understand, and use our philosophical and 'factual' knowledge and experience, in conjunction with our personal responsibility, can open a new dimension in our analysis of the challenges and solutions that humanity faces. Thinkers have always had to consider propaganda and censorship, and the manipulation and strategy of public life. However, we have a new understanding of both the psychology of how we think and the way our own brain and other people can manipulate our feelings. This includes how we think as individuals and how we think in groups, and how our deeply learnt biases may shape our opinions and actions. It must be an essential task of a modern, global, and independent citizen to understand our new ideas of how people gain knowledge and form opinions, the context and assumptions of their thought, and how that might be influenced by others.

Understanding Thinking

One mind can be both a creative genius and a murderer. Modern neuroscience is showing us how different parts of the brain shape and react to different emotions and different circumstances. We know that in groups we may act and feel differently than if we are alone. We understand that brains at different stages of development work differently. We also know that as adults we have the capacity to plan beyond what we can see, to analyse, to use logic, and yet we also feel intuition, to act emotionally without control, and hang on to predetermined or established ideas that have little logic. We sense that there is community memory without fully understanding how that is entrenched in an individual's thinking brain. We know that having a bird's-eye view and a worm's-eye view is both beneficial and a skill. We think we understand various Stone Age types of thinking or instincts, such as 'fight or flight.'

Our need ranges from understanding the point and subtlety of semantics in news articles, of advertising, of product or idea placement, and the use of false imagery. It must also include how an opinion-forming argument is constructed, an old skill, and the potential use of digital technology, including Artificial Intelligence (AI), and bioscience, to shape and manipulate thinking of the present and future. It will have to include how any of our senses might be used to trigger different emotions, something, again, not new, but capable of being done in new ways with new subtlety. Both the old and new forms of propaganda and censorship need to be understood.

One aspect of developing our updated awareness is to enhance our debating skills, which is not just about 'winning' a debate, but constructing a logical argument, and an ability and confidence to learn from debate. This also means looking beyond the information to assess its integrity, to avoid dismissing non-specialist or new knowledge; and to think of a burden of proof. This involves understanding the origins, the probabilities, and interpretations of written, visual, statistical, emotional, character and body language-based evidence, and how to put these together in the context of things we find it difficult to imagine, such as very small percentages of a national probability. This goes back to our biases. Most of us, at some point, overestimate or distort our knowledge of public topics. We must also remember the fact that people who live morally in one aspect of their life can still justify to themselves what could be considered an evil action in another aspect of their lives; and the systems we create give more or less chance for such actions to arise. We also need to watch out for powerlessness, of which stress is a symptom, and recognise that it may take away our ability to think independently or objectively. To deal with all this, a good citizen must attempt to develop their eloquence in the aspects of speech and listening, as well as of words, numbers, and emotions. Language is more important than ever in the accurate understanding and presentation of thoughts and knowledge.

Especially when added to the aspects of leadership discussed elsewhere, this is a dizzying list, and so once again, we need to depend on others for what no single person can do, which points again to the collective element of citizenship and democracy. There are some simple techniques that we can employ to practise and develop our thinking skills. One is the idea of 'CCC' – 'calm,' 'context,' and 'curiosity.' Calm thinking involves going through a process, over time, in order to avoid the 'fast thinking' that is often impulsive but wrong. Context involves relating facts and knowledge to the world in which they are placed – without context, measurements and numbers are meaningless. And curiosity points to the importance of always asking what the following question might be. CCC helps us to think through and clarify our thoughts and the evidence. Other established strategies include the idea of 'counting to ten' to slow our impulsiveness, and making checklists to create objective routines. This takes practice, for knowing the pitfalls of poor thinking does not automatically mean avoiding them. Knowledge of the world is power. Knowledge of oneself is arguably a greater power. Just as powerful is a real and deep knowledge of how others think. Upon such knowledge also stands reputation. Social dynamics, or social capital, are based on reputation and power. A small aspect of this is also knowing when to tune out, including not focussing online at the expense of real-world relationships and the need for rest. Giving ourselves time and new perspective are important. We must teach ourselves and our children how to do this.

Whether people at birth start with a 'clean slate' is therefore almost immaterial. If you believe that people can change, can learn, and can be influenced, then it barely matters if there are predetermined 'human characteristics' or 'personal characteristics' in someone's family or 'communal DNA.' Neurologist V.S. Ramachandran has spoken of how individuals' view, or their 'indifference,' is shaped by the narrative their brain adopts to rationalise what they see, hear, and feel.[*] They react through the lens of their own rationalisation. Logic is only a part of what makes us act; our chosen narrative produces our intuitive, or 'fast thinking,' and is the reason behind why someone with a fixed view can rarely be argued out of it logically. To change their view, they need to change their emotional connections and override their past experiences. Initially, this is likely to be destabilising. This is why a tipping point in society only happens when enough people feel a different emotional connection to an event or each other. This is why there is an emphasis on 'changing' or 'claiming' 'the narrative' by people who want to see change – and by people who do not. Individual narratives are the result of, among other things, the overlapping spheres of advertising, of behavioural insights, national and lifestyle 'myths,' education, and propaganda. One of the difficulties in healing rifts caused by differing narratives is that the baseline from which each individual begins may itself be a constructed narrative or myth, even if those narratives or myths are widely accepted.

If we seek to appreciate some fundamental challenges to our established worldview – such as that progress comes from competition – which can be destabilising, then we must challenge some of the fundamental foundations of what we think. The good news is that every single one of us as individuals can understand how we think better than we already do. The bad news is that understanding how we think can be dangerous as well as liberating.

---

[*] Rajan, 2022, 283–287, and in conversation on *Rethinking Brains* [podcast] BBC Sounds, 6 July 2020.

INDIVIDUALISM, SOCIETY, AND CITIZENSHIP

Thinking About Ourselves

Robert Greene's *The Laws of Human Nature* explains how he believes empathy, self-opinion, our 'dark shadow,' and irrationality all coexist to form our view of ourselves and our worldview. Most people have empathy that can enable us to understand others, but it is manipulated, or in more neutral terms shaped, by how we are raised. This creates our sense of what is normal, acceptable, agreeable, safe, what is love and compassion, tolerance, and fairness, and all their opposites. We also learn the narratives of our communities, and what to count as familiar and what is 'other.' We may learn, for example, what separates our family's or nation's values and characteristics from others. Many teachers will tell you that a young group of classmates reflects the personality of their class tutor, and this is similar to businesses reflecting the culture of the CEO. We need to minimise our self-absorption, engage our empathy more, and turn outwards in a kind of personal global dialogue. Most people additionally have a positive view of themselves, but everyone has a dark side, a 'shadow,' according to Carl Jung. Jung's shadow is part of the unconscious mind comprising weaknesses, repressed ideas, desires, and instincts kept in the shadow behind the conscious curtain we project by adapting to our cultural norms and expectations – much of which we call maturity. However, it is always with us. This is why anyone may be a murderer or see others as a mortal enemy if the conditions of stress are met and our triggers become engaged. Everyone has the potential to go to Darth Vader's dark side. We also see this in others before ourselves – 'the homeless will spend extra money on drugs,' or 'I am more likely to hand in that found money' – but we must recognise the shadow within ourselves, our insecurities, vulnerabilities, and misjudgements. We need to understand how we think to really engage our wider empathy. This can be channelled to become empathetic leadership and emotional intelligence. Greene also wrote about the idea of irrationality. This is the brain simplifying and rationalising emotions to justify what we 'want' to think, to fit in, or to take risks, or to act in a self-satisfied way, for example, 'I'm doing this bad thing for the best of intentions so it is OK,' or, 'if they did that, then I can too,' etc. This is the irrationality and emotional side of us that may be exhibited in the 'fast thinking' of

WHERE ARE WE GOING?

Kahneman and that might be cleverly manipulated. Evidence is good, but without engaging emotion and empathy, it is not enough. As for the effect of how we think in these poor ways, one needs only to consider attitudes towards regulation, welfare, discrimination, and conflict. It is a major driver of the Behavioural Insights promotion of 'nudge' theory, persuading people to act in a particular way, from eating less sugar to reporting crime. Despite the evidence presented, personal actions and attitudes and national policy are often at least partly determined by irrational feelings about others, while we have a high opinion of ourselves. As much as 95% of our decision-making is based on this intuitive, emotional, or fast thinking. Some of this is evolutionary, such as how we have evolved to sense danger for self-preservation. This is often what we call 'human nature' and might be considered the puppet master of what we do. However, the more we understand and recognise this, the more we can help ourselves and others to think better and believe that humanity can improve.

We can use systems and routines, accountability and transparency, and friendship and communication too, to improve what we do and improve trust. This is institutional, communal, and personal. This is about improving business, governmental decision-making, and making relationships better. Understanding how we think in all these ways is also at the heart of cognitive therapy, addiction, and understanding some forms of mental illness, and recognising the traits that make some people unsuitable for leadership or power.

The Psychology of the Masses by Gustave Le Bon, allegedly read by key Second World War leaders, predicted that in a crisis, people would go to their baser instincts to survive.[*] This is the *Lord of the Flies* approach (first published in 1954 during the Cold War), also known as 'mean world syndrome.' As Rutger Bregman points out, there is plenty of evidence to the contrary, from pandemic responses, and the Blitz, the story of six Tongan boys in 1965–66 marooned together on a Pacific island, and Danish resistance to the deportation of Jewish citizens.[†] However, it is the prevailing orthodoxy, and we must challenge it. If we expect, plan for, and 'see' distrust, then that is what we will get. If we believe that as

---

[*] Bregman, 2020, Prologue, xv.
[†] Bregman, 2020, 28–36, 177–180.

a species we can do better today, individually and collectively, and in the distant and unknown future, then we must challenge why our calculation is often negative, even dystopian. We have seen the effect of different biases and various other psychological traits that we veer towards. Why do we persist with these negative thoughts? It is not a lack of education, for we are more educated than ever before. It may be political conviction, or a leadership preference – but while we are apparently more polarised on the surface, all sorts of recorded trends show consensus. It may be because major religions have a basic assumption of sin. Perhaps it is Stone Age instincts of survival. It may be that the prevailing model of capitalism, now centuries old, assumes that we will act in self-interest. It may be our environmentalism, either that humanity is a superior species in control and that we can do anything, or that we are a destructive plague out of control. It is part of the philosophy of this book that we can improve. There is enough evidence in our daily lives and historic events to know that good things can happen, that a virtuous circle can take place, as well as a vicious one. No-one is doubting the capacity for 'bad thoughts,' or the need for transparency and accountability, but there is a greater need for positivity, and a belief that this is also realistic, and can be encouraged in the actions of individuals and groups.

In the origins of humanity, Neanderthals are known to have had larger brains and muscles than *Homo sapiens*, but they died out. Why they died out is one of the great questions of our origins. One theory is that of the Genius versus the Copycat. The genius, the stronger, does things on their own, even if they are creatively survivalist, and therefore no-one learns from each other. The Copycat is a co-operative species where people therefore learn from each other, act together for strength, and in this way, knowledge is passed down and built upon. Learning is communal and longer lasting or permanent. The idea is that Copycat communities survived longer, even if on any individual occasion they might succumb to a physically stronger foe. In such a way, Neanderthals gradually died out, to be replaced by the Copycat species of *Homo sapiens*. Frankly, no-one can know if this is true. It can, however, give us a framework for the belief of humanity as primarily a co-operative species. This also supports the idea that a society cannot be built on conflict and dishonesty, and that dishonest societies eventually implode. Mentioned previously, Bregman recites a much earlier Russian experiment with generations of Silver Foxes.* Even a commercial business cannot be run on a premise of allowing dishonesty. Our hope for humanity in a global world needs to be based on something more positive than the general orthodoxy of competitive development, whether that comes from our species' origins or from the most recent phase of our lives as urban-dwelling capitalists. There are reasons to be cheerful. Even our genetics may be pushing us towards further co-operation.

We need to put a more positive outlook into action. In daily life, we often feel faced by dishonesty and conflict. We know that intelligent people are just as likely to use their intelligence to justify their own belief as they are to engage in objectivity. It is not easy to be less cynical or avoid thinking of others as naïve. It is not easy to change existing power structures. These, however, are the things that we must do, and they can be done. Part of the solution is within us all. Some things are relatively easy to do if we want to do them, for example, creating more positive news stories, recognising one's own cues and rewards within our own habits, and more collegiate leadership. The aforementioned techniques, such as creating checklists, may seem boring, or even robotic to complete, but the human version also provides more objectivity and efficiency. Having a positive attitude to change does not mean ignoring the bad, nor does it mean diluting a need for accountability and transparency; indeed, it heightens that need. If we understand, for example, the role of confirmation bias – looking for things that confirm an existing point of view – availability bias – our propensity to only make judgements on what we see, or tangibly gain, in front of us – and the knowledge illusion – thinking we know more than we do – then we can build into our lives, and our governments, a new-found evidential check on our fast and slow thinking, screening out the excess 'noise,' and make our lives not just more positive but more effective. This can be done on an institutional and network level too, reworking the local and global systems we promote for co-operation. At his time of writing, according to Pinker, one-third of World Bank Reports were not downloaded a single time, and $3.5 trillion per year could be saved

---

* Bregman, 2020, 66–68. The experiment, led by Dmitri Belyaev, in Russia, began in 1958 and continued for generations of animals, being reported publicly in 1978.

globally if current good practice were followed in governments around the world.* If we acknowledge these guardrails, then we can genuinely debate for improvement and on merit, rather than to win an argument in a rhetorical exercise. If we can train our muscles, then why can we not train our minds, our empathy, and objectivity? This is not positivity for its own sake, for while that can be useful, that only takes us so far. Nor is it brainwashing in some inevitably progressive mindset, for we are not revoking individual thought or accountability. If we better understand these biases, then we can more effectively tackle a whole range of issues from discrimination to international conflict, and see the difference between competitive and conflictual. The key remains whether we are prepared to pursue a positive philosophy that sees ourselves as a co-operative species rather than a conflictual one. The argument here is that this is as much an individual choice and state of mind as it is an idea of group thinking. Indeed, without the individual foundation, there would be no stability in this philosophy being pursued by groups and nations. Psychologist Steven Pinker brought this possibility to a wider Western audience with the very title of his first bestseller *The Better Angels of Our Nature*. In this book he pointed out the slow decline of violence over centuries due to the development of individual experience and constructs such as the rule (and trust) of (fair) law and rights, growing accountability of government, and development of trade requiring peaceful interaction. It is these things that economists like Douglass North and Marianna Mazzucato say make the difference between economic progress or stagnation and decline. The latter writes about a re-moralisation of the public or common good to re-value it. It is these things that bring an end to slavery and feudalism and develop welfare support, mass health and education, and communal peace. We are clearly, therefore, some way down the road of both individual and collective positivity, often a hard road with real struggle, but the mindset we need is not a new one. Some people question Pinker's 'violent-to-peaceful' timeline of humanity and will have a 'nomadic-peaceful to urban-competitive-capitalist-violent' perspective, but in either case it is clear that we are now finding our co-operativeness, even if we are just re-finding it from our pre-modern origins. It is clear that we can change

---

* Steven Pinker, "Nudges and Noise," *Think with Pinker*, BBC Sounds, 2022.

what we do, either because we have been different before or because we have made progress. We just need to know that we can still do much better, know how we can do so, and continue to adapt to the changing circumstances of its application, most notably the growing globalisation of the problems we must address. This is why the growing positivity of global dialogue is a whole new level of development for humanity as a species. It is hard to see progress and easy to ridicule the naivety of this approach, and yet the evidence abounds of effective positive social interaction, if we choose to see it. The 'veneer theory' is an idea that the acceptance of a sinful nature has become just a convenient thing to blame for when we do something 'bad' or 'evil.' We need to recognise its validity in our current thinking.

Economist Tyler Cowen has spoken of being suspicious of simple, or simplistic, stories.* It is too easy to blame someone else or see good and evil as sharply defined, and to want a tidy ending. Conspiracies that last are not accidents, they are constructed. The process or debate of that construction is important. We need to ask the extra question, look for the unintended consequences, look at the detail and evidence dispassionately, and be comfortable with things that are less clear-cut. Justice is one such area of thought. Understanding justice often requires clarity of cause and effect, and with complexity, distance and in numbers is harder to recognise. Whether this is welfare claimants from a group we have little in common with or cheap labour in a different country, the difficulty of assessing what is just can in those circumstances become more difficult. Usually, we personalise an issue, perhaps making another group seem like a naughty, annoying, or distrusted neighbour; we use individual illustration, such as focussing on one orphan boy or dead child migrant, to represent a story; we may create a complex conspiracy theory or mystery to justify our preferred emotion-rich or bias-led explanation; or create an all-knowing theory or creed. These provide us with moral certainty, but they do not provide justice. We can do better if we understand more about how we ourselves, and each other, think.

---

* Tyler Brown, "Be suspicious of simple stories," *TEDx Talks*, YouTube, 9 Nov 2009.

Citizenship

Going back to the Ancient Greek idea of living a 'considered' life, replicated in all the world's old and current belief systems is a recognition that we can and should all be making an active and positive contribution to the life we lead, and to the relationships that we have. Our perspectives and the world around us are always changing. This is aside from whether you believe that we can change our character individually or whether humanity can change its nature over time, although a belief that we can do so may add to our motivations. That we often do not agree on the changes we see happening or that may happen in the future is an added complication to overcome. All this means that being a citizen is difficult. It means that one person's citizenship is different from another's. It means there are high expectations of a good citizen, and that those expectations are likely to change over time. We must be literate literally, emotionally, philosophically, financially, scientifically, politically, and in how we think – it is a big ask, too much for most people as they live their daily struggles.

A Good Citizen

Thomas More wrote that treaties themselves were a sign of distrust between people. Machiavelli condemned the idea of noble citizenship and said that most people were fickle and ungrateful. Schopenhauer wrote that any moral freedom we may have is not natural or part of the 'real world' where real choices and compromises must be made, and is not based on knowledge or education, or religious faith. When writing about India and Japan, Tagore wrote that the path to post-colonial modern freedom lay in freedom of the mind rather than slavery either to their traditions or to all things European. Keynes thought the 'economic problem' of humanity could be solved in 100 years and humanity's permanent problem would be how to use their freedom from insecurity and poverty. Nietzsche, whose ideas are easily misinterpreted to support power, saw a weakening of human core beliefs and character and believed that 'supermen' were therefore needed to prevent humanity plummeting into the abyss. For the Stoics, tranquillity was achieved by being true to oneself, by being moderate in all things, and by ensuring that adversity does not have power over you. This array of approaches across the ages reflects that there are many ways to think of citizenship and people's personal aims. But it also puts forward another possibility – that these ideas are all 'of their time' and that instead of looking to the past, we need to define a modern idea of citizenship for the circumstances and challenges of today, one that can have global resonance.

The wellbeing of society and economy can never just be left to develop without any form of law, whether that is explicit and specific or more general moral guidance. There must be some form of reciprocal obligation and public interest. This needs to be a starting point. There must be room for individual rights and for civic responsibility, including governmental rights. Society and individuals cannot thrive without each other. A citizen must accept this. The exact balance may seem an eternal dilemma, but some form of balance there must be. This also leads to a responsibility to engage in what that balance ought to be. Whether it is a religious-style 'love' or secular respect that is a framework for engagement is less important than the acceptance of a responsibility to take part in society, and therefore also to help in its decision-making when called upon. One cannot be a good citizen and nor can there be a sustainable society if members have no power to, or choose not to, engage. That is a dereliction or deprivation of duty to others and to those individuals themselves. In the sense that 'democracy' is the participation of people in a civic society, then clearly it is easier to be a good citizen in a democracy, whatever the specific political style of democratic government. Naturally, such engagement flourishes where there is trust between participants, and so some balance of faith in others and accountability as a citizen. Engagement and trust must, therefore, over the longer term at least, have some mutual benefit to sustain the effort. A successful society of citizens would be where the collective actions are an efficient sum, or greater than the sum, of individual actions. But this is not a pre-condition of an individual's effort. Where someone's active citizenship is 'against the grain,' then their efforts will either result in reform, be rejected with exposure to debate, or compromises will be found. It is a lack of opportunity to be heard, or for debate to occur, that is likely to make citizens feel that they are living in an authoritarian society – whether this judgement is objectively right or wrong. That would result in citizens either disengaging from society and becoming introverted, or in them calling for revolution. Both scenarios negate the kind of democracy that most people strive for.

For many people, Covid-19 became a reminder of the interdependence of citizens. Good citizenship was shown by those who engaged. They may have expressed an opinion, 'obeyed the rules,' been vaccinated to protect others, given time and effort or money in supportive voluntary action, or held actions to account after the worst was over. Some of these things can voluntarily be done in a non-democratic society, but that is either an expression of self-interest, or an expression of community despite the prevailing authority. Covid-19 has shown that philosophically and practically there is an enormous contrast between a citizen in an engaging democracy and a person in an authoritarian state.

There are many other examples established in everyday life. These include the acceptance of tax, progressive or single rate, namely that one's own taxed money may be given disproportionately for someone else, with a measure of need not just right. We also accept that there should be a minimum pay and conditions of work, and dignity in work, but also differences according to experience, skill, and qualification. This is not, here, a debate going over the individual rights – civic responsibilities balance again but is a recognition of the rights and responsibilities of citizens, and the opportunities of citizenship. It is for individual specific societies to work out their balances, but a citizen can accept a range of frameworks and demand that there is enough of a satisfactory result to not alienate themselves or others. We know that, as standards and circumstances change, the practical implementation of these balances is a matter for debate – or (party) politics – but these must be within the boundaries of mutually beneficial citizenship. This is as true of shelter and food as it is of work, tax, or health, as it is of seeing the mutual benefit of paying for roads and the emergency services.

When people call for clearly sectional interests, with no compromise, with no mutually advantageous outcome, or compensatory action in another field, then those people can be said to be straying from the path of good citizens. They, at least, are separating into a different society, and fracturing the nation or other community that they are officially part of. They may want a different type of society, but they are calling into question the fundamental bonds that hold that society together. When their society splits, they may also become the victims of new sectional interests. Again, this precludes no specific governmental type. A small-state government or an interventionist one can, and should, still place citizens at their heart. The subsequent decline of a citizen's engagement through a decline in their apparent power to influence has become the key challenge of globalisation in countries of every democratic form all around the world. It is one of the key reasons why the idea of citizenship needs a re-boot within the context of the global dialogue and changes taking place.

There are some clear actions required. The right to vote is a responsibility to be fulfilled, even if the expression of view is seen through a deliberately spoilt ballot paper. Employment opportunities need to exist for all, for people to contribute directly through the work they do and indirectly through the financial, social, and other consequences that result. The protection of freedoms such as speech, assembly, and religious belief are clearly the responsibility of a good citizen who accepts a mutually beneficial society in which individual rights and civic responsibility coexist. The responsibilities to inform oneself and think for oneself should be entrenched. These are basic and relatively obvious requirements. In some places, they have become so accepted that there is a complacency about the need for citizens, as opposed to an expectation of government, to fulfil and defend them. J.S. Mill's requirement for debate to re-learn and reinforce even accepted norms is relevant here.

We also need to look at the rights we give as well as those we expect. If asylum seekers are deprived of the right to work despite delayed judgements on their case, then they will not be seen as willing positive citizens and clearly have little chance of being so. When does a good citizen that accepts the idea of a mutually beneficial society decide the gap between executive and 'shop floor' pay is destructive, not motivational, or reasonable reward? At what point does someone not support ever-rising property prices in the face of greater housing shortage and homelessness and division between generations in inherited wealth and lifelong opportunities? A good citizen needs to have a view on the balance of punishment and rehabilitation in relation to criminal justice. These examples show the difficulty of choices for any citizen. People will have their own views, but in the aggregated view of a free and fair, informed democracy and civic society, a balance will be reached, acceptable by the fact of its collective opinion. A good citizen will have expressed their view and accept the collective result. This is the implementation of both responsibility and trust in others, as well as mutual benefit, that a good citizen accepts in a society of more than one. And their engagement gives them the moral right to continue to peacefully argue for a different outcome. One foundation of this mutuality is accepted across cultures and has been so across time – the notional 'golden rule' of religions, to only do to others as you would have anyone do to you.

Many people see voting in elections as something that does not affect them. Or they abstain because candidates do not represent their views. In any reasonable intention of democracy, this is the approach of an immature citizen or a misunderstanding of elections. Firstly, voting gives someone a moral right to criticise, for they have taken part in the process. This gives people a sense of power and can make us all leaders, every voter equal on that day, and is the single most powerful source of engagement with authority and our society at large. Secondly, we need to live in the real world where very few people get everything they want. People compromise every day. Practically, any government will typically either benefit you by £1,000 or take that from you, in all sorts of ways. The balance sheet of promises may not always be clear, but in what other hour or half a day of time could someone benefit from or safeguard their interest so directly? Thirdly, there is the power of aggregate voting. If no poor people vote, then they will never be represented, and of course, this applies to all sorts of groups. Voting is worth it individually and for the common good. While groups may 'balance out' in simplistic terms, this is less like 'giving with one hand and taking with the other' and more like a biosphere where the complex interaction is what makes the whole work 'efficiently,' or most fairly. Whenever a citizen has the chance to vote, they should. That is, they should inform themselves as best they can, and then vote.

Socrates said that the soul could be protected by 'good.' He also said that the only good was knowledge, as opposed to illogical opinion and materialism. His 'knowledge' was a philosophical knowledge, and he was saying that it was a duty to be certain of the underpinning philosophy of one's life. If this can be debated, thought through, and adapted with experience, the question 'what beliefs and values do we hold most dear?' is one that all modern citizens would find clearer to attain. An understanding and acceptance of other points of view being made in a widening global dialogue requires the foundation of confidence in one's own philosophy first, otherwise the ship is rudderless and is moved by the latest wave. On such a foundation, one can also feel self-aware and informed enough to engage responsibly. There is something to compare with the new.

The most essential aspect of being a good modern citizen must therefore be the taking of personal responsibility. While it is not true for everyone everywhere, and for few people all the time anywhere, we are more able to control or influence our own lives than in previous ages. Personal responsibility is therefore a possibility, and in most cases we have gone well beyond that in our development of individual rights, to make it an expectation.

Global Citizenship

A modern liberal view of citizenship in the West tends to emphasise the individual aspects. They expect a citizen to have a stake in society – for their own benefit. They expect free speech and other freedoms for the development of the individual. There is certainly recognition of relationships with others and the idea of society, but it is the individual that decides society. A global dialogue about what makes a good citizen will also look at it the other way around – society has a stake in the individual, and perhaps the society does, or even should, decide for, or decide the parameters of, the individual. John Rawls' 'veil of ignorance' approach, explained earlier in this chapter, is one attempt to moderate a heightened individualism with a societal responsibility. More frequently, however, Western individualism comes with a suspicion of predominant community interests, and 'community' is often interpreted as 'government' interest, which means 'being governed.' It is the legacy of a more libertarian-inclined Americanism to see this as bad. This is one of the greatest consequences of the American struggle for independence – a fight against 'being governed' as subjects, not as independent citizens, and a resulting distrust of government. To a large extent the USA has taken this as its creed, and communal interests that might limit individual action are almost by default viewed suspiciously. This fault-line is a permanent feature of American politics. A social liberalism has flourished to a greater extent in Europe. This, however, is still based on the idea that society is made up of people who have a stake in it, through work, through property, even as this is competitive for most people. The idea that a person can be a corrupting influence is, in a suspicious Western mind, adjacent to them being a controlling influence. Vigilance for liberty is often not seen as individual vigilance but governmental and becomes a government 'power.'

A global idea of the role and beliefs of a citizen must find a better understanding of the individual rights – civic responsibility balance seen from the direction prevalent in many other societies. Westernism believes it is individualism that has given it entrepreneurship and given it superiority in the modern world. It needs to look at the fundamentals of Confucius' idea of duty, and Buddha's idea of Karma, and other older non-Western ideas of humanity's relationship with each other and the natural world, if there is to be a globally accepted idea of what a good citizen should be like beyond individualism. It also needs to remember that most people in the world continue to have religious faith. These ideas can also encourage those in the West who seek a greater predominance of the positive and co-operative nature of humanity over the competitive and conflictual. On the 'other side' these ideas of duty and karmic intention, and others of community responsibility for individuals and for the whole community, need to be taken away from their politicisation, a political (or religious) interpretation to justify a specific type of government, which take away significant individual freedoms. Just as a purer communist idea of enforced individual equality at the subservience of the state imploded due to a practical and theoretical inability to work, so too will a modern communist-lite idea of providing material benefit in a sea of individual powerlessness be dissolved by the natural human characteristic of wanting a sense of power over one's own life. Although to some extent this has been the Western hope for a dissolving communist control of China that seems to have failed, it does not mean that the idea itself is either dead or illogical. When a demand for an end to individual powerlessness rises – because the drive for materialism as 'the opium of the masses' stalls or is spiritually unfulfilling – then the more fundamental and positive versions of Confucian duty, Buddhist Karma and other global beliefs about the protection of, and protection by, a community will come back to the fore. The East and the West need to differentiate civic from governmental, and to recognise the collective power and legitimacy of individual power, with enough regulatory framework to prevent a tyranny of the majority. This is especially a lesson for authoritarian and religious-based political authorities, but it also reveals that these regimes are about having power and do not have any legitimate long-term philosophical basis.

Another path to such a middle or new ground may be found in ancient indigenous beliefs and their relationship with nature. Individuals can be individual, and communities can be different, but neither should imperil the natural world they live in. This provides real limits to both individual and communal action and provides motivation for the most important co-operation between the two. While indigenous communities have little global power, this may be most likely to find a voice, and that power, in Africa, where a residue of it still survives. The indigenous, and Pacific, and African global citizen may be more likely to see the parallel between the stewardship of nature and the stewardship of communities and individuals. Learning from the cradle of humanity in the context of species-threatening climate change would indeed be an ironic sight for the future global citizen. It may be Africa's way into the global debate about the future of the planet. It also has the benefit of taking us beyond the Western industrialisation of the last few centuries that emphasised materialism, exploitation, and competition. This would seem a long way off, but is, nevertheless, one path forward to that global citizenship, and one path that gives the huge and growing continent of Africa and the heritage of humanity's birth place a better and positive influence. It also shows a path to how we might genuinely engage in a more global dialogue, as opposed to one of East-West power blocs.

Most countries and traditions also have their version of a social contract or a social psychology that can contribute to being a global citizen. Japanese *Ikigai* is a concept of having a purpose or direction in life that gives a sense of fulfilment. One's own passions can be pursued, but in the pursuit of bettering society. A good pursuit of *Ikigai* uses passion, 'mission' (what the world needs), 'vocation' (what you can be paid to do), and 'profession' (what you are good at). It involves civic balance and awareness, personal confidence, self-discipline, and the use of one's talents. Danish *Hygge* is a focus on contentment with an 'everyday togetherness,' encouraging the experience of safety, equality, and a spontaneous social flow. It is about the quality of one's life in relation to others. *Ubuntu*, in Bantu language cultures across sub-Saharan Africa, translates as a 'humanity' defined by 'I am because we are.' It is denoted by values and practices that make someone authentic as a human being, such as trust, caring, and sharing, and therefore make them part of a larger community and spiritual world. Recognition of the collective good is to be authentic as an individual. There are many such national and cultural ideas. They have a lot in common. They are all about doing the right thing for oneself without harming, or by actively helping, society or community. None of them are limited by method. All can be harnessed in the service of, or seen as seeds of, the global dialogue encouraging a new philosophy of a citizen who thinks co-operatively and positively on our new global scale.

Daily, and Democratic, Citizenship

It is realistic that people are good and want to do the right thing. Give people a chance as a default position, but without ignoring fair and transparent accountability and evidence. Thinking good of people is not a pass for naivete. How you think good of people is about treating others as you would want to be treated. Understanding others is worth the effort. Empathy is fine, but encourage it to lead to more positive action. Understand the limitations of your natural, or initial, feelings about, and understanding of, people, and ask if you are limiting yourself to what you know already. See that most people want for their children and themselves what you want for yours and yourself. This is even more about fairness than equality. See another perspective. Be prepared to debate established orthodoxies and taboo topics. There is not a mono-cultural or one-size-fits-all way of looking at people. Practise listening as well as talking. Engage to persuade, not confront to win. That means compromise too, but compromising based on confidence in yourself. Realise that cynicism is a learnt behaviour, and often a defence mechanism. Don't cover up good deeds. Instead, remember that one good deed often leads to another; and that we often remember a single bad experience more than ten good ones as a psychologically protective measure to keep us aware of danger. Understand how you and others think across words, images, statistics, and emotions. Take encouragement from the modern belief that *Homo sapiens* outthought Neanderthals and won through co-operation, not physical strength or conflict.

All these things will seem to some like clichés or impossibilities when applied to daily life. Being a good citizen is not easy. Personal responsibility is hard all the time, but accept that no-one is perfect, including yourself. Be confident enough to learn from mistakes. You know that often decisions can be hard and might not satisfy everyone. You can take comfort and pleasure in being individual but also from being part of a community. This is why people put up with family, join gangs, identify with a specific fan base, and accept the restrictions or expectations of a nation. Groups by definition have a collective will and care. Within all these are the right balances between individual rights and civic responsibilities. Be more persuasive while still being open to the views of others – views which may over time change your opinion. Individuals are not a set of random atoms bouncing off each other; each is a contribution to the whole, and none are completely independent.

For this to work, the architecture must be in place. A good citizen must have an education, formal and informal – both from school and in society. A good citizenry must have opportunities to express a view. Authorities must be genuinely accountable. There must be a mechanism for compromise and decision-making, and fundamental rules that 'the people' decide, and that people abide by, and that people can peacefully challenge. This is 'civic society': free and fair elections, education, investigative journalism, free speech, independent pressure groups. This is democracy at its finest. This is how a society tackles discrimination, corruption, economic and health inequality, and maintains mental health and resilience. Democracy as a form of government implementing this development of civic society may be eternally imperfect, but it has nevertheless set societies on a clearly recognisable path of improvement, which in recent times, globally, has been rapid. This is why 'democracy' has a moral argument in its favour as well as a practical one. Democracy is not a panacea to solve everything just by virtue of its existence, and a recognition of that is part of the political maturity people need. However, the fundamental point of people having power over their own lives within a community that works co-operatively to make that possible is what distinguishes it from other forms of organisation and gives it purpose, power, and legitimacy. People are also capable of learning from experience to make what comes next better. Scientific and technological development, adherence to a religious creed, new understanding of how individuals and communities work physically, intellectually, and emotionally, and how they interact, are all important but are tools for the task of how we choose to live and must be critiqued as such. The architecture that allows a good citizen to thrive is not therefore compatible with an authoritarian or technocratic government.

The notion of 'well, I wouldn't start from here' is not available to deal with the challenges we face. We need not abandon anything competitive or deny our own heritage. The global solutions we need do mean being able to see our lives and ambitions in perspective and recognising a fair playing field, including the place of materialism for some while others struggle first for a life above the poverty line. It means re-evaluating the balance of quality, purpose, and fulfilment in our lives. It means demanding for yourself or for others the possibility of these things. This might be said to be a mid-life crisis for humanity. Having a wider compassion, a greater knowledge, more openness to others, and willingness to engage, are ways to 'level up' society, domestically and internationally. Nor is this just about redistribution in some socialist utopia. It is about ways to do things better that work for more people. Redistribution, whether in proportion or actual amount, can also be in self-interest, as is sharing the practice of good governance itself, to lessen the cross-community dangers we perceive. The idea that charity begins at home might be fine but it cannot also end at home, unless home is isolated from the other problems of the world, which would now be rare or impossible. Any citizen can affect local change but needs to think globally if they are to help their locality most effectively. This is a change of mindset. It is not party politically based on business or worker, small-state or interventionist government, international co-operation or not losing national sovereignty. It is about the power of individuals to shape governments through enacting a positive co-operative philosophy. Again, this does not preclude accountability and transparency, or helping those in need on your street. It merely widens the solutions to be more comprehensive and, therefore, more foundational. In that sense, it is a revolutionary philosophical change, and yet one that we already tiptoe into to varying degrees.

One intriguing aspect of our development is that our increase in life span – maybe the greatest change in the history of humanity – could give us quite a difference in perspective to previous generations. Climate change, to give one example, may be educating us to think much more carefully about both unintended consequences and a future well beyond our generation, in a co-operative context.

Some things are easy to do, such as giving up meat one or two days a week, contributing to an international charity as well as a local one, voting in elections, ridding social media of algorithms that promote only already-favoured opinions, reporting more positive stories on national news, re-modelling business plans towards fairer pay and longer-term investment, encouraging good international governance in preference to promoting self-serving aid budgets, etc. Of course, some of these are not really easy, but given the philosophy of a global, positively engaged citizen, they become about how, not if. There used to be the phrase 'think global, act local,' and this is as applicable now as it was then (in terms of the environment and recycling). All this applies to citizens above the poverty line in a developing nation, not just Western 'rich' citizens, for there are things that everyone can do, and things that they can demand, of themselves and others and their governments. If they are starting from a poor governmental base, then things that they must demand include the good governance and civic society that are required to be a good global citizen and to have the opportunities that such a person should have – opportunities that go well beyond economic comfort. When in positions of power, people must look at what they are doing to contribute to opportunity, and must not separate themselves from the different communities they profess to believe in and represent. We look to athletes and celebrities to be role models, but we must apply that to business, cultural, and political leaders too, for the same reasons. People can be the positive change they want to be, and, to paraphrase President Obama and others, if not now, when?

Some things are harder to do. One of the reasons climate change is such a big challenge is that its solutions question large parts of the economic models and lifestyles of those that have been so successful. The change from progress by permanent materialistic improvement to quality of life will encompass what we need to do to deal with climate change, but is a wider concept. Tackling inequality on a global scale by levelling up rather than destructively levelling down means finding new creative ways to promote healthy cities, mass educational opportunity, and opportunity in work or other societal contribution. It means thinking about the balance of taxes, wealth, and income between rich and poor, the morality of increased inheritance, and thinking about the purpose of regulation. Change will still mean, for many people around the world, establishing basic sustainable levels of health, education, housing, and employment. Internationally, a commitment to the fairness of global citizenship means co-operation or agreement on everything from technological development, the power of international companies, conflict arbitration, shared infrastructure, and governmental standards. It means finding ways to cancel international debt, making aid effective, and responsibly preventing nations from falling into 'failed state' status. In science, we must assess the uses of bioscience/technology, digital communication, and machine learning, and even the purpose and role and power of science itself. Culture is where the global dialogue is already well established, and creative talent is more widely recognised – from fashion to music to sport to food to cinema to architecture.

The openness to being global and co-operative is the core value that we need to keep hold of. An informed, compassionate philosophy for a global age clarifies what we are trying to do and moves even some of these enormous problems into the 'how' rather than the 'if' category. None of this is a libertarian or nanny-state philosophy. It is reasonable self-interest, self-preservation, and morally the right thing at the scale we now live in. A modern notion of citizenship must also pass the test of what can be done and believed in by people who work too much, are not generally political, have a conservative or traditional strand to their opinion but also want progress, yet daily just want efficient government, and think that politics can't solve everything. Citizenship must be practical and believable in its motivations and benefits, not just for its activist adherents, and that is another reason why it must be collective.

In an authoritarian nation, very little of this is possible. Even individual citizenship is by nature seen as suspicious. It is within individual morality, and individual action, when possible, that such citizens must find their beginnings of global compassion and struggle. No-one can deny that this is hard, and can cost lives, but it is still a historic struggle that must be undertaken, if only for succeeding generations. The border, physically and philosophically, between democratically engaged and dictatorial nations is therefore one of the harder challenges for this philosophy to face up to, especially from the democratic perspective, and for those peaceful democratic nations more directly under threat. Security does indeed require vigilance and defence spending. However, a nation's greatest strength is the support of its people. Such a supportive people are resilient and able to make sacrifices in times of crisis. Such governments need to be more democratic not less and stand up for the moral foundation of their legitimacy as much as the procedural one. They need to keep open the olive branch of co-operation, differentiate between people and government, and focus on governance and legitimacy above all. They cannot force revolution across a real geographical border, for that can only truly come from the people who are seeking it themselves, even though that may mean the blood of martyrs being shed. In reality, there is no national narrative that does not involve sacrifice to realise that value. Enforced change by a democracy is only international authoritarianism, belying its own claims to respect the will of the people. This forces uncomfortable decisions, but we must be confident without complacency that a spectrum of democracy will be the winner, and can play 'the long game' better than any other form of government. This, equally, does not mean that there is nothing we can do. The longevity, resilience, and progress of our own example is a factor for change itself. If indeed citizenship and even democracy are in crisis, then like any carer, we need to look after our own in order to be able to help the others we care for.

III

GOVERNMENT AND LEADERSHIP

> *... crisis is a time for democracies to redouble our commitment to accountability...*
> Kang Kyung-wha, Foreign Minister of South Korea.*

> *The P.R.C. is a socialist state under the people's democratic dictatorship'*
> *... The citizens... enjoy freedom of speech, of the press, of assembly, of association, of procession, of demonstration.*
> Constitution of the People's Republic of China.

Our success as a species has been judged in 'modern times' as equating to our production of 'government' to improve ourselves, as measured by things such as physical security and quality of life. As history has increasingly been seen in 'big picture' form our re-visiting of the origins of government lead us to re-visit the origins of society and of hierarchy and may teach us more about ourselves, and the future that we could have. Theories, however, are products of their time. Even what we label as scientific proof in one era can be reinterpreted or discredited in another era, and even discredited beliefs can linger to shape, or poison, what may follow. It is social science that is providing most of the logic of our current mainstream theories. Some theories have a foundation in religious faith. These should not be dismissed because they still affect

---

*Kang Kyung-wha, Foreign Minister of South Korea, quote taken from Amol Rajan, ed., *Rethink: Leading Voices*, 2022, 178-179.

the ideas and practice of government in many parts of the world. The Stone Age instincts of Man can still be seen in the male-dominated warrior attributes of hierarchy and leadership. Yet overall, co-operation prevails, perhaps from the development of settled farming and religion.

Government We Recognise

As circumstances have changed so has our interpretation of what government is for as well as how it should be administered. All forms of technology, from writing to printing, from the development of transport to mass media in the home, have shaped government, and new technology continues to do so. 'Living' or personal philosophy has developed from ideas about supporting tight-knit groups to being part of geographically and historically extensive nations where most people are anonymous to us. Ideas vary from stressing individual freedom and liberty to a duty for communal stability. An increasing global dialogue also shapes the government that people experience. Feudal and colonial authority have dissipated. Education, awareness and experience of wider surroundings, and alternative ideas, have mushroomed and accountability increased. All these factors have contributed to government that we recognise today.

Government, and Human Nature, Nurture, and Character

In the earliest hunting, all played a part in the hunt, the meal, and in the exploitation of an animal: fur for clothing, hide for shelter, etc, just as Native Americans used the buffalo. The !Kung tribes of the Kalahari in Namibia continued until recently to have deliberate hierarchy-defying rituals after each hunt. Similarly, those who took part in fishing, or in gathering naturally growing food, had shared existences. Over time climate played a part. Whether people settled on, periodically returned to, or continually moved on from the land added settlement or fragility to life experience, and the resources available for exploitation. Tools developed. Groups began to join. Different climates and resources produced different tools, and new skills. Eventually farming was

GOVERNMENT AND LEADERSHIP

developed with animals and crops.

People encountered each other more often. They had to compete for resources. Our centuries-old predominant theories of leadership and the origin of government based on conflict begins to come into view. Conflict needed people to make decisions, and decision-makers became leaders. Leaders needed people to support their leadership, and hierarchy developed. Such leaders got used to power and began to take control outside times of conflict too, for that was 'preparation' and 'efficient,' and ambitious. War created chiefs, as well as kinship. Men became leaders, and the world became more violent. The physically strongest and most appealing needed to be role models to lead their people into battle, and have the mental toughness to survive the decisions they would have to make. These were the warrior virtues. We take it for granted these days that this meant that men became leaders and women were either designated for childbirth and family, to farming, or took the role of spiritual advisor. Logically, there is no inevitability about that distinction of roles in leadership, but they have been predominant ever since in authoritarian regimes and in democracies.

Close combat with axes turned into fortresses. As conflict became less commonly face-to-face, more strategic leaders were needed. Localised groups settled into peaceful coexistence, and united against 'foreign' marauders, and more powerful leaders needed loyal and efficient hierarchies to carry out their wishes from a distance. These hierarchies required clear advice from the spirits, developing into ritual and organised religion, and clear advice on how to rule, with advisers beginning to fulfil a 'civil service' role. A collection of people with different roles and skills could be increasingly defined as 'castes' or 'classes,' and 'society,' that needed direction and control. This approach holds conflict as the greatest reason for the development of government and leadership.

For other historians and social scientists farming is at the centre of governmental development. This shares a belief that we are still actively subject to our Stone Age impulses and psychology. The ten thousand years of farming development have, in this scenario, had far more effect than the mere four or five thousand years of modern co-operative or competing statehood. Farming required co-operation, planning, stability, and settlement. Land had to be secured, needed constant attention, to be sown and harvested, and Man had to work with nature. Crops, animal husbandry, and farming skills became specialist. Toolmakers developed technology and traded. Development provided more food and populations grew. This is also a convenient fit for the idea that mankind's development has become a complex entangled dependency on what it invents. Exchange of goods and ideas increased. This would not work without co-operative agreement and decision-making. Agreement on a small scale might be consensual, on a larger scale at least needed representation, and enforcement required leadership. Farming required organisation. Trade required regulation, and stability, including dispute resolution. In this way hierarchy and society developed, later followed by urbanisation. The leadership that farming required was based on co-operative skills, rather than conflictual ones. Farming illustrates that by nature humanity is a co-operative species.

'Rice theory' is based on the difference between wheat and rice farming.* In wheat farming of non-equatorial cooler climates individuals can be relatively responsible for their own crops. Rice production requires a more co-operative community and a larger scale. With wheat individuals might experiment, they might take risks to be more successful, to satisfy ambitions of simply having more food or to have a surplus with which they might trade and expand the orbit and resources of their lives. In this scenario wheat producing areas of the world became more entrepreneurial and more individualistic; while rice producing areas became more communal and an ordered community was more important than individual merit. Confucius stressed duty and order, ritual, and the predominance of community. It may or may not help explain a 'north-south' divide of 'development'; and the 'east-west' divide of individualism v communal order. This may confuse cause and effect, assume the present must be linked with the past, and may even have an element of stereotyping different peoples. It does not negate the general theory of humanity's successful co-operative development through farming. Of course, farmers also needed organisation and

---

*T. Talhelm, X. Zhang, S. Kitayama, et al, "Large-scale psychological difference within China explained by rice versus wheat agriculture," *Science*, May 2014, Vol 344, Issue 6184, 603–608; Michaeleen Doucleff, "Rice theory: Why Eastern cultures are more cooperative," *NPR, The Salt*, 8 May 2014.

military skills to defend themselves against competitors and invaders. Whether farming or conflict came first as the origin of leadership and government – and one source of conflict will have been nomads with farmers, just like homesteaders and cattle-ranchers in the 19th-century American West – is like asking what came first, the chicken or the egg.

Another theory places religion as the predominant origin of leadership and government, and of society as we know it. This is also, sort of, a theory based on the co-operativeness of Man, relying on modern sociology and psychology. It does not make assumptions about the truth of different religions or religion in general. The oldest religions were animalistic, or nature orientated, or they applied to characteristics or behaviours of Man. Individual Spirits or gods could be appealed to and were all around us. Such religions had no artificial boundaries created by communities. They have been overwhelmed, in the main, by an entirely different approach to religion: the all-seeing moralistic religions that are predominant today. It may be these that encouraged the development of a more formally co-operative society. An all-seeing, permanent, authority made judgements on people and therefore made them think about their behaviour all the time. These religions punished with eternal damnation or subservient lives, or rewarded with enlightenment or heaven. Rituals were communal and self-reinforcing, as they sometimes had been previously, but the reinforcement was the importance of actions towards one another as well as towards oneself and directly towards God. These beliefs therefore encouraged co-operation and social order. There was no other God or spirit to appeal to. Religions became sets of rules to live by. Hierarchies reinforced and clarified the rules, and in doing so reinforced their own importance. Even Buddhism emphasises community, seeking its nirvana through one's actions towards others in co-ordination with internally seeking enlightenment. Such religious societies became more co-ordinated and self-supporting.

Such stronger societies were more resilient, and therefore more likely to last. An all-seeing God would also be useful to a ruler, and rulers may have been more encouraged to adopt such a religion, hoping they could use it to their advantage, even using conversion of the conquered to expand the power of a religion whose hierarchy might be beholden to them as well as to God. Problems might be explained by the mysteriousness of, and inability to truly understand the mind of, God. We should have faith. The larger communities became, the more need there was for God to be all-seeing, for who else could keep everyone in order. The communal nature of these religions required communal participation, and galvanised commitment. Religion and societal government developed in parallel and then in many places they became intertwined, even to the extent of religion becoming nationalistic in nature. Claiming a belief in a judgemental God, or whatever the prevailing creed, to be on the safe side, is still a co-operative action, even if on the complicit end of the scale. There may still have been murder and mayhem in society – but if you could justify it in the name of your Faith and be absolved from the sins of your actions by a forgiving God then that is simply the successful perversion of its meaning. The nature of competition between religions also still needs more research. This is the understanding of religion as a created narrative that serves our own purposes, rather than the spread of convinced genuine belief. It also shows how religion can change. Religion may have been our first and most successful ever communal ideology. People who may not believe in God still take notice of cardboard police officers in shops and statues of children when driving near school zones. These are the governmentally secular versions of an all-seeing judgemental God. As Voltaire reportedly said, 'if God did not exist it would be necessary to invent him.'

Devotees still needed food production and organisation, and still needed defence (or took on a more attacking missionary zeal). The need for a co-ordinated military, religious, and food-production leadership is clear. The sociability required in modern religion and food production must coexist in some way with the warrior attributes required for self-defence and preservation. These skills and attitudes and instincts are not either/or. They therefore again raise the characteristics of human nature, and the nature v nurture debate, and a debate about multi-level selection, i.e., how different attributes can coexist. The development of reflective philosophies may be said to be a manifestation of the importance of nurture. Yet most people seek comfort in follow-ship not exposure as leaders. How natural are the Machiavellian warrior attributes of leadership, or are these learnt according to circumstances? Traditionally we have also concentrated on the belief that humanity has learnt from nature itself in its adoption of competition and that like other animals we can be, or are naturally, competitive, even ruthless, and it is this that brings both survival and progress. However, as we study more, we also learn that nature reflects, or we reflect from nature, that co-operation and empathy are also essential for survival and can produce progress. Perhaps it is that humanity is more naturally sociable because that is what produces the food for us to survive, which is our most fundamental need. Yet a society at war needs to be co-operative within itself to be efficient and successful. This also feeds into the idea that we can change and choose our path; especially if you believe in the superiority of the human mind and a unique human ability to reflect and analyse and then act.

Modern psychological, sociological, and even neurological studies appear to confirm that we can be sociable and conflictual. The neurological advances we have made allow us to now understand how different emotions highlight different parts of our brain, and through their exercise or stimulation strengthen them. If we are persistently angered, we become permanently angry. This must inform our attitude to government – and make us put into place effective checks and balances. These are in effect the checks and balances of nature or nurture, and what allow people to be both individuals and communal, to be different to each other but accountable, in government or leadership. This is the effect of culture on evolution, although when we talk of such evolution we should be careful to differentiate a long hard-wired physical change from a cultural and social change that appears historically very recent, and to remember our own, usually Western, context. In fact, we have no authoritative guide to the timeline of social change within a species in terms of behaviour that becomes widespread and truly evolutionary. Pavlov's dogs – repetitive rewards and punishments that change behaviour – are of some but limited use in this respect, but Stone Age instincts and Evolutionary leadership remain with us. Why, after all, are governments and leaders still predominately male?

This rubs up against a traditional liberal view of history, that humanity makes continuing progress, which is part of a European Enlightenment model. This is not necessarily a global perspective, or one that stands up to increasing knowledge about how people work, how they change with leadership, or one that acknowledges the weaknesses of the democratic model it promotes. Viewing government only from a liberal perspective could be outright dangerous, hence the common understanding of the phrase 'the price of liberty is eternal vigilance.' However, the changes of humanity over the last 10,000 years would seem to be substantial, and that this is a short period in terms of physical and neurological evolution would seem to give a strong indication that cultural evolution is also important. Things do change and we must continually re-evaluate. Indeed, the global nature of our learning is at its greatest since the original global migrations that populated the planet. That there should be some form of government is indisputably accepted.

The Path to Modern Government in the West

Athenian ideas of 'democracy' are said to be the foundation stones for Western systems of government. Plato's *Republic*, based on the ideas of Socrates, discusses different city regimes; and Aristotle followed this up with *Politika*, formalising ideas of citizenry, constitution, and different types of regimes. However, within the area and time of the Greek city-states democracy was not the only idea on offer, and frequently not the most accepted, and Europe largely ignored these ideas for over a thousand years. The Spartan notion of harsh and warrior leadership has also had a lasting impact. Nor was 'democracy' anything remotely like our modern idea, for the Greeks still had slavery, women could not 'vote,' they had their own elites, a panoply of Gods was paramount, and small city-states were much more manageable than modern nations. Much of the Greek, including Athenian, democracy was underpinned by strong men safeguarding their city-states from local and more distant threats, and the democracy they sought was more about support than accountability. A century or so before Socrates, Confucius was outlining a quite different philosophy for Chinese life and society, and the empires of Persia were completely autocratic. What some of the Ancient Greeks did outline was that a man could act with some free will, if only to stoically cope with the Fates, could seek his 'full virtue' through intellectual development, and could develop a specific and individual understanding of such ideas as justice and truthfulness.

GOVERNMENT AND LEADERSHIP

These are the ideas that we have developed. However, it may also be said that we have looked in the depths of time for the roots of what we now believe, to justify ourselves and provide an historical and philosophical underpinning. Ibn Rushd, latinised as Averroes, in 12th-century Spain, criticised the Plato he translated for not accepting that everyone had an entitlement to happiness, and in contrast to Plato, accepted the equality of women.

Thomas Hobbes, an English philosopher writing at the time of the shocking execution of Charles I at the end of the English Civil War in the mid-17th century, is said to have ushered in the modern era of political philosophy based on social theory rather than mystical or divine tradition in his *On the Citizen* and *Leviathan*. His view was essentially of brutal Man who must surrender some of his liberty in favour of a ruler who would impose order. After the confirmation of the ideals of parliamentary superiority over monarchy were confirmed in the 'Glorious Revolution' just over thirty years later his compatriot John Locke reflected and shaped the new reality, that governing came from the consent of the governed. Furthermore, he acknowledged that the opinions and judgements of the people could change. This was a much more optimistic, and participatory, view of the Ancient Greek ideas of democracy, and of humanity.

Part of Immanuel Kant's answer to 'What is the Enlightenment?' in the next century was that Enlightenment rulers believed in intellectual freedom, and that Man is not a machine but has free will and intellectual capacity (i.e., it was not cannon-fodder for a monarch's desires). He denoted two types of government: Republican and Despotic. In the former he identified equal freedom under the law for all, and representative government. Despotism would include autocracy, the effective rule of an aristocracy through monarchy, and the tyranny of a majority in a democracy. This was the language used by Jean-Jacques Rousseau writing in the context of pre-revolutionary France, and Thomas Paine writing in the context of rebellious American colonies. Rousseau wrote of a 'social pact' in which a ruler and the ruled should willingly and equally share authority, or power, or 'sovereignty,' to better preserve both the individual and the community. The 'general will' was always right but not always enlightened, and could be compromised by

WHERE ARE WE GOING?

sectional groups, and therefore needed a Civil Liberty of law and justice through a shared morality. Thomas Paine wrote of a monarchy having taken power by conquest not moral or intellectual pre-eminence, prone to unsuitable successors and its own interests. A representative democracy could fulfil the general will, the sovereignty of the people, and control or eliminate sectional interests. He wrote that a democracy itself must avoid extremes of wealth and poverty or dependence that would entrench such interests. The framers of the American Constitution themselves were worried about a tyranny of the majority and the corrosive nature of 'party politics' i.e., sectional interests. Hence America's separation and balance of powers between executive, legislature, and judiciary.

In the United Kingdom developing parliamentary reform to avoid the revolutionary fate of the American colonies and of France, encouraged J.S. Mill to speak of a ruler that was checked by constraints, which would become constitutional. The general will would prevail. Government had a right to compel citizens or subjects only in the event of harm being done to others, or in few cases of common benefit, such as common defence or jury service. Otherwise, individual liberty was absolute. Mill also wrote in favour of women's suffrage. Divergence began to emerge between the 'old world' politics and the 'new world' beyond monarchy or presidency. Jeremy Bentham's ideas of pursuing 'the greatest happiness of the greatest number' – Utilitarianism – became the bedrock of Victorian British government intervention and the development of welfare. The political and social contract – now between electorate and elected – became the foundation of legitimacy of elected government. There could be different strategies to achieve this, including light regulation capitalism and social democracy.

European conservatives were concentrating on suppression of change, leading to repeated 19th-century revolution and the greater influence of 'ism's.' Socialism and then Marxism moved beyond social democracy to a more radical embracing of change, spurred on by the inequality of industrialisation and urbanisation. In the 'new world' space of north America there was a greater concentration on individual liberty and freedom – the land of opportunity and self-reliance through 'rugged individualism' – and therefore the role of government became more limited. At its more extreme has emerged libertarianism – the complete freedom of individuals in virtually all things. Of course, in each world – social democracy or reforming conservatism, and 'the land of the free,' these were the ideals, and plenty missed out. Elsewhere the reason and liberties of the Enlightenment were selectively applied by colonialists, and therefore this Enlightenment itself was brought into disrepute for millions around the world.

Now we have a variety of 'democratic' governmental systems in the Western world and have exported them globally. Individual liberty and freedom jostle with common benefit in the application of rights and responsibilities. Property and ownership often define success, in parallel with materialism and consumerism. A government's role is to work for its people – either by intervention or getting out of the way. The majority rule, with a care for minority. The people interpret and judge the success or failure of their government. The will of the people is sovereign, and governments are held accountable, and can change, and sectional interests and entrenched power should be resisted, through elections and the freedoms of civic society. Governments not adhering to this are called authoritarian, although one day in any democracy will tell you that permanent, philosophical, constructed, and human flaws make it fragile.

The Journeys to 'Democratic' Government Across the World

Some governments across the non-Western world are on a par with, or on the way towards, a Western-style democracy, others clearly not so. Some lay claim to democracy despite obvious misuse of the term. Governments each have their specific national origins as well as commonalities. Very few at least pretend not to be representing their people's will. Progress to recognisable democracy may be fragile, with significant countering factors or groups. These nations may have the symbols of democracy: elections, some non-government media, the right to protest and demonstrate, a government that appears to attempt accountability, and that professes respect for human rights and the democratic process. These may also be nations where press freedom to investigate is legal but very limited, or insecure, or shadowy physical intimidation prevents it in practice from anything that might question government legitimacy. Civic society may similarly be hemmed in by difficulty of taking part, of association, of getting its voice heard, of criticism allowed. Opposition to the government may be characterised as unpatriotic, perhaps foreign-supported, or inspired by 'foreign' ideas. Judiciary may be technically independent but under constant pressure to conform to government wishes. Corruption within society may range from endemic to persistent low level – a bribe to get into a good college or be heard by a local politician. More direct criminality may be tolerated: 'white collar' financial, planning, bureaucratic; or protection money, or laundering money, accompanied by the threat of more direct violence. Most of all forces beyond democratic accountability may be having an influence on government formation, or policy, or accountability. A country struggling with these, all of them possible along a spectrum of light to severe, is very much an emerging democracy or struggling to be one. Such nations may have a written constitution that is idealistic but not genuinely accepted or plugged into everyday civic life. They may not have a history of tradition and precedent that has delineated red lines for politicians, institutions, or the public. Transference from one government or another may be haphazard, violent, and with outgoing leaders rarely allowed to live in peace as elder statesmen, and perhaps prosecuted for corruption or simply to discredit them as an alternative voice. At the more severe end of not-yet-democratic nations may be interference from a Head of State or Armed Forces not recognising the need for them to be above the political fray, unable to give up entrenched control or influence, or uncertain of the boundaries of their changing power.

This may seem like a never-ending list of dangers and challenges on the path to earning the title of 'democracy.' It is. We have learnt in recent times how established democracies can weaken and fade and fall into something not quite democratic. Possibly no country in the world can say that it has achieved the right permanent answer to all these issues. Democracies are also subject to pressures, sometimes malign, from outside their borders. However, if a country is transparently struggling with some of these challenges, and the direction of travel of its democratic processes is clear, it may be able to call itself a working democracy. Many governments around the world are working democracies that have many of these flaws. Earning the label of democracy must include the support of most people for the democratic process. If a democracy is complacent enough to think that every problem is solved, then it is likely to be already failing to maintain that support.

Middle Eastern and Arab states generally have elected or part-elected parliaments with a form of monarchy that remains predominant. UAE, Saudi Arabia, Kuwait, Qatar, and Oman introduced female suffrage from 1999. They may have independent political parties arisen from grass-roots movements to only parties or independents authorised by the head of state who may be widely understood as, and legally be, the arbiter of who can stand for election or be a minister of state. The UAE has no directly elected chamber or official right of free speech. More localised 'government' may be less Western and more based on traditional councils and traditional leaders. Jordan and Morocco have strong and established monarchy but freer elected representatives who form a government responsible for domestic policy, with limited direct monarchical interference. Periodic political crises do not negate their emerging democracy. Iraq is to some extent a transplanted democracy. Various sectional interests from different traditions and modern political ideas have been forced into a Western imposed parliamentary style with no free political or civil tradition in the country. It passes from crisis to crisis, but its parliamentary structure and political cut and thrust are becoming more accepted in the public mind and helping to crystallise a new Iraqi sense of independence. Afghanistan – whether Taliban led or not – has given greater emphasis to traditional councils and leaders but a parliament has been established, with more women's voices and more attempts to impose national policy. It will be interesting how much the post-2021 Taliban government uses the Afghan parliament, or abolishes it; and how the world chooses to engage, or not, with a Taliban government, and on what terms. The idea of a national parliament giving a national voice – or various voices shouting at the same time – may be more difficult to erase from people's minds than they expect. Across the wider Arab world these institutions are reaching varied accommodations with often nationalist Islam, and nationalist Islamic parties are adapting. Libyan instability has become a specific regional problem, sucking in other nations; and Tunisia's retraction from its Arab Spring success is incredibly disappointing, as is Egypt's reversion to authoritarian rule.

Across South East Asia nations appear further along the democratisation of their politics and national life. Malaysia, Indonesia, and Singapore are all established democracies by most definitions. They each have faults, from one-party predominance in Malaysia to ethnic-religious conflict in regions of Indonesia, but each has a thriving critical media, robust participation in elections, and a general acceptance of the democratic process itself. Thailand suffers from a democratic process subject to background influence of, disregard by, or hindering deference to, the monarch and the influence of the military. Both are struggling with an historic decrease in their power at the expense of the masses now engaged in the political process. The Philippines is playing with its history. The 'peoples power revolution' of Corey Aquino after the overthrow of the dictator Ferdinand Marcos in 1986 was one of the first modern people's revolutions. Its last President, Rodrigo Duterte, was seen as dictatorial in style, but in 2022 relinquished power at the end of his single constitutional term. He was replaced by a son of Marcos. However odd that may seem, turnout was 83% and notwithstanding the criticised role of social media there was a vocal and relatively free press, an open campaign, and visible pressure groups arguing their position on the issues of the day. In Taiwan a thriving democracy has taken strong root. Out of the authoritarian Kuomintang that fled China in 1949 emerged the predominance of a single party, but over time a Western-style democracy has emerged. So too South Korea after the Korean War, and Japan after the Second World War. All three have a thriving civil society, independent media, all-round respect for the democratic process, healthy electoral participation, and peaceful transfer of power between genuine political rivals. In fact, given the time usually needed to establish these things they have become genuinely democratic very quickly. China appears ideologically determined not to go beyond one-party rule.

South and Central America are areas traditionally beset by military interference in government. This past still casts a shadow but is not as strong as it once was. In Argentina and Brazil, South America's largest nations, people are accepting the democratic process. Anti-democratic forces and ideas have relevance but not a hold on the levers of power. Like some in East Asia the roots of democracy appear to have become reasonably entrenched in a relatively short time. Chile has just, by democratic and peaceful means, engaged in wholesale review of its constitution. Mexico is hesitatingly shedding its preference for the continuous rule of one party, its democratic process is relatively accepted even though its society is far from peaceful, and in that context has a reasonably free press and civic society. Other parts of South and Central America are trying, but the power of the military in nations still recovering from, or still fighting, separatist conflict or extensive criminal power or corrupt practice, or a combination or entwining of these, is often still a strong influence. Security in the name of stability can still be suffocating to civil society, deliberately or through circumstance. An element of this in the past has been the influence of the Cold War, where nations became embroiled with one side or other. It takes time to free oneself of such influence and find an individual national path to building the circumstances that encourage a trusted democratic process, or at least one where people are prepared to participate in it and defend it.

In Africa it is the colonial and Cold War legacies that have hindered democracy most. These encouraged factionalism within nations, separatist conflict, and as in South America, a side-stepping of social policy in preference to security and stability, often built on actual corruption or the corruption of national priorities either internally or from external influence, or both. An added layer of nation-building required onto often artificial borders encompassing multi-religious, ethnic, and tribal divisions has been a further complication. Then there are added issues like extensive rural-to-urban migration with rapid urban growth, a young population, and the difficulties of international trade and aid. The lessening of Cold War and colonial burdens has cemented borders and raised governance. Developing civil society including media and social pressure groups, women's voices being heard far more, technology helping business, and a greater international emphasis on supporting the development of education and health services have also made the building blocks of the democratic process far stronger. Problems remain: leaders that stay in power too long, corruption, factional conflict, economic inequality, and susceptibility to the winds of international harms from the environment to war elsewhere, and to trade restrictions and fluctuations. Professed Islamic aligned violent groups across the Sahel are a particular problem. However, elections are more common than coups; investigative journalism and public accountability are more common than ever before; opportunities for more formal education at secondary level and higher are more widespread. The one-party dominance of government is less common as independence parties lose their lustre, and army interference is less common as peace prevails and armies professionalise. Elections are now the norm. The chaotic but apparently robust democracy of Nigeria, the tribal and prolonged leadership-tested democracy of Kenya, and the highly accountable and civic strength of South Africa are all more typical of Africa these days than the one-party-rule government of Zimbabwe, or the failing state of Somalia. Africa is a big place, and variety remains along the democratic spectrum, but the majority of countries are somewhere on it.

People and leaders in Europe and America often forget how long it took for their own countries to develop a level of societal education that made political participation realistic and peaceful, how long it took for a universal suffrage to emerge, and an independent media, and to end interfering monarchy and establish democratic and parliamentary precedents. William and Mary were invited to be the monarchs of England on the condition that they accepted, again, parliamentary supremacy in England. This was about forty years after a civil war won by Parliament; and yet George III a century afterwards still believed he had the right to dissolve Parliament on a whim and had to be resisted. That alone is a 150-year timespan. Several nations of Central and Eastern Europe have seeds in previous centuries but are primarily constructs from 1919, lasted barely twenty years with independence, and re-claimed that independence only fifty years later after the fall of Nazism and Soviet Communism, barely thirty years ago. Yet these nations too had quite long-established education, media, and what we would call civic society. The United States of America did not suddenly appear after the colonies fought for independence. Its creation was a deliberate act setting aside the thirteen colonies' independence, and its federal-state tensions brought it to catastrophic civil war about seventy-five years later. Its democracy remains imperfect: with issues from that civil war that remain over race and states' rights, to political appointees deciding constituency boundaries in a partisan way, and the corrosive amount of money required to run a campaign to get elected. It may even now just be beginning to see the downside of a fixed Constitution needing reinterpretation for changing circumstances. There are tolerance, differences, and lessons we seem to have forgotten when we judge the progress of others, the challenges they face, the imperfect nature of the development of democracy around the world, and its changing nature in our own nations. We still focus on helping leaders who are supportive of our interests in the short term.

In an historic timeframe the global spread of democracy has been nothing short of incredible. Nationalism has accommodated democracy. Ruling monarchies, colonial overlordship, and army control are almost at an end. Government accountability through media and education and the ability of ordinary people to have their voices heard are all much more widespread than 100 years ago; and a focus on economic development and services far more likely. Globally, what we have now is the widespread acceptance of the principles of the democratic process, its nationally individual implementation, and a struggle against its imperfections. Non-democratic nations stand out as exceptions much more than they did even fifty years ago. Most of those offer no cohesive ideology that is an alternative template for others to follow.

Contemporary Democracy

Today's democracy is often said to be in decline or facing challenges that it will struggle to meet. Trust or good governance is eroded by lack of transparency, perceived lack of effective participation, and disagreement over whether services and opportunities are efficient and available. New governments so often start with the best of intentions which soon fade away in favour of their self-proclaimed necessity to keep power. Most people believe the maxim that 'power corrupts, and absolute power corrupts absolutely.' Good governance in established as well as emerging democracies cannot be taken for granted. It must be safeguarded and updated in the face of foreign influence, domestic inequality and disengagement, demonising of opposition and civic society, and unexpected events.

The Challenges to Democracy: Interests

These are many and varied. Churchill allegedly said that democracy would be discredited if you spent two minutes with any voter. That misses the point of democracy and hints at some of its current dangers. Democracy is about the collective. It is the collective wisdom. We have representative democracy in practice. No single person should be democracy, whether the richest person in the world, the elected politician, or the person next to you putting the world to rights in the pub or cafe. Democratic decisions are formed from the collective experience and will of the participants. We have therefore, by definition, an imperfect system. The preponderance of 'interests' above the collective is one of the greatest problems that democracies face. Interests act as one voice with power over their specific issue/s, and this has been an ever-present danger. The founding fathers of American independence and its Constitution were afraid of a party representing a section and doing so efficiently by allowing minimal internal debate. The 'tyranny of the majority' is one aspect of this. Representative democracies must be effectively participatory and representative. Different voices need to listen and empathise as well as talk. The failure of many democracies to engage large numbers of their population is the most ignored and serious problem those democracies face and is endangering the collective enterprise that is democracy.

Two examples of this illustrate these points in different ways. Firstly, the effect of the Covid-19 pandemic. Jonathan Sumption, former leading UK judge, represented many when he said that people had too easily given away freedoms to the state. His view was that individuals were responsible for themselves and their own decisions. His view had an in-built assumption that people could be so, in terms of the information to make informed choices and the practical or physical notion of being independent in their health. However, those that could not be – such as those unable to be vaccinated for medical reasons – clearly depend on the responsibility of others. It seemed that in Sumption's view democracy is individualistic, and educated, with the ability to assess 'fair' or 'true' or 'clear' information. However, his comment was also, like many, a matter of timing. He was not questioning first essential steps for combatting a virulent disease or saying that government had no role or responsibility. His concern was persistent loss of individual freedoms to government decision-making. That more nuanced argument had more sympathy. Following the peak of the pandemic the collective will changed. The point is that collectively it did so. Democracy may be individualistic in its personal opinion-forming, but it is not so in its decision-making. The language of combatting Covid-19 – the state being 'at war' – allowed democracy to move onto a war footing. A working democracy can summon the collective will to act differently when under threat. That democratic collective must then be strong enough to recognise the end of the threat, and the necessity to return to the democratic norms of peacetime. Not all democracies make it through to the other side of conflict. It is the collective nature of democracy that allows it to do so. An individualistic version is too prone to both a single leader making that turning-point decision, influenced as they would be by their burden of responsibility and their political or personal ambition; and prone to a division of action that breaks down society and renders a democracy unworkable.

Participation problems have been caused by, and led to, the outsize importance of 'property' as a specific 'interest.' This is the second example. Property ownership historically denoted a stake in society and a level of responsibility that made a citizen qualified to make decisions, and to gain the vote. Arguably, the eligibility of women to vote represented an historic, even revolutionary, shift away from property towards rights – therefore also benefitting poor property-less men. However, the strength of property ownership as an 'interest' within Western democracies remains very strong. Property is seen as a continually rising investment in the future, and a reflection of someone's success, and of their worth. Government policies in relation to property are distorting investment and government spending, generational balance, social mobility and opportunity, and therefore faith and participation in democracy itself. Property ownership is being promoted and valued as an inalienable right, like education or health, that surely people would want. A strand of conservative thought even maintains that a 'small state' should only exist as a 'nightwatchman' to protect people's property. The ambition is for all to own their own property – it is in that sense inclusive – but the competition it encourages and value it is given are destructive to the collective will upon which an effective democracy depends and thrives, and is another symptom of the imbalance towards individualism and 'interest.' This is not saying that property ownership should not be allowed, just that it currently serves as an example of the danger to democracy of specific interests at the expense of the whole. For property, so too wealth itself.

The increasing importance of property and wealth are also indicators of the rise of the middle class. This will soon become, globally, the largest economic and social grouping, expanded by the development of China and India and South East Asia. A rising middle class comes with more education and critical citizenship, and with higher expectations economically, politically, socially, and culturally. A middle class 'needs' or demands more attention, more resources, is more confident in initial change until it has more to lose, and is more confident in its opinions, which may not necessarily be progressive. This will be a major change for the world in ways we cannot foresee. For example, will the Chinese middle class demand more peace, or feel more confident in promoting assertive nationalism? Nations must reconcile the alleviation of poverty, the demands of a rising middle class, and increasing inequality between the richest and the poorest. Looming over all that will be the even bigger 'interest' of girls and women's rights.

Interests have created our modern, misunderstood, identity politics, and misnamed 'culture wars.' These are used to appeal to a specific group, whether to claim legitimacy, power, or victimisation. Partisanship in this context is far more than policy division. If it is an exclusive group rather than an inclusive one, and the same group remains in control, and then fixes the rules and the culture to sustain its control, and inevitably becomes less empathetic and less knowledgeable of others, then democracy is dying. If such control is acquiesced in, or results in a perception of powerlessness and disengagement, then democracy is dying. The result is not a democracy of shared intent, or common benefit and sacrifice. Nothing keeps it together. Power becomes power for its own sake, lost in the fear of losing it and losing everything, or lost in the conceit of always knowing best.

The original issue of an 'interest' may be a reactive or a progressive one. Belief in a nationalist purity may be a general example. Brexit in the UK might be said to be a specific one. The creation of wealth itself may be another, with its spectrum of how much the means justify the ends. Identity politics is just as likely to be used by majorities as minorities, whether as a compliment or insult. The original point is making people equal not to promote them as a special interest. The point about Black Lives Matter is not that black people matter more; it is that they matter as much, and to address historic inequality. The feminist and *#metoo* movements are instructive in this respect. They are also about addressing historic inequality even though women make up roughly 50% of the population and in that sense can hardly be called a minority – but they are seen as an 'interest.' And democracies have chosen to address this 'interest.' Democracies choose what interests to promote. It is the collective will to choose equality for women. It will eventually be successful as long as it remains the collective will. It is education and awareness and leadership and people's lived experiences that will make it and sustain it as the collective will. Any interest, given that backing, can become part of the working collective will, the mainstream, of a democracy. There are dangers – the imperialist mindset was supported by an education system which shaped colonisers and colonised. Any interest can lose the collective will if it loses that support by overplaying its hand or working out surprisingly badly. Thankfully the imperialist mindset is dying, the one encouraging female equality of opportunity continues to thrive.

Identity politics is fought through 'culture wars,' which essentially mean anything that can define that group being fought for or against, positively or negatively. Any group needs to define itself. It is the same with nations, which is why identity politics used divisively is a threat to the unity of a nation. We are all members of multiple groups within society, from religious grouping to ethnicity, from educational level to income group, etc. It is when we cannot acknowledge the value of different groups, or support or empathise with more than one group at a time, that we become isolated in our views and susceptible to 'evidence' that may trap us within a dominant narrow identity. At that point we must break free again of the emotional commitment and restrictions imposed, or accept their overwhelming importance, and from then onwards seek our care and comfort, our dependence and understanding, in that one group alone.

Language is key. Communication on any serious issue requires the willingness to accept language that explains difference, and to accept and cope with disagreement. A culture war is a war in the sense that the enemy is demonised. 'Political correctness' or 'wokeness' becomes a matter of free speech. Free speech becomes about the right to offend or to not be offended. The claim that one should not be offended is claiming the right not to be questioned or challenged. Without common understanding of the language empathy dies. The collective shared intent of a democracy is then weakened or lost. Free speech must include the right to offend, most clearly the right to offend with a point rather than gratuitously. We can divide offence from intimidation and hatred. Democrats must defend this right to offend even when they are offended. New language, which is what political correctness often is, denotes a new point of view, or a new standard. We may talk about 'black people' and wonder if that is the up-to-date phraseology but at another time that was the new politically correct alternative to what today we would find offensive. Some politically correct language will be commonly accepted over time, some will not, just as the standards that they describe or reflect are adopted, or not. Only those concerned with developing divisive sectional interests highlight issues as culture wars and selectively demonise language. A minority seeking change, for example in law enforcement or housing provision, is often negatively characterised in identity politics rather than wider justice or equality. This promotion of specific interests at the expense of others can be defeated. 'Feminism' was once a term of protest for outsiders. The issue has become part of the common will, and the language now commonly accepted.

Inequality is the most important problem that might eat many democracies from the inside. Increasing inequality is the result of special interest politics. Inequality breeds contempt for the democratic process.

If you never win, then why play the game? If no-one represents you, speaks your language, and acts in your interest, then why follow anyone? There are many things that can be done to reduce inequality, some short term and some longer, some easy and some hard: taxing wealth as well as income, raising wages to a level where benefits are no longer needed but needing to do so without raising inflation, and changing executive pay through worker representation or shareholder power or restrictive law, etc. Everything has consequences and we have made the uncertain and the imperfect the enemy or master of the possible. We teach children not to take risks rather than assess risk, and we are doing the same as adults. In democratic terms the economic model, or at least the aims within it that we set ourselves, have become twisted. We have got ourselves in a position where the people serve the model. We are losing the ability to compromise and to make decisions based on a consensus interpretation of the evidence. We need to re-find the common good. We need to review the narratives that we tell ourselves are set in stone and find a better balance of rights and responsibilities towards each other if we are to maintain economic progress and opportunity as a driving force, and a foundational stone, of a thriving democracy. We are finding that economic imperatives are harder addictions to ditch and what should be good moral attitudes towards one another are harder to implement, and even sometimes too hard to see or acknowledge. As people – leaders and public – feel powerless to change the economic landscape, so then other divisions are reinforced to protect their position. Hence the protection of identity and culture become more important. Economic man may not be the be-all and end-all of progress but while some think we cannot change inequality because the problem is too big or inevitable, others may feel that it is not so important. This is a lose-lose scenario, fed by interests and the pessimism and isolation they feed. Inequality cannot be effectively challenged without a shared sense of benefit and sacrifice. This applies whether you think humanity makes progress competitively or co-operatively. Without a sense of the common good democracy is doomed.

WHERE ARE WE GOING?

Specific Challenges to Nations Around the World

The American Dream is alive and well in general, but what Angus Deayton called 'deaths of despair' through, for example, drug overdose, suicide, or by firearms, and the levels of imprisonment, are serious societal problems that are proving difficult to address. The communities affected do not see themselves represented in American politics and leadership. The increasing partisanship of politics with little middle ground, reflected in communities that seem to be geographically and physically separating out politically, at local, state, and national level, are a threat to American democracy. In the UK disengaged groups relate more directly to inequality. However, the USA, UK and the EU also share another tension within themselves, that between centralisation and localism. They are unions under pressure, wanting central efficiency and local engagement. The union of the UK itself is under threat from appeals for Scottish independence and Irish union. Brexit has highlighted the political notion of 'taking back control.' The EU is struggling to develop a political and cultural conformity that can keep it together. Inequality, identity, and disengagement threaten democracy in the Western world.

India is pursuing the development of a different path for the nation away from secular Western ideals to a more specifically Indian Hindu association with government. How it is doing so may be exemplifying a tyranny of the majority and is concerning for democracy. Japan remains an essentially inward-looking and conservative society, while trying to maintain a liberal and globally outward-looking economy. Within a very different political context India and Japan are on the same spectrum of governmental conservatism and economic globalism as China. This is a core part of the stereotypical Asian problem with the advance of individualism and individual liberties in the face of maintaining their distinctive identities, cultural heritage, and strength in community. It is, however, a wide spectrum and clearly India and Japan, in their different ways, have much greater opportunity and openness to adapt to changing circumstances and global trends. South Korea's dangers to democracy are population decline and the unpredictable threat of real-world conflict with North Korea.

GOVERNMENT AND LEADERSHIP

In sub-Saharan Africa the issue is the provision of livelihoods and modern social living for younger populations when that group does not have a controlling interest in the power structures. Economically, politically, and in terms of Western liberalism, these are developing nations, sometimes at rapid pace, attempting to maintain their cohesion and often a social conservatism. Similarly Middle Eastern and North African nations continue with economic and technological modernity, youthful populations, politics emerging from the shadow of monarchy or colonialism, and conservative Islam. These are competing interests in a battleground of increasing urbanisation and Western individual, especially women's, rights.

Australia and New Zealand and parts of South America exhibit some of the problems of the Western world elsewhere, and, distinctively, are seeking a greater accommodation with their indigenous cultures. Australia is now also recognising that it may be more susceptible to climate change extremes than any other large nation, while New Zealand continues to portray itself as a steady refuge of co-operative Western values. Pacific Island nations are increasingly fighting for their very survival against climate change extremes and are increasingly being drawn into choosing between a Chinese or Western sphere of influence.

Russia and China are becoming more surveillance orientated, integrating political rulers with holders of economic and social power, institutionalising corruption, and in general treating general populations as threats not partners. Leaderships are increasing nationalism, international isolation and allowing oligarchy. Both are at different stages of 'interests' dominating national life, but in their different ways both can only commit to that path. Neither are even keeping to their own proclaimed versions of democracy.

Every nation has its specific issues. It may be that the struggle against 'interests' is permanent and that is what creates the 'tension,' or entrepreneurial and creative ideas, and ambition, for change. However, development at different rates does not preclude change or progress on a more co-operative footing than that of conflict and competition. Urbanisation also continues apace. Then there is the role, whether threat or opportunity, of developing science and technology.

WHERE ARE WE GOING?

The Challenges to Democracy: Science and Technology

Both social science and physical science are having an increasing bearing on democracy. One of the benefits of Covid-19 may turn out to be the public understanding that science can be reinterpreted, be used, and something to be regulated by ethics and cultural norms. We also believe that science cannot be 'unlearnt,' and that science will lead wherever it will lead itself. However, we are not keeping up with thinking through and preparing for the consequences, socially, economically, emotionally, morally, or politically, of our current level of invention and discovery.

To know one's opposition, to know the 'electorate,' whether feudal lords or the public, and to know one's own mind, are all essential long-standing holy grails of politics. They are about understanding and shaping behaviour, because politics is the art of the possible, as opposed to philosophy which seeks the 'truth.' Whether ambitions are good and moral, or immoral and self-serving, is irrelevant here; this is about the method to achieve success. American thinker and politician James Madison in the 18th/19th century had said that governments reflect people's beliefs, but studies show that people overestimate themselves, seek confirmation and social conformity, are often persuaded by emotions and images more than data, tend to remember the most recent not most important, and dread losses rather than appreciate gains. Advertising is an ancient art that appeals to these instincts. Daniel Kahneman's *Thinking, Fast and Slow* and subsequent works have deconstructed the instinctive and the deliberative, the 'fast' impulsive and intuitive thinking from the 'slow' methodical, thoughtful, care that can more effectively screen out the 'noise' of irrelevance and misdirection all around us.

A new theory to change behaviour in the light of these ideas emerged from about 2000: nudge theory. We know that just because people are aware of biases, they do not necessarily counter them in their actions, they usually think 'fast.' We also know that if they are being told to do something many people instinctively have a mistrust of it. We also know that trust in government is generally in decline. How, then, can governments produce the behavioural change that is often missing from their ambitions and predictions? Nudge theory is behavioural insight that uses intuition and engages emotion in a targeted way to produce behavioural change. It is also about developing processes in institutions to produce more 'slow' thinking and therefore better planning with more long-term effectiveness. Sweets are near the tills of the supermarket to encourage an impulse buy but if you want people to be healthier the same impulse can be used to buy healthier food placed there instead. The Delhi metro now uses colour-coded footprints to guide people to the right line.* Researching nudge theory from the bottom up as opposed to top down, i.e., using real-world data to understand how people make decisions, is called 'human design' or 'design thinking.' In Chicago its school-based 'Becoming a Man' programme (from 2001) intervened to get young men to act less impulsively i.e., more maturely, with the recorded result of reduced arrest rates and improved graduation rates.† In New Zealand since 2017 advertisements that presented prospective police officers as helpers and representative of a more diverse population produced more women (up 29%) and Maori-heritage (up 32%) officers and a different profile of character – in contrast to American law enforcement promotional and training videos that present officers as enforcers, emphasising suspicion and strength.‡ This is psychology as part of public policy, helping to determine people's choices. Yet if it is in the background and not accountable it may be manipulation rather than education and nudging. Nudge is good but 'sludge' is bad, and can weave dark patterns, i.e., the theory can be used to promote controlling messages and choices. It is important to remember that like a computer it depends on the input. We must learn to recognise this technological and modern updating of old ideas. Behavioural science will influence government in the future in parallel with, and as much as, policy development because it is key to implementation and success in the real world. Our future education must include more about understanding how we think, and how other people may try to shape how we think. Sludge can clearly put democracy in danger.

Another age-old aspect of behavioural science is the use of 'fake news,' disinformation, and distraction. Exciting news for free is a distraction

---

* Sowmya Rao, Anirudh Tagat, "India's nudge unit: An idea whose time has come," *Mint*, 17 February 2016.
† Hallsworth, Michael and Kirkman, Elspeth, 2020, 183.
‡ Brian Klaas, 2021, 53–55.

WHERE ARE WE GOING?

technique used by authoritarians and democrats from gladiators in the Colosseum to an eye-catching policy distracting from scandal. In an overarching way the promotion of consumerism might be considered a general distraction away from political questioning or engagement. This is a charge against the current Chinese government and might also be a charge against (unhindered) capitalism as a constructed narrative. The news is about perception, and governments will try to control the story. President Trump's administration came with the promotion of the idea of 'alternative facts,' and the suggestion that people should not believe what they see. Narratives that last and become accepted have a usefulness and real world relevance or recognition for people, something that comforts or inspires them, or binds them with others. The person who points out that the emperor has no clothes, the whistleblower, takes a gamble between being called a truth-teller or traitor. Social media algorithms promote stories and opinions in people's news feeds that they may show an interest in, based on their previous reading, or even their friends' reading, not based on any objective importance or truth. Critics believe this narrows opinions, increases isolation, erodes the concept of objective truth, and therefore decreases the compromising and co-operative instincts, empathy, and communally accepted evidence required for a working democracy. This is as true and maybe even more dangerous in developing nations as developed ones.[*] In 2020, 23% of Americans said that they 'often' got their news from social media, although it was 42% for those aged 18–29.[†] A modern democratic citizen has the responsibility to understand their own biases, and to verify their sources as much as that may be possible. Evidence, or stories, that are consistent between different independent sources is a staple requirement of any research, journalism, or historian, and has been for centuries.

The development of the physical sciences, including neuroscience, is potentially a far more insidious danger. Elections are about feelings, informed by information. Having many sources of an independent

---

[*] Odanga Madung, "If it cared, TikTok could stop itself being used to stir up tribal hatred in Kenya, *The Guardian*, 27 June 2022.
[†] Elisa Shearer, "More than eight-in-ten Americans get news from digital devices," *Pew Research Center*, 12 January 2021. "Half of people now get their news from social media," *Ofcom*, 24 July 2019.

media, investigative journalism, an ability to meet anyone else and experience anywhere else, to try things for oneself, and the freedom to speak out even as a lone voice, all combat the control of information. This is why all these are controlled during wartime. Influencing education, creating an enemy to rally around, or creating a scapegoat such as Jews, or 'the elite,' or 'extremists' as defined in any way someone wants, can all manipulate information and feeling. Algorithms and big data may be able to look at a billion experiences, tests or words and make predictions. We might want to know if we are likely to get cancer, or if our teenager is a risk-taker. We may have second thoughts about whether that information should be given to our life insurance company or if our child's future employer should know. We may meet someone who says that if the process is, by track record, accurate, then what right do we have to withhold that information, for example to stop health services knowing and being able to intervene. We already live in a Meta and Amazon era where they believe they can predict what we will want to buy, or want to know, and where information about us can be bought by a political party to predict how we may vote, and that political party may tweak a message towards our preferences. The individualisation of messaging allowed by modern technology is one form of manipulation. Supposing those messages we receive are negative, are critical, are propaganda, and make us think that the views we hold are out of the ordinary, or abnormal, and isolating, or alternatively that the extreme views we hold are natural and common. The potential for algorithms to define the boundaries of what we think we know, and to produce personal isolation and personalised discrimination, are just beginning. One example: inputs that look at a track record of racially biased convictions to say more criminals are black will identify more black people as criminals, and this becomes a self-confirming algorithm leading to a narrowing of 'intelligence,' or our interpretations, and resources, that results in self-sustaining discrimination.

People who exercise may look at their watches to check their heart rate. Neuroscience can now check what parts of the brain light up when we are angry or sympathetic, frustrated, or happy. As computers learn from exponential examples they recognise patterns. That may be a pattern of lifestyle that will result in diabetes or predicts conformity, or individualistic behaviour. As the effectiveness of computer facial recognition grows AI will recognise if we are angry or happy. If the biosensor on our wrist shows elevated heart rate or other chemicals in our body such as prolonged high adrenaline levels, and that is sent to a central 'computer' able to look at that information in real time our mood may be all too clear. These developments may have perfectly beneficial uses, but who would have that information? Anxiety and high heart rate might result in us getting a call from our local automated doctor asking if we are OK. The health 'authority' may be upon us, in our own interests of course, pursuing their targets of preventative medicine. However, a regime with less noble intentions may look at an angry expression and high heart rate and think potential political extremist, with a likelihood confirmed by profiling which denotes your ethnic, racial, religious, cultural, geographical, or educational background. The magazine you bought on your app about going to live elsewhere or how to control privacy settings on your computer may not have helped. The visit may not be from the health authority but from the real police. Today we are not far away from all this technology and science being possible, most of it is already. It will improve, and at least parts of it may become more centralised in the name of efficiency. And if you are not wearing the wristband, or object to facial recognition, which helps identify criminals and health issues which are both clearly for the public good, then the questions 'why not?' and 'what are you hiding?' will be asked. We must be clear that these are nightmare futures. Let us remember that technology is a tool, its algorithms and sensors and boundaries and definitions are man-made. There is no inevitability about this. However, nor is there an inevitability about somehow it not happening. For those who already live in an undemocratic state it may already be being perfected. For those who live in a democratic state 'the price of liberty being eternal vigilance' is a two-edged sword. How easy would it be for a health, retail, insurance or employing company to decline to give the information they have when the nation seems under threat, and afterwards when keeping access to it may be a good preventative measure for the next emergency? AI algorithms, big data, and biosensors can prove beneficial in all sorts of ways but let's not pretend either that they can't also destroy individual freedoms and collective democracy. We may find that individualised discrimination is far harder to protest against than group discrimination. The technology may not even have to be very efficient. It is our perception that it is there, and one or two high profiles examples of its use that may provide enough incentive for self-censorship. As for the character of person who would use it, how would they balance individual risks to innocence and national security or the public good, within a claimed '99% accuracy'?

Democratic Recovery

In Albert Camus' 1947 novel *The Plague* 'the only way to fight the plague is with decency.' This is an imperfect answer to the struggle between social solidarity and individual freedom. Individuals find their level of decency amid their rights and responsibilities, and a consensus emerges from the whole, but individual voices can also raise the standard or alter the direction, and provide leadership. This means that in a democracy there is always a chance of new ideas and self-renewal. The consensus is buttressed by the quiet majority who, in a real democracy as opposed to other forms of government, get to be heard. How this happens depends on politics, political will, and collective struggle.

We live in a world of global economics, cultural importance and identities, expected liberties and freedoms, and inequality, powerlessness and stress, but the issues through which democracy can be rejuvenated are already here. Quality of life feeds into cost of living and climate issues, and the bigger picture of too much consumerism and materialism. Women's equality, which still has so much further to go in employment, family and other spheres, and ending all forms of discrimination, feeds into a bigger picture of individual opportunity, fairness, and the common good. These struggles in democracy are about new opportunities to contribute, new sources of entrepreneurship, and new empowerment. They are global. They are not just 'left-wing' social issues but 'right-wing' issues of innovation and wealth, or how to make money and pay for it all. A mass democracy expects financial responsibility and security, but also expects more. All this is really about engagement. While leaders should lead they must persuade too, and listen. When a third or more of people do not engage in the democratic electoral process – whether through disinterest or lack of energy/time or thinking their opinions are not being represented – something more needs to be done. When many of those are showing an interest in specific issues, and it is the democratic process that they lack faith in, then there is a door to be pushed at and opened further.

Around the world several ways of pushing at that door are being explored. Some are dealt with in the chapter on the Economy including local devolution, participatory budgets, co-operatives, and open-source entrepreneurship and research. Specific democratic ideas are being explored which include constitutional conventions as recently held by Chile in the remaking of its constitution, and citizens' assemblies as exemplified in the Republic of Ireland's abortion debate and subsequent referendum. These are big projects that build on a history of genuine local consultation from economic regeneration to housing and facility planning. These need to be genuine sources of decision-making or proposal outline for wider democratic consultation. They need financial and organisational backing but most of all they need political and communal will. Authorities need to make it clear that participation will be worthwhile, not in money but in an increase in influence at the decision-making table. This can reduce powerlessness, and unite people in compromise. The mixed economy of private, state, charitable, and 'expert' organisations and approaches all remain. If we engage greater numbers of people we can renew a more accurate and effective collective will and common good. Such projects must not be endless talking shops, although must also not negate the accountability and power of an elected authority. This is not easy, but we must have more faith in ourselves, in the level of education and civic society that we have, and in other people. We can choose to be a socially co-operative species. Kang Kyung-wha, South Korea's first female foreign minister, emphasised, during Covid-19, her country's democratic approach to the crisis: in a crisis she said governments must extend and reaffirm accountability through transparency, communication, knowledge, and science. The contrast to a populist, technocratic, or more autocratic approach is stark.

In crisis or not, in new approaches, we will still need to recognise the dangers too, those of the charming public speaker-wannabe leader, those of the megaphone social media voice, the lack of diverse representation in debate, etc. Nor does it negate big government responsibilities for big government issues of long-term planning, infrastructure, security, and foreign relations. This democratic revitalisation is aside from things like term limits and administrative efficiency; citizenship education and freedom of information; an independent judiciary and freedom of expression. These and others remain bedrocks of any working democracy worth its name. Democracy needs to be felt as personal, local, and national. Religions have changed practices over time and integrated localised customs and continue to do so. If democracy is the common creed of our actions towards one another then it must be able to do that too – while, like religion, maintaining its core beliefs.

The Alternatives to Democracy

We like to think of the multiplicity of voices in a democracy being its strength. Two heads are better than one. If both have a voice both can have power, and hope, and better ideas can emerge. Listening may take time and then action take longer, but when democracies act they do so with better foundations and more solidity. That is what we like to think. It may be continually battered by the lack of engagement of one of the heads, their lack of trust, their smaller voice. What if they no longer believe that the other voice has a shared intent and shared sense of sacrifice and benefit? How natural is their belief in the positive benefit of co-operation, and how inevitable their trust? Negative answers call into question the roots and strength of the liberalism that any democracy requires to work. People's trust is determined by track record and perceived efficiency. Remember J.S. Mill said that we should from time to time debate even our most basic beliefs to reaffirm them, to update them if necessary, and re-educate ourselves and the next generation on their importance, especially in changing circumstances. Disturbing foundations can be liberating but also dangerous. At that moment our opinions may be manipulated, or the debate itself may produce a divergence of language, of intent, and of commonality. Even in established democracies we may find that democracy does not have the foundation we thought. Most people, if something isn't working, will try something else. That is an open door to an undemocratic alternative efficiency to make their lives better. An open door may have other forces to push it, such as leadership ambition or cultural and identity politics, or external influence, but its opening is because of the failure of democracy to work for its people and their inevitable search for something, anything, better.

Acquiescent 'Democracy'

Lack of transparency, lack of competency, an apparent inability to react to changing circumstances, faltering economies, inflexible partisanship, the tyranny of a majority or a minority, and the emergence of a political class out of touch with ordinary people, all call into question the viability of established democracies. Personal insecurity, corruption, or an inability to maintain one's health or find educational and entrepreneurial opportunity, all call into question the viability of developing democracies. Young populations, religious tension with government, and between farmers and rapid urbanisation, also set a very difficult scene for many developing nations. In some places – economically and politically developed or not – the to-and-fro of partisanship has exhausted the goodwill of people who see little change, or who see a lot of change but then its reversal a few years later. Across an historic era democracies have undoubtedly improved people's lives but on a day-to-day basis in a world where every individual has a voice and thinks that it should be heard, there is a sense that they are failing too many people.

Populism calls itself democratic but emphasises division not co-operation. It may identify as either right or left wing and may be neither. It places the wants and concerns of one group distinctly ahead of, or in opposition to, others. The easy way to do this is to scapegoat minorities. Those minorities might be ethnic or cultural groups, they may be 'big business' or 'the swamp' of 'self-serving' politicians who despite either their best or their incompetent efforts have not given you what you needed or wanted. Big corporations, outsourcing, institutional power, bureaucracy, inequality, and failing meritocracy, can all be populist targets. Populists claim to represent the forgotten. They move with changing circumstances and elude both responsibility and principles. Democratic leaders can turn into populists at that point when power is close, or when losing it is close, and they decide that they know best, that they know what is good for people, and that they can fulfil the wishes of the people if only they had that chance, a chance worth dealing in the Machiavellian arts for. By not listening to all its people, democracy only has itself to blame for the success of an undemocratic-minded populist. Such a populist believes only they make the right decisions, they may mould the existing system or create a new system, and manipulate perception, and may move onto using intimidation and even violence. Populism is a response to an opaque and unresponsive democracy not working for the common good. Many democracies need to do better.

A democracy might itself choose to support a technocracy. If people want government to be efficient and then want to get on with their own lives, why not choose experts. They can be objective, not subject to the whims, or the excessive influence, of interests. Since the 1980s about 20% of Italian ministers have been appointed from outside its Parliament, including four prime ministers. In Italy, in 2011 a technocratic cabinet government was appointed – but rejected by the electorate in 2013, unable to persuade the country of its decisions. For a decade or more this is how Italy increasingly reacted to governmental disruption and political deadlock. A technocracy is a place where the electorate do not have faith in elected leaders but find faith in 'experts' that should make things work, but may be appointed without the same accountability as democratic politicians. These may be experts with or without personal ambition, able to resist or not the maxim that power corrupts. This is benign technocracy that works, or corrupting technocracy that works for a few or doesn't work. Neither is a democracy. Neither respects the will of the people beyond a flimsy idea of representation. There are many experts who demonstrate the skills of persuasion and explanation in words people can understand, but there are also many who cling to a complete belief in their own judgement or who say the data cannot be wrong. A technocracy that lacks a foundational respect for the will of the people and an aim to reach a consensus across different groups of society is not a democracy, and its acceptance is an acquiescence in undemocratic government.

If technocracy is to be avoided ask yourself if you can think of, or believe in, a meritocracy. No meritocracy currently exists anywhere. Many people believe we are getting there. A false meritocracy can sustain itself if a democracy lets it. Meritocracy can be false through perception and real-world unfair opportunity. We judge people with our biases. Our 'fast' thinking promotes people that are similar to us, and charmers, good speakers, people who have the skills to get through the interview but not necessarily the skills to do the job. Rarely do we look at someone completely new and different and say we have faith in them. Sometimes we excuse that by saying such a person wouldn't fit in, or wouldn't understand us. Someone who makes it past those biases is a true pioneer. When we believe that we have a meritocracy the next danger arises: a meritocracy that corrupts itself, that pulls up the drawbridge after itself, that believes in its technocratic merit. If you are at the top of the hierarchy for long enough it becomes harder to empathise or understand those that are not. Associated with that is a danger in the belief that expert knowledge is best passed down through the people you already know or those steeped in familial or group knowledge. We so often fail to look beyond the candidates to see who is not a candidate and to ask enough about why. Furthermore, if you are told that you cannot do a job because no-one from your background has done it before, you may be more likely to believe that the next generation of the current officeholder is a better choice. That meritocracy becomes not only self-perpetuating but one reinforced by everyone else. This is a democracy where people acquiesce in the process but cannot take part. Our actions are not currently enough to qualify society as a meritocracy. We struggle for group representation, but nor is representation a meritocracy. We have much further to go to achieve success through individual merit. A failing or misunderstood meritocracy can be as anti-democratic as a technocracy.

Populism, a technocracy, and a poor meritocracy can all exist under the umbrella of a democratic process. They can come crashing down if the will of the people were to assert itself. They are hollow versions where democracy has eaten itself from the inside – or not yet matured enough and found enough substance and depth. People acquiesce for as long as they have their necessities or their perception of influence, or are intimidated physically or by knowledge. We must be continually vigilant that our democratic processes and our ideals are not being subverted by our own actions.

Nationalist, Conservative, and Economic Anti-Democracy

Another subtle alternative to democracy is nationalist conservatism. Globalism, with its cross-cultural dialogue and its economic development, has clearly taken millions out of economic poverty and is in the process of educating the world about itself and its differences, to the extent that it feeds the transition of social improvement from one part of the globe to another. Why then are some nations refusing or faltering in their adherence to liberal democratic principles that have allegedly fostered this open globalism? The answer is that liberal democracy may not be at the heart of globalism and may not be essential for it. In nations without an historic strand of individual liberty and freedom, and nations outside the European Enlightenment tradition (old discriminatory or new open version), conservatism is much more entrenched. Economics may have become about business efficiency not a service to the people. Individualism and consumerism may be disruptive or dangerous ideas to a community trying to hold itself together. Conservatives, by definition, seek to protect the established institutions and ways of life. They may do that with slow incremental reform so as not to lose the essence. They may do that with a rejection of change, or a fear of it, even if selective modernity helps them to do that more efficiently. A more natural conservatism may come to the fore: slow down, don't take risks, don't let change happen too fast, let's not lose the power we have… In translation this may reject the immigration of people and ideas from elsewhere, whether that is people of a different faith, a preponderance of the English language, feminism, the Black Lives Matter movement, international business, or trends in education. It may reject shared sovereignty and decision-making. Instead, hold on to what is uniquely 'ours,' our traditions and customs, the way we look as a nation, our self-perceived values, our lifestyle, our ways of doing things. This can be presented positively as well as negatively. It is not just that 'the Luddites' have been left behind and are fighting back, that is a patronising attitude.

Around the world this alternative to democracy may be a conservatism born of a backlash against the imposition of colonial attitudes and rule, and the reawakening of traditional ideas and hierarchies. The conservative backlash to shared sovereignty, to the pace of change in traditional societies, to globalisation and loss of cultural or political power, is a potentially democratic response, if it has that collective support. However, what we see in its implementation is populism and isolationism, and neither of these are democratic impulses. Democracy must be true to itself. It must be an open, collective, and inclusive effort, not one that is simply driven forward by its activists because they think they are right, from whichever end of the political spectrum they come. Democracy must exhibit a collective will that includes persuasion and offers real benefit, that outweighs risk or loss, to those who doubt it and see no future for themselves in it. Reforming conservatism can cope with this, it is one step back but still two steps forward. Regressive conservatism, especially one manipulated by self-serving or arrogant leadership, is a retreat from democracy and needs to be resisted.

The mix of economics and politics is also re-shaping non-democratic regimes. This is seen from Russian oligarchs to Iran's Revolutionary Guards' businesses, and the combined business and political influence and beyond-the-law attitudes of China's leadership families. In 2012 the wider family of the Chinese Premier (2003–13) Wen Jiabao, who had often talked about his poor upbringing and was seen as an ordinary 'Uncle Wen,' was revealed to have assets of $2.7 billion. Chinese leaders' 'princeling' children are frequently seen as having, using, and providing privileged access to power and business, leading elite privileged lives.[*] Russian opposition leader Alexei Navalny, whose death in a Russian prison in February 2024 provoked international condemnation, concentrated on revealing the hidden wealth and its lawless origins in the post-Soviet collapse of Russian political leaders. Russia is seen

---

[*] David Barboza, "Billions in hidden riches for family of Chinese leader," *New York Times*, 25 October 2012.

by many in the West as a state where someone's extreme wealth is allowed to exist only in return for non-involvement in politics.* Iran's Revolutionary Guard Corps (IRGC) is commonly understood as being the bodyguard and enforcer of the theocratic Iranian Islamic Revolution and government, and responsible for intelligence, internal and border security, including the suppression of discontent in 2009 and 2019. The IRGC uses 'front companies,' charitable foundations, moves goods into and out of Iran without paying tax duties, bids for contracts abroad, partners with foreign firms, and is controlled by a small number of people within the heart of government. Mohsen Sazegara, a now-exiled Iranian dissident who helped found the IRGC, said in 2010, 'It's also like a huge investment company with a complex of business empires and trading companies, while also being a de facto foreign ministry…'†
Books like *Kleptopia: How Dirty Money is Conquering the World* by Tom Burgis have popularised knowledge of the link between globalisation and the flows through nations and institutions of money from opaque or corrupt origins. Taking control of national assets is added to a day-to-day corruption of how things get done. As well as actual violence this is enabled by the rise of 'jurisdiction over jurisdiction,' i.e., the subversion or hijacking of existing law in those non-democratic nations, and further afield if they can. This can be much more subtle and gradual – such as intimidatory law-suits – but equally strangulating for democracy and free enterprise than more obvious lack of law in developing nations, or outright obvious corruption. These examples from China, Russia, and Iran illustrate the importance of modern economics to keeping authoritarian regimes in power.

Aspects of nationalist, conservative, and economic anti-democracy exist in most places, restrained by real democracy. Iran, Russia, and China are further down the line. Much of Iran's conservatism originates in, and is buttressed by, the theocratic nature of its regime. At the end of the spectrum is the People's Republic of North Korea, effectively

---

* Luke Harding, "Pandora Papers reveal hidden riches of Putin's inner circle," *The Guardian*, 3 October 2021.
† Julian Borger and Robert Tait, "The financial power of the Revolutionary Guards," *The Guardian*, 15 February 2010. Also see Ali Reza Eshraghi and Amir Hossein Mahdavi, "The Revolutionary Guards are poised to take over Iran," *Foreign Affairs*, 27 August 2020, which explains its operating methods, strengths, and potential weaknesses.

a monarchical military dictatorship, with global relevance only in its military threat, its self-fulfilling victimhood, and the possibility of humanitarian disaster.

The People's Republic of China

The Chinese Communist Party (CCP) led by Mao Zedong grew and fought for its survival in the 1930s and 1940s in the Chinese context of a failed Republic, warlordism and civil war, and internationally in the context of the rise of fascism in Europe, Stalin's totalitarianism in Russia, and Japanese expansionism. It learnt the lessons from these of taking and keeping power through force, complete belief in its ideology, a need for whole-population change through education and worker control, and rapid modernisation. It had to change everything. The greatest achievements of the CCP have been the effective reunification of the Han Chinese, under its own dominant power, while bringing China into the modern scientific and technological world, and in so doing taking more people out of real poverty in a shorter time than any other known regime. Under Mao, however, the speed of change also produced tragedy: complete quashing of dissenting voices, extensive famine, and failed industrialisation in the Great Leap Forward of the 1950s, and the disastrous Cultural Revolution of 1966–76 that set the nation back a generation. All these continue to reverberate today. During these times the CCP fought for its survival and its survival became paramount above all else. It also moved from under Russia's shadow with a split in the 1960s.

The successful China we know today began in the post-Mao era of Deng Xiaoping. Its fundamental justification has five strands: Firstly, from the Book of Lord Shang in the third century BCE it has taken the belief that when the people are strong the state is weak. This is an approach of rulers who want permanent rule. Secondly, its misuse of a Sun Yat-sen saying that the Chinese are 'loose sand,' and that nothing naturally holds them together. In 1912 Sun Yat-sen had sought a unifying democracy. Thirdly, a misuse of the Confucian belief in order and stability through duty and the respect of authority. Confucius had written about the responsibility of the ruled to respect and protect the people, and only if that was done did the people owe authority their duty and respect. Deng Xiaoping's 'socialism with Chinese characteristics' has become a fourth strand. It encouraged capitalist-type competition and money-making, made China the manufacturing hub of the world economy, and therefore given it global economic strength and significance. It also acts as a contract between restrictive CCP rule and rising living standards. Deng's rule prioritised economy over politics. Xi Jinping has returned to the primacy of politics. The fifth and most recent strand is Xi's promotion of Chinese nationalism. His stated ambition is uniting greater China and making it the predominant world power. Nationalism is being made into a pillar of the state and a justification of Party rule. In these ways the Nation, the People, and the Party are presented as indivisible. Its apparent stability and economic successes are globally presenting the most coherent contemporary alternative influence to Western Enlightenment-inspired democracy.

China has learnt that if it does not control history, and the history it is currently making, then its actions can be questioned and faith in it weakened. There is no mention of the 1989 Tiananmen Square massacre in any public Chinese text. There has been no public recognition of the Cultural Revolution in recent years. Criticism of Mao is once again ill-advised. Coming to terms with the past – as for example Germany has done with Nazism or Rwanda at least to some extent with its Tutsi genocide in 1994 – has been called 'historical nihilism,' seen as destructive, and which can now be prosecuted. This has led to historical amnesia, even if it is 'zhuang-she,' a pretence of ignorance. This can be effective deception or persuasion, confusion, or intimidatory, and produce effective self-censorship. It may become generational, for what should parents teach their children. Such manipulation of history distorts a community's identity, and wipes away general knowledge and context, essential to accurately understanding the past, present, and future. Chinese students abroad are often in complete denial about Tiananmen Square events when faced with commemorations abroad. Education works, or you choose not to believe anyone or anything but not knowing an alternative, ideals and knowledge die either way. If you stand up against it, regardless of the enormity or absurdity of the lie or propaganda, then you are marked out as abnormal, or subversive, or the enemy. Can you risk that? This is the trend within China today. Dissident Ai Weiwei satirised the government approach to dissidents: 'dissidents are criminals... only criminals have dissenting voices... if you think China has dissidents you are a criminal... does anyone have a dissenting voice regarding my statement?'* The trend is one firmly established by the Cultural Revolution that encouraged children to denounce their parents and teachers, and neighbours and workers to denounce each other. A stated aim of the Cultural Revolution was to destroy the old traditions, the old history, the old ways of thinking. China's enforced historical amnesia extends to current events, such as HIV abuse in villages, or badly or corruptly built schools collapsing during an earthquake. Investigation, comment and commemoration call into question the effectiveness of, and the support of, and for, the Party. It becomes dangerous to have ideals, or fixed opinions, and maybe even certain memories. This is institutionalised distrust deliberately created by the state. It is a form of mind control. It is a route to the permanence of an authority and effective totalitarianism. All of this is reinforced by modern technology that is making China a surveillance state. Like the Soviet Union it is impossible to know how effective this really is. How free-thinking are people naturally, how can they ignore their own lived experience, how effective can technology be, and how does it deal with national events that cannot have a line drawn under them so neatly like Covid-19 and environmental protest?

'Document No. 9' from April 2013 outlined a key element of 'Xi Jinping Thought': it rejected 'universal values,' which were equated with 'Western values,' and which included civil society, independent judiciary and media, separation of powers, and questioning history.† The document effectively authorised the purging of scientists, media, academics, artists and entertainers, and other groups, and of historical interpretation to re-place political ideology at the forefront of national life – 'you don't need to know about Tiananmen Square to invent an iPhone.' How effectively the identity of the Chinese people can be changed and shaped will be one factor in determining the extent of

---

* This is a shorter version of Ai Weiwei's satirical piece written on *Twitter* (now known as 'X') quoted in Kai Strittmatter, 2019, 30–31 (Eng. pub.) with original footnote.
† Strittmatter, 2019, 147 (Eng. pub.).

GOVERNMENT AND LEADERSHIP

the challenge that China may pose to the Western democratic style of government, and how extreme the disruption in society if the CCP fails and falls.

That is its unity and coherence. Another factor will be its effectiveness. There are four main strands to this: the law, technology, physical action, and its economic success. The interpretation of law is officially and entirely determined by the CCP. Rights of individuals and communities are determined within the constraints decided by the Party to serve its own ends. Part of the response to Covid-19 was to outline 'crimes' related to the epidemic which included 'stirring up public sentiment' and 'inciting subversion of state power.' The interpretation is fundamentally different to a Western view, to whom the language used seems like Orwellian double-speak.

The surveillance of people, and traditional propaganda in print, continue in China but it is the application of technology that is most frightening. With the introduction of the internet the demise of such regimes was almost taken for granted. It was assumed that not every secret could be kept and not every action watched. Such regimes sought to crush the internet, and then tried to control it. China exploited the emerging ability to technically turn it off, selectively, but also decided to pro-actively use it, and link it to emerging AI technologies. CCTV is increasingly real-time, co-ordinated, and centralised. Facial and voice recognition is being rapidly developed, including the ability to recognise emotions and ethnic minorities.* Systems like WeChat (think combination of Amazon and Apple) are doing away with the need for cash and making the whole range of products and services payable digitally, and therefore able to be monitored. From 2003 China has been working, like other nations, on a 'Golden Shield,' i.e., an internet with Chinese characteristics that can be separated from the worldwide web. Words, characters, and images can be censored, as well as websites. On Xi Jinping's altering of the constitution to allow him unlimited terms in office, even the phrase 'don't agree'/'bu tongyi' was briefly banned from digital media in China. Skynet, being developed since

---

* Paul Mozur, "One month, 500,000 face scans: How China is using AI to profile a minority," *New York Times*, 14 April 2019, stated that this was the 'first known example of a government intentionally using artificial intelligence for racial profiling, experts said.'

133

WHERE ARE WE GOING?

2015, is essentially a police digital cloud of information that collects, among other things, medical history, DNA, facial recognition, methods of birth control, product purchases, fingerprints, location, transport used including when and with whom, and online behaviour. The Social Credit system is also in further development. There are different systems on trial for this, and it is not yet clear whether there will be a nationally co-ordinated and centralised system. What is clear is that any approved system will depend on the Party interpretation of the actions people take and the required consequences. Much of this can be justified. A cashless society is safer and easier. Facial recognition catches criminals. Health records can help control public health. Social credit in China is characterised as a system for developing social trustworthiness, giving people confidence that others are also doing the right thing. Did you get the Covid-19 App, and did you expect others to do so too? However, like all technology it is subject to the inputs, to the interpretation of information found, the transparency of the gatekeepers, and trust in them. In October 2016 the CCP Central Committee and State Council published 'Warning and Punishment Mechanisms for Trust Breakers.' 'Trust' meant adherence to Party-decided norms. Punishments might include not being allowed to apply for a government job, limited access to insurance, or internet and transport use restrictions. The Sesame Credit system, one of those being trialled, advertises that 'one person's credit score can be affected by their friends' ratings': so be careful who your friends are, tell your friends if they are doing something wrong, or discard and isolate them. This system is operated by the private company Alibaba that has 600 million customers in its cashless payment system. The need for physical intimidation is decreasing. Have a phone and be tracked, or not have one and be asked officially as to why, and be under pressure, and under surveillance. According to a leaked report in 2020 abnormalities in majority-Uighur Xinjiang Province that may be subject to investigation and detention include having a relative abroad, a 'minor religious infection,' and 'thinking that is hard to grasp.' In practice these include having a beard and using a back door excessively. This was confirmed by a leak of police records and state documents in 2022.* In Xinjiang DNA may be taken at any medical check-up without

---

* Strittmatter, 2019, 210 (Eng. pub.), referring to a leak known as the 'Karakax list.'

permission, a car must have GPS, and every phone must have a 'Clean Net' app.

Xi Jinping's 'Little Red App' has become required use for Party members. However, the Berlin cybersecurity company 'Cure53' revealed it had a backdoor spying tool that could view a phone's downloaded material, websites visited, appeared to have the possibility of changing files, detecting keystroke use, and that location data was sent daily to a centralised location which was created and managed by the company that had programmed the app… Alibaba. Beyond China's border Chinese registered companies are also expected to comply with National Security laws compelling co-operation with Chinese law enforcement, even in foreign jurisdictions. These laws, introduced since Xi Jinping came to power in 2013, are the reasons for an increasing number of countries separating themselves from Chinese technology. Most disturbing of all: these systems don't have to work that well. If you believe the government is doing this, however imperfectly, can you afford to take the risk of losing everything, and with consequences for family too, by going against the tide and being found out?

Real physical consequences of crossing the CCP include social, familial, and professional isolation, public shaming and televised confessions, prison without others knowing where you are, or the victim knowing how long for, given by an opaque judicial system where the Party has a 99.9% trial conviction rate. This can and has applied to ordinary non-Party members of the public and to internationally profiled business or sports stars, Nobel prize winners, and leading politicians. There are recorded instances of Chinese citizens abroad, often students, being pressured to report on others or cease actions under the threat of repercussions for family back home. In 2015 five Hong Kong book publishers, including a Swedish national, disappeared, seemingly kidnapped from Thailand and taken to China. They all appeared some months later in China making televised 'confessions.'*
That was well before Hong Kong's security law and effective dismissal of the 'one nation two systems' policy. The CCP has shown ample ability and willingness to follow through on its threats of consequences for

---

* Ilaria Maria Sala, "In Hong Kong's book industry, everybody is scared," *The Guardian*, 28 December 2016.

individuals, groups, institutions, and businesses.

Selling 5G IT infrastructure and increasing its armed forces capability are two ways of pursuing its interests. The military threat is being seen in the militarisation of claimed but disputed islands in the South China Sea on which international judgements have been made against China's interests. Military intimidation of Taiwan has also increased. Its propaganda is also international. It supports students abroad and the setting-up of academic links, from Confucian Institutes to collaborative scientific research and business projects.

China has pulled millions out of poverty. the Chinese method means rejecting the universal values that in Beijing's proclaimed view cause division and slow development. This is the alternative to a West that may be seen as acting in its own interests historically and now, and that can be presented as becoming economically and politically weaker. In this scenario China can influence the world's future and make itself safer. Its alternative is not a communist state; it is a surveillance and one-party state that efficiently promotes and manages economic success at the same time as 'social stability.' Economic success has also helped to weaken others. China has made itself the manufacturing hub of the world and within nations, including Western ones, buys up debt, offers credit, builds infrastructure, becomes an essential business partner, and influences culture. This is its view of its reach, and these are its reasons for its confidence on the world stage.

Liberal democracies need to find their confidence again by re-finding their political stability and engagement, their economic success, their unity, and clarity of values. There are also, however, dangers for China from within. Covid-19 exposed to the world the moral vacuum and disinformation created by distrust within its totalitarian system. Whistleblowers like Wuhan Dr Li Wenliang were punished, and investigations hindered. Lower-level politicians could not analyse, adapt, criticise, or therefore contribute to, the Party line. Its successes such as rapid hospital building became overshadowed. Mass and forced quarantine, and persistent economic disruption, is what the world that China hopes to influence also came to see more clearly. In contrast the Western world opened economically and socially and regained its stride sooner. China has been damaged internationally by its actions. Its reversal of policy, and sudden opening up of economy and society, raised other questions: how much of its previous messages were therefore wrong, how could it be seen to be successful when TV showed a football World Cup populated by other peoples of the world not wearing masks, how much was the reversal of policy the result of high-profile and widespread public protest, and how much could and will people's own experience be successfully replaced by the CCP narrative?

Its rising nationalism is a turn-off for others. Increasing integration, power, and influence on world affairs will lead to increasing responsibility and if it is seen to act in self-interest alone it will not gain friends but increase suspicion. Its relationship to international law is currently determined by its nationalism and its victim-narrative. Its actions in Xinjiang, Hong Kong, and even Tibet are not internationally settled issues. Its reach can be seen as another version of colonialism, just like the 'American suffocation' it criticises. Its pained, conflictual but distant reaction to the Russian-Ukraine war and what it learns from the experience for itself, its relations with Russia, and about its competitors, is unclear, but it is not currently a comfortable one. There is also a tension, if not contradiction, between China's growing independent power and realpolitik, and the necessity to continue international co-operation and compromise on issues like climate change. The West's response to Covid-19, in the end, and its unity in the face of Russia, may make China think harder about its international ambitions; and could become, with a renewed economic drive, a triumvirate of effective policy against Chinese influence around the world.

Within China, the Chinese government has taken on board, at least to some extent, people's environmental protests, but there is little sign of China's *#metoo* movement, or any obvious reaction to the worldwide trend towards racial/ethnic/cultural diversity. China's social and economic inequality is rising not falling and discredited by continuing high-level and familial corruption. CCP legitimacy is resting increasingly on its economic success and its nationalism, and its consumerist bargain in return for accepting Party rule, but as its economy matures economic progress will slow, and people will look at the quality of their life. Economic development may not have produced democracy in the way the West hoped fifty years ago, but it may still be producing the building blocks and circumstances in which there can be political development. Furthermore, for those that claim that China has no history of liberalism or democracy and needs a firm ruling hand, now come two answers: is this a Western racism that devalues Chinese aspirations and abilities? and most of all: Taiwan, the living embodiment of a thriving Chinese democracy from the same political, social, and economic starting point and time, as the People's Republic itself.

China can find leaders who can think through the options, but this was the reason why the term limits that Xi has overturned were introduced in the first place. There is no inevitability about the course it may take. What we can say is that a continuation of Xi Jinping Thought will make China an imperfect but viable alternative to liberal democracy, at least in China, maybe in other places too, but not without risk to itself.

Leadership

According to Dacher Keltner in *Power Paradox*, forty-eight studies have shown leaders in hunter-gatherer societies to be: generous, brave, wise, problem-solving between groups, good speakers, fair, impartial (i.e., 'open'), reliable (i.e., focussed), tactful and calm, morally upright, strong, assertive (including enthusiastic), and humble. In these 'original' societies he opines that power is given, not taken. If the list of qualities given here is predominant then one must also ask how many leaders were women, and if not many, based on these qualities, then why not? Keltner goes on to explain in his studies that power does indeed corrupt, and that people in power may become essentially different characters to those that attain or accept it. Has everything or nothing changed? We tend to think of the leaders we have as being a product of the governments or governmental systems that we have. We also think of the governments we have as being a product of the leaders, reflecting their strengths and weaknesses. Systems have certainly changed over time, but have leaders?

GOVERNMENT AND LEADERSHIP

The Leaders We Have

Bertrand Russell, as quoted by Keltner, said in 1938, an interesting time to write about leaders: 'The laws of social dynamics are laws which can only be stated in terms of power.' When social dynamics meant feudalism, deference, family ownership, and inheritance, then 'power' would mean exercising of a particular type of power. It's nature may have changed but is still to some extent about access and force. This is true even in non-state institutions, including public and private business. Physical force or inheritance – individually or by belonging to the right group – was most likely to get someone access to that power. This applies when war was more, if not actually, commonplace; and when there was no or little state responsibility for services or industry, meaning less incentive to be representative. In democracies deference to authority may be weaker than in times past but it is still the norm, and elected leaders may easily and quickly move on to feeling unaccountable. Keltner's leadership of hunter-gatherer societies is not the norm we think of today. That version infers sociability, progressive co-operation, and the common good. We tend to think now of Machiavellian strategy, and competitive instincts. Empathy or emotional intelligence played little obvious role in the leadership skills of Julius Caesar or Henry VIII. Even worse, we often think of duplicity in employing sociable tactics to win power and then more ruthless and selfish instincts when in power, to keep it.

Today we also think of systems and hierarchies, of checks and balances, to keep leaders in check, as much as a greasy pole to climb, or masculine shoot-out, or literally killing rivals along the way to dictatorial leadership. Modern democratic leadership is not about striking fear into subordinates or rivals it is about offering understanding, and persuasive, hopeful, and exemplar leadership. Even though individual real decision-making power, and professional intimidation, can still be wielded by democratically elected leaders – especially if supported by legislative majorities, the power of patronage, and an unwritten or unclear constitution – there is much that they cannot achieve. They cannot control the international money markets or free media or simply tread all over the laws of the nation, at least not by themselves. That even a democratic leader with real power has so much that they cannot do emphasises the need for the 'soft' influential skills. Even authoritarians rarely have absolute power invested in them alone and need an instinct of the limits of what they could force others to do, or what they can get away with. No such instinct means they do not last very long, if successful at all.

The biggest obstacle to exercising complete power is stultifying bureaucracy, whether it is corrupt or cumbersome, or because it is contrary to its boss. Controlling the army still doesn't collect the taxes. Dictatorships need hierarchies and systems – a consistency and clarity of government, of roles, and the role 'the people' are expected to play – if the man at the top is to be successful and stay there. This is also true in a democracy, but built within it will be checks and balances, ranging from tradition, law, ethics, educated into government workers and the population at large, as well as systemic routines. Hierarchies and systems have proved as essential for civilisational development in large groups as individual leaders. Individual leadership, system, and hierarchy can still shape each other, for good or bad.

Studies across the Western world tend to focus on who succeeds in attaining power, not who desires it. Those who succeed in any place have succeeded in a particular culture or set of circumstances. It is not just about character. Those who desire it may be unsuccessful because they are not the familiar and traditional: in the West, white and male and of an expected age. Appearance also still counts, so looking mature not 'boyish' narrows it down further; height and a look of strength helps too, and someone seen as 'good-looking' further still. These are realities from political leadership to sports teams, not exclusive but certainly common. In other regions aspects of these can also be seen but the different cultural context is much less studied. The preponderance of the familiar and being good-/strong-looking is sometimes called 'evolutionary leadership,' where qualities useful in the Stone Age remain our basic instincts. Character counts but it may not be the first thing we think of or notice in our 'fast thinking' brains. How much we can counter these instincts is a question that would help to answer whether we can change our own fundamental character. If we can widen our familiar circle of 'understood' (which means 'acceptable') people, think more slowly to get past the appearance, and assess character dispassionately, then we may get a better quality of leader. It is character that is judged when assessing the reality of promises made and how unforeseen events are dealt with. This also would allow a greater consideration of motive and policy.

We do quite a lot already to mitigate the Stone Age instinct: people apply for jobs, write application forms and personal statements, supply references, have interviews, do interview 'tasks,' fulfil probationary periods, have periodic appraisals, subject themselves to the questioning of an electorate, etc. Yet clearly there is some way to go. We have improved, in general, our collective performance in who we choose as our leaders, and role models, but the pool we choose to pick from is still relatively shallow. There are others still given little consideration who desire leadership, and more to the point, might be 'good' at it. We usually still look at a photograph and a name before reading an application, and our judgement is already set on a path with that. We look at appearance and accent and sociability and decide if someone 'fits in' or is part of 'the norm,' and frequently decide these before we have even one answer about policy, motive, or vision. We often look at, or look for, experience as a confirmation of our expectations rather than as an opening to someone's character and ideas. And while these may to some seem outdated or stereotypical statements we need to ask ourselves why leadership in politics, in business, in so many professions, lacks diversity, even to the basic proportion of men and women so long after women have been educationally and legally 'equal' and there has been enough time to gain requisite career experience. We need to look again at who we have as candidates for leadership, not just at who is chosen from those putting themselves, or encouraged or allowed to put themselves, forward. We need to see more. The diversity of leadership should be a strength of diverse democratic societies.

This also means moving past the idea of 'representation.' Representation may be a stage along the journey but does not fulfil the requirements of a genuine individual equality of opportunity. We must also be aware of how we adapt to changing circumstances: interviews can simply lead to smart charmers. The wider inclusivity we should be promoting will either wither away, or will be constrained, by a lack of diverse leadership. Developing a genuine equality of opportunity in leadership choices may be more difficult than resisting the Stone Age need for sugar, but if we cannot then what is our vision of progress, and our vision of the future in a more global world? Our globally found leaders in music, sports, fashion, and other 'social' or lifestyle areas, where we instinctively choose the music or style that we like from a platform of wider-than-ever-before access, is an interesting contrast to the formal leadership we choose. In being both instinctive and the product of deliberate decisions about wider access, are we not proving to ourselves than we can reject the narrowness of traditional choices and ways of thinking? Nor should people outside the 'Western world' think that these are only Western problems. They are applicable globally. 'Tribalism' with a small 't' is a problem the world over.

Perhaps we have nature to blame for our fast, intuitive, familiar, thinking. Or we choose to blame nature. We have always accepted contradictions in our view of nature. We come from animals but have moved beyond them. We use their competitiveness and ability to survive, and perhaps propensity for conflict, but often ignore that animals also co-operate to learn and live together, within and between species. We believe that we have heightened emotions and feelings that we do not assign to animals, while also understanding more than ever about the biological processes that determine or highlight them. In leadership we seem to instinctively believe in a difference between men and women. We have studied apes and chimps, as our ancestors, and seen that males are hostile and aggressive and dominant. Have we put effect before cause? Have the wars of humanity confirmed the need for, or naturalness of, aggression and hostility, and that men are, or should therefore be, dominant in leadership? Bonobo apes, cousins to chimpanzees, have equally similar DNA, but while males can also be aggressive they are less so, and females are more dominant than males. Bonobos have a different social structure. Why do we not highlight that example? While we are still in the process of learning much more about the natural world we should hold our judgement about whether the gender and style of leadership in humanity is natural or learnt. Our preconceived ideas may yet still only be a matter of nurture rather than nature, of how we have educated ourselves to interpret our experience. Brian Klaas has pointed to 'recent research' that 'fight or flight' is a phenomenon more applicable to men than women, and that 'tend and befriend' i.e., protect the vulnerable and seek allies, is a more accurate description of the approach of women.[*] There are some that think of our 'progress' into 'civilisation' as a feminisation of history, an increasing adoption of sociability and co-operation that are seen as female characteristics. Firstly, this would seem to infer that humanity can collectively change its character. Secondly, it may or may not be seen as a return to the 'original' hunter-gatherer qualities of Keltner and a pre-conflict era of humanity. However, it also ignores the co-operative and empathetic qualities that males can show, and have needed, in the real human world and in the natural world. Leadership itself, and our view of it, remain bound up in our views of character and its permanence, and our confusion over nature or nurture, and even gender is caught up in this.

The Corruption of Power

If our ways of, and reasons for, choosing leaders and role models is suspect then it can be no surprise that we sometimes end up with the 'wrong' ones. This is increased if the candidate pool is already 'polluted.' Sociopaths and psychopaths are over-represented in leadership. These two labels are alarming, and may even evoke criminality or evil, so let us be clear what we mean, and that they are on a wide spectrum. A sociopath is someone with an anti-social personality disorder. They lack a conscience and empathy, and disregard social norms, they have aggressive and impulsive tendencies and may take risks, and because of all this may live a less 'normal' life. Psychopaths are more manipulative and can be more charming, they can dial up or down their empathy, and measure risks, and as a result psychopaths can appear to live a more 'normal' life than a sociopath. We consider empathy an essential for (democratic) leadership. Empathy, however, can be of two types: the natural, intuitive, 'mirroring' empathy of recognising others' emotions and feeling or understanding them; and a deliberative empathy where the person tries to 'work out' someone else. Related to empathy is the idea of shame, from conscience. A leader with no shame does not or

---
[*] Klaas, 2021, 171.

chooses not to recognise hurt and wrong and is less likely to abide by the rules.

People who put themselves before others and think more of themselves than of others, are attracted to leadership roles at all levels. A psychopath who can dial up and down their empathy can read a room and adapt accordingly, getting the job. This might be useful in a real-world way: the combination of distance and level of empathy required to fire someone, or to fire a gun at someone as a soldier, is a difficult balance to achieve in a mentally healthy way. However, it is not a substitute for integrity. There are levels of sociopathy and psychopathy, and most people learn the limits of what is acceptable, often in childhood and early experience, and often intuitively. Most people know and take care of the perceptions that other people have of them. To be deliberately manipulative, without a real conscience or genuine empathy, can be dangerous traits in anyone with any power. An intelligent psychopath who can hide their true selves behind charm and confidence is more dangerous. People want leaders to be confident, they want people who show them empathy even if they show different empathy to different people, and may judge intuitively rather than more deliberately. These are important reasons for the checks and balances that any and every institution should have. Psychological testing, ethics advisers, the law, a supervisory board, an independent regulator, majority decision-making, independent investigative media, double authorisation for financial transactions, etc are all examples of these checks and balances. One would think that a psychopath would find it difficult to attain and to stay in a position of power in a democratic context.

Studies in this area are not conclusive or extensive either in sample size or geographic and cultural variety but they appear to show that about 1% of people have the potential to be psychopathic, scoring about 22/40 on a scale, and about 0.2% clearly are so, scoring 30 or more. In research quoted by Klaas the average score for male convicts in American prisons was 22. In a small study of corporate professionals, some already quite successful and all put forward for higher management training, 6% reached the possible threshold for psychopathic traits, with 4% reaching the 'are psychopathic' threshold!* The answer to 'why

---

* Klaas, 2021, 96.

would anywhere else be different' is either not good for America or not good for everyone else. This albeit small study shows the danger of not taking this seriously and not having effective multiple checks and balances at virtually every level and in virtually every context of leadership and government. Once in leadership psychopaths may dial down their empathy, while successful ones will maintain the veneer of integrity. There are other non-social traits that would also pose risks, such as narcissist and paranoid personality disorders. They will be by most definitions 'corrupt' and may corrupt others. In a healthy system of checks and balances they will be restricted or found out. Such systems have a reinforcing anti-corruption culture and are less obvious fields to apply one's efforts to. A belief that there is a high chance of getting found out is a major hurdle and deterrent for most, but not all, such people. Some psychopaths and others will, however, underestimate or deny the system, test it, and take advantage if it is found wanting. This applies to anyone with a natural or a nurtured belief in their own superiority. The checks and balances need to be universal.

Thankfully not all leaders are psychopathic, sociopathic, or otherwise deceptive. Most leaders of people have genuine reasons to be leaders. However, at the same time, most people believe in the maxim that 'power corrupts, and absolute power corrupts absolutely.'* In fact, the quotation should begin 'power tends to corrupt,' and we have a distorted idea of that corruption. The idea that leaders can't be trusted has both benefits and dangers. It helps to produce accountability but can also hinder action. We often exaggerate and misname 'corruption': Firstly, leaders often, if not usually, have choices that whatever the course of action some are disappointed or disadvantaged or put in danger. Secondly, with experience they get 'better' at making such difficult decisions. Thirdly, they have greater opportunity to make decisions that to some may seem corrupt, and given their position and power may be magnified in consequence. Fourthly leaders tend to have extra scrutiny of their actions, and therefore also greater chance of getting caught. Many people feel disengaged or powerless, and it is easy to lay 'corruption' at the heart of that – 'they're all in it for themselves' being

---

* Klaas, 2021, 128. Original Lord Acton, 1887, about the power of Popes and Kings in relation to the historic Spanish Inquisition.

the most common refrain about politicians we do not know - but often not about those we feel we do know.

Nevertheless, leaders, of whatever democratic or other persuasion, have opportunities to be substantively corrupt. Openly, they can use patronage, a democratic majority can become a tyranny of the majority, a leader can be populist or cultist and act in the interests of themselves or their favoured groups. Corruption may be legislative or financial, or in the criminal justice system and law enforcement. Like any criminal, open acts depend on the confidence to either not get caught or not be held accountable, and may be opportunistically available. Opportunities arise when the qualities needed to gain power are different to those needed, or possible, to keep it. Being a 'good' person helps you persuade, and earns trust, and credibility. However, the difficult decisions and speed of government encourage different traits: less empathy, less listening, less reasoning, quicker judgements, and more stereotypical views of others. These help a leader to de-clutter a decision, they get rid of the 'noise' that complicates it and that might erode the confidence to make it. They also make it more possible for low-level and substantive corruption, and disregard, to thrive. Being in leadership can erode social distance from those effected; can expand the time difference between decision and effect; can erode spatial distance – not seeing the consequences within the geographic orbit or 'sight' of the leader; and can erode experiential distance through separation from ordinary lives or demonising an opposition. In some contexts these may be useful or understandable, but still be problematic: controlling a drone at war hundreds of miles away may be conscience-pricking but distance may make decisions easier; but on the other hand, justice is usually better understood and accepted if a fair process takes place in good time. In all these ways a leader must not become divorced from the consequences of their decisions. If they do, empathy and integrity may be lost as well as losing the actual knowledge of consequences of their actions. Being too close may be equally challenging. Leadership is and probably should be difficult. The checks and balances of a democratic system can help this – not least facing an electorate – but it is the democratic culture of a society that may be just as important here. This is the civic society of pressure groups, independent, free, and accurate information, the right to assemble and protest, etc. We must always recognise the possibility of honest leaders with the best of intentions becoming 'corrupt.' Whatever the reason, being dazzled by wealth from a poor background, by the power to influence from a belief in righteousness, or frustration of action, this is our fear of the corruption of power. Systems and culture must be developed and maintained, but a virtuous circle can proliferate.

A whole different type of corruption of the political process derives from its adopted conflictual nature, a sort of 'game theory' approach. This is the notion that politics is always about winners and losers, and that not just winning, but showing others as losing, is important. The global approach to climate change may be an example of this. Geopolitical rivalries and long-term power struggles disrupt negotiations, as one nation worries whether compromise will help another nation more. This is a very political view of politics, rather than an issue-based view. In some sense this is inevitable, and we should not underestimate the sincerity of different political views and philosophies. However, it is still an approach that is neither inevitable nor often productive. In the real world people co-operate every day on what they think is a realistic enterprise. People understand self-sacrifice even if the context of fairness is also essential. The more people understand each other the more they are prepared to compromise and see the picture beyond themselves. This does not minimise self-reward but on the contrary sees the benefit to one's own side of shared action. The 'knock-about' party politics, win-lose scenarios, masculine toxicity, loss of shared intent, and aggression of language, all contribute to the breakdown of a democratic culture.

Democratic Maintenance and Improvement: Systems, Hierarchies, and Leadership

Democracy is never static: citizens' assemblies, open-source information, etc. These are in practice all about engagement, renewing the commitment, understanding, and shared intent of a community. They all require the continuation of dialogue – listening and talking – and that requires a commonality of language, accurate enough to be effective. They also imply that whatever governmental system there is it must have the ability to change by deliberate design or gradually through changing circumstances.

One area of challenge and change to leadership and governance is technology. This is a tool. We must make sure of relatively obvious things like its security. There is also the danger of quick and direct decision-making being at the expense of what needs more evidence, time to work, and reflection. See-saw decision-making may be responsive but we already know this does not produce good governance. On another level we must be aware of and address the corrosive effects of some communications technology. This ranges from unchallenged disinformation, either deliberate or just mistaken, from bots that multiply specific messages for a specific or general disruptive end in a planned and large-scale way, to isolated individuals. The former is up to technology companies and regulators and can surely be managed by overseeing technology, but it is also up to all of us to learn how to recognise disinformation and manipulation (from sloganised messaging through selective arguments to deep-fake videos) and to regularly evaluate our trusted sources. We must have trusted sources in the first place, including our own individual and communal experience, hedged by their weaknesses. The isolation of individuals with a keyboard is a social problem. We need to engage these people more, and beware of labelling them as having a mental illness or addiction at the expense of free speech. The lone voice may be right, or be the pioneer, or the original thinker, or a whistleblower. On a third level, much more subtly, the ability of organisations to collect, trade, or use information and personal data about individuals to produce targeted individual messages, whether commercial or political, and to do so understanding the effectiveness of images, intuitive thinking, the importance of familiarity, personal biases, etc, is clearly open to misuse. That path leads to division, mis- or non-understanding, unreality, and conflict. Part of an effective future democracy will be people's understanding of their own data, control over its use, and recognition of its misuse. The regulation of technology, and the democratic oversight of the regulators, is therefore key. This needs to be part of any democratic system and become part of our civic society and our education. However, technology can also be a boon for democracy: if transparency is harder to avoid, if information can be distributed far and wide, if usually silent minorities can have their voice heard, if the best of education can be widespread, if geographically separated groups can be brought together, if new ideas and decisions can be more easily shared and explained and tested, then technology can engage more people, more ideas, more democratically. These also show that technology is a tool, and dependent on its inputs and the motivators of those inputting. They also confirm that the views exhibited through technology that we do not like are not the fault of the technology. It is the origin of those views that we need to address as much as the ease and speed of their distribution.

We need to do more to encourage a diverse stratum of leaders. We need to be more representative, on the way to being more genuinely meritocratic. That means removing obstacles, from educational opportunity to internet trolling, across all the under- and mis-representations that our societies reflect. It means changing some of the deep mindset characteristics that we have lived with for generations or longer, like conflictual leadership and win-lose decision-making. We need to think about how we think, and not just be more aware of our bias towards what and who we already think we know but put in place systems to counteract that. We need to understand that our perceptions are the result of our emotions and our individual character, and context, as much as of reality, and how we can counteract these subtle distractions, this 'noise.' We also need to understand more about leadership, the reality and complexity of it; and how leaders can change through the attainment of power, and even just through the experience of the decisions they make. Leadership and governance can decline with complacency. We must also get back to recognising the imperfect nature of whatever form of democracy we choose. We fundamentally may not agree with others' principles or policy, but we must maintain some belief that we all share a genuine intention to safeguard and improve the community that we call ourselves part of – without this being blind assumption. Mutual toleration of ideas, institutional resilience, common norms, resisting polarisation, resisting the rise of anti-system groups and social segregation, protecting the gatekeepers of the rules such as the regulators and judiciary and free media, maintaining professional ethics and the rules of society through law, all need active support and engagement. In these things we all need to have the courage of our convictions. If we do not then systems, hierarchies, and leaders will fail, and consensual rule enters a death spiral. We need to be the leaders we want. We need, collectively, to be active citizens.

At some point all societies change. When a new consensus emerges, democracy is reconfirmed and strengthened. The struggles to achieve that new consensus through new ideas, reinterpretation, or just coping with changing circumstances, are danger points. Today the combination of gender and racial equality movements with climate and biodiversity changes, in the context of a new global dialogue and integration, and disruptive technologies, is almost certainly an epochal change. Permanent revolution, as opposed to reform, is also dangerous. Democracy cannot leave groups of people behind and cannot let argument or change continue without some eventual consensus and consolidation. A downward tipping point is not reached when everyone is disengaged but when significantly large sections of the population are. A democracy is a mosaic whose recognisable picture depends on most of the pieces being stuck together.

In any organisation checks and balances will be known, transparent, inspire confidence, and be resilient under pressure. Corrupt leaders do not enter a system they will be found out in, unless they believe that the system is not sufficiently resilient to withstand the pressure they are prepared to place it under. Good-natured leaders are less likely to become corrupt in an effective system. A majority, term limits, open questioning, the legal system, interested groups, etc, therefore become a positive part of government in which people become stakeholders. Modern states may be the most hierarchical, or bureaucratic, yet have the most effective law, be the safest, and most resilient, as long as they remain receptive to their stakeholders, including those at the poorest end of the ladder of power. Leadership in such a democratic context is about influence more than power. The power wielded is to get the judgement implemented. The best judgement is the sum of all the participants in the process. A good leader gets the participants to buy into the process with their own opinions, evidence, and their best judgement. The skills to persuade, through integrity, oratory, detail, and logic, are required. The power to challenge while being supportive, and to both enthuse and hold accountable, are required. The ability to set out a vision and maintain an organisation's efficiency are required. Such a leader must be empathetic and engaging, as well as clear and far-sighted. They will not get everything they want for they know they are not 100% right all the time and will have at some point doubts that make them seem 'human,' 'in touch,' and help them to respect the democratic process of another 'head' talking – the electorate, advisers, experts, or bureaucracy. If that seems idealistic let us remember that there may be no right answer to a challenge, a problem may be both unforeseen and unprecedented, the evidence may be unclear, our judgement may be clouded by the last decision which may have suited everyone else but not us, etc. Democratic politics is the art of the possible and the possible can only be redefined in exceptional circumstances or by exceptional leaders. Democracy will only be maintained with care. It remains the best philosophy and form of government that we have.

IV

THE ECONOMY

As long as my purse contains money it secures my independence ... The money that we possess is the instrument of liberty...
Jean-Jacques Rousseau.*

The white man's desire for material possessions and power has blinded him to the pain he has caused Mother Earth by his quest for what he calls natural resources.
Thomas Banyaca, Hopi Indian leader.†

In 2021 the science journal *Nature* reported an Israeli study that all man-made built things now outweighed all natural things.‡ It was a remarkable statement, which on the surface must surely be a guesstimate rather than concrete. Furthermore, they wrote that in 1900 it had only been 3% of natural biomass. It would confirm to many that man is primarily 'economic man,' a competitive and exploitative species. Adam Smith's *Invisible Hand* and *Wealth of Nations* elevated the idea of 'Economic Man' to policy. Since then, economists have argued over variations, measures, and success.

---

* Jean-Jacques Rousseau, *Confessions of Jean-Jacques Rousseau*, Book 1, 1782.
† Quote from letter given to President Nixon in 1971, Joe Jenkins, *Introducing Moral Issues*. Heineman Educational, 1994, 88.
‡ See article Ron Milo et al., "Global human-made mass exceeds all living biomass," *Nature*, 9 December 2020, in which it was concluded that man-made mass was doubling every twenty years.

WHERE ARE WE GOING?

The idea of Economic Man can be used to support both a competitive and a social view of humanity but is more likely to be used for the former. It explains the nature of capitalism through self-interest. It encourages continual 'growth' through entrepreneurship, to be richer and 'better.' This is the economic model that we have today. At worst Economic Man lacks empathy, and is unable to relate to others except through contractual terms. This has clearly had a defining effect on our approach to society, politics, and government. It frequently frames our judgement of a 'successful' person and has monetised or made materialistic our ideas of wealth. It has made many people more comfortable in their lives but has also been corrosive.

The oil crisis of the 1970s was followed by the 1980s feeling, the world over, that the gap between rich and poor was widening. In the 1990s the end to the Cold War seemed to confirm capitalist victory, but also gave some more room for genuine independence. Liberal cities were being divided from the more conservative hinterlands where there was more social conservatism and distrust of the government. Freer trading regulations encouraged multinational companies separated from national control; and global communications began to emerge. The Common Market of Europe flourished and expanded; China's limited capitalism roared ahead; but the Soviet Union's economic implosion was scarring the democratic nature of political change. Economics seemed to be the key to 'progress.'

The 'financial crash' of 2008 led to severe economic depression around the world. China continued to grow but elsewhere adopted austerity policies. These reduced safety nets and restricted opportunity policies that had expanded education, healthcare, and welfare. Many people believed that governments put 'wealth creators' above the welfare of 'ordinary people,' and that those responsible were not held to account. From origins in California student protests and Spanish Indignados, the 'Occupy Movement' was born. It spread into 82 countries and 951 cities where protesters called themselves 'the 99%.' It decried 'bailed out bankers' and demanded more responsive government action. It helped publicise startling figures, such as the American increase of 275% in income of the top 1% in the previous thirty years compared to middle-incomes rising by 40%; and similar figures were seen to apply in nations across the world.* It was a global movement and a localised one, socially and politically progressive. The angst came from conservative and progressive heartlands. Demands were often not crystallised into policies – except perhaps a 'Robin Hood tax' on financial transactions – and it seemed to fizzle out. However, this was the forerunner of the populism that emerged soon after, and an indicator of the new internationalisation of protest. Inequality and opportunity were now front and centre of national politics the world over. At the same time global environmentalism had become an economic, political, and moral issue as it morphed into global awareness of climate change. For some people economics and economies had to change. For others economic control seemed impossible and their battles turned to cultural issues that could give them some continuity, comfort, and value.

Yet... hundreds of millions *have* been taken out of economic poverty. Some form of free trade is an expected precursor to a more peaceful world. Some form of contract between governing and governed is the bedrock of all political systems currently employed in the world. Continual innovation is testament to the creative free will of humanity. Whether success comes from collaboration or competition is almost a moot point because there are paths from either. On the other hand, in societies not forced to concentrate on national security, how we employ our principles and seek to regulate them at any one time is of profound debate. How we limit the extent of self-interest, deal with extremes of wealth, and provide opportunity and basic standards, is the nature of our politics. How we use the law to promote or control wealth is seriously in question, as is the morality that we apply to 'the poor.' How much the principles of competition have shaped and encouraged empires, discrimination, and wars, and therefore need changing, have been debatable for a while; how much they are threatening the sustainability of the very planet we live on is a relatively new debate. Judging by these issues, there were always going to be winners and losers. The question now is how we employ our morality, character, and virtue to keep the

---

* "Congressional Budget Office Report USA," November 2011; Robert Pear, "Top earners doubled share of nation's income, study finds," *New York Times*, 25 October 2011; Deborah L. Jacobs, "Occupy Wall Street and the rhetoric of equality," *Forbes*, 1 November 2011.

balance of wealth, opportunity, and need at levels that have common consent, are sustainable, and allow for change.

Systems

Mainstream ideas about wealth creation, economic control, and the levers of change, have not changed much in recent times – apart from the apparent demise of communism as an alternative – but as we stand now inequality is the centrepiece of economic and political policy. This is both global and domestic. This is still a struggle over the balance of state and 'private' control, investment, and innovation, encouraging dependence or the provision of opportunity.

The Theory

Adam Smith wrote of an 'invisible hand' whereby the self-interest to do well would result in the betterment of all, and that this was natural for every person.* He wrote, in *Wealth of Nations* published in 1776, that 'little else is requisite to carry a state to the highest degree of opulence from the lowest barbarianism, but peace, easy taxes, and a tolerable administration of justice' i.e., little or no government interference in business and markets. He talked about supply and demand. His economic ideas have been fully understood, but the accompanying views about their context and limits and uses have often been forgotten. He also wrote that governments should provide infrastructure, education, defence, and collect enough taxes to administer small regulatory government. His ideas implied that government could not control the economy, but could shape it and should make competition fair. Smith believed that people knew their business best and therefore monopolies and treaties restricted trade, hence 'free trade,' even within the empire, not then the consensus. He also wrote against extreme inequality and the over-powerful rich. He wrote that labour was the key but did not write in a time of accumulated unearned wealth and the easy global

---

* In *Invisible Hand*, published in 1776, he wrote that it was 'not from the benevolence of the butcher... that we expect (our dinner) ... but from regard to their own self-interest.'

movement of either labour or money. His ideas were as much about a level playing field and the chance for people to benefit from their labour as they were about making money without interference. Manufacturing goods was the key to increasing wealth, he said, because agriculture could not be increased in an on/off fashion, although a free trade in agriculture would prevent the poor having to pay higher prices and give them greater choice. This was to be the industrialisation of economics. His efficient economy extended internationally, namely that if one country produced specific goods expensively it would stop doing so, buy cheaper from abroad, and pay for that by the export of its better value goods. Economist David Ricardo soon made this into 'comparative advantage' and argued that this export specialisation would then produce higher wages. The ever-increasing manufacture of goods to increase wealth may be blamed for our obsession with materialism but Smith believed that the wealth of a nation should be judged by the value of goods to the nation and its revenue, not just by the money exchanged for them.

Shortly before Smith's influential book Frenchman Jean-Jacques Rousseau's *The Social Contract* (published in 1762) merged the idea that no man should have authority over another with the reality that individuals have a 'Natural Liberty' through free will, and therefore that some will be more successful than others. Rousseau also required a natural right to what people needed, and a Civil Liberty. His pact envisioned willingly and equally shared authority ('sovereignty') to better preserve the individual and the community. It decried the use of force to gain power, promoted the rule of law, and said that with free will in decision-making came responsibility and moral significance. He argued that with extremes of wealth came self-interest and with poverty came over-dependence. Thomas Paine, of *Common Sense* (1776) and American Independence fame, wrote specifically of 'landed property,' which was becoming synonymous with progress and wealth, and even with civilisation, while causing inequality. Paine suggested free trade and an 'inheritance tax' paid into a common fund to compensate people for their loss of the natural right to benefit from the common land. This was limited redistribution of wealth, with the rule of law, and faith in the election of men who would be representative. The ideas of Rousseau, Paine and others form the philosophical basis of our economic model today within the principles of Adam Smith: freedom to make money through free trade, with the rule of law; ownership of property and goods; a monetary system to manage it; and a trade-off between rich and poor.

Central European economist Joseph Schumpeter, in the first half of the 20th century, wrote that capitalism was an ongoing process through the creative destruction of innovation. He presumed capitalism to have an honourable and communitarian aim, not a selfish materialism and worship of wealth, or dominant companies buying up competition. Economists like Friedrich Hayek and Milton Friedman have stressed that only free trade and non-government interference creates entrepreneurs, who use that liberty to create wealth. This means less regulation, that inequality motivates people and is therefore OK, that free markets will deal with the inefficient and unscrupulous, and that government is responsible for the rule of law and a basic social and economic safety net for the most vulnerable or poorest. Interestingly Friedman also wrote of a negative income tax for the poor, which could be interpreted as a form of universal basic income, except not universal, instead of complex spending on a welfare state.

It is the ideas of these and similar economists that currently guide Western economics. These ideas led to austerity in times of economic depression, aiming to motivate people, free entrepreneurs, and limit the interference, spending, and therefore size, of the state. These arguments supplanted the post-Second World War economics of Alfred Marshall and John Maynard Keynes. Marshall said that economics must help people by accounting for their personal and social responses. He saw business greed, increasing wage inequality, and the emerging danger of the global movement of capital and people without regulation. Keynes, writing after the destruction of the First World War, argued for active government investment in infrastructure and welfare. He wanted government planning and spending power, even by borrowing, to stimulate demand when necessary, which could then be paid back in boom times when private investment would be able to take on growth. Economist Robert Solow went on to pronounce more clearly that public investment helped raise the value of private investment. The moderate political battle of economics is generally between

THE ECONOMY

Keynesian government intervention and 'free markets' enabled by 'small government.' Fundamental beliefs about the motivation of a person to act are separated between co-operation and support, or competitive instinct and individual liberties. All the moderate versions of economics anticipate 'growth,' with or without a measure of redistributing wealth.

The primary revolutionary alternative to this debate has been some form of Marxism-Leninism, Socialism, or Communism. The *Communist Manifesto* of 1848 and volumes of *Capital* published between 1867 and 1893 evoked history as a class struggle. They were born from observations of urban industrial impoverishment and the rise of 'capital' in social and political importance. Workers were being exploited and needed to benefit from the fruits of their labour, which would only happen when they were in control, instead of the selfish landowning and business owning classes, the bourgeoisie. Communism needed a social, cultural, and political revolution as well as an economic one. Labour would stir – workers of the world, unite! – when mechanisation produced a crisis of unemployment. In time this anticipated crisis was supplanted by the idea of inequality. These ideas foundered in the last quarter of the 20th century on overpowering and corrupting government control at the expense of individuality and entrepreneurial renewal. China altered course to accommodate a more rural population and to allow some entrepreneurial development within a strong but ideologically looser government control. The failure of communism left the field of global development to an unfettered and triumphant free market economics. Any economic model we employ and the way we measure it, are from their time, whether the 1770s or 1930s. The interpretation of these, and the importance we give to them now, is of our own making.

'National income' was an idea from the late 17th century. Gross Domestic Product (GDP) came along in the 1930s. GDP is how we measure the economy of nations. Value comes from measurable production, which can be used to determine 'progress' and 'growth,' and therefore also status. It is economic. It makes an incomplete sense of the difference between quantity and quality. It measures long-term benefit badly. It makes no sense of quality of life or of relationships. GDP is statistical, although forecasts are notoriously poor. It only indirectly applies the efficiency of saving money through new processes or technology. It rewards the replacement of a broken window because that is economic activity, but it does not reward not breaking the window. It does not recognise unpaid work such as that of 'housework' mostly by women. It does not perceive what a good life may be. It could be said that GDP has taken over as the message, not the messenger. How is this working out for us now?

The Practice

It must be repeatedly stated that hundreds of millions of people in a rising population have been brought out of real poverty over the last few decades. However, inequality has increased with more inherited income, a top few controlling more of national income, with stagnating average wages in most Western nations for three to five decades. Even in China the richest 5% own over 50% of the national wealth. In the USA a CEO of an American top 350 company in 2021 was projected to earn 399 times that of a typical worker, compared to 20 times in 1965.[*] Increasing automation will increasingly take away low-skilled jobs, manufacturing jobs, and outsourced service jobs; and mid-level developing countries may therefore be having improvement cut from beneath them. Many new technology-based companies require few but highly educated or skilled workers, and profits are concentrated in few hands, not contributing much to the tax-based investment possibilities of a nation in which they work or make profits.

Economically, the 1980s were about deregulation and the separation of 'markets and government.' Socialism became an economically and politically toxic word. Relatively lower taxes for wealthy people and business was intended to result in more jobs and higher wages as companies invested and competed. This, in simple terms, was 'trickle-down' economics. Stakeholder capitalism became shareholder capitalism, which thrived, but 'Main Street' did not. Money was spent on dividends for shareholders and executive pay, fewer jobs were needed from investment that was made, or companies moved production and those jobs to cheaper jurisdictions with less regulation. In 1964 the four

---

[*] Yu Xie and Yongai Jin, "Household wealth in China," *Chin Sociol Rev*. 2015, Vol 47 Issue 3, 203–229, National Library of Medicine (USA); Josh Bivens and Joro Kandra, "CEO pay has skyrocketed 1,460% since 1978," *Economic Policy Institute*, 4 Oct 2022.

largest American employers averaged 430,000 workers, in 2011 it was less than a quarter of that, but they were 'worth' twice as much.* As a result, pay and worker rights including those through trades unions, stagnated. For the public, consumerism from the 1960s, through inflation of the 1970s, became the debt of the 1980s. Governments often did not invest in infrastructure, whether engineering or social. While a simple explanation, the crash of 2008 again brought this into focus. In many nations government chose austerity rather than state investment, because 'small state' conservatism had come to dominate politics. Greater welfare costs for higher unemployment created another circle of lowering regulations to make employing people easier and cheaper – hence the rise of zero-hour contracts. Apparently, richer people needed encouragement through lower taxes, but welfare support was seen as 'subsidising the poor' and would be de-motivating. Well-off people had funds to weather the storm, even make new opportunistic investment, but others did not. 'In-work poor' are now recognised as a group, still requiring state benefits or charitable help to supplement stagnating wages, unable to afford rapidly rising property prices, while soaring rents reduce the chances of saving. Hardship is not just rising but harder to escape. A generational gap has also emerged. For the first time, in many nations younger people have a lower economic expectancy than their parents, with others depending on inheriting what is usually property-based wealth. Where is the social contract, or the 'common good'? The Occupy Movement's disdain became politically divided between being more 'populist' or more 'progressive,' but not necessarily in either case less radical. Inequality could create motivation but it also created resentment as upward 'social mobility' became a myth for many people. In many developed and developing nations fragile social and economically supportive infrastructure was again highlighted by Covid-19.

Work itself has become distorted. Better-off people employ lawyers, stockbrokers, accountants, private healthcare and education, etc, to sustain wealth and insulate their way of life. They are not directly wealth creators or innovators; they are not manufacturing goods. It

---

* Derek Thompson, "This is what the post-employee economy looks like," *Atlantic*, 20 April 2011.

may be a little simplistic – and this knowledge economy also includes innovatively creative and entrepreneurial people – but many of these jobs do not clearly contribute to the value of the nation. Significant income comes from bonuses, investments, lump sum pension arrangements and interest. A large part of the knowledge economy has become the profit economy.* During the Covid-19 pandemic, where developed infrastructure existed, so-called 'key workers' were in healthcare or education or law enforcement or essential supply chain work. Many, though by no means all, were in state sector employment and significant minorities on zero-hour contracts. Many, though not all, were not well paid. Key work was shown not to equate to valued work as a genuine market would have us believe. We have come to value jobs by income not usefulness. Furthermore, through an academic professionalisation of work education has become a key indicator of wealth and of politics. State sector work has traditionally been lower paid than private sector work, compensated for by supportive regulations and rights, and more stable pensions as well as a rewarding sense of public duty, but now these benefits are more questionable in their effectiveness or questioned in principle. We are also more aware of the inequalities between gender and between majorities and minorities within nations.

Inequality within nations is challenging our politics and social cohesion, therefore questioning the working of, and measurement of, our economic model, in parallel with climate change questioning its sustainability. Inequality is challenging the 'social contract' that is at the heart of modern government the world over.

The Social Contract: Is It Working?

Is work still working? If not, then is the social contract still applicable? What can be expected of it now for welfare, education, health, and old age? Do we still have a public morality, a civil liberty, and a common good, that maintains it and will do so in the future? These are questions that governments face as they come to a new reality of what levers of

---

* As defined as an economy in which growth is dependent on the quantity and quality and accessibility of information rather than the means of production.

economic progress they control within a new globalised context, with new communication, disruptive technologies, climate change, demographic change, and questions of national identity and culture. If there is to be government support then why, and what taxes should there be and on whom, to pay for it? These questions are much more 'political,' or party political, even ideological, than the general alleviation of poverty or climate change. They go to the heart of people's motivations, what sort of society people want to live in, and even whether we are naturally co-operative or competitive.

Work

Work is seen as an essential element of looking after those we care for and belonging to a community, whatever the actual work we do. We also realise that we will not be looked after by a community without making some effort to contribute. Work serves to give us purpose in our lives. If we believe that we are doing well our self-worth and self-confidence rises and we see more opportunity, although the reverse is also true. Work also allows us to use our talents and our education and makes the effort we have put into those aspects of our lives seem worthwhile and useful. Sometimes we overlay our sense of worth through work with a sense of public duty or responsibility to others. Work is seen as an indicator of maturity, and we tell school students to prepare for work as a sign that they must be prepared to enter adult life with all of its responsibilities as well as its rights. Every part of this applies to all communities, including those where work is less formalised, where it may be family orientated such as in farming, where education is still familial and local rather than 'schooled,' and whether the state enables or regulates the work people do.

As settlement increased jobs became more specialised and people depended on each other for their needs. Education remained centred around the knowledge and skills directly needed to be a useful member of the community. For some that meant learning the skills of reading and writing, especially as religion and government became more formalised. A working life often remained a hard one, subject to the chances of peace, injury, illness, and then to old age. All of this applied to women as well as men, although women also gave birth to and looked after children, who were the safety rail against loneliness and poverty in infirm old age. Much of this still applies in parts of the world. As the influence of religious authority was curtailed, and therefore its welfare provision too, government was forced to step in and replace their 'essential services,' however limited, with some of their own.

Urbanisation and industrialisation have changed the way we work most radically. Hours and times of work, physical working conditions, worker rights, pay, and the skills required were then set by an 'employer.' Early on women and children still worked beside men in much the same way as they had on the land. As workers felt exploited they demanded more intervention from authorities to curb the worst excesses of unscrupulous bosses. Trade unions developed, and government responsibility through regulatory laws was slowly accepted for the nation's workforce. It was realised that a more educated workforce would spur government efficiency, trade, and growth, and the money that could be collected by government. It was realised that provision for healthcare would similarly make a workforce more productive. Taxes developed to finance a balance between necessary government action for individuals and for the nation. Army pensions became worker pensions. Governmentally, the connection between provider and supported became more anonymous and more 'professionalised.' All this took hundreds of years, but this was the development of the 'social contract' of Rousseau. Government would protect and people would work, and the latter would pay for the former. Work was still meant to offer self-worth, fulfilment, opportunity, and a way to support oneself and one's family, and it was still a communal enterprise.

For most people in developed nations this social contract still works well. For an increasing number it does not. Part of this is expectation of continuing 'progress.' However, work may no longer do what it promised. For these people work does not afford sufficient resources, i.e., pay and pride, to allow them to live a reasonable life. For some this means a streaming subscription and regular visits to the pub, but for others it means adequate heating, healthy food, and an adequate coat or shoes for growing children. The 'in-work poor' have increased in number; they have experienced increasing healthcare waiting lists, state pension put off until they are older, and rising and possibly exploitative prices from landlords and private providers of essential services without sufficient government regulation to protect them. People, especially women with less complete working lives, do not have the financial or other infrastructural resilience they need. Regulations, the responsibility of governments, have not prevented exploitative work contracts, including ones without sick pay or paid holidays, expecting worker payment for work materials, and for training, or probationary periods ended without explanation, or 'fire and re-hire' with different contracts. A still increasing awareness of workforce gender or minority discrimination adds to people's protestations.

Governments still collect taxes, still spend on health, education, welfare, etc, and are expected to provide services whatever the economic health of the nation, but part of the expectation people have is a perception of fairness. Government is seen by many as unrepresentative of them. Some of these people vote, some do not. Governments face distrust and disengagement. Lack of leadership, corruption, self-interested politicians, being 'out of touch,' and incompetence are all blamed, fairly or not, for allowing a lack of fairness in society. Symptoms include sky-high executive pay compared to that of 'the workers,' a perception of tax evasion by better-off individuals and big companies, and a perception of politically partisan support for one area or group. We are in danger of a toxic mix of genuine unfairness, difficulty of government decisions, declining resources, distrust through partisanship, disinformation, and partial personalised perception, all contributing to a breakdown of belief in the social contract that keeps communities together, and keeps government tethered to its communities. The increasing difficulty of many people to see that work can provide fair opportunity or fulfilment, that it can provide for oneself and one's family, that people can contribute or save in good times and get support in difficult times, is leading to a fracture of that social contract. This is not a majority of people or yet a tipping point of numbers, but nor does it need to be. It needs only to be an undefined substantial number whose declining mental or physical health, or inability to economically survive prospective illness or old age, threatens that work may in fact not pay, and for whom paying taxes and contributing and voting may in fact not make their life any better.

WHERE ARE WE GOING?

Expectations and transparency are part of the burden of developing and keeping the social contract alive. There is no inevitability of further progress in any nation. The secret is leadership. Wise governance can provide regulations, manage expectations, and provide essential services to build on over time, and efficient government can collect taxes and show the benefits of how the money is spent. Economic fairness in development and gaining and maintaining government legitimacy are what enables and upholds the social contract.

Health

In the UK, reforms before the First World War introduced Old-Age Pensions, Free School Meals, and National Insurance. During the Second World War, the Beveridge Report outlined familiar causes of poverty: Want (from poverty of income), Squalor (poor housing), Ignorance (a lack of compulsory education beyond primary level), Idleness (unemployment), and Health (or rather ill-health). From wartime came the moral consensus to implement its most fundamental proposal of the NHS: free healthcare for all at the point of delivery paid for by national taxes paid by everyone. In the UK this was state intervention on a scale never seen before outside a wartime economy. Enormous political battles were won to implement it. It was seen as in the public and national interest, accepting public health and the health of the national workforce as in people's self-interest too. The moral standpoint of a nation was as clear in that moment as it had ever been, even while private care remained an option. Its expense was enormous, taking up almost 4% of GDP immediately; and it has become the nation's largest employer.* It was a roaring success and immediately came under pressure from the volume of expectations and 'catch-up' health interventions required. Its prime idea remains politically sacrosanct in British politics. It has enabled relatively cost-effective, high-quality, large-scale healthcare, responsive to national demands, able to change

---

* John Appleby, "70 years of NHS spending," *The Nuffield Trust*, 21 March 2018. It became nearly 8% by 2020. Also see Emma Hawe, "Sixty years of the NHS: Changes in demographics, expenditure, workforce and family services," *Office of Health Economics*, September 2008. Also Nick Triggle, "The history of the NHS in charts," *BBC News*, 24 June 2018.

THE ECONOMY

with the times and adopt new technology and science. While not without its critics and operational flaws it is accountable. It has been adopted in some form or other in many nations, though noticeably not the USA, although critics may claim that state intervention in national health as a priority is inevitable, whatever the model.

It suffers from surroundings of general social and economic inequality, disinvestment in public services (sometimes to provide more for the NHS itself), and renewed partisanship in political attitudes towards it. Successes are easily forgotten, like the large reduction in smoking and virtual elimination of diseases like measles, as new problems are encountered or faced up to and old problems still fought: obesity, alcohol abuse, environmental ill-health, the connection between social care and healthcare in an ageing population, increased awareness of mental health, cost of new developments and technology, and variations in outcomes for different ethnicities or regions. Its greatest problems remain the level of expectation, and that for some it is increasingly seen as an overhead cost not an investment. The moral force behind its model is being lost. The state intervention required is out of fashion, even as Covid-19 brought out the best in the NHS and showed up the continuing weaknesses in the nation's health. Across the world health systems face these pressures and have acted in this context. While the 'final' effects of Covid-19 across the world are yet to be seen, it will renew calls for structured health systems and for addressing the overall health inequalities, not just medical care, within nations.* In the USA there has been an unprecedented three-year fall in life expectancy.

In England the Marmot Review into health inequalities was published in 2010 as Fair Society, Healthy Lives. It showed a seven-year gap in life expectancy between England's poorest and richest neighbourhoods, with more years of disability or ill-health. It showed a gradient of ill-health, not just a top and bottom. Its explanations were sadly reminiscent of reports over the previous 100 years. It went

---

* Up to 2022, the WHO estimated that 14.9m had died worldwide because of Covid-19, as judged by an estimate of excess deaths; Naomi Grimley, Jack Cornish, Nassos Stylianou. "Covid: World's true pandemic death toll nearly 15 million," *BBC News*, 5 May 2022. The Spanish Flu probably killed between 25 and 50 million. Currently both may have infected about 500 million worldwide. In May 2023 WHO declared the end of the pandemic as a 'global health emergency' although it was still a 'threat.'

WHERE ARE WE GOING?

further, in stating that health inequalities were largely preventable, and in establishing in modern terms the business case as well as the social justice case for addressing them. In 2010 the economic cost was placed at £36–£40 billion in lost taxes through inability to work, in welfare payments required, and in cost to the NHS in picking up the problems caused. It asked for a renewed political consensus, long-term planning for consistency and co-ordination, addressing health by including social and environmental factors, and called for 'devolution' to localities and individuals for them to take control of their own lives, with mixed use of government, voluntary, and private sectors. The Marmot conclusions could be replicated now across the full range of developed and developing nations. The review was, hopefully temporarily, lost in the fog of post-2008 economic austerity, and Marmot has subsequently renewed his conclusions. What these need the world over are three fundamental conditions: a willingness for state spending (whether in partnership with others), political consensus to allow generational perspective, and a renewed sense of self-interest in the 'common good' within societies.

Covid-19 spread across national borders with frightening speed enabled by modern travel. Data sharing in identification and vaccine development became astonishing and unprecedented. Whether that continues beyond Covid-19 will determine if that is truly revolutionary. That sharing has been by research academics publishing data for free and open use, and by private companies and governments to develop vaccines and other treatments, often quicker than ever thought previously possible. Continuation depends on government–private partnership, which is about government priority and expenditure, and the balance of investment and profit allowable for private companies. Will other nations be allowed to copy medicines more cheaply or will patents be held and monetised by a relatively small number of, and geographically concentrated, big companies, for extended periods? Companies often need to spend many millions developing treatments, and this cannot be ignored. New technology, including big computer power for data and DNA (or other original solution) research, and more 'open-source' sharing may solve or lessen this problem, but at some point mass production requires extensive investment too. These are economic, political, moral, and practical issues: economic strength prevents every nation developing its own vaccines so there is a moral incentive to help those who can less help themselves; diseases may reach everywhere else in weeks, so there is self-interest too in helping others; and the cost of failing healthcare has been shown to have global consequences economically, socially, and politically. The facility of global co-operation is complex but it can also be a series of deliberately taken decisions. Covid-19 could potentially produce a new benchmark for addressing international health standards and inequalities – but those involved in HIV/AIDS or malaria treatment may say that they have been here before. The business case for international development must be made. The practical and moral balances between domestic and international help are yet to be found. The balance of investment, in comparison to immediate priorities, for possibly rare but catastrophic disaster is judgement and guesswork. A nightmare scenario would be a succession of new diseases enabled by ever-closer wild animal to human contact until co-ordinated action is forced by mounting death tolls. It is up to humanity, but especially those holding the purse strings and technology, to prevent this. Covid-19 has shown the varied international dimensions of health in our globalised world and the increasing strain being placed on the social contract within nations. Its imperatives for action are already being lost, just like those of the Marmot Reviews.

The Economic Generational Divide

Perhaps a generational divide is inevitable. People want to live their life differently as they get older. There will naturally be more thought given to health and pensions, or maintaining family support. Younger people, whether that is considered under 21 or 25 or 30, tend to think about careers and earnings, and starting families, and having somewhere and somehow to live that gives them independence. These are natural differences.

In recent years the generational divide in nations like the UK has come to mean an unfairness, a lack of balance in rights and responsibilities, and in opportunities and risks. Younger generations may have new solutions for old problems, and sometimes find new priorities to begin with, and they want their opportunity to put them into practice. Fairness requires the older generation to have made a reasonable effort to solve its own problems when they were younger, not leave a drag of previous burdens for the young. The state of this fairness is being questioned.

Property prices and rents frequently out-pace wages and savings. In few countries are these specifically controlled, although rent controls have been employed by some, such as Germany. In many countries property has become a symbol of being a fully-fledged stakeholder in society, the notion of a 'property-owning democracy.' For an extra decade of their life younger people cannot afford to be on the property ladder, if they can conceive of the possibility at all. This means they are living with parents for longer or living in shared accommodation. This has repercussions for how they live their life, particularly for when they feel able to marry or start a family, which in turn may influence their maturity and personal development. For some only a deposit by parents or inheritance allows affordability. Rising property prices have become economically 'essential' and socially destructive. They seem to have become a sacrosanct indicator of wealth. The divide between those that may afford property eventually and those that will not is now a key block on social mobility.

Some have benefitted from the very significant expansion of higher education in the last decades. However, as government has withdrawn from public investment it has moved from grants to loans, and from free tuition paid for through general taxation to individual tuition fees. The reason for this was to finance the expansion of such education. The consequences have been that many students are saddled with extensive debt for two decades or more after graduation. Another consequence has been that some students from poorer backgrounds do not pursue this option. Support may have been offered but if your family background is one of being careful with your spending, not getting into debt that you would not be able to pay off without high-rate loans, or alternatively being saddled with the worry and restrictions of debt, then the thought of having £30,000 or more of debt at the end of your course can alone be a negative decision maker. The generational unfairness is seen through the change to this system when previous generations had grants and tuition paid and therefore much more limited debt. One part of the context is the increasing imbalance towards paper qualifications as against built experience. The generational divide will in fact become an educational-socio-economic divide.

Pensions have also changed. In the way they are now calculated most work-related pensions are less generous than they were, or currently are, for older people. In terms of a state pension some governments have kept this related to wages or inflation, but most are now extending the age at which it can be claimed, so younger generations will need to work longer. They may live longer, but they will not necessarily live in good health longer, or live longer at all, the poorer they are. The younger generation is therefore being asked to work longer for the elder generation to maintain their pension affordability. In a time of falling workforce numbers and rising pensionable-age numbers this appears to have lost its balance of fairness if you are younger.

Relatively simple action is being, or could be, taken: fairer repayment of educational debt, minimum or living wages, rent controls (around deposits and security of tenure as much as rent rates), long-term funding of social care in a generationally balanced way, etc. The issues indicate a generational divide that needs to be faced and that will have longer-term consequences. Inheritable wealth is becoming an indicator of standard of life. There is a growing divide between those with higher education following into higher incomes, able to pay off debt, and attain the indicators of maturity and independence; and those without skilled and higher-level paper qualifications destined for less dependable and regulated minimum-wage jobs, a lack of savings, high rents, and permanent family economic struggles with associated stress and health consequences. The generational divide as it is seen today is another fueller of the increasing inequality of tomorrow.

It must be said that the arc of each generation is different. We must look over the whole length of a life to judge it. We should also realise that young people care for their grandparents' generation; and that grandparents in general want better lives for the generations that come after them. There is no lack of care. Most of all, inequality within generations remains as concerning as that between them. Many younger people expect to live longer with technology that makes life and health more comfortable. However, we also know that if you are poor then you have more chance of eating unhealthy food, being unemployed for longer, less chance of gaining educational qualifications, more chance of disability, greater dependence on state pension alone, and more chance of dying earlier than average.

Then there is the legacy burden. This is the feeling that a younger generation is being forced to find solutions, and pay the price of those solutions, for the failures of older generations. This is surely one aspect of the movement from any one generation to another. What was not seen as a problem is then seen as one, because of new discoveries, new attitudes, or new events. However, there may be some legitimacy in the idea that the current younger generation is being presented with bigger legacy problems than previous generations, specifically continuing to come to terms with gender inequality, minorities' discrimination, and climate change. These issues will change the life of our younger generations in ways we probably still do not know. The context will be an increasing globalisation, and a feeling of having to build, as well as the opportunity to build, a wider community that they will need to be a part of. The challenging size of these issues is either extra stress inducing, or more creative inducing – and that may depend on your character, beliefs, wealth, position, and how you are represented.

There is plenty of evidence to suggest that younger generations are interested in a whole variety of specific issues, but they vote less in elections. If as many younger people voted as they could then the balance of the electorate would be quite different. That would result in the voice of younger people being listened to more across the whole policy area of government – wouldn't it? Well, it may do so. It should be noted that it is highly arguable whether governments around the world are more responsive to female issues and points of view despite the established voting rights and turnout of women. Most legislative bodies around the world remain male-dominated. Nevertheless, at least in an electoral period, politicians do pay attention to the electorate. Young people are not one monolithic group who all believe the same thing, but if more young people voted that could change the policy landscape of elections. There is no excuse not to. The responsibility to do so should overcome obstacles of how, and thinking that politicians don't change anything or that they do not represent 'you' and offer what you want. Politics is about idealism when running for power and the art of the possible when in power. That is a mature reality to come to terms with. That is not to say that politicians and electoral systems in many countries could not be more responsive in making sure that voter registration is easy or automatic, that voting is easy as well as secure, that voter representation is fair, that more attention is paid to those numbers that do not vote as a deliberate decision, and to those who are not engaged at all. There must be a greater responsibility on both those promoting elections and on those who want to see themselves as citizens.

The Morality and Future of Taxes

Two things are most well known about taxes: no-one likes paying them; and 'only death and taxes are certain in life.' When Donald Trump, in reply to a comment doubting whether he paid income tax, in an election debate in 2016, said 'that makes me smart,' some were amused and some shocked.* If he meant it seriously it was one of the most destructive single statements of attitude he has shown to the country he came to run. Taxes pay for government expenditure, and in most places that means the roads we drive on, the schools and hospitals we use, the law enforcement we depend on, and the regulations on all walks of life that are the infrastructure and the boundaries of the society we live in.

A Value Added Tax (VAT) on goods bought and paid by the individual consumer is increasingly common around the world, and increasingly used in preference to raising individual income tax. Most business taxes are on income or profits. Few people fully understand what have become complex tax systems, and most have an inaccurate idea of who pays what. In 2023-24 the independent Institute of Fiscal Studies forecast that in the UK, the top 2% of taxpayers would pay 39% of all income tax, paying at the highest rate of 45% over earnings of £125,000, while 36% of adults would pay no income tax.† Income tax will account for 28% of tax collected in the UK, followed by National

---

* His opponent Hillary Clinton then said 'maybe you haven't paid any federal income tax for a lot of years' to which Donald Trump replied 'it would be squandered ... believe me.' *USA election debate*, September 2016.
† "Income Tax Explained," *Institute of Fiscal Studies TaxLAB*, https://ifs.org.uk/taxlab/taxlab-taxes-explained/income-tax-explained.

WHERE ARE WE GOING?

Insurance, VAT, and 'Company taxes' (about 18%, 17%, and 11% of tax collected respectively). Tax revenues as a percentage of GDP in the UK will be 41%.* In 2021, the latest year for international comparisons, in the UK it was 33.5%, near the Organisation of Economic Development (OECD) average of 34.1%; with higher nations often being Scandinavian/West European, with the USA being near the bottom at 26.6% complicated by there being state and federal taxes. Illegal tax evasion and legal tax avoidance are major industries. Most income tax systems are 'progressive,' i.e., the more you earn the more you pay, but VAT is often seen as 'regressive' because it takes a higher proportion of income from lower-income households. This contrasts with a 'flat rate' on income tax where everyone pays the same percentage, only implemented in nine countries with eight at between 10% and 20% of earnings. These nations are generally criticized for lower welfare provision. Until 2021 there was no international agreement on tax rates for multinationals.†

Morally there has been a general acceptance that the wealthier you are the more you could and should contribute, up to a point, and in so doing contribute to the infrastructure you use and to the less fortunate. The former of those two reasons being practical, the latter moral. Higher earners may have taken more from the state, in such ways as staying longer in subsidised education, and clearly use the same roads, law courts, etc as everyone else. They also need workers and customers to have access to healthcare and education, etc. 'Up to a point' means up to the point when it seems that the tax you pay on the money you make is disproportionately high, seen as unfair, and encouraging tax evasion that reduces tax collection. A higher tax rate now tends not to exceed 50%, although it has done in the past. There is a safety net of state aid paid for through taxes for the poorest or most vulnerable, often those hindered in some way from a full working life, perhaps through disability or ill-health; and aid for those who could be deemed temporarily out of the workforce, such as those looking after young children. Corporate taxes

---

* "Where does the government get its money?" *Institute of Fiscal Studies TaxLAB*, https://ifs.org.uk/taxlab/taxlab-key-questions/where-does-government-get-its-money.
† "How do UK tax revenues compare internationally?" *Institute of Fiscal Studies TaxLAB*, https://ifs.org.uk/taxlab/taxlab-key-questions/how-do-uk-tax-revenues-compare-internationally. Also "Countries with Flat Tax 2024," www.worldpopulationreview.com.

are frequently tweaked, such as to encourage investment or claim more for the treasury when needed. The tax system is a series of moral as well as practical balances.

The tax system is also coming under more pressure. When a rich person does not use the same hospitals, schools, etc as everyone else they become more divorced from the society around them, less appreciative of it, and separated from the social contract that to work must apply at the top end of the wealth scale as much as the bottom end. Some people with a more individualist morality will complain about others having no incentive to work harder to be successful; and complain about ineffective government use of their hard-earned money. This restricted view of government action is called 'small state' government, and this attitude is commonplace, not just in the USA.* This argument minimises the self-interest involved in the common good and often dismisses causes of poverty that are beyond someone's control. The less scrupulous look for tax avoidance, or tax evasion. The richest can simply move somewhere else with the world their oyster in a kind of personal survivalist mentality. The same applies to companies. Politicians are often not careful enough to prevent the perception of favouritism. Ordinary taxpayers and poor non-taxpayers perceive a decline in fairness when they think this is happening. The most vulnerable feel a decline in the safety net through austerity or deliberate ideological design – or indeed a country simply getting poorer, which no-one likes to accept or recognise. Their options, in the context of stalled opportunities for upward mobility, are official but more exploited jobs, deeper poverty, or the 'black market' unregulated economy, and own social networks to help each other, which furthers their own disengagement from society at large. These trends accompany inequality across the world. The more fundamental failure to collect taxes is an indicator of a failing government itself.

A more 'libertarian' point of view would argue that if people did not pay taxes they would have and use more choice in how to spend their money in ways that suited them, choosing from a pick and mix

---

* USA President Ronald Reagan said on 12 August 1986: 'The nine most terrifying words in the English language are: "I'm from the Government, and I am here to help."' He remains one of the most popular (Republican) presidents of nearly 50 presidents to hold office.

of private company education, health, transport, etc, choosing when to contribute to a larger pot for larger projects. This is the citizen's ultimate control and choice. It would destroy the idea of general community and cohesive society in the process, ending effective government and regulation. It assumes that people will make logical and moral choices, for themselves, for their families, and that communities would then inevitably benefit. It depends on accessible and reliable information, the regulation of those offering services, and compensation in law for those exploited. It depends on even the poorest still having access to, or money to pay for, a public or private safety net that keeps them afloat and out of an unheard, unseen, forgotten underclass.

As low personal taxes are meant to encourage independence and choice, so in corporate terms lower taxes are meant to encourage innovation and investment, and hence increase employment and competition for workers, thereby raising wages and standards of living. This 'trickle-down economics' is highly controversial. Many would say that it has not helped to raise the living standards of most people, or has done so very inefficiently or haphazardly. As an increasing number of companies require less workers through efficiency or technology, are more beholden to shareholders, face less government regulation, less connection with local communities, and more opportunity to move capital between jurisdictions, corporate taxation as an instrument to raise living standards is becoming harder to rely on, if it ever worked. Possibly the signature law of President Trump's presidency was known as the Tax Cuts and Jobs Act and was signed in December 2017. It slashed corporate tax to encourage business back to America, to increase investment, to raise wages, intended to simplify the tax system, and to pay for itself from increased growth. In practice US corporations brought money back from abroad but often used it to pay higher dividends to shareholders with more limited investment and more debt pay-off rather than raising wages, it has paid for about one-fifth of itself, and with lower taxes on foreign profits there seems no incentive to bring back business activity to the USA.*

---

* "12 Terrible things about the Trump-GOP tax law (as of 8 March 2018)," *Americans for Tax Fairness*. Lydia O'Neal, "The Trump tax cut: Promises made, promises kept?" *Bloomberg Tax*, 26 January 2021.

Nor have personal tax systems kept up with the changing nature of society. It remains income that is taxed at a time when wealth is not measured entirely in income. Property and inheritance are key modern measures of wealth and success. While income is available money, and therefore practical to be taxed, 'unearned wealth' of property values and shares (even if they can go down as well as up) can increase faster than wages but not be so easily accessed. Nor is unearned income literally unearned, a conundrum that also needs to be faced more honestly. However, what we currently call 'unearned income' is increasing social-economic divisions and inequality, by 'artificially' increasing some people's life chances and personal economic stability. A rented house that cannot be passed on to the next generation and a minimum wage or 'just in the tax-paying bracket' job precluding the ability to save, point life in a different direction to that of loans based on a mortgage or using inherited money to get on the property ladder or pay off tuition fees, etc. Our current tax system may or may not encourage this, but it certainly does nothing to prevent it. Yet whether there should be high inheritance or property taxes is also a moral question. If someone works hard to earn money with the deliberate aim of passing that on to their children, is it morally acceptable to take that away from them? Such an act, however, requires nothing from the inheritor, no skills or actions, no contribution, no merit on their part, so what have they done to earn that largesse (aside from the love of their benefactor)? Where is the meritocracy and equality in that? If unearned wealth simply reinforces the difficulty of upward social mobility for others – the hope and possibility for a better life beyond one's own born circumstances – then resentment and disengagement are winners too. It then becomes more difficult to maintain a cohesive and stable society, putting in danger the life that even the successful may lead. We need to address the inequalities that are being created and sustained by the tax system that we employ. It is making a consensus on the common good harder to achieve, and it is endangering the social contract that stable societies need and that legitimise governments. It is also stressing the competitive character of humanity and calling into question the morality that people should help each other.

WHERE ARE WE GOING?

Changes

Changes are taking place in the productive economies of nations both fast and slow. These include a divergence from the fossil fuels of coal and oil, and eventually from natural gas too. For biodiversity and permanent sustainability plastics development and production will change or end, and the extraction of many minerals from land (and ocean) used in mobile phones and computers must be short term. Historically, one way of measuring civilisations has been by the amount of energy they use, but now the types may be just as important. Innovative system and technical solutions are needed, and some are already available.

Other changes relate to the way business works. Labour determining business success is no longer true. Capital, i.e., money, is more essential. Instagram was sold to Facebook for $1 billion in 2012 when it had thirteen staff and bought either because it was competition or to stop a competitor buying it, rather than trying to out-compete it.* Capital can be moved across the globe. Trade is global and can be done by individuals and multinational companies. The type of work we do, how we do it, where, who does it, and even when, are all in a state of change. Digitisation and automation are doing this, and capital is adapting to them. Worker rights and conditions, pay, education and skills, and mobility, are all in a state of flux. Rights and expectations are less secure than many people thought. Within a newer global context, changes in work and business are also calling into question how a nation controls the levers to raise the money that allow it to fulfil its expected functions. Those functions are therefore coming under scrutiny too. The social contract that binds people to government and underpins developed societies, and is an aim of developing ones, is coming under pressure. We must then add in the physical disruptions for people of extreme weather events, and domestic and international migration. Additionally, one consequence of the Russian–Ukrainian conflict is a level of insecurity or actual military action unknown for seventy years in the Western world, although more known elsewhere, producing

---

* Salvador Rodriguez, "As calls grow to split up Facebook, employees who were there for the Instagram acquisition explain why the deal happened," *CNBC*, 24 September 2019, retrieved 15 June 2023.

THE ECONOMY

further layers of complication and division – who are the producers and consumers of raw materials, energy, technology, or foodstuffs affected?

Inequality is being seen in all these changes, domestically and internationally. Trust in government is therefore coming under a cloud. Democracies must respond, but so must authoritarian leaderships whose primary legitimacy is usually that people can still get on with their lives peacefully. This is a complex mix of continual change that makes a stable economy very difficult to achieve. Already nations know they can only shape and influence, not have complete control.

What will be our morality towards those in less fortunate circumstances, at home and abroad? Do we see humanity as a socially co-operative exercise or a fundamentally competitive one? Does our humanity use the planet and seek complete control of it, or does it recognise a stewardship of it as something greater than itself? Changing livelihoods of people within our economies will play out over time, with our actions softened or harshened by domestic political, internationally strategic, technological, and physical realities. We must be prepared to review and reassess in our own lives, in government, and between governments, without predetermined conclusions. There must be a resolve not so much 'to leave no-one behind' but more to 'take everyone with us.' Our decisions will be moral as well as technical and practical ones. As things change, we must have an idea what sort of life we want to lead. That means what sort of livelihoods we expect, or think, are possible, or are prepared to cope with, to allow that life to happen.

We should control science and technology, not leave it unregulated or be viewed as inevitable.* Automation, AI, bio-human development, etc may need new guidelines, laws, or ethics from legislators, entrepreneurs, and scientists. However, our problem is currently more basic than that. Why do we want continuous scientific and technological development? We want easier lives, cheaper and more reliable goods and services, but we also think that we cannot stop development. We believe that in our competitive world someone will always use it to gain an advantage.

---

* See Liis Vihul, "International legal regulation of autonomous technologies," 16 November 2020, part of a series of essays *Modern conflict and artificial intelligence* from the *Centre for International Governance Innovation*, based in Canada, an independent international think tank, www.cigionline.org.

Such developments can be in physical materials, of robotics, relating to computer power, and the development of 'thinking' AI. These may vary from graphene as a new super light and strong material, to 'the internet of everything' where all sorts of goods are connected, to Blockchain recording of origins, mechanical delivery systems, robotic replacements for jobs now done by real people, millisecond advantage in money markets, and 3-D printing of perhaps anything including untraceable guns. The development of electricity from its invention or discovery took thirty to forty years to be generally understood and widely used (from the 1870s to the 1910s). Forty years after the development of computer power we are now in a new era, or a 'Second Machine Age,' or another 'industrial revolution.'

Automation

We have already seen the enormous changes that technological development can make to Work. The printing press revolutionised the distribution of information, literacy, whole industries rose and fell, and was an important factor in the decline of the power of the Church in Western Europe. Another, more recent and on the face of it much more limited, example is the development of containerised shipping. One example: Liverpool's manufacturing base and working port almost ceased to exist within the 1970s after 150 years of internationally renowned success. The economic decline was catastrophic. Unemployment rose and population fell, both sharply. The decline in confidence of one of the British Empire's great cities was perhaps as damaging. Containerisation saw a parallel rise in ports across East Asia, from Hong Kong to South Korea as manufacturing centres changed too. Technology changes people's livelihoods, their environment, their aspirations and confidence, and their political power. When we think of scientific and technological changes in the world of 'work' and 'economy,' most commonly thought of as 'automation,' we must consider as much as we can the depth and complexity of the changes they will produce.

Drones began as small tech surveillance. Now they are being used in war to deliver explosives to a target. In contrast they are now also being used to deliver humanitarian aid to remote areas. They are on the cusp

THE ECONOMY

of being a key tool in the surveillance and regulation of environmental change, making that job more extensive, accurate, and safer. Drones are set for multiple purposes by individuals, companies, institutions, and governments. In warfare drones may offer a viable alternative to the development of a traditional air force, perhaps not for a major power but for minor nations whose armed forces can therefore become a concerning opposition to a would-be aggressor. Drones may alter the infrastructure required and distribution possibilities of a nation. In the USA driving is the second most common job skill in all fifty American states. What happens to those jobs when driverless vehicles are deemed just as safe and efficient? Perhaps personal driving skills wither away, in a similar vein to navigation instincts being killed off by the satnav. How would our roads begin to look, and what happens to insurance? Who programmes the car with ethics so that it can choose whether to avoid a child running after a ball hit into the road or to avoid an oncoming car with occupants that it might hit if it swerved? Automated customer service is already common. As it learns to better detect human emotion how will this change the nature of what we think are our relationships with people, or with companies, or with authority? Amazon's 'Alexa' is clearly an early example of this – automated, internet-connected, to some degree personalised, for some people it has become one of the family. One can see how it could become extremely useful for people with disabilities. One can also recognise fears of surveillance and gathering information for exploitative profit-making. Japan has one of the most ageing populations in the world, and one of its increasing problems is therefore social care for the elderly. One of the solutions being trialled now is robotic carers, i.e., carers that are robots. Caring employment may wither away to a few managers and technicians. The ethics questions are also relevant here: who programmes them? They could reduce the cost of care, making it more widely available. What about the personal relationships that are what it is to be human, when we are suffering an epidemic of elderly isolation the world over. In Japan 'customers' of robotic care are giving them names and 'characters' and creating their own relationships. Robotic carers, at least in theory, will never be late, will never forget to do something they promised, won't forget your medication, or be embarrassed by something you do.

WHERE ARE WE GOING?

As big data and real-time data become more expansive systems can learn from millions or billions of interactions with real people in real situations. This is how they will come to recognise the difference between a cry of happiness and a cry of anguish. At least that is how they will be sold. They will seep into people's professional, personal, family, and public lives. They will cause the decline of occupations and whole industries and create others. No-one knows if the creation will be comparable to the decline. Unskilled jobs may more comfortably be done by automation. Technical jobs may be done by more accurate and reliable automation. Jobs requiring the skill of judgement may eventually be done by automation weighing up a judgement from millions of programmed scenarios and experiences. Creative jobs? In 2022 Ai-Da became the first robot to make its own art, to 'paint like an artist' where its 'algorithms prompt the robot to interrogate, select, and decision-make to create a painting' so that no two paintings are the same. A 'humanoid robot' named after pioneer Ada Lovelace, created at the University of Oxford, UK, in 2019 by Aidan Mellor with robotics, AI, and engineering teams, it can already 'create' poems.*

The problem of automation will not be whether it can achieve something but whether we want it to and whether it should. The world is talking about automation but not at all prepared for its consequences, in work, purpose, income, or the wealth of nations. We need to think about the moral choices that automation will also put before us, about who controls it, who makes a development acceptable or unacceptable: automotive sex toys or people using holographic images at work? No-one knows how automation will affect the development of nations in the work they can offer and the finances they will have. Changing jobs, or having multiple jobs, is one thing, but people may be unable to keep reinventing their skills and may not want to. Retraining availability, psychological stability, and maturity of age and outlook, all come into that. Does automation give us more comfortable leisure time or more desperation to find income; will it up-skill or de-skill us; will it make the world more or less equal; will 'work' still be a measure of adulthood and maturity; will we come to treat robotic engineering as 'like us,' and

---

* Caroline Davies, "'Mind-blowing': Ai-Da becomes first robot to paint like an artist," *The Guardian*, 4 April 2022.

how might that effect the real relationships that we have that might be less reliable, less sympathetic, or less helpful? The ways in which our economy and work change in the next few decades may have a profound effect on who we are. We must prepare for automation across our built environment, our government, our sense of fulfilment and self-worth, and in our human relationships. We must deliberately make automation an inclusive opportunity, not a nightmare of exclusion, inequality, or isolation. We need to effectively place automation within humanity's narrative of progress. We must learn to see the automation of our economies as something that we want, and can have, direction over.

Openness and Innovation

Innovation in ways of working may be an alternative to new disruptive invention, and to the rise of bigger and bigger business. The expansion of 'big business' and 'big tech' appear to initially offer greater consumer choice but go on to control choice through their buying and selling scale and through their profile. Amazon makes it easy to buy a product but it offers less of a cut to the producer than other companies. Supermarkets squeeze their suppliers to give consumers cheaper products. Suppliers gain a market but they may make no profit to invest, running on debt and subsidy. High streets may be hollowed out of 'independent' or locally run business. Larger companies sometimes act like a competitive business – surprise! surprise! – by hoovering up talent and buying up companies that may become rivals. The bigger they are the more distant they become, and the more automatedly efficient the more impersonal they may seem.* Some of this is unfair, but perception as well as actions count. In 2022 California's Proposal 22 was an electoral ballot initiative led by Uber and other app-based companies to exclude their app-based workers from nearly all employee rights under state law including minimum wage and compensation laws. It proposed its amendment

---

* Miguel Helft, "Google's buses help its workers beat the rush," *New York Times*, 10 March 2007. "Google to use driverless autonomous vehicles to transport employees within San Francisco," *CBS News*, 30 March 2022. Jennifer Elias, "Google's plans for a mega-campus in San Jose lurk behind its recent $1 billion housing pledge," *CNBC*, 11 July 2019.

only with a seven-eighths vote of the state legislature, making it almost impossible to overturn. It passed, but the State Superior Court has since ruled it unconstitutional, and that is now subject to appeal.* Add a potential to threaten to leave unless its lobbying is successful and such business can be dangerous to a community. To 'achieve' all of this would be rare but it is the nightmare of democratic politicians and communities.

There are emerging alternatives and traditional counterweights. The most obvious of these is the political process. Where democracy of some form exists politicians can change the law. Laws relating to monopolies and cartels, and corruption, may be established and need updating to make them relevant to multinational companies and new sectors of business and employment. Improving zero-hour contracts would be another example. Politicians must be independent enough and representative enough to make this happen, and this is one of the current struggles of democracies. It is a struggle that must make sure innovation is for the good of the nation and its people. To succeed it also needs civic society, such as a free press. Legislators need to learn and be engaged. Fortunately, it is difficult to keep secrets these days. One example suffices: The Pandora 'papers' were nearly 12m confidential records obtained by the International Consortium of Investigative Journalists, published in various media globally in 2021, that showed the hidden, often denied, and previously unknown wealth of thousands of leading figures around the world. Some was clearly the result of tax evasion or avoidance, of deliberate opaqueness, or political influence. So-called open democracies cannot afford to be complacent about lack of transparency and the connections between wealth and politics in their own societies.

Autocratic nations cannot embrace some of the different ways to extend economic enterprise and participation being explored in democracies. The continuing life of the co-operative movement, share-buying by individuals on a modest scale, business-like analysis of charity and investment effectiveness, increasing necessity to bid for funding by

---

* Brian Chen and Laura Padin, "Prop 22 was a failure for California's app-based workers. Now, it's also unconstitutional," *National Employment Law Project*, New York, 16 September 2021, www.nelp.org.

local government and non-government groups, people holding multiple jobs, the better-off retiring 'early,' and the rise of crowdfunding, have all begun to lead to a revolution in attitude of what some people can do. This is a mishmash of democratisation, analyses, competitiveness, and individual actions that are merging into innovation. If something can be crowd-funded, then why not have 'crowd-invention' – individuals working together to make something better through their accumulated ingenuity. If people can retire early or work part-time why not exercise those interests and talents not involved in, or actively constrained by, their everyday job, and contribute to something 'more worthwhile' or 'more interesting' as part of a like-minded community. Some people are reassessing what they can achieve for others as well as themselves and working in a more altruistic pattern. All these can combine for the creation of crowd-invention, and for more 'open-source' distribution – i.e., the foregoing of patent and copyright exclusivity in favour of free access to that knowledge. This can become a more democratised knowledge and entrepreneurship. This is a possible antidote to the development of impersonal, constrained, and competitive big business. This is a different way for people to employ themselves and to make money, and to 'do good' for others, and to feel part of a community, and to use their talents in a fulfilling way. Self-developing groups can become hybrid entrepreneurs. They can be inventive and investment groups, they can be completely inclusive or exclusive – understandable if that is about sharing expert knowledge, though also concerning if exclusivity is based on any form of discrimination. Ease of communication makes all this possible. That is why it is a scenario for democracies and democratic renewal, not for authoritarian governments to allow. Such groups can increase diversity in business, and be consumer led. They can be global or very local. A very small number of companies are beginning to catch onto this potential. Innovative companies can encourage and reward this practice in partnership, resisting the impulse to control and buy up and see everything as competition. They can at least partly outsource innovation, offering reward for success and successful development that they then make more money from. Consumers can be designers. It can be related to creative activity not just strictly scientific and technological invention and discovery. Companies can become hubs of entrepreneurial activity connected to real people and local communities. Not all innovation can be done in this way, but ideas and shared experience can ally with the computer power and big data of a company whose expertise would become development and production. Wikipedia began in 2001: there were previous iterations, it is funded by donations, and is participatory in content development. This is an early example of the potential. The development of Covid-19 vaccines through the co-operative work of academics, scientists, and pharmaceutical companies is a more recent and different, more expertise-based, example. The potential of crowd-invention, open-source knowledge, and hybrid entrepreneurs to re-shape how we could work, and how economies can develop is great. Their potential to ally a significant share of economic power with democratisation and engagement is serious. It is quite a different context but the apparent international collective effort of hackers to act in a cause they support in the Russian–Ukrainian war may give a different glimpse of this potential; could Ukraine put out similarly successful calls of support in its reconstruction?

The Co-operative movement is arguably an origin of all this. Begun in 1889 it lives on. It supports community engagement and individual action and co-operation. It works in the space between profit and non-profit groups, and outside government, with regulation. Three million co-operatives around the world have one billion members and do $2 trillion of business annually. They remain an 'invisible giant of the economy.'* Participatory Budgets is a relative newcomer: the deliberate and planned devolution of spending power. It can revive the idea of 'the common good' with modern accountability. The keys to participatory budgets are fourfold: courageous political leadership to give up power; regulation for basic consistency, structure, understanding, accountability (including diversity of participation), the prevention of exploitation or (big) business intimidation, and a 'safety net'; the availability of expertise; and citizen participation. Building up voluntary participation is never easy, but there are clear steps along the way to make it work that are already widely known. Participatory budgets can widen minority engagement, and reduce corruption, if they have regulation. They can be

---

* Ann Puusa, "The Case for Co-ops, the invisible giant of the economy," *TED*, YouTube, 27 May 2021.

heavy in local dialogue but at ground level they are more practical than ideological or party politics. They can take a share of budgets, leaving issues like massive infrastructure to national governments. The largest early example was in Porto Alegre, capital of Brazil's southernmost state, created in 1989. It involved 17,000 citizens at its peak, distributing about $160 million of public money. It was effective in engaging lower-income and minority groups. Elected councillors can accept or reject proposals made but have a limited role, and funding has shifted towards poorer parts of the city.* Placing workers on the operational boards of mid-size and larger companies is a step that some nations encourage and others shy away from. Such representatives would help to present a more rounded view of the consequences of a company's actions and decisions, from working practices to investments, from pay structures including executive and main scale pay balance to political lobbying and donations. Such worker representatives would soon understand the complexities of business, its pitfalls, and fragilities. They can be a conduit to the ideas of workers, and for their education and engagement in that business. Its primary obstacle is an us-versus-them attitude, and a professionalisation and separation of running the business from working in it.

Participation builds – like democracy itself – on the notion that we share more than we often realise. We share the roads we use, the streets we live on, we share compliments and language, we share ambitions for the next generation and care for others, and we share a wish and a need for things to work. This is the solid moral and philosophical foundation of participation. What we do not directly share we often still have a self-interest in preserving or developing. Co-operation from each perspective is hardly new. We need to maximise a use for it and methods to make it work in our modern lives and our modern economies. Crowd-invention, open-source knowledge sharing, hybrid

---

* "Case study: Porto Alegre, Brazil," *Local Government Association*, 12 December 2016; William W. Goldsmith and Carlos B Vainer, "Participatory budgeting and power politics in Porto Alegre," *Lincoln Institute of Land Policy* (USA), January 2001. Also see www.citizenlab.co as an organisation and online platform encouraging participatory projects, working with communities and authorities across the world, winner of awards including Best Social Impact Startup of Europe, and the World Summit Award for Government and Citizen Participation.

entrepreneurs, co-operatives, devolutionary participatory budgets, and worker representation are all ways that innovation can be as important as invention and discovery, and some of them are not even very new.

A Four-Day Week

It has been a prediction for decades that we would get to a far shorter working week. Individual working hours have generally gone down since about 1850, but family working hours have gone up, i.e., more women work. That's good for equality but is also often out of necessity. Many people have the same instinct, about others, as the Victorians, that more leisure time would mean more vices pursued: drugs, gambling, sex, alcohol, and now 'screen time addiction.' From a business perspective this has been a horrific idea for a century but calling it 'less work for the same pay' feeds into a misrepresentation of it. Yet let us also be very clear that we are talking about no reduction in total pay. From a philosophical perspective its objections include it being more 'nanny state' interference, more 'something for nothing,' more of business paying for society. Then there is the idea of how this would change judgements and comparisons – wouldn't production just go down by 20%, and what would that do to a nation's reputation as well as its wealth?

These are all outdated views that can be faced head-on. When Henry Ford, one of the great businessmen of the industrial era, and definitely not a socialist, reduced his company's working week from six days to five he found that productivity remained the same. In the 1970s when Edward Heath's UK government reacted to the oil crisis by temporarily instituting a three-day week, productivity reduced by only 6%.* Firstly, there can be less stress, less accidents or mistakes, people may be better rested even if they live an active 'fifth day,' and with more buy-in for a company, although if it is the norm then perhaps the latter falls away. The Covid-19 period has helped companies to think again about how they can efficiently use their workforce, even though working at home and a shorter working week should not be confused. Secondly, a shorter

---

* Bregman, 2018, 141; Andrew Simms, Anna Coote, Jane Franklin, "21 Hours, the case for a shorter working week," *New Economics Foundation*, 13 February 2010.

individual working week does not have to mean a shorter working week for a company. Continuing a five-day week with four-days-a-week workers opens possibilities of job sharing and part-time work. This can help women back into work after childcare, or seniors stay in work in a time of more flexible retirement. Unemployment can in fact be reduced, as well as having the personal benefits for these people. Productivity can be maintained as well as workforce diversified in skills, experience, and character. While employing more part-time staff has training and other employment costs, the costs of worker absence can be reduced, which, together with societal and governmental benefits of reduced welfare and better health, could allow subsidies for companies to set up such schemes, and pay for the key infrastructure necessary including the availability and reasonable cost of greater childcare. There is nothing to stop a company working six or seven days a week, as many do now, if individual workers work four days. Clearly there are ways to do this well and fairly, and ways to do it exploitatively with the aim of saving money. A financially neutral settlement in the business case for a shorter working week is both possible and should be enough.

The all-round social benefits may be more consequential (which in turn will have benefits for the businesses people work in). What would people do on their 'fifth day'? Most people, especially if this applies to all workers of all ages, will remain restless, and while the fifth day may or may not be a slower pace they will want to 'do something' with their time. It may not be rest; it may deliberately be more physical activity or more family time. We have introduced paternity leave as well as maternity leave in recent years to strengthen initial family relationships in that time of change, stress, and required energy. Some grandparents will spend more time with grandchildren for the benefit of parents, children, and themselves, resisting the opening of generational gaps of understanding and appreciation. Wide-ranging gains in family, health and welfare benefit each generation. Subsequent improved school outcomes and reduced health and welfare issues for youngsters would far outweigh the benefits to society in relation even to the parents of the time. All this is saving the government money, and if that were the case then that means reduced taxes, which would help individuals and companies, or more money in a financially neutral settlement to set up

WHERE ARE WE GOING?

the infrastructure that allows this to happen or to spend on dealing with the reduced number of social issues that would remain. To those that think this is pie-in-the-sky nonsense they must address the logic of these changes, and honestly review any long-established opinions. And for others, or the same people sarcastically, who say why not work just one day, or two? At some point fair and extended trials will show a decline in benefit. Nor is this a reason to pursue the complete automation of all work leaving nothing for humanity to do. Humanity is a busy species, we like to do things, and there is reason to suppose that will continue. As we have noted already, work plays a part in the fulfilment of our lives. 'Work,' in whatever form it takes, will not just end, and we must have the confidence and self-belief to acknowledge that, and those purposes of work, too. Furthermore, as companies can still work whatever number of days per week they want, there is no reason to judge that even materialist-driven measurements of national wealth like GDP would decline. The case for a shorter working week, without negative effect on business, is strong.

Companies have increasingly embarked upon their own trials, such as the small family-owned British manufacturing/engineering company Chilwell Products in January 2022. There was no reduction in pay for their four-day week (or reduction in numbers employed), it followed an investment in new technology, and workers at all levels reported more family time, healthier activities, and more positive attitudes to work. The campaign for a four-day week acknowledges UK companies that have met its standards. Currently most are 'new' or knowledge-economy businesses. Few are manufacturing companies with a more traditional production line.* This is a global interest. Reykjavik city council has trialled a four-day week, as has the FTSE 100 consumer goods group Unilever, and Japanese electronics company Panasonic. Another example is the Spanish government's agreement in March 2021 to a trial for a thirty-two-hour week for three years in one area of Spain that will involve about 200 companies and thousands of workers.† Announcing

---

* Nicola Gilroy and Jennifer Harby, "Four-day week: what we do with our extra day off," *BBC News*, 3 April 2022. Also see www.4dayweek.co.uk.
† Ashifa Kassam, "Spain to launch trial of four-day working week," *The Guardian*, 15 March 2021.

another private-initiative multi-company larger-scale trial in the UK in April 2022 Joe O'Connor, chief executive of 4 Day Week Global said there was no way 'to turn the clock back' to the pre-pandemic world, and that '[i]ncreasingly managers and executives are embracing a new model of work which focuses on quality of outputs, not quantity of hours' and '[w]orkers have emerged from the pandemic with different expectations around what constitutes a healthy life-work balance.'* How the campaign is boosted by the change in attitudes and routines of work from the pandemic remains to be seen, or copes with a business backlash to work more to 'get economies moving again.' It also needs to encourage 'front-line' and 'production-line' companies, or risk widening the working conditions difference between those and others. It also remains to be seen, given economic developmental pressure, whether the campaign translates effectively beyond a Western business model of management and a Western social context. How would developing African nations view it, or east Asian 'work-ethic' and 'work-as-personal and national-duty' contexts adapt?

As well as rest or family time or 'leisure' people may choose to do another area of activity: voluntary charity work, from local environmental projects to national organisations. Some may even choose another part-time job to supplement their income further. There is a third and more radical new work that people may choose on the fifth day: creatively or entrepreneurially exploring their own talents and ambitions. This can be organised and group-related, or ad hoc and individual. It can be business-like or entirely for personal development and enjoyment. People might take up painting, or improve their cooking skills. Equally people may choose to spend their time, resources, and energy in money-making or invention. This is the open door to the previously discussed 'crowd-invention' and 'open-source' society. This has the potential to hit the jackpot of individual, civic, and business benefit. During Covid lockdown in the UK the Meteorological Office asked for volunteers to digitally input decades of historical handwritten data on rainfall. It believed that recording 5.2 million individual observations would take

---

* Jasper Jolly, "Thousands of UK workers to take part in four-day week trial," *The Guardian*, 3 April 2022.

several months. So many people volunteered it took sixteen days!* It must also be clear that mandating anything specific for the 'fifth day' defeats the object and would be authoritarian in character and practice.

What is central to this idea is a review of what we are living our lives for. If lives are about money and wealth then many will want to work as much as they can. If we are beginning to place, or re-place, quality of life at the core of what we want, then a shorter working week must be a consideration. Obstructive arguments from business can be answered. There is a business case for it, and a civic society case, a governmental case, a family case, and an individual case. There is a logic that it could significantly ease social pressures, health and welfare problems, and civic cohesion. If it did that by one-fifth, or most of one-fifth, that itself would make a massive difference. The case for it in terms of government expenditure and change can be neutral at worst, and it may well be beneficial for those who want better government, those who want smaller government, and those who want government to help in people's everyday lives more effectively or directly or both. Of course, it can be done well and done badly, it can be trialled or blustered into. Like most changes in life it would take time to adjust to. The way we work is changing, and we can embrace that and make it work for us. It might even be argued that the only governments that would be against this are authoritarian ones. A shorter working week gives people more control over their lives and more time to think for themselves. A shorter working week may contribute to a freer society, and it can even be a selling point for free societies in comparison to others.

Universal Basic Income (UBI)

If a four-day week is a serious consideration for modern work, then UBI is a serious consideration for modern welfare and support and more widely renewing the social contract. It gets to the heart of what we have been doing wrong in relation to poverty over the last 200 years, and in particular over the last fifty. Let us be clear first though that this is in relation to one nation.

In 1968 USA Republican (Presidential candidate) Richard Nixon

---

* Press Office, "Victorian rainfall data rescued," *Met Office*, 25 March 2022.

proposed a UBI. He proposed a family of four being given $1,600 per year, equivalent now to about $10,000.* He was a strong conservative, and a less obvious reformer, but perhaps therefore in a position to carry many of his more naturally sceptical followers with him. There were multi-state trials that showed, among other results, a decline of 9% in work although mostly from young parents, and High School Graduation up by 30%. Nixon saw that UBI could lessen dependence on the state – as Republicans wanted – not increase it. However, to get it through his party he was persuaded to add a 'must work register' to the proposal, which contradicted the essential idea. Congress defeated it, and in today's USA UBI is seen as a radical left-wing idea. Alternative 'work for welfare' programmes lasted into the 2000s. Government and middle classes saw poverty as something that people had got themselves into, through laziness or vices. Welfare therefore became something to be earnt and dealing with the poor took precedence over dealing with poverty.

At the turn of the last century a 'poverty line' became characterised by living in a state of 'merely physical efficiency' allowing no expenditure on transport, insurance, tobacco, beer, church donation, paid doctor, newspaper, etc, and when with young children, being ill, unemployed, and too old to work. Over time these were all softened by policies from old-age pensions to unemployment insurance, child allowance, and now a minimum or 'living' wage. However, arguably, we still deal with the poor not with poverty, and we still promote having to 'earn' welfare. Modern support for people in poverty includes extensive bureaucracy, distrust, punishing sanctions, supervision, negative language, compulsion, and lack of free action. There is of course an importance in spending taxpayers' money wisely, and this is essential in gaining support for action, but we have given efficiency and government austerity a predominant say over welfare. This is where we are now; and its complications and repeat spending doesn't work in helping people out of poverty, or for government.

---

* Peter Passell and Leonard Ross, "Daniel Moynihan and President-Elect Nixon: How charity did not begin at home," *New York Times*, 14 January 1973, quoted in Rutger Bregman, "The bizarre tale of President Nixon and his basic income bill," *The Correspondent*, 17 May 2016.

WHERE ARE WE GOING?

We know that people under stress act with poorer judgement. We know that people need to focus on more than their next meal or bill. UBI is not a panacea of problem-solving on its own, but it is a different approach with advantages that can work. A basic income would be given to everyone. Everyone means everyone, whether in work or not. This is its fairness. Everyone has a stake in it. Those who do not want it can donate it, and that is not meant sarcastically, to a cause of their choosing. The income level set would not lead to a comfortable life, it would be enough to cover basics and keep people above desperate levels of poverty. In so doing it does not take away the motivation to work, it does not make life easy. It means that people can make their own choices on the priority they believe will make their life better.

We know from trials and other schemes that the great majority of people do not 'waste' it on superfluous materialistic or addictive items. Nixon's trials showed very little 'waste' of money by participants. Trials often concentrate on people below the poverty line, such as the Los Angeles $3,000 per month basic income programme that was for 3,000 L.A. families drawn by lottery from eligible citizens with no strings attached, begun in 2021. Stockton is a below-state-income multi-ethnic Californian city. The *Stockton (USA) Economic Empowerment Demonstration (SEED)*, launched in February 2019, offered a two-year, $500-per-month income with no strings such as work requirements, and that was protected against losses to key existing benefits. First year assessed results included improved health and job prospects, and an improved sense of self-determination and personal and family stability, with only 1% of money spent on alcohol or tobacco. Exemplar participant benefits included better relationships because family and friends were not being asked for money on a regular basis; having the funds to leave a 'bad marriage'; and being able to take time off work to gain qualifications for a more stable and higher-paying job. Over time it also reduced involvement with payday lenders and has begun to improve trust in government employees. This was a small sample of only 125 but included median and lower-income participants, and a control group.* An earlier trial in eleven villages in Madhya

---

* "Preliminary analysis: SEED's first year," *Stockton Economic Empowerment Demonstration*, www.stocktondemonstration.org.

THE ECONOMY

Pradesh state in India for one year in 2011–12 with longer follow-up was determined to have beneficial effects including improved welfare issues, stimulating the local economy, and emancipatory effects such as less bonded labour, less loans, and greater female influence: 'I have money. I am fearless. I am liberated,' said one recipient.[*] The Indian government's 2016–17 *Economic Survey of the Union Budget* stated that UBI is 'ripe for serious discussion.'[†] Larger trials are badly needed. UBI also needs to have options of support, which might include support in planning, in financial management, or links to expertise to explore options for someone's ambitions. There is a logic in ensuring the same stability and ability to plan for individuals as we expect of institutions. If employers thought that they could reduce wages then a basic guarantee of an income is a safety net that allows someone to look for another job instead. UBI can also simplify welfare with no means-testing forms and discriminatory or priority judgements within constrained budgets. It does not allow benefit-withholding or lack of take-up, and bypasses feelings of shame. Women, minorities, and other 'hidden' groups do not lose out. There would still need to be welfare support, but this would have more chance of being targeted at solving specific issues for people: a drug addict with a UBI still needs drug addiction treatment, and the onus is to make that more available to be able to use their new income wisely; a woman seeking refuge from domestic abuse still needs the availability of a refuge and immediate support to get life back to safety and on a new track. UBI does not solve every problem and should not be expected to. It does get us nearer to dealing with poverty itself. More hope and planning mean less stress and less debt, with better health and less conflict. All that means less pressure on mental health, physical health, and child and adult welfare services; less chance of homelessness and associated dangers; less pressure on law enforcement and the courts; less isolation, and less dependence on hidden welfare such as sofa-

---

[*] Guy Standing, *Basic income: A guide for the open-minded*, Yale University Press, 2017, and the 12-minute film he also showed at a *TED Talk* in 2018 illustrating the trial in Madhya Pradesh.

[†] Vanya Mehta, "The great Indian basic income debate," *Open Democracy*, 14 November 2019 (outlines India's path to UBI so far). See also R. Ratchana, "Impediments to successful implementation of Universal Basic Income scheme in India," *Times of India*, 28 January 2023.

surfing hosts and relatives' handouts. It can mean less loan sharks or rent arrears; and released prisoners getting a more realistic new start. What applies to adults receiving UBI and seeking to make positive change applies even more to the effect on children in benefitting households whose early stability will have an effect for the rest of their lives through less material and mental hardship.

All these things are difficult to quantify or put an accountant's number on. There could be greater demand on some services as people seek, with advice and planning, to move away from the parts of their life that hold them back. UBI is not a solve-all solution, and good UBI will be part of the increasing recognition that we already have of wrap-around services that some people need. Some people will not respond well and will continue destructive lives; some people will take time to realise that they can make positive change and take time to seek or accept advice. Economists may worry, for example, that people moving to better-paid jobs by gaining higher qualifications, may stoke inflation. We must not be so 'scientific' or 'efficient' in our approach to demand every penny is accounted for by each person with a receipt. Dependence will only be reduced and personal confidence increased if we allow more freedom and more control for those receiving UBI, even as we promote advice. We, people and government, must avoid preconceived assumptions or criticisms. It can help people to address the causes of their poverty on the individual and family basis that is best for them. Nor does this forego any form of democratic accountability for sums spent and operational efficiency of the system itself; or minimise long-term research into real-world effects.

UBI needs specific, political, or politicised, decisions on issues such as the level of payment, does it apply to all adults individually or is it family-based, what current welfare payment could be expected to end, and how might others change or raise criteria for provision. If it is given to children's accounts is that expected to replace child allowance and can it be built up over years; does it begin at an age when they can have more say in its use, etc. Any system and payment level must make sure that those currently depending on welfare – long term or short term – are not made worse off. To which some people then ask, why give it to those that do not need it? How can we possibly afford it for everyone?

THE ECONOMY

Affordability is in two things: savings and priority. Taking the need for welfare from more 'in-work' poor reduces the number of claimants, even if this is not a 'gain' because it is balanced by the greater awareness of need for wrap-around services and guidance asked for, encouraged by the stability given from their UBI. Currently most countries already have some form of tax-free level of income – potentially a step already made towards UBI. For better-off but not rich people more spending power is good for the economy, and to choose more savings enhances their own and general economic resilience in tougher times; and is part of the civic benefit of giving it to all. Giving more may not reduce the inequality gap but does at least reduce absolute poverty and raises the prospect of upward mobility. If more spending power stokes inflation that is an issue for the government to address. Money could even be spent by people on those activities made possible by a shorter working week, with a multiplying value in its consequences. National health services are brought about by a shared philosophy of helping others that we could help, of 'my neighbour's health is my health,' and of 'there but for the grace of God go I' self-interest. In an age of widening inequality we need to rekindle that approach. We must have the values to help, build the systems to help, and have the incentive to help. UBI can be made to work. It would be a big change that requires a political and societal consensus, because it cannot be something over one election cycle. Like any major governmental initiative it is the job of leadership to provide such vision, integrity, consensus, transparency, and accountability. To many these are increasingly elusive talents but there is no inevitability about that, nor an inevitability of automatic partisanship in the face of well-constructed trials and legislation. As Nixon thought, UBI can be a policy with benefits for all sides of the argument. It can also be a policy with benefits for democracy. Less inequality and more productive engagement mean more cohesiveness and a stronger society. UBI is about giving people a renewed sense of worth and a renewed actual worth. UBI is a democratic response to a creaking social contract.

During the Covid-19 pandemic local authorities across the world were encouraged to house the homeless. Bigger projects like reducing homelessness cannot be solved by UBI, but it can contribute. For many homeless people it was their first stability for years, and their first safety. Successful schemes accessed health services, and 'contact' services to advise on housing and benefits and education and finance. Unsurprisingly people got healthier, happier, and more hopeful. Some rekindled their ambitions to live what many others would call a normal life but which to them was inaccessible. It didn't work for all. Some improvements were temporary, some preferred life on the street, but many people's lives continued to improve, and a better chance of work followed too. This homelessness example illustrates that 'universal' support schemes are not a panacea but can make a difference.

Saving Capitalism for the Capitalists

In conclusion, unless you want a complete revolution, then, ironically, society must save capitalism for the capitalists. However, we need to reassess what capitalism – making money through invention and innovation – is for. Specifically, who it is for, and we need to reassess how it works now. Adam Smith's *Theory of Moral Sentiment* clearly lays out that its aim should be to raise the standard of life of the citizens of a nation as well as the nation's wealth. More people than ever before understand that capitalism is constructed, an artificial set of rules and routines and traditions and values and beliefs promoted to serve a narrative. We need to be clear what change we want to promote. We have largely forgotten that free markets depend upon non-free markets, on the infrastructure of roads and laws to make it, or allow it, to work. This balance needs re-stating and re-working. Trickle-down economics doesn't work. Those in the middle in developed nations have seen their real incomes stagnate. Those at the bottom have only survived through state action. The rich have got considerably richer. Capitalism has moved away from balancing labour and capital. Profit capitalism has narrowed further to shareholder capitalism. It has become exploitative. Incomes have risen but so has inequality. 'Low' wages have been allowed to be supplemented by government, rather than business being forced to pay a real living wage. Too many people live on credit or debt, or with the fear of one unmanageable setback. Life expectancy is no longer rising and for some in developed nations is falling. At least half of people

THE ECONOMY

think their children will be poorer.* Either inequality is a problem or people (or groups, or whole nations) think there is enough opportunity for it to be motivating, or they think they can isolate themselves from it and its consequences, which themselves are a failure of morality and understanding. Big business seems to get more thought than smaller or self-employed business. In the USA 99% of all businesses are small businesses (less than 500 employees). According to the Small Business Administration in 2019 small business accounted for 44% of GDP, created two-thirds of new jobs, and produced sixteen times more new patents per employee than large patenting firms. Thirty-six per cent of small businesses were owned by women, and 15% had black, Latinx or Asian owners, making them more representative of the community. For each $1 spent at the business a small business funnels back into the community 68%, but large businesses 46%.† In agriculture, supply chains seem to work in reverse, more demand than supply. Producing food in many places is effectively uneconomic without subsidy. In Germany in 2018–19 one kilo of milk sold in shops for about 50 cents but cost 64 cents to produce.‡ Developing nations are being suffocated by the international demand for completely open markets. This chokes the development of a solid base from which to develop the infrastructure and the domestic economic strength they need to place their own economies on a surer footing. Internationally, bananas serve as an equivalent example to German milk.§ These are our current economics. We measure what can be bought and sold in our GDP and the more we do so the less we pay attention to why we do so. There is an array of 'national health' rather than 'national wealth' measures available to

---

* "Poorer than their parents? Flat or falling incomes in advanced economies," *McKinsey Global Institute,* McKinsey&Company, July 2016, 4.
† "Small businesses are the backbone of the economy," *Better Accounting,* 11 August 2020; J. Mariah Brown, "How important are small businesses to local economies?" *CHRON,* 15 October 2018.
‡ Graham Ruddick, "Milk price row: the key questions," *The Guardian,* 11 August 2018. "Milk production: what really drives the price of milk," *Food Unfolded* by the European Institute of Innovation and Technology (EIT), an EU linked body under Horizon Europe. Like other foodstuffs, supermarket competition, demand fluctuations, cost of fertiliser, fuel, etc may all affect the price.
§ Joe Fassler, "Bananas are getting cheaper. That low price comes with hidden costs," *The Counter,* 2019. *The Counter* is a non-profit, independent newsroom 'investigating the forces shaping how and what America eats.'

WHERE ARE WE GOING?

remind us why we work and make money, from the Happiness Index of Bhutan to the UN's Human Development Index to the OECD's Better Life Index, looking at health, education, security and safety, human rights, environmental health, civic engagement, natural wealth, and personal fulfilment. To resignedly decide that a nation must manage a decline is overly pessimistic, and itself a view bound by the expectations and measurements of our current economics.

A second reassessment is therefore about the responsibility our economic model plays in the provision of the social contract that binds people to people and people to government. The social contract in developed nations is cracking or falling apart. It is inhibited from development in nations where it is not already fully formed. Wealth and inheritance need to be taxed in different ways to now, achieving a new balance with working income, which alone no longer reflects the wealth of too many people. Since the start of the Covid-19 pandemic 651 American billionaires have on paper gained $1 trillion in wealth, enough to give 'every American' $3,000.* How much money is it reasonable for people to accumulate, or to set up their children for life with, until it becomes obscene to everyone else, $10million or £100million or $1 billion? Inequality breeds resentment as well as motivation. How many times an income should a leader be allowed to have more than the average of their workforce, 100x, 200x? How does share price (affecting dividends, investment, and status) balance standard of living or worker conditions? We have allowed property prices to become a free market touchstone. 'Key workers' are not key when it comes to pay or conditions. What role is there for government, shareholder governance, or legislative action? How effectively are we addressing discrimination in careers, pay, and conditions? We have lost sight of the 'common good.' Someone earning far more than they need can choose to give it away or agree a lower salary if they want – how many do so? Our economic values have become lost in a mist of individualism and materialism. We compare our pay with others rather than with what we need or want, and we constantly convert wants to needs. We must not leave our humility at the door of our workplace, or the shopping

---

* Robert Reich, "Trickle-down economics doesn't work but build up does – is Biden listening?" *The Guardian*, 20 December 2020.

mall, or anywhere else. Individual liberty and freedom have become competitive rather than a matter of true opportunity and have become sacrosanct at the expense of community – that we also benefit from. Other cultures have maintained a stronger focus on community, but they have to fight to hold onto it in the face of Western materialist and competitive philosophy. We have lost our individual responsibility for the social contract and outsourced it to government, who have in turn outsourced it or given arbitration rights to a fixed and inflexible legalism and, arguably, to lobbyists. The social contract for the most vulnerable, providing security and a reasonable standard of living for paid work, has become neglected. Economic man is not all that man is, but it has become pre-eminent in our government. Yes, there are many, many, things that governments do to help people, but we have not addressed the core issues of this failing social contract for at least forty years; we have only tried to manage them.

As we reassess how our economic model is working and who it is working for, we must also acknowledge that the circumstances in which we are living are changing profoundly. Even if manufacturing companies are enticed back to the developing world away from cheaper labour nations they will return with increased automation, and only with tax breaks. Over the next fifty years automation will affect unskilled and technical jobs, and then jobs that allegedly require creativity or 'reliable judgement.' New industries will be created, but enough jobs, and with what sort of transition? Labour itself has become less essential. Global communication and travel also means global comparisons and knowledge, and more migration, with consequences for economics, identity, and politics... right up to the point when working populations begin to fall, which is already producing other problems. Climate change-induced extreme weather events will also encourage migration. Just as labour can move so can capital, and more international agreement will be needed if capital is not simply to be moved about, avoiding the regulations of a country it does not like. The economic strength, political influence, and profit-making models of multinational companies therefore will need greater attention than received at present. If governments cannot reassert more control, either individually or collectively, over the economic levers of power they will be unable to fulfil, or control, the social contract expected of them, and they will lose legitimacy. Their focus may then instead turn to culturally identifying or divisive issues to maintain their relevance. This is happening now.

There are many dangers that can derail the progressive reassessments that we need. A lack of ethics in business management and around automation would make political leadership harder. A lack of leadership in government could be fatal because the result of that is either popular disengagement or more radical campaigns and movements. Poorer-quality governance may set the right path while being done badly, but perhaps not irretrievably. In the end poor governance must face the wrath of an electorate or an explosion of radical feeling from a resentful populace. An unresponsive democracy fails as a democracy and moves along the spectrum to rule by sectional interest. This is just the other side of the coin to an idealistic communistic workers' rule. One scenario we do not yet fully understand is what happens when an economy is encouraged to grow, innovate, and change only within the confines of a specific ideology or one-party or person control. We once thought that economic growth and prosperity would naturally, as part of the human character, produce independent political thought and confidence, but it seems that materialism may be the modern opium of the masses.

Other dangers are international: Developing nations may be left without the support or resources to build up their own domestic economies, and their own social contract. Cheap jobs may not become better-paid ones that can pay for improving infrastructure and services, resulting in unstable government. This may also happen in the event of emerging defined economic blocs that exclude them; or if international institutions like the WTO or World Bank are ineffective and unrepresentative. Another scenario is war. While war can inspire elements of invention and innovation its destructive power can wipe everything off the chessboard and a whole new game is begun. War changes governments, alters the priorities of a generation, and reduces infrastructure, capital, and even available labour. A new 'cold war' scenario between different blocs of nations may result in the end of economic globalisation for generations, and a radical altering of priorities and capabilities. Only anarchists and megalomaniacs really want to use war as a 're-set' mechanism. To this list can be added those persistent and extensive extreme weather events that make areas inhospitable or produce intensive destruction; and as we now know such a global disaster as a health pandemic of unknowable length. All these dangers are real. We have seen that all these dangers can test the most resilient of nations.

Yet we must not automatically look for a dystopian future. OECD research estimates that by 2030 (perhaps add a few years due to Covid-19) 50% of the world's population will be 'middle class,' up from just over 20% as recently as 2009, and two-thirds of them will be in Asia. This is global change on a grand scale. Douglass North also wrote that 'we are just beginning to see the serious study of institutions.' We appreciate the central impact of governance and civic and governmental institutions and stability in economic development more than ever before, i.e., the very nature of society makes a key difference to economic growth and development.* These two trends alone can produce a foundation to cope with the dangers we face in our economic outlook. However, what we have now at the very least needs refinement. Greater global and democratic dialogues can play their part in this. A reassessment in new circumstances of our competitive Enlightenment-style capitalist economic model, based on permanent 'progress' as defined by materialistic and individualist gain, can produce new opportunities. In reviewing the purpose of what we do we can reimagine the world of work. We can address inequalities and discriminations in the system and use new technologies and innovations to work for us. We can reconfigure what is important to us personally, nationally, and internationally… if we re-find our willingness to work co-operatively. If we can do that then we can find democratic opportunities for renewal that non-democratic nations cannot do, and that rebuild trust in government and add a new shine to democracy itself. Fairer tax systems, hybrid entrepreneurs, open-source research, a four-day working week, and a domestic UBI may or may not play a part in that renewal. Without belief that we should, and that we can, influence or control that renewal, then inequality and dysfunction will continue or get worse.

---

*Yueh, 2018, 264, quoting North, 1990, 140. "Earning between $10 and $100 per day, enough to buy a fridge – a global measurement of middle-class earning power!"

V

CONFLICT

...travel is fatal to prejudice, bigotry, and narrow-mindedness.
Mark Twain.[*]

Conflict is often thought to be a 'survivalist' aspect of human nature. However, our current science, and a growing movement to go back to the origins and establishment of humanity, increasingly bring this into question. We must look again at the problem of conflict. Unless we want to believe that only conflict drives us to make progress, or gives us 'enemies' necessary to define us, then we have a duty to work out how we can reduce or eliminate it. That means all types of conflict, including crime such as domestic abuse, discrimination, and war. It may seem odd or controversial to think of all these harms together, but the moral problem is surely the same: why do we harm others, and can we stop?

Thomas More's *Utopia* in the 16th century, wrote that Man's humanity was itself a treaty to others. This was both his common humanity through his Christianity – 'do unto others,' etc – and his politics, in the context of oaths of loyalty in the time of the developing Reformation. He believed that treaties, between men or nations, were borne from mistrust. This was not the same as Law, which was the policy and practicality of 'Ethics.' Ethics being the boundaries of belief.

---

[*] Mark Twain, *The Innocents Abroad, or The New Pilgrims' Progress*, 1869, quote taken from Rutger Bregman, *Humankind: A Hopeful History*, 2020, 364.

WHERE ARE WE GOING?

We do not by consensus or in scripture, believe in 'murder,' so we have laws that forbid it, such as the original 'Thou shalt not commit murder/kill,' Sixth Commandment for Jews and Christians from Exodus 20:13 which we place a faith in 'government' to enforce.* We have also defined murder more specifically than 'killing' to fit our own preferences. For some people abortion is murder, but they may support the death penalty. For some people going to war may be justifiable but discrimination based on race or gender is not. On a very fundamental level there are clear inconsistencies at work between societies around the world, within them, and within individuals.

Religious or cultural beliefs do not act as clear dividers between accepting conflict or rejecting it. Women have been and remain much less responsible for conflict although there is a perception that there are more violent women now than before. Women make up just under 5% of the full UK prison population and about 10% of the USA federal and state prison population, partly from the mid-1980s' 'war on drugs,' having been a flat line since 1925 until then.†‡ Globally they still make up only 7% of the prison population, but this has risen by 33% over the last 20 years compared to a male increase of 25%.§ Neither perceptions of physical strength or empathy are decisive in deciding the approach of women themselves towards conflict. Nor is there evidence of one race being more prone to conflict than any other, although the last 250 years of colonialism and world war don't present white Europeans in a good light.

Many people think that we have lost the 'art' of peace, despite a preponderance of the 'architecture' of peace through laws and institutions. Steven Pinker's *The Better Angels Of Our Nature* paints a

---

* 'murder' in the *New International Version* of the Bible, 'kill' in the King James Bible, although they can be interpreted differently.
† "Women in prison," *House of Commons Justice Committee Report*, UK Parliament, July 2022, https://committees.parliament.uk/publications/23269/documents/169738/default/.
‡ Aleks Kajstura and Wendy Sawyer, "Women's mass incarceration: The whole pie, 2023," *Prison Policy Initiative*, 1 March 2023. The American criminal justice and prison system is complicated by having federal, state, local (and tribal) differences. The 'non-profit, non-partisan' Prison Policy Initiative advocates for criminal justice reform in the USA and was founded in 2001. https://www.prisonpolicy.org/reports/pie2023women.html.
§ "Global prison trends 2022," *Penal Reform International*, https://cdn.penalreform.org/wp-content/uploads/2022/05/GPT2022.pdf.

picture of the steady (but he does not say inevitable) erosion of violence. He identifies different stages of progress, such as development of government, consistency and faith in law enforcement, and individual rights. He identifies reasons such as the development of education. Writers like Rutger Bregman do not agree with this 'violent Neanderthal to peaceful modern humanity' timeline. He argues that humanity itself must be viewed in the entirety of its history and that this determines a different interpretation. The journey of human nature is different, the positive idea that we can be more peaceful in the future is similar. The two acknowledge that humanity has changed, and can do so again. The idea of nomadic hunters and pastoralists being co-operative *before* giving way to competition has more recently gained a foothold. In this approach communities developed through shared farming and belief, which produced specialism, hierarchy, and government. Urbanisation began. Property ownership developed. Individual rights to gain property, gain 'wealth,' gain status, all developed, and in doing so a competitive system of living emerged around the world. Chiefs, monarchs, city-states, and nations arose. We now call the economic aspect of this system a 'market economy,' after the market trading towns of the Middle Ages. Industrialisation magnified this competitiveness into what we call Capitalism. This model was then exported around the world to become dominant over subsistence and mutually supportive work. Government, money, and urbanisation changed people's relationships to each other. This did not happen quickly and was not without subtlety. Nations formed to unite people in a common narrative often defined by threat or competition and so intentionally and internationally competition was channelled. People and resources were exploited. Religion moved in alliance with governments and nations. In these ways competition led to conflict. Different theories can still be squared together: there was resistance by the oppressed, reflections by philosophers, a self-interested moderation of power, and in time institutions arose, and the idea of rights. Thomas Hobbes' idea of naturally brutish Man was moderated, or managed, or controlled, by the 'social contract' of Jean-Jacques Rousseau. But all of this had, and has, conflict built in.

The acceptance of conflict is based on an acceptance of winners and losers and of some being better than others. Now we see this on an international scale. Modern sciences show how we separate people into 'familiar' and 'other' and therefore justify conflict and discrimination. Those who argue it is natural to think of people unlike ourselves differently must ask themselves why. 'Murder' and 'crime' are defined by whether people conform to our norms. Equality has parameters of whether people are on 'our' side, familiar, or competitors.

The United Nations Charter Preamble, signed in 1945 includes: '... *to reaffirm faith in fundamental human rights, in the dignity and worth of the human person, in the equal rights of man and woman and of nations large and small... to promote social progress and better standards of life in larger freedom, ... to practice tolerance and live together in peace...*' These were radical concepts in the 1945 context of much of the world not being independent, socially progressive, or democratic. When we look at them now, we see a very mixed picture of success. We should remember that historically the time has been short, that the world has changed a lot for the better, and that we know there can still be positive change. We also know that often change is fragile, and that economic depression, authoritarian regimes, and natural disaster can all result in backward steps. What we do not often entertain is the idea that the systems that we promote can also act against progress and co-operation. Liberal impatience often ignores the depth of social, behavioural, governmental, and economic movement needed in societies, and hence the historic nature of what we demand. Aristotle said that some people were born to be slaves. Hobbes said that rulers were superior by nature. Yuval Noah Hariri wrote in *Sapiens* 'Complex human societies seem to require imagined hierarchies and unjust discrimination.'* Surely this is an attitude that can be changed through communication, education, and different government, shaping new knowledge, understanding, and perspective.

Competition and conflict, it should be noted, are not the same. In 'good' society regulation is not arbitrary or random; it is 'law.' Not everyone is the same, naturally. Someone will do something first, or worse, or better, or differently, or just out of immaturity or experimentation or creativity. Angels may only need a common philosophy, but real people need boundaries to ambition and relationships. Within fair, consistent,

---

*Yuval Noah Hariri, *Sapiens*, 2014, 253.

understood and generally accepted law, competition may thrive and yet conflict may be accountably managed and suppressed or minimised. This is a key role of government. Rousseau's social contract was a shared *Will* and a *Sovereignty*, to better preserve individuals and community. This is domestic peace, but can surely be applied to conflict between individuals or nations too, and if not, why not?

Crime, Punishment, and Justice

Crime varies from opportunistic 'petty' crime, premeditated violence, anonymous scams, large-scale corruption, and gender-based and hate crimes. It can be local or international. The cause of a crime may be poverty, earning power, or the exertion of power, and be psychological, sociological, or ideological. These include peer and social pressure, individual isolation, self-esteem and worth, and health issues. It might be said that the only pre-requisite is nerve. Crime has changed and is changing through advances in technology and communication, and what we think of as crime has changed over time. Most criminals think they won't get caught. Most people committing 'day-to-day' criminal acts are relatively young. Most adult criminals would prefer a worthwhile and respectable legal income, but reoffending is relatively high. Most people do not commit crime and think of punishment before rehabilitation for those convicted. Crime costs everyone either directly or indirectly, emotionally, financially, and in their view of other people and the world at large. In short, crime has a multiple number of forms, causes, and consequences.

Before we consider solutions and our ideas of justice let us quickly touch on three aspects of what we may consider about crime that seem to have increasing currency: the science of committing crime, discrimination in crime, and crime as 'self-harm.' Crime as 'self-harm' may appeal to our sense of enlightenment by questioning whether anyone would wish to commit a crime of their completely free will. This may either encourage support or encourage us to see a character defect and relinquish responsibility for context or circumstances. If we want to 'solve,' or at least seriously address, crime we need to look at context and policy too. Our perception of crime (and justice) is also likely to be influenced by discrimination. As we interact with many more people we have readjusted the antennae that determines the level of threat we see to our safety *and* interests, with 'familiar' or 'other' self-reinforced, usually from a preponderance of 'negative' news. This has a fundamental effect on our perceptions of fairness and justice. The responsibility of news organisations to present balanced or alternative or simply explanatory and reasoned news is therefore enormous. People also have their own civic responsibility to understand the sources of their news. Thirdly, physical sciences think they see parts of the brain aligned to, or influenced by, character traits — honesty, stubbornness, deception, violence, etc. This is a work in progress and science has not always been right in the past. There is a danger, as with other foci of science, that we expect definitive unchanging pronouncements to affirm current views or to justify a specific future course of action. We should remember that we are nowhere near understanding the complexities of the brain's interactions, although this will not stop science offering different biological, psychological, and sociological perceptions of, and 'causes' of, crime, and imply remedies. We should bear in mind these developing ideas, and nature and nurture, when we consider 'Crime.'

Punishment and Justice

Ask any cross-section of the public what the outcome of a conviction should be, and the collective answer is usually harsher than judges would pronounce. Recompense to the community, education, or rehabilitation are not necessarily ignored but are frequently downgraded. Victim-perpetrator meeting in the context of some form of listening, discussion, reconciliation, or 'restorative justice' is not the norm. Nevertheless, it is generations since blood feuds formed the basis of justice in Europe, and we have deliberately moved away from the victim or their friends and family deciding the punishment; or punishment for violent crime being a financial penalty or boon to the treasury. However, crime will always feel personal for the victim. The public gets its say in the laws passed in their name. Even where judges are elected or politicised the notion of justice being independent, fair, consistent, and transparent, proving guilt not innocence, and with justifiable decisions, are key differences between free democratic societies and authoritarian ones. However, in many countries unofficial blood feuds, public shaming, and legal family consequences remain acceptable or acquiesced in, and these can range from tattoo 'branding' in a Russian prison to house demolition across the Middle East. This is both societal discouragement of crime and societal intimidation – remember, the West is often seen as soft on criminal punishment – although it may also be misused as governmental political intimidation. This divergence is part of the individual–community tension across the world. No system is perfect, because people (police officers, lawyers, witnesses, jurors, judges) are not perfect, but free societies seek to improve justice, un-free ones seek to preserve or improve control.

Some form of historical hypocrisy or inconsistency is common: when the Islamic State put people in cages for display or for public burning it was thought of as a zealotry unseen in Europe since the Inquisition of the 16th and 17th centuries, although slavery and the Holocaust are just two more recent examples. Public executions under judicial directive still take place in various places around the world, as do public floggings; and trial by media and paramilitary police forces are widespread.

The current conditions of many prisons around the world whether by design or lack of resources still shout of degradation and neglect. In 2020 Haiti's prisons were the world's most overcrowded at 454% of normal capacity. By comparison USA is at 103% and ranked 113th. Studies in the UK, Sweden, and Australia show about 60% of the prison population have difficulties in basic literacy, although these figures are not so different to the averages for people from similar socio-economic backgrounds. Twenty-four per cent of UK prisoners reported having been in social care at some point; 42% reported having been permanently excluded from school; 29% had experienced abuse, and 41% had seen abuse as a child in the home, often of alcohol or illegal drugs.[*] There must be punishment and the protection of society, yet although few

---

[*] "The world's 10 most overcrowded prison systems," *World Atlas,* accessed April, 2022; Christina Clark and George Dugdale, "Literacy changes lives," *National Literacy Trust,* November 2008. UK figures from "Prisoners' childhood and family backgrounds," Ministry of Justice, 2012, www.justice.gov.uk.

remain in prison for the rest of their life, we have morally abandoned those whom we recognised as vulnerable when they were young. We expect growing maturity, understanding of society and stake-holding within it but so often little is done to encourage those things after the switch is flicked from child to adult for those we called vulnerable. For some this will just be 'nanny state' left-wing nonsense that ignores the protection of society, or order, even of the 'character-building lessons' that might be learnt through conviction and punishment. In many Eastern or Confucian societies order and community come well before individual rights, and it is possible that Western nations have not paid enough attention to this. More fundamentally it may seem to mark a dividing line between the idea of humanity as naturally aggressive or co-operative.

However, it is still true that most convicts are at some point set free with the expectation that they will then be law-abiding positive contributors to society, and we do not give them much help to be so, as their literacy, housing, health needs etc, remain. In the UK from 2021 a Discharge Grant of £76 is now given for living expenses in the first week, having risen from £46 in 2020, the first rise in twenty-five years. In the USA eleven states restrict voting rights for some or all individuals even after they have served a prison sentence and are no longer on parole or probation. As of 2020 one in seven black citizens are disenfranchised in seven US states.* What citizenship do authorities expect? Or even the return value of resources put into imprisonment? This latter example also illustrates the historic origins of some of our actions that we have not addressed. On what foundations are our justice systems based, or how were they shaped that still resonate now? What past does feudal class, historic slavery, or political ideas of 'the mob' or idleness play? By what means do we compare 'white collar' to 'blue collar' crime? Using what balance sheet of expenditure and return do we judge the effectiveness of our convictions, punishments, and release? This alone should cause us as a society to reflect on what we do. Nations that prize communal order far above, as opposed to slightly or level with, individual rights need to ask themselves whether fear and justice directed from an authority

---

* Jean Chung, "Voting rights in the era of mass incarceration: A primer," *The Sentencing Project*, July 2021.

above result in a better society? The answer for some people will still be that society is safer, though that may be temporary, and law-abiding citizens can get on with their life. This may be an aspect of Rousseau's social contract – but is the lawgiver democratically and evidentially responsive, or repressive? Eternal vigilance may be the price of liberty but mercy, or in modern parlance justice, is also a mark of humanity.

Punishment for spectacle should have no place in a moral justice system. Independence of the judiciary from deliberate revenge is essential. In some form the punishment should fit the crime, in recompense or proportion, and make society and the individual better off. This is not about making the convict's life easier. It is about future prevention. It can re-establish a broken link between perpetrator and society at large. Even a consideration of expenditure and value in (prison) punishment needs to go beyond the time they are in prison. That may have serious benefit, but what comes next? How does society improve and prevent the next generation repeating those failures?

When a teacher has a class of thirty with two troubling students the teacher knows that concentrating relatively more (not all) resources on those two will reap dividends for those two and the rest whose lives, or lessons, are more peaceful and more fruitful as a result. This approach is not easy and nor can it be done on the cheap. However, a lifetime of welfare and social security and health and law enforcement spending might also be saved. Nor should the lack of a perfect answer or perfect results cancel recognition of more limited success. This sees not so much crime itself but justice as a personalised 'health and welfare' issue, like addiction or depression, maybe even like education, and for the benefit of all. This is the moral change or standpoint that society needs to develop. There will still be people that commit crime – especially when young people test the boundaries – and victims should still be able to highlight the personal and perhaps devastating effects. There will still be long-term career criminals impervious to help and crimes so heinous as to warrant a life term of imprisonment. Prisons will still be needed but nearly all prisoners are eventually released. Where is the leadership and investment needed to cut crime and to prevent reoffending by say, 50%? In the UK reoffending constitutes 80% of all cautions and convictions and costs an estimated £18billion per year.* In the UK and USA about 25% and 44% respectively of those released reoffend within one year. Norway has one of the lowest rates, 20% reoffending within two years. These three nations had incarceration rates per 100,000 people of 130, 639, and 49 respectively in 2021.† Why are incarceration and reoffending rates so different in comparative countries? Are we trying to improve, or just to control and manage? How successful have we been so far?

In a practical sense we think of understanding crime and criminals in terms of Motive, Opportunity, and Means. A police detective's ABC might equally resonate in terms of how we study crime and criminals: make no Assumptions, Believe no-one, and Check everything. Is this the rigour we apply to our own thoughts and policies on crime and justice? Self-improvement books, habits of effective people or good leadership, and addiction recovery, all include the ideas of knowing oneself, clear aims, marshalling resources including others, being self-critical to build, recognising success, and building up systems and behaviours to sustain that success. We already have various theories and strategies that allow us to critically evaluate our relationship with crime and criminality. The question is whether we have the moral clarity and willingness to act.

Evidence: The Bystander, Golem and Pygmalion, and Pluralistic Ignorance

We know that perceptions influence how we think and the judgements we make. In 1964 the murder of Catherine Genovese in New York was used at the time to prove the 'bystander effect,' namely that people do not naturally help each other.‡ That is a nightmarish view. However, later study has cast a different light. When people heard screams they telephoned the police. They *did* try to help. Only a few days later members of the public intervened in a burglary and caught

---

* Ministry of Justice, UK.
† Ministry of Justice UK October 2021. Bureau of Justice Statistics, part of Department of Justice, USA, www.bjs.ojp.gov. Various sources incl. www.worldpopulationreview.com and additional information from independent group World Prison Brief at www.prisonstudies.org. NB. Not all national figures measure the same thing.
‡ Bregman, 2002, 182–187.

the murderer of Catherine Genovese. Community-based police forces know that public engagement is key to fighting crime. It is common to believe that nowadays people stand around filming an incident rather than helping. The death of George Floyd in 2020 in the USA was filmed by bystanders, but they included bystanders making a deliberate choice to record as witnesses, and bystanders clearly attempting to help the situation by attempting to get the police officers involved to act differently. In 2020 at a Black Lives Matter demonstration in London a BLM supporter physically lifted and carried away a counter-protester from a conflict for his own safety.* These latter two examples may be 'highlights' or exceptional, but they are not so unusual. It is possible that telling the good news of these examples and others, and providing some education about 'how,' can help to create a virtuous circle of action by others. It doesn't make it easy, but it makes it more doable. It could be as commonplace as how to use a defibrillator or a fire extinguisher.

American philosopher William James' 1896 lecture *The Will to Believe* promoted the idea that it was possible to believe something without first having evidence. British philosopher Bertrand Russell coined the phrase *The Will to Doubt* in 1958, which encouraged a concentration on the facts, not allowing oneself to be shaped by, as we might say now, our biases.† Social scientists think of a 'Golem Effect' which essentially translates as 'if you expect less of people, you will get less from them.' Let us first consider the opposite: the 'Pygmalion Effect,' if you expect more of someone you are more likely to get more from them. Considering these 'effects' can alter the balance of how we think about our relationships with people we know and people we do not know at all. We must remember individuality but these ideas can be applied with success across a whole swathe of areas. Teachers know that if you denigrate a student they are more likely to fail and to fulfil that negative characterisation. Teachers know that if you expect more of a student they are more likely to try to live up to that expectation. It does not mean they don't need support and confidence-building or

---

* Widely reported, e.g., UK newspaper Clea Skopeliti, "BLM supporter speaks out after carrying counter-protester to safety," *The Guardian*, 14 June 2020. Patrick Hutchinson said 'you just do what you've got to do' and lamented the lack of similar action by those policemen at the scene of George Floyd's death.
† Bregman, 2002, 255–257.

trust-building measures to do so but the positivity is more likely to be rewarded. Education also knows that if you characterise a whole group in a certain way then people – within and outside that group - will see that group in that way, and the characterisation, or stereotype, is hard to break down from *all* sides. Understanding this is a potentially transformative foundation of modern education with target setting and mentoring of students. It is foundational to the idea of role models. It could be equally transformative in business and social policy. Implementing this understanding in relation to tackling discrimination or welfare could have huge positive benefits. In government this is a foundation of Behavioural Insight and 'nudge theory,' nudging people with examples, information, rewards, and positive messages to do 'the right thing.' It still requires integrity in the message and application. It still requires practical resources to help make possible the actions you want to encourage. Hollow insincere slogans are counterproductive.

There is also the idea of 'pluralistic ignorance.' This is the idea that individuals go along with something they don't understand because it seems to them that everyone else understands, and accepts. Therefore, no-one questions the status quo. This is societal complacency, or maybe even complicity. We have a view of crime and justice that may be the result of pluralistic ignorance. Thinking 'beyond the box' or 'blue sky thinking,' to mention just two of the current clichés, is severely constrained in this sphere by the emotional engagement experienced by those directly involved, especially as victims, or representatives of victims, which in practice is also the stance understandably taken by most politicians and policy deciders. However, the apparent permanence of crime and reoffending should lend itself even more to a Pygmalion approach – with monitoring, evidence, and regulation. This would be courageous, but new approaches can be debated, trialled, and independently assessed. The dangers of reoffending are real and serious, but the potential benefits of change are also enormous. A good detective will acknowledge where the evidence takes them.

A relatively well-known example of the approach of stricter law enforcement was the 'Broken Windows' crime enforcement of New York and other places in the 1980s. The theory was that cracking down on minor crime would stop its escalation into other more serious offences;

and that people would see criminals being caught, they would feel safer, and their communities would in practice be less damaged (and they would appreciate the police more). Crime rates went down, it was hailed a success and copied by other forces. It seemed to show that harshness or 'tough love' worked. However, in subsequent years with a longer perspective and more analytical evidence other consequences became clearer: more offences were criminalised, and more people ended up with criminal records that hindered the rest of their lives, and many of these people were youngsters and otherwise law-abiding. Immaturity as much as criminality was being punished with long-term effects. A higher proportion of those people were from minorities, because the biases of the criminal justice system had not been addressed, and so some groups of people felt more victimised, not safer, and more criminalised. More serious crimes were also less likely to be recorded, investigated, or solved to fulfil the targets and specific policy priorities that had been set. Elsewhere, in places that had not adopted this approach, crime also went down. Evidence had been at best short term and at worst manipulated to fulfil the desired end. This is something to be constantly aware of. 'Broken Windows' was not the only example of this. The USA's 'three strikes and out' in the 1990s, whereby three convictions could result in life imprisonment, also seemed like necessary 'tough love' but resulted in extensive imprisonment for people convicted primarily of relatively minor crimes. It was implemented while supportive welfare services were being reduced, and in a context of increasing demonisation of those who needed welfare. The American ideology of 'standing on your own two feet,' a lack of empathy, a liberal 'tough love,' and a denial of or lack of rigour in evidence, combined to enhance a criminal justice system that promoted the anger of people who saw, or thought they might be affected by, rising crime. Like the 'Broken Windows' approach 'three strikes and out' is now a discredited policy.

Most prisons are 'total institutions' of 'static security,' of strict rules and regulations. Norway has adopted 'dynamic security.'* Rather than

---

* Sven-Erik Skotte, "Dynamic security – perspectives from Norwegian Correctional Service," *European Penitentiary Training Academies Network*, 2019, https://www.epta.info/wp-content/uploads/2019/08/Norway_presentation.pdf. Also see Jessica Benko, "The radical humaneness of Norway's Halden Prison," *New York Times*, 26 March 2015, for a comparison of the American and Norwegian prison systems.

mirroring or confronting the attitudes of its inmates when they arrive in prison it is 'non-complimentary.' It actively seeks to rehabilitate by exemplifying good treatment and expecting that in return. It aspires to release people in a condition where they can become someone's neighbour rather than release someone who has been merely contained for their prison time. Active housing and employment support is given to people on their release. The reward is greater community safety through less reoffending, less further victims, and released prisoners with stability and more likelihood of paying taxes. Even with the support offered it has been shown to be cost-effective. To those that say somewhere like the USA has too many convicted felons and this is too liberal, they need to ask how they believe their own system is working. Privatised prisons, especially those run for profit, find it too necessary to compete on minimum costs and too tempting to exploit prisoners as workers, and are not accountable enough for reoffending. To say that American criminals, or those of other nations, are more violent, or more prone to criminality, begs the question why? And what is being done to change that? The Norwegian approach was taken up by the traditionally law and order Republican American state of North Dakota in 2019. Minor rules were dropped, conversations between wardens and prisoners encouraged, and prisons re-designed. It has worked, with falling prison and reoffending rates. The head of North Dakota's prisons commented: 'I'm not a liberal, I'm just practical.'*

All this doesn't mean that serious crime can be explained away or solved by more welfare. It doesn't mean prisons aren't needed. I have also written about law enforcement, the justice system, prisons, and reoffending, and these are not to be confused. It does mean that understanding criminality is at a premium, that targeting different crime in different ways is at a premium, and that with some crime and some offenders a health and welfare approach within a clear and accepted justice system can work, can be cost-effective, and is more humane. 'Community Policing' is not a perfect solution. Resources and intelligence gathering are needed, serious and organised crime need to be treated differently to individual and community-based crime, and

---

* Quoted in Bregman, 2002, 348, and see 346–348. Also see Cinnamon Janzer, "North Dakota reforms its prisons, Norwegian style," *US News*, 22 February 2019.

biases in criminal justice systems need to be addressed. However, a policing and justice system that does not recognise the context in which people offend or show some faith in the ability of at least some offenders to change, is a failing one.

Domestic Abuse and Violence Against Girls and Women

If one role of government is to promote safety and minimise conflict, why hasn't more been done to eradicate domestic abuse and personalised violence? Modern conventional arguments often come up against provision of 'proof' in law, or interference in private matters, or definitions of abuse. The latter has always changed through history. Rape within marriage was once accepted and now it is not. Domestic abuse is now accepted to include manipulation and neglect as well as physical violence. The idea of 'proof' in a crime often witnessed by only the perpetrator and victim is a difficult legal problem but it also acts as a distraction. Why haven't we put much more effort into the prevention of the problem as opposed to an over-reliance on the judicial process? Taking people to court will always be necessary and difficult but prevention requires far greater effort, including: recognising the damage of financial or familial insecurity; counselling and refuge availability; and a review of male and female attitudes towards partnership. These are policy questions we choose not to do enough to prioritise, or significant social and moral questions we do not do enough to address at either a young educational or societal (i.e., adult educational) level. These are some of the major steps to preventing domestic abuse. Would they cost money? Yes, of course. The average length of stay in a UK Refuge is four months (six in London), often determined by availability of onward housing. A commissioned NEF Consulting report estimates a social return to the public sector (savings in health services, in the criminal justice system, etc) of £4.07 for each £1 invested. The Women's Aid 2020 annual report estimated a real world 'total unit cost' (incl. staffing and support) within assessed quality Refuge services of £31,059 per year per place; a requirement of 5,598 spaces; totalling an estimated £173.8 million annually, but also remember the need for onward support in such as housing and longer-term safety.*

Beyond these costs new policy reflects a more fundamental attitude. Abuse has lifelong effects for adults and witnessing children including alcohol/drug use and other dependencies, mental health issues, and relationship issues. More specific policies like Child Family Allowance or UBI to address family financial insecurity can be massive, but the specific dividends can be equally massive: from addressing part of a mental health epidemic for children and adults, less A&E visits, less work for law enforcement, to the greater engagement of (mostly) women's talents and ambitions in society. The argument about not having unlimited resources and therefore targeting change is a valid one, but what is the direction of our travel? Is the argument about resources, or government power or individual responsibility? How clear is our moral message to the next generation of what is acceptable and what is not? For the year ending March 2021 the police recorded 'domestic abuse-related crimes' at 845,734; which was 18% of all recorded crime (74%/26% of whom were female/male victims).† The UK wide charity SafeLives estimates that female victims on average endure fifty incidents and wait up to three years before seeking help (not necessarily police help), and the ManKind Initiative estimates 49% of men and 19% of women do not tell anyone they are a victim of domestic abuse.‡ There is always likely to be a need for having to deal with difficult domestic harms but is understand-to-prevent driving our policy and our attitudes, or is punishment-after-the-fact being given centre stage? Are we currently striving to solve a problem or striving to manage it?

The World Health Organization in 2021 estimated that about one in three women globally had been subjected to physical and/or

---

* Lucy Hadley, "The whole housing approach – whole housing toolkit," *Domestic Abuse Housing Alliance*, 2020.
† "Crime England and Wales: Year ending March 2016," *Office for National Statistics*, 21 July 2016. And see also year ending March 2021.
‡ "How long do people live with domestic abuse, and when do they get help to stop it?" *Safe Lives*; "Male victims of domestic abuse and partner abuse: 70 key facts." *ManKind Initiative*, June 2023. Both these organisations provide a wealth of factual research in these areas. For the effect on children in abusive households see CSEW for year ending March 2016, Office National Statistics, 27 September 2017. Joanna Moorhead, "Breaking the cycle of abuse," *The Guardian*, 17 September 2013.

sexual violence in their lifetime.* Women's safety has become a part of the *#Metoo*-inspired global movement of protest not just in the Western world but across Latin America, Islamic nations, India, and elsewhere. It draws attention not just to assaults of women but to assaults on women's rights, and to how they are dealt with by (usually male-dominated) governments, the media, and in the criminal justice system; and to patriarch-dominated family life. Some progress has been made, from changes in the law in relation to birth and abortion rights in Latin and Central America; and following several internationally profiled cases, police handling of assaults on women in India. Across the globe the reasons for gender-based violence and poorer treatment of women are varied and common, from pressures on domestic and family life, to cultural traditions, and institutional discrimination. The preponderance of pornography and abuse on social media is also thought to be an increasing factor. Rape as a feature of war is now also more acknowledged as a problem but remains common. Assault, primarily against women, remains under- and inconsistently reported the world over (and therefore figures are not always easily comparable). What most reasons have in common is that abuse is about power, demonstrating power, or keeping someone in their place. What nearly all abuse shows is a lack of respect for, or valuing of, the victim. This is why it is part of the global spread of human rights, and gender equality awareness and protest. In many parts of the world communities struggle with acknowledging the prevalence of domestic (and other) abuse, and victims are often shunned. These latter statements are true in developed and developing nations.

Addiction

The Oxford Dictionary says 'addiction' is 'having formed a dependency on' something. It can apply to anything: chocolate, shopping, gambling, illegal or legal drugs, pornography, and perhaps even conspiracy theories. Buddhists would talk about the need for moderation in all things. We know from our own life experience that anything that dominates our

---

* "Violence against women," *World Health Organization*, 9 March 2021, based on an analysis of data from 2000 to 2018 across 161 countries.

life, our time, our emotional energy, and focus, especially at the expense of real relationships, is likely to be unhealthy for us. Addiction itself persuades into irrationality and self-justification. It induces stress that people want to avoid when they plan to ditch it, even as it causes stress to continue. An addiction, by definition, is something that many people cannot rid themselves of alone. Therefore, just as addiction is a societal problem in the dysfunctional relationships it causes it also requires a community solution. The answer to addiction in all its guises is not simply seeking abstinence; it is connection. While character-based risk-taking may bring neuroscience and maturity into the discussion, the notion of addiction as requiring health and/or welfare intervention is becoming more prevalent. Knowing for example that a twelve-week absence can produce lasting behavioural change and a control mechanism is the sort of science that can be useful in formulating policy and planning resources. However, if the solution to addiction is social and communal it is the skills and courage of human interaction that need to be understood, improve, and applied. Persuading a gambler to accept the consequences of their actions on their family and friends, or a 'couch potato' to get out and about in the fresh air whether alone or with others, are difficult skills. They require empathy, time, integrity in voice and listening and body language, perhaps experience threaded into the content of a conversation, and possibly some specific knowledge. We all need to be a coach or mentor or counsellor now, to know the difference between them, and to know our limitations. While walking clubs or the Samaritans can exist through voluntary action or a charitable business model and grants, professional advice and help usually cost more serious money for expertise, experience, and real resources. In past societies religion may have taken the lead in prevention and addressing these needs with moral-based advice and practical social welfare programmes. Now people expect government to take the lead. Again, there is the debate to be had about state interference and individualism.

We must also consider more the often-youthful origins of addiction. Why are we so lax on children under the age of sixteen having social media accounts and having access to internet gambling, pornography, or self-harm videos? Where are the standards being set? Where is the help being offered to parents without that elusive parent handbook?

For those that say adults would be affected, which in turn infringes their rights, we need to stress that there is a responsibility of society, not just parents, to bring up its children. We need to stress that not acting harms the rights and opportunities and circumstances of both children and adults. There is self-interest for these people too. It might even be argued that this is a dividing line we need between a Western emphasis on individual rights and a more authoritarian or Confucian emphasis on societal order – seeing children as a whole society responsibility. Adults can learn about gambling, unhealthy food, pornography, etc when they are adults. While we give more space to, and listen and debate more, with adolescents to encourage their maturity and forgive them their early sins and mis-directed adventures, let's not pretend that children are just small adults. Deciding on the dividing line between adult and child, and changeable ideas of what is a 'harm,' both need a transparent public consensus. Maturity will not always take hold. Reason, logic, duty, shame, and regulation will not always work, but if this approach reduces the foundations within adults of their addictions by 25% in a generation, then 25% in the next generation then that is an enormous improvement in many people's lives and gives us a better chance of helping the other 50% who need help as adults. This approach would have a profound effect on our health, welfare, and law enforcement agencies. Why, for example, are youth clubs and leisure facilities not widespread, accessible, and free to under-sixteens or even under-twenty-ones? The benefits of social cohesion, informal education, health and fitness, both physical and mental, and laying the groundwork for an adult life encompassing these, have been known for years.

Having started writing this section about addiction, I have finished writing it about children. It is a realistic admission that there will always be addictions that people have, not least from the pressures of adult life itself, but it is also a realistic approach to prevention, not just containment. It is a longer-term approach that requires strategy and perseverance, and leadership and political consensus.

Capital Punishment

In an arguably much more violent age Thomas More wrote that the killing of animals or people, by the death penalty, removes one's humanity and should therefore be done by slaves, if at all. This remains one of the fundamental moral arguments against the death penalty. Who are we to kill another person? Christianity says that we are all from one God, and that God is within us all. We may not know how to reach God in someone we may consider evil, but is that failure, from a Christian point of view, reason to kill someone? It is true in the real world, however, that people may believe in the sanctity of life for the unborn and for law-abiding citizens and yet still believe in the death penalty for others. Let us be clear that this is a moral contradiction. It presupposes that we decide, that we *can* decide, on the boundary between unforgivable evil and forgivable sin. Is therefore, the taking of another life not assuming the decision-making role of God? Or is the ultimate penalty allowable if the free will given by God has been so abused?

The Old Testament, the scripture of Judaism, says that the death penalty is allowable but only as a last resort to protect society and if the consequence of the crime was known and there were witnesses. Reform-minded Jews place pre-eminence, like Christians, on the Commandment 'You shall not murder/kill.' Islam also accepts capital punishment, but forgiveness and peace are constant themes of the Qur'an, as love is for Christians from the New Testament. Capital punishment is, in Sharia law, appropriate for two causes: intentional murder, which the victim's family can insist on or not; and 'spreading mischief in the land' (fasad al-ardh). In some countries this means what may undermine authority or destabilise the state. This in turn can be used to punish apostasy – denying the faith – and such as rape and drug-dealing, but also adultery and homosexuality. These are seen as crimes because they are seen as undermining the values of the faith, and the state, which may be publicly the same or indivisible. Public punishment reaffirms the power and place of those values. Historically, Christian nations have in the past used the same justifications.

Beyond acting for God is the question of whether a society is confident enough, or is so fragile, in its lawgiving and judgement to decide that justice can be fairly and transparently given and have the support of the people. Fragile in the sense that the state or religious authority feels the need to prosecute justice to the extent of capital punishment to defend its authority or position. While upholding the values of faith or state may be the stated aim, and genuine intention in the face of perceived human weakness and temptation, this is an authority or authoritarian-led judgement, more about power than faith or morality or public safety. A fair trial is the minimum expectation but is there a society that can with sincerity believe its judicial system contains no bias against women, or the poor, or minorities, or other group? Can any system of judgement by men and women guarantee not to make mistakes, consciously or unconsciously? Many of the 142 nations that do not now practice capital punishment do this because they recognise that mistakes are made, either in their perception of people, i.e., their biases, or in their search for, handling of, and interpretation of, evidence. They recognise and are not prepared to accept the fallibility of human judgement when someone's life is at stake.

Discrimination

Discrimination is one form of conflict. Treating it as such should inform us with a further moral urgency. This type of conflict may be violent or psychological; it may be open or hidden. In some places specific attitudes and actions may be seen as negative prejudice and discrimination but in other places they may not be. Attitudes and policies in relation to homosexuality and same-sex partnerships are one example. This is often tied to Christian or Islamic beliefs, and is sometimes, especially in the former, seen as originating in colonial attitudes and laws. Prejudice and discrimination in all their forms prevent people from finding and using their talents and contributing to their own and their communities' wellbeing. They produce a trauma within individuals and within groups. Class in the UK, race in the USA, caste in India, tribe in African nations, minority ethnicity and political allegiance in China, all may play a part in deciding employment, livelihood or dependence, health outcomes, government engagement, treatment in the justice system, having a public voice, and in relationships including marriage. Discrimination is intensely personal.

WHERE ARE WE GOING?

The Reach of Discrimination

Anupama S. Chandran's new-born baby was put up for adoption by her high caste parents without her consent because they were unhappy that the father was from the Dalit (previously Untouchable) caste (and ten years older and previously married). Across India only 5% of marriages are cross-caste. Chandran said that her parents, local dignitaries in relatively progressive Kerala State, tried to persuade her to abort the baby, kept her confined, refused contact with the father, and allowed her only three days with her baby before it was taken away by force; saying that the police and local politicians refused to investigate. One state minister had told the media that Chandran's parents 'had done what any parents would do.' After thirteen months the courts ordered her baby to be returned to her. Her parents denied most of her story. This was about caste prejudice and personalised corrupting influence within local politics.*

In the Islamically orthodox Gulf States well-off women can seem to be at ease with a guardianship system for their protection, with relatively liberal male guardians, and a high level of education, health, personal safety, wealth, and comfort. However, for many this remains a 'gilded cage,' dependent on the attitudes of men, with a difference between the practice and letter of the law, with political under-representation, and various degrees of gender separation in social settings and careers. For poorer women the gender discrimination is more obvious as well as being wound up in class and nationality, and the cage is not gilded. A World Economic Forum 2021 survey put Japan 120th/156 in gender equality. Feminism is seen as a largely foreign concept, and there is a large gulf in the mainstream view between an acceptable lifestyle for single and for married women, in public, career, and home-life. 'Ojousan Power' denotes modern Japanese women extending traditional roles.† Women's and girls' rights are part of a globally and deep cross-cultural dialogue.

In England in 2019 24.7% of 'disadvantaged' students in state schools achieved Grade 5 (a 'good pass') in GCSE English and Maths

---

* Hannah Ellis-Peterson, "Give me my baby: An Indian woman's fight to reclaim her son after adoption without consent," *The Guardian*, 9 December 2021.
† "The real loves of Doha's housewives," and, "Ojousan Power," *The Documentary* [podcast], BBC, October/November 2022.

compared to 49.9% of non-disadvantaged students.* In developed nations success is increasingly associated with formal educational qualifications, and in the UK, class has historically been seen as a key factor in opportunity. Education standards may have risen but despite much focus the attainment gap has barely changed. Educational experience is also now being seen as becoming a key factor and identifier of political persuasion.

In the USA, it is race that is the great and obvious division: infant mortality stood in 2021 per 1,000 live births at 10.55 for the non-Hispanic black population, at 7.46 for American Indian, and at 4.36 for non-Hispanic whites. Gaps relating to employment and life expectancy closed from the 1960s but stopped closing from the 1980s.† Sometimes race covers other issues: poor white life expectancy has not improved as much as it has for the black middle-class; and rich Americans have lower life expectancy than rich Europeans. Nevertheless, these and other measures illustrate the historic nature of factors affecting minority race-based discrimination in the USA and show how discrimination can be 'cradle to grave.'

In Nigeria, in 2019 a public opinion poll stated that 44% of respondents believed that people of all tribes in the nation were equal, and 56% did not. Nationally 48% said they themselves or people they knew had experience of opposition to inter-ethnic marriage.‡

---

* 'Disadvantaged' defined as being poor enough to have had Free School Meals (FSM) during secondary education, or having been officially 'looked after' for at least one day, or having been in state care. Changes in educational provision and assessment due to Covid-19 were seen to further widen the gap between these groups. "Key stage 4 performance, 2019 (revised)," (see page 9), *Department for Education*, 2020. https://assets.publishing.service.gov.uk/media/5e3adeeae5274a08e4a7db2d/2019_KS4_revised_text.pdf.

† "Infant mortality rate in the United States in 2020 and 2021, by race and ethnicity of mother," *Statista*, www.statista.com; "Historical unemployment for Black women and men in the United States: 1954-2021," *Brookings*, https://www.brookings.edu/articles/historical-unemployment-for-black-women-and-men-in-the-united-states-1954-2021/; "Table 4. Life expectancy at birth, age 65, and age 75, by sex, race, and Hispanic origin: United States, selected years 1900-2018." *Centers for Disease Control and Prevention*, https://www.cdc.gov/nchs/data/hus/2019/004-508.pdf.

‡ "Poll report on Perception on Tribal Discrimination in Nigeria," *NOIPolls*, Sept 10, 2019, https://www.noi-polls.com/post/poll-report-on-perception-on-tribal-discrimination-in-nigeria. NOI Polls Ltd is a West African specialist polling organisation partnered with Gallup USA. See also Abdul Raufa Mustapha, "Ethnic Structure, Inequality and Governance of the Public Sector in Nigeria," *Centre for Research on Inequality, Human*

Across Africa, and elsewhere, tribalism remains a factor in opportunity, livelihood, social connection, and political influence.

In 2014 the Chinese Communist Party (CCP) under Xi Jinping published new 'Detailed Rules' for party membership in a deliberate effort to make the Party more selective in quality and more representative of the nation, presenting changes as part of his anti-corruption drive. The proportion of women rose (although they remain woefully small in higher positions in the Party); and blue-collar and rural representation fell from 41.5% in 2007 to 34.8% in 2019.[*] His efforts to re-model the CCP have been partially successful but show how difficult it is to overcome traditional discriminations and widen opportunity despite having the absolute power to set the rules. Party affiliation is often seen in one-party nations as the path to success, but it is not so for all.

Roma are officially Hungary's largest minority, at 3.18% according to the 2011 census. Only one-third of Roma children continue from primary to secondary education. An ECHR Report in 2017, based on a specific far-right attack on a Roma village area in 2012, found that perpetrators of anti-Roma actions 'remained virtually without legal consequences' and that law enforcement discrimination was common.[†] Elected leader Victor Orbán has publicly called the Roma Hungary's historic unwanted burden. Discrimination can be a deliberate policy of politicians, can be 'used' to define identity and culture, and can be successfully promoted, especially if it has historic roots. Ireland would be thought of as historically more accommodating to the Traveller community. Irish Travellers have an 11% suicide rate, 80% unemployment, and a life expectancy fifteen years lower than the average in Ireland, and (like the UK and elsewhere) laws tend to discourage

---

Security and Ethnicity (CRISE), CRISE Working Paper No.18, May 2005, Oxford University, https://assets.publishing.service.gov.uk/media/57a08c97ed915d3cfd0014aa/wp18.pdf.

[*] Neil Thomas, "Members Only: Recruitment Trends in the Chinese Communist Party," *Macro Polo*, July 15 2020, see Part 3, Figure 8), https://macropolo.org/analysis/members-only-recruitment-trends-in-the-chinese-communist-party/

[†] Barbora Cernusáková, "The Roma people's Hungarian hell," *Politico*, Jan 25, 2017, https://www.politico.eu/article/the-roma-peoples-hungarian-hell/. See also, Bernard Rorke, "10 Things they said about Roma in Hungary," *European Roma Rights Centre*, 27 Oct 2015, https://www.errc.org/news/10-things-they-said-about-roma-in-hungary.

their travelling culture in favour of them being a 'settled population.'* Discrimination is intensely personal, often historic, institutional, and frequently in plain sight.

To think that prejudice – the thought behind the action of discrimination – may be an inherent part of human nature is both possible and depressing. Alternatively, we may believe that prejudice has always been a learnt behaviour. If we believe that human character can change, and that we choose our virtues, then we can change our ideas around prejudice and our actions around discrimination. If it is based on power, and fear of the unknown or losing what you have, then logically it has changed over time. People's circles of community have changed. The stage we are at now is unclear, as it usually is in historic movement. We have gone well beyond local communities and now think in terms of nations, underpinned by specific cultures. Tackling different strands of discrimination may also run along different paths with different timescales. In 1893 writing in Germany the pan-African William Du Bois wrote anti-Semitically, even though Du Bois in his entirety showed a clear anti-racism both in relation to and beyond the black American experience.† This mirrors the work of some original Enlightenment philosophers like Hume who had written positively about slavery. Class and gender prejudice may be as old as the first communities and hierarchies. Our confidence in systems of government and lifestyle may appear to harden other prejudices. War tends to encourage long-lasting hatred of the enemy through stereotypes. As we meet new groups we are forced again to reassess, and we have become generally accustomed to the idea of civil rights. The globalisation of our knowledge may even give us an endpoint to our prejudice.

The concept of civil rights, while from a Western point of view an Enlightenment offshoot, has both travelled and been adapted all over the world. Discrimination as a concept, and in terms of individual action,

---

* Chris Page and Chrissie McGlinchey, "Irish Travellers' mental health crisis driven by discrimination and deprivation," *BBC Report*, 18 April 2022; and "Ireland and the Convention on the Elimination of Racial Discrimination – Submission to the United Nations Committee," *Irish Human Rights and Equality Commission*, 28 Nov 2019, https://www.ihrec.ie/documents/ireland-and-the-convention-on-the-elimination-of-racial-discrimination/.

† Appiah, 2018, 125–126 (and re. Du Bois, 123–126).

has become a matter of law, deliberately and pro-actively, although it is understood that prejudice in the mind cannot be ended by decree. In the West the idea that individual prejudice is in the eye of the receiver, rather than its identification being decided by the originator, has become rooted. This is a not always accepted attempt to address effects not just intentions. Institutional and state discrimination is still commonplace, whether official or not. State-to-state 'discrimination' may still be said to be commonplace however hidden by justifications of self-interest, alliances, and traditional relationships. States and institutions are the 'powers' clearly in 'control' in most situations, and while individuals can talk, listen, offer explanation and nuance, and subtly change, 'powers' find it harder to do all those things. For a 'power' there is their power, perhaps even their legitimacy, at stake. There are arguments about clarity of the law or rules, consistency, and precedent, that are often used to avoid change or reflection. These are arguments about 'stability' and the 'controversy' of change and are as likely to reflect an unwillingness or inability to reflect, to serve a whole community, and to make the most of 'all the talents' that could be at their disposal.

Sometimes this unwillingness to change the physical and cultural profile of their power is simply to keep out other less familiar, less established, less agreeable people. It is self-interest, or arrogance, or fear. For individuals too it may be fear of the unknown or apparently strange, a desire to hang on to their familiar environment and accepted interpretation of their history, or a common concern about losing out on their slice of the cake if the cake must be split into smaller pieces. Even if the cake itself is unsatisfying and their slice seems insufficient for their needs it is the slice they have. The accumulated or aggregated rejection of newness is what is in essence institutional, or societal stagnation, and institutional or societal discrimination can be understood as one manifestation of this.

One view of human history explains discrimination as using the 'other' and 'difference' as easy identifiers of the competition or the enemy. It is Rousseau's blaming of 'civilisation' for mankind's poor relationships with each other. It builds on Hobbes' 'brutish man' theory that justifies or naturalises it. The original European Enlightenment of the 17th and 18th centuries remains a case study of how even 'modern' philosophy can be fashioned to fit the desired attitudes of the time. It justified discrimination based on superiority. It has taken us another 200 years and counting to return to its origin, or see its logic, of equality, or at least empathetic consideration based on an equal or fair hearing. We continue to unwind the consequences of our original abuse of the true principles of the Enlightenment.

Addressing Gender, Race, and Class

Anti-Semitism, other non-Christian 'uncivilised peoples,' and gender have been entrenched discriminations in Europe for centuries. Colonialism added race based on skin colour. Recognition of discrimination due to disability is also rising. Racial and cultural differences are now increasingly being used to explain each other ('they're blue so they do things differently...') and are used to justify contemporary discrimination. Tackling it may even be weakened by our short attention spans and our need to think that what we have done so far has been successful. While we should recognise specific differences in these types of prejudice and discrimination, we should not ignore some of the common features.

In 1930 Julian Huxley, as Chairman of the Eugenics Society in England, wrote: 'What are we going to do? Every defective man, woman and child is a burden... an extra body to feed and clothe, but produces little or nothing in return.'[*] At this time terms such as 'defective' and 'mentally deficient' were commonplace, Social Darwinism popular, and Eugenics hotly debated as a branch of science. Disabled people were often separated from society. From the Second World War disabled veterans, and their better treatment, began to change attitudes. In some nations eugenics became more associated with race. This was similar to, maybe the same as, colonial elimination of Indigenous minorities on the grounds that their 'backwardness' and 'difference' would weaken a nation or that their culture was 'offensive' in some way to 'civilised' standards. There is a reasonably straight line between the

---

[*] G.R. Searle "Eugenics and politics in Britain in the 1930s," *Annals of Science*, Vol 36, 1979 – Issue 2, 159–169.

'superman' philosophy of Nietzsche disparaging moral and physical weakness, measuring the length of noses, and the Holocaust: prejudice, identification, action. For many people old and discredited ideas of race continue to play a part in sociological analysis of contemporary issues. In 2020 Marius Turda wrote: 'Unfortunately, as long as the underlying structural conditions, shaped by Europe's slaving and colonial past, are not directly confronted and addressed, the unexamined social attitudes that caused them will continue to fester and generate new forms of scapegoating and stereotyping.'* History and science have much to offer but still require respectful accountability.

For centuries we have believed, or acted as though we believed, that women were less capable. Are women's brains smaller, less complex, are women less decisive, more sociable, less ruthless, instinctively and fatally less violent, fitted for motherhood, and to be protected, not for leadership, etc? These are the arguments thrown up by previous centuries of 'science,' and 'philosophy,' that have led to women being deemed less capable of education, less capable of the Machiavellian skills of leadership, and therefore incapable thinkers and leaders. This is the 'men are from Mars and women from Venus' argument. While hopefully these statements seem dated, like modern racist justifications gender discrimination is based on trying to explain 'difference,' rather than blatantly informing groups of their inferiority. Sometimes it is expressed as a need for difference. Gender discrimination has arguably been with us even longer, and more deeply, than racial discrimination; and within different racial and cultural groups there exists gender discrimination. Arguably this is as old as the history of hierarchy. If the first hierarchies were family, which were dependent on physical power to attain food and for defence, and included the vulnerability i.e., need for protection, of a mother to ensure the family's future, then gender discrimination might be said to be the original sin, and the protection of women the original justification.

How much does our Christian-world gender discrimination originate from the lack of recognition of female voices in Jesus' disciples,

---

* Marius Turda, 2020. Marius Turda is a leading European historian/writer on the relationship of eugenics, racism and politics and is Professor and Director of the Centre for Medical Humanities at Oxford Brookes University, UK, member of the Royal Historical Society, and of Academia Europaea.

in the acceptance of only four male versions of the life of Jesus, and in the hierarchy of the Christian Church? How deep is the root in what we in the West call Hinduism of the division of the caste system, and the all-male Brahmin, and how does this still affect how hundreds of millions of people live their lives? In Islam how much of the role, independence, and respect of women is from traditional power that has been cemented into place in the name of religion? How much are 'respect for' and 'protection of' women code for making women subordinate to men and enforcing policies denying education, independence of movement, or the ability to work with men, in many varied communities? These examples are given here not to damn religion, which could be and sometimes is at the forefront of positive change, but they show some of the historical and complex roots and confirmations of prejudice and discrimination.

These scientific, religious, and traditional rationale can be challenged. They can, over the full course of human history, be considered short term. If you believe that humanity can change then they can be seen as learnt behaviours, which with deliberately different attitudes and policy and changing circumstances, can be unlearnt. Once we knew only maybe 300 local, and therefore usually broadly similar, people. Now we can know as friends people of different colour, of other religions, of other social attitudes, of other locations around the world, and of other life experiences. This may be perceived as retraining our brains to accept something else, to redefine how we think about the unfamiliar. This is the argument that mankind can change because it is in fact a sociable being, whether optimistically to all mankind naturally, or whether through enlarging the circle upon which it realises it is inter-dependent, therefore learning new relationships and behaviours for its own interest. We know that now and in the future condemning groups (however defined) within nations, or whole nations themselves, who do not seem like us, is damaging and can rob them of health, education, entrepreneurship, and safety, and result in societal instability. Internationally this will result in unrest and migration. If women are one of these disregarded groups the result is under-achieving families and missing out on the talents of half the population. One example of this in action is the social media sexism that is a 'go to' method of criticising women today and undoubtedly discourages public roles. Society's, and our own, prejudices and discriminations limit opportunities and talents, our personal development, and weaken our own nations.

We also know that many people do not accept the reasoning of that last sentence. Some people see a successful narrative of their history and their pride entwined with these actions, presented through rose-tinted glasses. Or people should 'pull themselves up by their bootstraps' and be 'self-made.' Isn't that what happened in the West, they may say, or what ambitious or successful people do? Both gender/racial rights, and therefore also immigration, evoke fears of an established group missing out. It is intuitive to many that a new group or another person wanting more means the established get less. For many people who live in the short term because they can only afford to do so, they must look out for themselves, because they believe no-one else does. It may seem as simple as 2+2=4. This need not inevitably be a part of the conflicts within society, which are sometimes labelled the 'culture wars' in political terms, but the elaboration of this fear is easily stoked to an emotional level, away from a practical or logistical or even moral one. If you can be persuaded that someone getting a part of what you have will make you worse off, will change the look of your town, will alter the way you have to do things, will take away what little influence you have or stretch limited resources in order to satisfy the new neighbours, then you can be convinced that prejudice or discrimination is self-protection, necessary, defensive, and in your interests, whether it is done loudly and proudly, or subtly and institutionally. In gender terms this view shows itself in a belief that a woman's place is in the home, not being a, or *the*, breadwinner. A transformed view of the role of women calls into question the power relationship between men and women, especially within marriage (or partnership). It can, for some, call into question the role of masculinity. Women going out to work, earning 'pin money' for some independence, 'helping out,' may have been a necessity for a long time for many families but accepting that is not the same as accepting role equality or even role reversal.

This is an element of the largely exploitative competition-based economic model we have. It applies to individuals and nations. It is the model that gave us modern slavery, imperialism, and wars over resources and status. It is a model that led to a religious-cultural feeling of superiority and the elimination of Indigenous groups the world over that modern society has yet to face up to. It is a model that leads to borders reimagined as walls. This is a key reason people are persuaded to discriminate, because the new is not a partner but a competitor. These are the economic battlegrounds of prejudice and discrimination and how the economic bleeds into the cultural.

Our confidence in our culture relates to its foundations in our history. Education may follow to celebrate achievements, but also precedes legislation and campaigns highlighting injustice or disaster. This is why education, traditions, history, and identity are added to political culture wars. The recognition of prejudice and discriminations lays within these fields, and to an 'activist' the acknowledgement and solutions they desire cannot be won without addressing these spheres of our lives. For those who consider themselves the established group under threat the new is not welcomed to enhance, to learn from, or to share. People prefer to hang on to what they have. This applies whether they are rich or poor. Both are in the same manner prone to the persuasion that their culture is changing beyond their own recognition and their willingness or ability, or both, to adapt. Worrying that GP surgeries can't cope because immigrants with 'imported' health problems or increased pregnancies/new-borns 'take up all the appointment slots,' etc, is a matter of logistics and communication, and some understanding and some perspective. Directing resources to hotspots is logistic. To empathise with the enormous changes involved in moving country is a difficult skill if the one expected to have that empathy has no experience to guide them. Women can be seen as too collaborative to be decisive leaders and too individual to be part of the club. In practice women will be the leaders and co-workers they need to be for their success and are trained to be by design or by example. Change is partly happening because it is a realistic feat of imagination to believe that our daughters can take a successful and independent role in the world as much as our sons. These practical and policy logistics – translation courses, health services, etc – can take place if we have the will to address them. It is possible to accept new energy and resources spent with empathy if you yourself have confidence in your own way of life. Disadvantaged and depressed groups within the established landscape may not have this confidence, and this too must be addressed. The attitude itself, the morality, is within us, and is a quality of leadership. Our confidence allows our morality to bloom. We can see prejudice and discrimination from a different perspective. Culture battles can fade away, in favour of morally accepting the differences and opportunities of others, within a practical logistical framework explained and achieved through consensus, which is in fact in our own practical self-interest.

We also need to know our history to better understand the current realities shaped by it. We need to understand the struggles there have been in the past for the rights of majorities and minorities. This is itself an enormous challenge. We need to understand that equality is not the same as diversity or representation, understand the slowness of generational attitudinal change in family life, realise the importance of the words we use to describe someone, and be confident in our belief in free speech and in our own ability to entrepreneurially adapt. To do these things, to have the foundation of self-confidence, requires education, both school and societal. It is why education is increasingly a dangerous battleground. It is why those that resist the changes these battles may entail decry educational change as propaganda or a derogatory 'wokeness.' If we get it right, if we try, then our leadership, our priorities, our empathy, and our everyday actions, follow. These are enormous changes to make. This is why addressing prejudice and discrimination and the success of a multi-cultural society, and a gender-neutral or gender-fair one, are seismic processes.

The role of 'affirmative action' – a very deliberate form of promoting social and economic mobility – is worthy of consideration here. A genuine attempt to give 'outsiders' a chance, based on their perceived potential and judging their perceived disadvantages, affirmative action in places like the USA and India (in relation to Dalits) remains controversial. Affirmative action is a judgemental art buttressed over time using historic statistics informing potential and success. Successful action should be non-permanent as the profile of entrants and decision-makers changes, unless the newly promoted simply pull up the drawbridge behind them. The real weakness of it is that it promotes the perception of winners and losers in a sometimes less than transparent way that can feed resentment by those in established groups that feel they have missed out. The identity politics that gave birth to it was an enabler to universalism. It was not about separation it was about unity. The fundamental misconception that affirmative action, and in the 2020s Black Lives Matter, are about emphasising minorities' importance rather than allowing the promotion of them to achieve equality by eradicating systemic obstacles, remains strong. Affirmative action has given a chance to many who would not have previously had that chance, however imperfect it may be. It may be a practical form of reparations for historic injustice.

Meritocracy, like social mobility, is a term we use positively, often in relation to Class, the third lightning rod of discrimination. There are inequalities of opportunity that prevent effective meritocracy. One simple example is unpaid internships that give candidates essential experience in their chosen field. For the vast majority the idea of unpaid but full-time work being affordable is practically unthinkable and so this simply serves to reinforce the access to such jobs by people who already have financial support from family or a network of modern-day benefactors. A more controversial example is the continuance of fee-paying schools that may well provide good education but whose popularity is also based on the creation of lifelong networks to know 'the right people.' Educating your children in what you yourselves do, because you naturally want them to succeed, can also result in a disconnection from others and the stagnancy or complacency of institutions. There is an associated danger in society of inherited or familial knowledge as much as there is in inherited wealth, even if there are benefits. This can be seen in any walk of life, including government, professions like teaching and law enforcement, and has been seen in the past in jobs from car manufacturing to printing press workers. None of us should be in favour of cronyism, the opposite of fairness and equal opportunity. The promotion of meritocracy within groups is the creation of a new elite and another aspect of social engineering. The point about real social mobility, meritocracy, and affirmative action, is who has a fair opportunity to succeed.*

The expansion of further and higher education in recent years, across

---

* See Michael Sandel, "RSA minimate: The tyranny of merit," *RSA*, YouTube, 24 May 2019. https://www.youtube.com/watch?v=dRolGQ3QIPE&t=12s.

the world, is therefore seen as a good thing. Mass education is sometimes said to have 'democratised' class. It has major benefits in terms of more educated citizens, more able to think for themselves, have confidence in themselves, and be more independent. It also results in people gaining a wider experience of other people, with positive consequences, overall, for their understanding and empathy. These are natural follow-ons from the comprehensive system of secondary education, one of whose aims was the greater socialisation, or integration, or democratisation, of society. These are large reasons for the accelerating decline of deference and accelerating promotion of accountability regarding those who have traditionally been nearer the top of our social, economic, and political hierarchy. More people understand the limits of experts, as well as being more likely to be experts, or independent thinkers. Deferring to Class has declined. The reign of meritocracy has begun but we still need to do more to make it realistic for many people.

The philosopher has their merits but so does the car mechanic. We live in a society where some work is valued above other work, even to such an extent that the monetary value of it is seen as hundreds of times greater, creating such a chasm between the lives of different citizens that nominally have the same rights but no longer have the same opportunities. Class defined by background or income of family at birth may be on the decline, but division by education and monetary value of work and wealth held is on the rise. These are the new inequalities that we are creating. These are choices we are making as a society, or are allowing to happen. This is part of the continuing belief that people are competitive and conflictual.

The alternative for some, at the other end of the spectrum, would appear to be a communistic equality, an enforced equality, resources given according to need. This would end a class system, a hierarchy, and 'if done properly' result in a democratic meritocracy. Of course, the point about a meritocracy is that it cannot be enforced, it should be organic. Who does the enforcing? Such an ideal society has never been created, thwarted by ambition for power, corruption, and by individual creativity and entrepreneurial ambition. It was once thought that class would inexorably diminish with increased urbanisation. Feudal classes faded as individual liberty and anonymity thrived in increasingly urban areas. However, modern Class grew up as division based on money, reinforced by new ranks of self-reinforcing power.

The extent of inequality must be addressed. Equality of opportunity to establish that level playing field is now what matters for many people. Yet even that is based on the logic of 'success' meaning one person is better in some way than another. This is the product of 'higher' education and the segregation of people who earn more from those who earn less. We need to more fundamentally re-value what we consider important and readdress the relative value of the jobs people do and the lives they lead. Imagine a discontinuation of the use of the terms 'higher' and 'further' education. Imagine an abolition of the preconceptions of the difference between 'academic' and 'vocational.' Imagine a limit to the pay gap between 'worker' and 'boss.'

Traditional class discrimination is still common but the present and future danger is its redefinition into an educational or professional patronisation of others, with a financial hierarchy from income or inheritance or familial access that bestows opportunities and freedoms on some but not on others, justified by an 'evangelical' belief in meritocracy. Hence comes the creation of a new self-sustaining nobility whose world is quite divorced from the world of others, as much as the world of kings and peasants ever were. It is these realities that call into question how far our democratisation has come. Our wished-for meritocracy must have better foundations and checks and a more honest appraisal. In practice change is not simple but new ways of doing things can produce a bigger cake to share from. A bigger cake results from new entrepreneurial ideas and perspectives, new workers, and new markets. Limiting discrimination might be seen as a challenge for capitalism to embrace, which then moves the argument onto an established group losing what they think is their share of power and influence, however limited or not that may be.

WHERE ARE WE GOING?

The Politics and Morality of Changing Discrimination

These pages identify power, identity, history, human fallibility, religion, science, economic competition, and our own DNA as possible influences in the development of discrimination, in the areas of gender, race and class, and in mentioning disability. That list indicates how deep-rooted this psychology is. It illustrates the magnitude of understanding and change required if we are to overcome it. We can baulk at the challenge, or we can see the permanence of migration and development of women's rights in human history, and see that they have regularly or constantly, encouraged or forced us, to face the consequences of discriminating against others. We can recognise an historic trend to increase equality. We can recognise that change is possible and has happened. People's attitudes follow legislation and yet legislation also requires positive expressions to make that legislative change possible and more likely, and successful. This might be termed 'the permanent arc of education.' Is there gold at the end of this multi-layered rainbow? Are there at least nuggets and diamonds on the journey that are worth the effort? Such change depends on both leaders and grass-roots movements, on campaigns and everyday individual contact. Sometimes the pace of change seems slow, and sometimes reflection makes it appear quick. Sometimes achievements are not recognised as we hurtle towards the next goal we set ourselves, or that 'activists' try to point us towards in a sort of permanent revolution. Most often change is of an inconsistent pace, consolidation is often needed to prevent leaving people behind, and its certainty is only assured when an entirely new generation takes it for granted.

We have, over the last mere two or three hundred years, begun to make real headway. Our renewed and more fundamental definition of Enlightenment, individual rights, education, female equality, multi-cultural experience, and migration, addressing the worst of poverty, and relative international solidarity, have produced remarkable results in this historically short period of time. In this period hundreds of millions have been pulled out of real day-to-day poverty and have opportunities to develop their talents as never before. In our time we have gone from very little outward or official female leadership to popularly elected female presidents and prime ministers in countries right across the world. A young woman in Myanmar can use the internet to watch an American soap opera with its product placement of individual liberty as well as Coca-Cola; a mobile phone can hold political leaders or law enforcement to account, or be used to self-educate academically or vocationally, and keep in touch with vital services. The extent to which our achievements so far are 'only' building blocks in addressing discrimination and the inequality it results in depends upon many things: we must keep listening to each other, find out about each other, be willing to stand back from our own lives to offer empathy and to find perspective, and continue to have ambition for ourselves, our children, and humanity itself. People continue to develop the courage and communication skills to point out what else needs to be done. This is part of the method of the aforementioned arc of education.

Deliberately addressing both gender and racial prejudice and discrimination may be the most fundamental moral earthquake we have yet attempted to bring forth and manage. The recently and currently emerging global phase of our society is taking a step to address its unheard voices, no matter who they are or their point of origin. This is the fundamental equality for which we must strive. The logistics of managing change, the worry of a changing environment, the fear of changing balances of power, addressing or understanding the historical nature of discrimination of whatever type, are all complex and difficult issues but are all bluster compared to, and subservient to, fighting for the essential moral attitude we should have now and for the future. The increasing globalisation of our world – economically, politically, socially, environmentally – has heightened our need to do this, and placed these issues on our menu or in our faces in ways that we have not had to address before. It is the moral focus that is the artist of our arc of education.

WHERE ARE WE GOING?

War

Is our attitude to international conflict different from that of other conflict? Should it be? What is practical in the real world? How depressed should we be about our current position? The underpinning 'philosophy' of the United Nations and countless international agreements is obvious, in the sense that it is obvious and right to say that nations should want peace. Who could, or should, or would have, argued against that in the shadow of two world wars? However, the reality is that some people may not want that. For some people conflict can seem beneficial. For many people the human species is naturally conflictual – the very reason for needing the UN, and its forerunner League of Nations, in the first place. The UN was also built on a mixed bag presumption of balance of power, of democracy, and in a context of campaigning liberation movements. While some of the causes of conflict in our world today seem ancient or permanent, like a struggle for resources or status, some of them were also sown in its formative years, like colonially imposed national boundaries. Evidence shows that over history we can continue to create reasons for war.

Our Current Warrior Virtues

The virtues of the Ancient Spartans of Greece, of Ramayana-inspired Hindu rulers, of Zulu Chiefs, and Central and Southern American emperors, were 'warrior virtues,' i.e., a belief that the character of Man, and that a man's leadership, respect, and credibility, were entwined in the abilities of a warrior leader who needed courage, decisiveness, ruthlessness, singular authority, and even physical prowess and stature. Subtlety and teamwork were very much behind the scenes if they played a part. Negotiation and compromise were weaknesses, and even feminine virtues. Throughout time good leaders have shown all these qualities but most kept the public perception of masculine strength. These were the qualities taught to any self-respecting male heir to authority. These leaders often did live in times of violence, times when men, including pampered leaders, often died before they outlived their physical ability to lead an army, and dead long before they had to rely on other skills. The average age of death of those that even made it to kingship in medieval England was about 48, of Alexander the Great 32, of Julius Caesar 55. Rare female leaders often took on these qualities to survive. They may have blended in a different charisma, even put themselves on a slightly different pedestal, but they lived in the same violent times. However, should we not question or analyse it a little more thoroughly? How much were violence and these leadership qualities reinforcing each other? Although the technology of war is more destructive than ever, we see more of it, and we understand the consequences of it better, the end of war is elusive. We have yet to really understand, or decide, if we as a species are naturally conflictual through competition to survive and succeed. We have yet to summon the belief that we can deliberately change the dynamics of how we coexist. Warrior virtues are still predominant or seen as 'ideal' or 'the right and necessary qualities' in leaders around the world. Leaders are not expected to sacrifice power – and are usually penalised for doing so – whether their own or their nation's. The competitive instinct still predominates. Authoritarian-minded rulers today clearly play up to these characteristics, but democrats are not immune to these attitudes either. 'Populist' democracy often thrives on the competitive emotions of the voters, whether manipulated or not. Enlightened self-interest and investment in longer-term co-operation remain difficult to explain and justify without short-term benefits. Constitutional arrangements may mean another leader reaps the benefits, or must continue with the same priorities. A decade for even a very electorally successful leader is a long time. The warrior virtues are still prized. The competitive model firmly in place.

There are co-operative states. We should not forget that the USA is a unity of different states that could have gone their separate ways, although it has significant problems of internal identity. It has thrived and continues to do so in an unprecedented way. The European Union is a standout modern exercise in co-operation, still young, still changing, different in foundation to the USA. Its success is not yet assured but the forces that brought it together, of war-prevention and economic rejuvenation, continue to be relevant. These two groups have the strengths and weaknesses of a democratic philosophy: they reflect and respond to their constituent people. The warrior attributes in these places have not been discarded, but they have been softened. The Union of Soviet Socialist Republics (USSR) is now seen as a failed exercise of co-operation but one that lasted about as long as the current EU has done so far. Imposed at a time of ideological revolution, unresponsive in the main to local and changing circumstances, it imploded in the face of mismanagement and outside pressure, unable to persuade its constituent parts to remain engaged at the first moment when central authority crumbled. African nations may offer a glimpse of the future. Many are superficially mini empires with central control over a multiplicity of peoples. However, within themselves, with some success, many balance the interests of historically different tribes brought together artificially in imperialism or decolonisation, doing so either through constitutional arrangements, cultural integration, or sensitivity to local historic leadership. The best do all three. Africa is a large, varied continent with more newer nations than any other, but growing peacefulness, stability and economic co-operation are happening at the same time as continuing nation-building, despite political setbacks, poverty, and under-representation of women in the political process. The diversity of interests, powers, and traditions within what we now call India is also an exercise in co-operation. It is a nation brought together through British imperial rule, filtered through the division from Pakistan/Bangladesh at independence, and maintaining a state/federal balance with a multi-cultural nature. It has its issues in all these respects and is a rough diamond version of democracy that many would say is still fragile, but its first seventy-five years have shown that it can adapt and thrive. It is a lesson in imperfect co-operation. China has taken a different course. One of China's current and future concerns should be how it avoids the pitfalls of empire. Xinjiang and Tibet are geographically huge areas, culturally different, but economically small; Hong Kong (and Taiwan) have forged different political foundations, economic strength, and internationally independent profiles. China's approach currently appears to be takeover rather than voluntary or complicit union, central control and change, not local accountability, and Han Chinese expansionism to dilute (or worse) ethnic minority culture. It is leading itself down the path of being a military state to maintain the control and foundational ideology that it believes it relies on to maintain its preferred style of ordered society, the primary focus of Chinese government for centuries, and to promote 'one China.' Its warrior leadership seems set to last for a while, but both its success and failure will eventually call it into question, and then China will need to decide what sort of nation it wants to be.

We remain in a phase of wondering if female leaders will naturally be more consensual, have less ego to satisfy, or have different priorities for their supporters or electors or their nation. This is another aspect of the 'men are from Mars and women from Venus' arguments. We must recognise that a leader is in a representative position to represent; and that a nation's interests may remain exactly the same whoever its leader may be – unless there is a deliberate decision to change priorities. There is no reason to suggest that women leaders understand this less than male ones, and therefore that female leaders will be substantially different to male leaders. Do we not believe in equality, and individual character? Female leaders in the first year or two of the Covid-19 pandemic were often seen as working differently and more effectively, but they often worked in different and differing circumstances, whether that was leading an island nation like Tsai Ing-wen of Taiwan or Jacinda Ahern of New Zealand, or seen as having a different background, like the scientific one of Germany's Angela Merkel. Shoulder pads and trouser suits remain the norm. As noted elsewhere, women who aspire to be leaders will look at the criteria required and seek to fulfil it. Society will set the example or train them in the way that it wishes, and they can hardly be blamed for then succeeding. We must expect female leaders to pursue the interests of the nation or institution they lead; to do otherwise would be a dereliction of their duty, and their representation. A slightly different personal style may emerge but the interests and the circumstances of their power, and their policies, will remain, including any consideration of sending soldiers into battle. Pioneering women who reject the current conflictual approach to international relations should be seen as pioneering leaders, as rare as such pioneering men. Women, like men who do so, may judge that only when having proved their strength can they influence the world in the peaceful way they want to. All this is true of authoritarian or democratic leaders, but authoritarian women leaders remain rare. Female monarchs of the past can more clearly illustrate the persistent need for a warrior mentality, from Elizabeth I to Russia's last female leader Catherine the Great. Female dictators who make it may be more, not less, likely to feel the need to demonstrate their warrior virtues. Jiang Qing ('Madame Mao') and the sister of North Korea's Kim Jong Un, Kim Yo Jong, are sobering thoughts for those who believe that a female authoritarian leader would have a different approach.

Causes of War and Dealing with Them

There are many general and specific causes of conflict that claim to be justifiable. War is usually said to be in the 'national interest.' Religious or ideological war, and historical grievance, may stand apart and within these. On the surface it may be to a nation's advantage, or necessity, to fight for resources such as land or minerals, control of water resources, or access to the sea. It may be encouraged by the demands of a rising population, or the necessities of a dwindling population. It may be that specific materials were once unused but now, perhaps due to new technology or lifestyle, are valuable. Two examples from the past include the place of opium in international trade that had a profound effect on the treatment of China as a nation; and the Transatlantic Slave Trade that fuelled the economic development of the Americas directly and of European industrialisation. These two examples show how long term the effects of such conflict can be, politically, economically, and socially: from China presenting itself as a power that can no longer be bullied, to race relations in the USA. While this cause of war may seem antiquated, it is not. It is playing out in Central Africa where sometimes weaker governments of weaker international standing struggle to control or regulate the mining of minerals now deemed essential to produce computer chips, or that may become essential for climate change-busting technology. It may play out in the future in relation to exploitation of the Oceans, or the Arctic and Antarctic. It is also, not incidentally, mirrored in the exploitation of minority Indigenous land within a nation, even as Indigenous rights are gaining more support. Resources have always been an indicator of a nation's power. Nations face a choice of action or inaction when their resources change: alter prices and therefore income, find new uses for their resources, or diversify away from dependence on them. This would seem inevitable. It is. It is currently playing out in relation to oil. It can be ameliorated by the developing global trading system with regulation and arbitration. This is increasing the chances of peace by the two-fold method of making war as a way of gaining resources less acceptable and necessary, and increasing economic development globally which places a greater premium on the fact that more people have more to lose in the event of conflict. There is a long way to go in the development of this system as a truly and globally fair mechanism for managing the world's resources, but we are well down the path of accepting it as one strand in our interwoven rope pulling us towards a more peaceful world. Prosperity increases the chance of peace, as does an ageing population that is more settled and does not want an only-child going to war.

The Western reaction to Russia's full invasion of Ukraine in 2022 is an interesting mirroring of this. It seeks to wage a more comprehensive economic war than has been seen before in modern times. The strength of this approach is the globalisation that has taken place so far, i.e., Russia's integration into global economics. The weakness of this approach is the limited globalisation that has taken place so far, in both economic terms and in the cross-cultural dialogue of what is acceptable in the actions of individual nations. The West's sanctions show their continued dominance of global economic structures, but this may further encourage a more diversified globalism, weakening their relative position in the longer term. The slow enlargement of the BRICS group and China's influence may encourage this. Russia is depending on the lack of a global consensus in principle and in action in relation to its aims and alleged atrocities, which are more subject to the vagaries, or development, of global public opinion than ever before.

Conflict is also sometimes related to, or justified by, a moral argument, historically related to religion: defence of the faithful, or of the Faith, or spreading the Faith. Armies have always professed that God is on their side. Nineteenth-century European empire builders invariably took missionaries as well as engineers and accountants in support of their armies and their colonialism. Where there is 'religious conflict' religion itself is often the identifier of the sides rather than the root or predominant cause of the conflict, although as an essential part of their identity it should not be minimised. Religion also still plays a part in internal conflict and religious minorities remain disadvantaged in many places. Where it plays a part in conflict it is now more likely to be used as another arm of the state, rather than one using the beliefs of the religion itself. Where the moral argument is not religious it has increasingly become one of human rights or political ideology.

Another aspect of conflict that may be justified in the national interest relates to historical grievance. The collapse of the artificially constructed Yugoslavia through repeated Balkan Wars over twenty years from 1991 remains a lesson in the necessity of accepted national identity. The consequences of 19th- and 20th-century worldwide empires and decolonisation give other examples. When one looks at a map of national frontiers it is astonishing how many are imposed artificial perfectly straight lines. The Sykes–Picot agreement of 1916 effectively decided the borders of Iraq, Syria, Jordan, and Lebanon for the purposes of a French/British power arrangement. In the Indian subcontinent Pakistan and India were separated when those lands had not been separately distinguished before. Partition in 1947 resulted in the movement of 10–20 million and the death of anywhere between several hundred thousand and two million. The Biafran War of 1967–70 in Nigeria pitted a secessionist region of Biafra against the national government, identified largely through religion and tribe, at the cost of 45,000–100,000 killed in war directly, two million civilians dead (often from famine), and 2–4.5 million displaced. Kenyan election violence in 2007 when over 1,000 died and 600,000 were displaced, repeated on a smaller scale in 2017, shows how this can be under the surface, come out, and be repeated, in apparently stable nations. Yet nation-building in terms of identity has often been successful. There seems surprisingly little appetite for redrawing colonially imposed borders. Part of it is likely to be a judgement about the balance of risk of opening a pandora's mix of history, identity, hopes, resource-division, the difficulty of agreement, and political tension or violence. In response to Russian recognition of independence for breakaway republics from Ukraine in 2022, the Kenyan Ambassador stated at the UN:

CONFLICT

> Kenya and almost every country was birthed by the ending of empire. Our borders were not of our own drawing. Had we chosen to pursue states based on the ethnic, racial, or religious homogeneity, we would still be waging bloody wars these many decades later. We rejected irredentism and expansionism on any basis, including racial, ethnic, religious, or cultural factors. We reject it again today.[*]

While nations try to adapt to imposed borders there is still a strong argument that much of the conflict in the world today originates in the colonial period and decolonisation as decided by the imperial powers. In the West there has, perhaps until very recently, been a successful tendency to put the colonial era in the past. This is not true of the previously colonised, and that is a disconnection that ex-colonial powers need to come to terms with. The origin of the phrase 'crimes against humanity' is African American George W. Williams investigating Belgian atrocities in the Congo under Leopold II in 1890. After the Second World War Raphael Lemkin formulated the idea of 'genocide,' using the British destruction of native Tasmanians as one of his case studies. Renewed study and public campaigns in respect of slavery and racial justice are bringing the consequences of colonial-era injustice to the fore again.

Israel-Palestine, Kurdish struggle for statehood, and Libyan chaos are three ongoing examples that show boundary change through the division of artificially constructed nations is not a thing of the past. In the best-case scenario there are democratic processes, such as may happen on the island of Ireland. In worst-case scenarios it means war. Nor, although they may only involve lower-level conflict, should we completely ignore the position of older or Indigenous groups within more developed or Western nations. Land issues within these nations have not gone away, and this includes Aboriginal peoples in Australia, Native American tribes and Nations in north America, and Indigenous peoples in South America. Nations like Australia, the USA and Brazil have faced up to these issues with varying degrees of empathy, historical

---

[*] Julian Borger and Andrew Roth, "Russia strongly condemned at UN after Putin orders troops into eastern Ukraine," *The Guardian*, 22 February 2022.

awareness, and legal interventions or protections.

The notion of 'fighting for the nation,' whatever the specific cause, can be a strong mover towards war. The latter might be dressed up in language like 'spheres of influence' or 'provocation' or simply 'patriotism' or find expression and justification in a specific and deliberate interpretation of a nation's history. This may also be mixed up with a national belief in being a 'chosen people,' or even just 'a regional power.' It is far harder to oppose a regime that successfully embodies the pride of the nation or who can put the reputation of the nation on the line. However, even dictators know that such a war is a risky business. While the whim or emotion of an authoritarian leader can clearly be condemned as a cause of war, the notion of a democratic nation standing up for itself is sometimes just as hard to resist. Fighting 'for the nation' is a complex psychology as much as its causes in policy and its consequences need unwinding or criticism.

Conflict may include a nation going to war to further the spread of its own values or ideology, even as a pro-active self-defence. Imperialism may be included in this in its deliberate promotion of a cultural superiority identified by race, or Christian missionary conversion, or European economic, scientific, and technological 'progress.' More recently this relates to the Cold War, and its proxy hot wars, between communist USSR and capitalist USA, a battle between different philosophies and lifestyles, promoted by and through different government, that shaped the post-1945 world. With the apparent end of the Cold War from 1990, this dissipated, although non-democratic nations, and many ex-colonial nations, may say, with varying subtlety, that the USA has been doing much the same for 'the American century.' The pursuit of American influence through economic power, military presence, political action, and cultural profile has continued. This is portrayed as a push to make the world a place of Democracy. In Western eyes ideology would seem to be less of a central tenet of government than in previous decades, but not necessarily to non-Western or non-democratic nations.

Three other protagonists are arguably choosing to use an ideological thrust of conflict: Firstly China, whose strategy includes, just like the USA, a full array of its economic influence as the world's manufacturing hub, its increasing technological development, its expansion of military bases and the use of, or attempt to control, its diaspora in other nations. In style the so-called 'wolf-warrior' diplomats of Beijing echo the warrior virtues of most other imperial nations through history. Its publicly stated values are directly anti-liberal, trying to portray the West as colonial, and in decline economically and morally – something which Putin of Russia has latched onto. Notably, the re-claiming of Taiwan is not put in terms of extending Chinese communism, only in nationalist terms. Secondly, there is theocratic Iran, defending and promoting Shia Islam in the Middle East, as a national defensive mechanism, a religious promotion, and the promotion of a particular type of government. It encourages internally driven power in other lands for Iran's own influence. Russia under President Putin has increasingly spoken of the failure of the democratic West, and sought to extend China's criticism of Western values, but does not refer to socialism, primarily referring to Russian peoples and security. In a State of the Nation Address in April 2005 Putin said that the collapse of the Soviet Union was 'the greatest geo-political catastrophe of the century' and in 2021 said that Russian people in newly independent countries found themselves cut off, calling this a 'major humanitarian tragedy.' National leaders with an historical perspective are good – but it depends on the integrity of the history. Russia's threat to the independent sovereignty of some of its neighbours had clearly not dissipated (actively supporting separatists and committing military forces in Georgia, the Crimean Peninsula of Ukraine, and eastern Ukraine between 2008 and 2014 onwards) before Russia shocked the world and began its full invasion of Ukraine in 2022. Putin's public pronouncements seek to leave a nationalist legacy. Direct opposition in war between major nations has not happened since the opposition of Chinese and American forces in the Korean peninsula, but there is nothing inevitable about this continuing, and ideological conflict remains a bedrock of international relations and megaphone diplomacy.

The effects of war are always widespread and serious. In Ukraine, millions of refugees internally and that have fled abroad, infrastructural and economic destruction, with thousands dead and wounded. Internationally, energy access and prices have been used as weapons with worldwide effects on the cost of living with subsequent domestic political consequences for many nations, and which may quicken reduced dependence on fossil fuels; and disruption to major global grain and fertiliser supplies causing shortages and price rises across a range of goods and nations. It is producing new geo-strategic decisions, including the expansion of NATO membership and spending, review of Russian-ex-Soviet state relations in central Asia, and possible alignment of authoritarian states; and a clearer cultural and value-laden division between the West and Russia, with significantly reduced individual and political freedoms and more fragility in Russia itself, and ever greater international disinformation. China may be forced to play a role in international affairs that it does not want, as it walks a tightrope between anti-Western rhetoric, potential active support for a key ally, the maintenance of an internationally friendly image amid strong UN General Assembly support for Ukraine, and maintaining international financial and trade networks to boost its economy. The level of economic sanctions is unprecedented and shows a Western control of the levers of economic global power, but also shows they are globally weaker than before, and the war may yet result in more multi-polar, less dollar dominated, and less Western controlled, economic global systems, whether these are China-led or non-aligned. The United Nations and its Security Council is again shown to be ineffective when having to deal with a veto-wielding nation. Drones have become a major component of warfare, and cyber war extensively used, while old-fashioned trench warfare predominates on the ground. There is an environmental impact that can only be currently guessed at. The effects of the Russian invasion of Ukraine are global. Around the world most wars do have some geo-political consequences. Outside sponsored and armed civil war in Yemen affects the stability or international standing of regional powers Saudi Arabia and Iran, and feeds into Islamic division. Continuing conflict in Central Africa, especially the Democratic Republic of the Congo, affects the world supply of rare earth materials. These are two examples of largely ignored wars in the West that are not forgotten elsewhere, nor should they be in the West. The Palestinian conflict remains a more obvious example and perhaps the world's most serious continuing conflict, as Hamas-led Gaza reminds us.

There are trends, however, that even war-willing nations will find difficult to resist. Decreasing poverty, smaller families making individual children more precious, international progressive-social and lifestyle trends and commonalities, and continuing development of international regulation, can all contribute to a greater global empathy and understanding, and more people with more to lose. Trumping these with nationalist ideology, control and culture wars are still possible, but will be harder, because across the world these are domestic as well as international changes re-shaping societies.

Nations and international institutions must be clearer in their analysis of whether to support a nation based on actions that are about its influence. This is difficult. In the 1990s–2000s UK Prime Minister Tony Blair enunciated the ideas of an ethical foreign policy and liberal intervention. The latter was done successfully in Kosovo, and in Sierra Leone where murderous leaders fighting a no-holds-barred civil war were overthrown, peace was restored, and a more stable and supported government took shape. The policy, however, was much more than military, calling with some success for global tackling of extreme poverty, co-operation on global issues, and reducing trade barriers. Iraq's invasion of Kuwait entirely for its own gain was successfully repulsed by a wide international coalition. The Second Iraq war (in the Middle East this is the third Iraq War, the Iran–Iraq conflict being the earliest and therefore first) sullied his reputation. Intervention publicly based on the fear of Iraq developing weapons of mass destruction (WMD) and defence of Iraqi human rights in the face of regime gas attacks and potential genocide against its own minorities and opposition were completely drowned out by the perception of fighting for oil interests, not finding WMD, and the lack of post-war planning. Intervention in several cases has been considered because we are ever more acutely aware of the effects of a failed state on other states. That awareness is of self-interest related to migration, crime, international aid, and other issues. We are more aware of, and increasingly supportive of, the human rights of others too, which makes it harder to look the other way and to offer no help to those who seem defenceless and are repressed by the prevailing power within their nation. The UN officially adopted a *Responsibility to Protect* doctrine in 2005 after the wars in former Yugoslavia and the Rwandan genocide, to promote international action against war crimes, genocide, ethnic cleansing, and crimes against humanity, both by one state against another and within an individual state. Since 2005 its effect has been inconsistent, but it continues to be official UN policy and has been invoked in eighty Security Council Resolutions to date.* It is these points that bring into focus the non-intervention strategy of nations who ask where intervention in the name of human rights stops, and does it apply to their own regimes? Intervention to bring down Muammar Gaddafi in Libya is one such example when action was taken, but again without clear-cut resolution, leaving continual internal, and internationalised, conflict. Often common interests between nations with different values must suffice for an active alliance but intervention must have widespread international support to be both justified and possible. And once destruction has ensued what comes next must also have common agreement. A temporary alliance with specific aims between nations of different interests may be stronger than a fixed alliance of like-minded nations automatically supporting each other. However, we must have a clearer approach to how we deal with nations and leaders that do not play by the rules. Morally, decisions should respect other nations, and respect the arguments of the case. It is a call to recognise the national interest of all in international stability. To some this is a 'Western' view. To some the guiding fundamental principle of non-interference in the affairs of another nation is sacrosanct, but for the grace of God may they go. As we become ever more global this will be increasingly unsustainable. Just as to act alone is to invite both defeat and condemnation, to never be prepared to act is a desertion of our principles and a dereliction of our duty.

The United Nations

The United Nations in its current form teeters on the brink of powerlessness when it comes to preventing conflict, although it tries to do much else with some success. The veto powers of UN Security Council members, deriving from their position in 1945, frequently prevent effective action. Nor has Council membership reflected changing demographics or economic power. Western nations frequently wish to

---

* See Global Centre for the Responsibility to Protect, www.globalr2p.org.

interfere in their rush to promote a Western-style democracy. This is what also serves their ends. However, non-interference should not be a sacrosanct principle. The principle of use for the veto is frequently that of the previously explained non-interference in the affairs of another nation, and while this is not entirely without merit it is often used to prevent a precedence that could in time be used against themselves, or their less powerful allies. The United Nations needs to rid itself of the current veto powers of individual nations, although that would not be without its own consequences. If it did so the question then becomes one of legitimacy of action taken by some nations but without the support, or with active diplomatic opposition, of others. This might lead to a fuller non-co-operation of some with UN activities. It might lead to compromise towards a consensus of the rules and criteria to follow when considering intervention, or different levels of intervention, precisely to prevent groups of nations taking control of UN action. The idea of veto power needs updating as does the use of the General Assembly (GA).

In 1948 there were far fewer politically independent nations than there are now. GA influence and decision-making would be world opinion based on the legitimate sovereignty of the varied nations of the globe. It would not be 'world government,' a separate institutional idea from the strength of national sovereignty and common interest. If the GA became more powerful it would then face calls to contribute more, financially, diplomatically, and militarily, and it would need to do so. The veto powers maintain their military, diplomatic, and financial reach to maintain their legitimacy within the Security Council. This reach in fact needs to be pooled into UN-led agencies, led efficiently by the administrative arms of the UN, whether given direction from the GA or the Security Council. This itself would be a major change of emphasis by the UN. This is more than financial contributions. If countries believe in the UN then why can diplomatic resources not be integrated, why have more than 100 ambassadors in a country when one UN ambassador could have 100-fold influence. This would need really working out, but what it needs most of all is commitment to the common principle even when a single nation doesn't get all it wants and might have to compromise. Ambassadors could be saved for immediate neighbours or perhaps historic relationships with more daily ties, or trade. It would need more representative policy and greater efficiency than is currently seen. The UN was conceived as a community of nations, acting through them, controlled by them, without power of independent action which would be seen as power those nations could not control. This lack of independent resources *under unified action* hinders the UN in all sorts of ways.

Two other major changes are needed: Firstly, criteria of what makes 'good government' needs to be agreed. In practice this may be an enunciation of Rousseau's 'social contract' for our modern world, and having to consider the tension between individual rights and societal order, without being general platitudes. Secondly, and even more fundamentally, independent arbitration by UN agencies with effective resources. This calls for a leap of faith in trusting an agreed criteria by nations that have different philosophies and potential fears of being subject to such criteria. Morally, how much respect do or could or would nations find in each other and how much confidence do they have in themselves? Imagine a UN with no veto powers in the Security Council, with majority GA votes for legitimacy of action, with independent and resourced agencies to act derived from the fair and proportionate contributions of its members that are not withheld in tantrums of disagreement, and that could even be pegged at a set percentage of national wealth. Nations with a unique governmental ideology can still be protected.

These would be mammoth changes, and yet... We already have Millennial Goals relating to standards of living; we have conventions on human rights and refugees; developing infrastructure and policy for climate change and biodiversity; we have international financial institutions and Interpol... These are all imperfect, certainly, but they are all accepted, and not just because they can be controlled or ignored by individual nations, but because they benefit nations. We have projects at very local level and international level encouraging good government, from community finance and accountability to the Aspen Global Leadership Network that highlights leaders of integrity globally across different sectors. Sovereign nations... mutual respect... and accountability for practising agreed standards... it may only take another 200 years! It can take less time if leaders of nations and people within nations were prepared to find the moral clarity to aim for the common good and go beyond staggering from one individual crises to another. They could recognise their own self-interest in giving up some power to invest in greater global stability. They could have the confidence that what happens in their nation is defensible within the debate of the community of nations – or change it if it is not. Morally, why not? There are many proposals out there for reform of the UN, but the UN itself has no formal proposals under active consideration beyond management and finance. It and its members need to do much better.

The emergence of 'universal jurisdiction' – nations taking it upon themselves to allow the trial of foreign nationals for alleged crimes against international law not committed on its own soil or involving its own nationals – is an interesting development.* There is the chance that this has the potentially disastrous effect of appearing to be a sort of legal imperialism. Chinese or other national attempts to bring to 'justice' their own nationals, or even foreign nationals, living abroad may be entirely self-serving mirrors of universal jurisdiction enacted in ways the West will find unacceptable. Perceptions must be considered as well as the intended result. If this is an extension of internationally accepted law, and the current UN International Court of Justice at The Hague, then universal jurisdiction can serve a very worthwhile purpose, but it may become a legal and contradictory confusion that embeds different values.

The Hardest Example: The Israeli-Palestinian Conflict

Antonio Gramsci wrote that history leaves its traces in our DNA and our collective experience, that we need to understand ourselves, our surroundings, our history, and others, that we need to work out how we fit together and move to a global view.† Nowhere is this ancient

---

* The International Justice Resource Center, outlines the current state of universal jurisdiction around the globe, with examples of prominent cases, and how it relates to the UN Responsibility to Protect, www.ijrcenter.org.
† Gramsci, 1891–1937, was a left-wing Italian, most known for writing about the idea of cultural hegemony, the dominance of one cultural group or norm in a more naturally diverse society.

challenge currently more obvious than in Israel-Palestine, which appears to be the hardest conflict to solve in the world today. Religion, land, resources, power, status, democracy, authoritarianism, individual rights and liberty, and everyday livelihoods, all play a part in this conflict. So does colonial history, stereotypical imagery, the psychology of resisting power, the Enlightenment, and a counter-Enlightenment. The conflicts of the Middle East, including Palestinian-Israeli, are ancient in origin – or at least strands of them are – but what we also see now are man-made narratives, deliberate decisions, entrenched positions, geo-political considerations, and ruling authority survival instincts.*

In 1948 Israel was placed in the Middle East by Western powers after the catastrophe of the Holocaust and building on increasing Jewish emigration, and immediately and automatically seen as the Western, modern, enlightened nation of the region. This remains the foundation of American policy towards Israel. Many Muslims saw this as the imposed creation of a Western state, except Jewish rather than Christian in nature. Multiple stereotypes and confining narratives in Arab nations of the history of Israel and of Islam need to be loosened if the current nations of the region are to coexist. Only when current narratives or interpretations change can the complex practical problems within the Israeli-Palestinian conflict, of settlement, the status of Jerusalem, security, and religious coexistence be seriously addressed.† The failure of Arab–Israeli peace initiatives over the years do not prevent the world still seeking long-term and immediate solutions, and confidence-building and tension-reducing measures, to build mutual understanding and coexistence. Middle Eastern governments, populist, monarchical or autocratic, may continue to be anti-Israeli and traditionally Islamic, but such governments must be more interested in and sensitive to the living standards of their people, must engage or be engaged internationally, separate anti-Semitism from Israeli policy and

---

* Edward Said, 1935–2003, was a Palestinian-American writer, born in Jerusalem, of American nationality, who transformed the study of non-Western cultures, most notably writing *Orientalism* in 1978.
† I have deliberately referred to the conflict as Israeli–Palestinian and Palestinian–Israeli. The order may well drive our understanding of who is more important, and therefore our vision of how it can be managed or solved.

strategy, and encourage religious leaders to feel so confident in their faith that they can separate it from the political interest of the state. There is a long way to go. This requires changes such as less overtly anti-Israeli education and media, a willingness to expand trade, and religious leadership for peace. Within Israel the dangers of creating a second-class citizenship for non-Jewish people, and of the moral position of creating what seems to many in the outside world an apartheid-type existence in occupied land, may change the very foundational balance established in 1948 of a safe Jewish home, socialist-style Kibbutzim, Western-style democracy, and international acceptance. At a time in history when geographical location still matters Israel is a part of the Middle East. Israeli and Palestinian/Arab peoples must resist the encroachment of the conflict itself changing or dominating what sort of people they want to be. Only when these considerations are faced can compromise be embarked upon and practical difficulties overcome. Hatred must not be allowed to officially, or by default, continually embed itself in the future generations of each side. This is the most worrying aspect of extreme settler and of Gazan Hamas pronouncements and violence. These conflicts are about facing up to history, leaving some of it behind, about self-confidence in identity, and having an inclusive or at least non-hostile idea of progress and coexistence. This is why the conflicts of the Middle East have commonalities with other conflicts but are also the hardest to solve. Leaders and people of the Middle East must find their way to the globalism of Gramsci, the ability to coexist with people who seem different. This needs the constant nurture of the rest of the world, and that may even need an element of imposition of the opportunity of, or circumstances for, peace by the international community, but the best and only sustained development is always from within.

Science and Technology

We must face the danger of not continually making progress towards peace before we destroy each other with old or new forms of warfare. The development of gunpowder, of rapid-fire guns, of aviation, of under-water machines of war, all altered warfare in multiple ways. More of the enemy could be killed in quicker ways, from longer distances. War could become less personal. It has become conflict between populations not just armies, across nations not just on front lines, from an enemy you may not see coming or one that gets up close, silently and not wearing a uniform. Conflict may not be the work of a soldier or seaman or pilot but an IT specialist.

The most up-to-date technology brings the consequences of conflict to catastrophic levels. We now live with the possibility of nuclear war that would not only destroy nations but make whole regions uninhabitable for decades. This acceptance is one of the dangers. Losing a collective memory of what war really entails is dangerous. Losing the shock value of what total destruction might really mean, and its actual possibility, is dangerous. Thinking that we can 'manage' such a scenario is more dangerous still. Nations are increasingly seeking ways to get around the Mutually Assured Destruction (MAD) policies of the Cold War era. In nuclear terms this means the specific development of more localised nuclear devices, so-called 'battlefield' nuclear bombs. Issues have proliferated: multiple nations engaging in nuclear bomb development, perception of multiple threat, or a small economically weak or politically isolated nation developing the technological capability to threaten a much more obviously powerful nation across the globe. Other problems are the increased threat of 'accidental' detonation or misjudgement, and lax regulation or control mechanisms. A truism would seem to be that we cannot un-invent technology. Another truism would seem to be that we cannot guarantee the suppression of technological development in major nations or remote corners of the world.

Since the use of gas in the First World War we have outlawed but not stopped chemical warfare, as shown by the use of Sarin on the Tokyo underground in 1995 which killed fourteen, to its use in Iraq and Syria since by national governments, to its use against individuals as a method of assassination even in the lands of another nation as in the failed Salisbury poisonings in 2018. It is a staple of fiction that ideological international terrorists or governments or unbalanced individuals must be researching how biological germ warfare or chemical warfare can be directed towards specific locations or specific individuals or specific groups of people. This is a terrifying prospect, but the logicality of this development cannot be denied. As we learn more and more about altering our DNA for medical purposes we will learn more about how that can be a threat to our very existence. How much can one nation be expected to deny itself this development in what it perceives to be an international community of multiple threats? How easy will this technology become, and how available?

Modern technology affords us the ability to wage war against an enemy we do not need to be personally near. Un-manned drones and orbital satellites are an addition to missiles that cover 1,000 miles. They make both local and international war impersonal. They even threaten to take our conflicts into space. Impersonal war – never impersonal to the victims of course – may redefine the very nature of conflict. In the Second World War armies met on battlefields and brought back memories of trauma because they were fighting a humanised enemy, despite propaganda and training, and even though many will have never killed in combat. Good military leaders are by cliché known for understanding the consequences of war better than political ones, and having a higher regard for the longevity of men (and increasingly women) under their command. These breaks on conflict are weakened by the im-personalisation of war. In the future how will this develop, and just as importantly why will this develop? Will there be a push to de-personalise war to make it more of a realistic policy alternative? Will robotic war develop to save humans from the cold-bloodedness of killing, based on an acceptance that such killing is intrinsically wrong? Or will robotic war develop to further the aggressive instincts of a nation or group, simply acknowledging its lack of emotional cost and remoteness as benefits, or even advantages, over an enemy? Similar things may be said of cyber warfare. It is remote, impersonal, technological not emotional, can be targeted or general. It can be widespread or local. It may even be relatively cheap. Furthermore, cyber war can be denied and done with no declaration of war, or even acknowledgement. In a similar way to understanding how we can use our new-found knowledge about DNA we can also dissect our knowledge about new technologies for their misuses. With each technological advancement a new cycle of opportunities arises. With a technical education, a 'have-the-nerve' or game-playing or following-patriotic-orders mindset, a few buttons can paralyse financial systems, health services, information networks, energy facilities, government services, and personal everyday services. Technology is just like the physical sciences in being in a constant race with itself to mitigate its potential misuse. Public debate, regulation, and enforcement are way behind. These new technologies even call into doubt the definition of war. They make it difficult to judge when we are at war, or who we may be at war against. They call into question the idea of proportionate responses. They are replicating a fragility of life and an eternal vigilance that we have not known for a generation or more and that many people in 'developed' nations thought had been consigned to history. In some places the balance between eternal vigilance and individual liberty will be wrong. In some places such eternal vigilance is the misuse of this same technology for regime control, perhaps in the name of societal safety and order, in a parody of the French Revolution's Committee of Public Safety that killed thousands in its Reign of Terror. Our values and virtues have not addressed the dangers of new technologies. This dystopian view of nuclear, biological, chemical, robotic, and cyber warfare is frightening but not inevitable. Science and technology are atoms and code. How we use them is up to us. The price of eternal vigilance is up to us; and the nature of it to.

Freedom Fighting and Terrorism

Terrorism is the desperate refuge of people who see no other way to get what they want. Whether it is the last such choice, coming after what we may call democratic resistance, is decisive in whether we decide to understand it sympathetically or not. One person's terrorist is another person's freedom fighter, just as crime to alleviate poverty elicits a different response to greed. Authoritarian regimes around the world have taken up the phrase 'war on terror' to tar any resistance to their rule; but Robin Hood is a wholly different matter. Terrorists themselves have failed in their attempts to convince others by more peaceful means or have decided not to try to do so in the first place. The latter may come from a belief that a system they seek to overthrow has no credibility and should not be engaged with as a matter of 'principle.' In working democracies there is no justification for terrorism. Significantly damaged democracies with ignored groups should not be surprised by increasing physical acts of resistance, though not starting with violent or terror-inducing acts. In dictatorial regimes where even disagreement is subject to intimidation or imprisonment, people will inevitably move towards physical acts of resistance, even when the fear of government retribution is very real. In Tunisia in 2010 Mohamed Bouazizi publicly burnt himself to death and in so doing began the 'Arab Spring'; an echo of the Buddhist monk Thich Quang Duc in Vietnam in 1963 who became a worldwide symbol of Vietnamese government repression. These we do not consider 'terrorism.' If there is to be violence against such regimes, then the question becomes how it is enacted and who are the targets. Terrorist acts that blow up innocent civilians, innocent by virtue of their lack of influence to change anything, however that might be dressed up as acquiescing in the regime, is still beyond acceptance. Terrorism that concentrates on military and governmental targets is more sympathetically received. It would be nice to think that no terrorism is ever justifiable, but the reality is that those who rule without any moral authority to do so and deprive otherwise law-abiding people of any chance of change, need to be resisted. Such resistance may then reach the threshold of 'freedom fighter.' Between damaged democracies and outright dictatorship comes another group. Iran and China, for example, are not democracies with free and fair elections, and opponents are often deprived of their liberty, but nor are they mass murderous regimes of their general population like Pol Pot's Cambodia, or Saddam Hussein's Iraq – although they kill, disappear, or imprison significant numbers and may concentrate on specific groups. Within strict limits determined by their guiding religious or political beliefs they allow elections, and allow protest. These strict limits can be suffocating and strangulating to Western ideas of individual liberty and civil society. There is no plural political or civil society in a Western sense. Protests are prevented from becoming movements or campaigns, prevented from questioning fundamental aspects of the ruling orthodoxy, election candidates are vetted, and people are subject to non-independent judiciary, and patriotism is aligned with supporting specific government or leadership. However, while there are forms of protest that are allowable, where there is a limited boundary that may over time be pushed wider, where there are international relations that can influence, then terrorism is not the clear or obvious option. In the place of terrorists there may be martyrs for a cause, those who push the boundaries and get punished for doing so. This is uncomfortable to a Western audience, but the change of ground rules of a nation requires the perspective of time; and examples of struggle and sacrifice to learn from, live up to and cherish. Only in this way is significance truly appreciated. Robin Hood can become a national hero. Change imposed from outside is rarely grounded in solid and lasting foundations. Change of some sort still needs to be seen. Hope, or rather 'only' hope, can kill you. An authoritarian state by its very nature slips into a military-security state, giving people no outlet for expression or hope of change.

Terrorism depends on creating fear. Fear intends to intimidate people into changing what they do, and governments into changing policy to accommodate demands, or into overreacting. On many occasions authorities fall for this latter trap. It is of course part of a government's core job to protect its people, but 'tightened security' often in practice increases suspicion and prejudice against minorities, which maintains or can increase the sympathy or support for what terrorists want or how they should be treated. A state becomes an authoritarian one when the surveillance, restrictions, and control, are on everyone's shoulders. Public vigilance is not the same, and the connection between the two must be one hounded by accountability, such as reasonable or specific suspicion and independent judicial review. It may be that the demands of groups are seen as 'wants' and are considered extreme or unreasonable, but this should be the judgement of the width of society, not simply a government or even a single majority group. Consensus against a terrorist group makes it easier to defeat them. A single life lost being one too many is also a common refrain and an essential and inescapable aim, but no government can guarantee to protect the life of every single citizen. Fortunately, in practice terrorism kills and injures very few people. The Global Terrorism Database (GTD) defines it as 'the threat or use of violence to achieve a political, economic, religious or social goal through intimidation or coercion by a non-state actor.' From 2009 to 2019 terrorism under this definition killed an average of around 24,000 people worldwide each year, with a high of almost 45,000 in 2014; in 2019 was responsible for an estimated 1 in 2000 deaths (0.0005%); and is geographically focused primarily in the Middle East, Africa, and South Asia.*

It is greater in our feared imagination than reality. In recent times there has been a slightly different approach. In New Zealand the prime minister vowed never to name the perpetrator of the 2019 Christchurch Mosque attack that killed fifty-one. People have a greater understanding that they should still live their normal lives. Punishment would be proportionate. Justice would be transparent. Media would not be sensationalist. This approach can withstand different causes of potential terrorism. It contributes to the resurrection of the democratic nature of a response that had been lost to legislative and security-led action. It begins to control the imagination of fear that terrorists depend on. A more democratic response begins to address the need to properly analyse and face up to the reasons why people choose to support or get involved in terrorist groups or campaigns. It does not mean that the loss of any single life is OK. It rebalances the attack on terrorist acts to a more even keel between root causes and reaction to the threat. These things are not possible in a non-democratic regime. Public opinion cannot be embraced by the regime, security and order is a greater aspect of their legitimacy, and root causes cannot be acknowledged without questioning the workings of authority.

Existential threats that can alter the fabric of society such as 'dirty' nuclear devices and biological or chemical threats must be treated differently. This is the role of real security services. International terrorism unrelated to a specific state requires the multinational action of international crime, with the same analysis. International terrorism supported by a specific state is in practice an act of war. International terrorism that does not explode bombs but does attack critical infrastructure must be subject to that same approach.

The Future of Conflict

There is an array of global experience that relate to international

---

* Bastian Herre, Veronika Samborska, Hannah Ritchie and Max Roser, "Terrorism," *Our World in Data* https://ourworldindata.org/terrorism (relying heavily on the *Global Terrorism Database*, GTD, https://www.start.umd.edu/gtd/about/).

relations and internal governance. There is a growing call for the rule of a consistent and accountable rule of law within nations. Economic prosperity is increasingly inter-dependent. Government is becoming more managerial and less ideological in the pursuit of rising standards of living which are becoming the centrepiece of the struggles for public and individual rights within nations. Both materialism and the need for a spiritual purpose to life are crossing cultural divides. A new global level of communication is furthering the understanding of others and their lifestyles, beliefs and circumstances, and their fears and ambitions. Within multinational groups nations are realising that they can keep their individual sovereignty at the same time as achieving common policy. This is a journey and there is no overarching plan. At some point the repetitive nature of conflict must be addressed.

There are significant actions, even trends, pulling against the virtuous tide. People will point to increasing political culture wars, and people living in their own silos of information or disinformation. In some places there is deliberate disengagement from authority. On the other hand, in many places people are impatient for change. There is often a lack of knowledge or strategy about desired change encompassed in a lack of leadership or unified vision. Localism itself can sometimes seem like a breakdown of unity, division without an overarching commonality, local voices separating themselves. This is sometimes the result of a lack of confidence in a larger authority, but localism can also be an expression of confidence from the larger authority. It is the criteria, the context, the goals, and the resources that make this a problem or an opportunity. At the other end of the scale multinational corporations or supranational institutions may deny local voices and individual or small community circumstances, and lose touch with ordinary people, losing the language that ordinary people use. They can seem to encourage competition or further the interests of some but not others. Few places around the world have achieved a good balance between local and national power, let alone local, national, and multinational power. All these can pose serious problems to progressive change and be further causes of conflict, directly or indirectly, large and small, international and domestic. A more global and longer-term perspective is needed.

Positively, more people around the world are engaging with each other in the transfer of ideas, in economic activity, in travel, and in their knowledge of processes that determine the running of their communities. This is a multi-peopled, multi-layered, multi-located attack on the causes of conflict. We must resist the balkanisation of the internet and self-reinforcing algorithms, resist disengagement, resist simply managerial government. We must resist the revenge motive for justice and the acceptance of others as not being like us. We must find it within ourselves to listen and engage with others who disagree. Opposition for the sake of opposition does not improve anything, it simply results in the development of opposition as an ideology, however dysfunctional that may be in practice. We must resist the misuse of technology. We need to be teaching ethics, whatever we may call it. We need to address the problems we have, not look the other way. We are beginning to recognise the dangers of globalism, that national problems can be common and globally linked too: crime, corruption, disinformation, as well as more obvious international issues like climate and pollution, migration, and health. We are increasingly understanding the internationally reinforced factors contributing to poverty and inequality. Nor can we ignore persistent domestic causes and consequences of conflict in the guise of discrimination and crime, including unfulfilled stressful lives, and economic hardship.

We cannot afford to ignore more traditional causes of international conflict, over resources, over status or pride, over historic grievance, or conflict serving the interests of a national leader; nor the attempts to retain power of a declining nation and the attempts to flex the muscles of a rising one. Around the world intractable pre-global problems persist, from drug cartel power in Mexico to warlords in Central Africa, from religious tension in Indonesia to old-style national animosity in the Indian subcontinent. Oppressive one-person dictatorships are almost a thing of the past, but outwardly benign dictatorships or one-party control not so, and cleverer more media-savvy techno-military dictatorships are on the rise.

We have not translated the values we have as individuals into consistent beliefs about conflict, either as it exists now or might exist in the future. We have not addressed the inconsistencies in our beliefs and actions when we consider different forms of conflict, from crime to discrimination to international warfare. There is not yet a consensus for those values in the emerging global world. We have not worked out how to put hopes and fears into regulation and enforcement. These are aspects of the arc of education that humanity is embarked on. It will develop depth and strength as the underlying features that prevent conflict continue to develop: education about each other, communication with each other, inter-dependence of each other. This applies to domestic conflict as much as international conflict. A growing list of worldwide movements continues to educate all of us, from climate change protests, to addressing discrimination. A growing tendency for communities to be multi-racial and multi-cultural grows understanding of others and of ourselves and can result in the growing confidence in both that allows us to address our problems from a position of communal and individual strength. We just need to make sure that we do not end the life of humanity – either by becoming billions of lone unconnected individuals or by mass extinction – before we realise it. We must continue to make progress in addressing all forms of conflict. We must continually develop the art and architecture of peace and co-operation.

VI

GLOBALISATION

*If the Earth
were only a few feet in diameter,
floating a few feet above a field somewhere,
people would come from everywhere to marvel
at it. People would walk around it marvelling at its
big pools of water, its little pools and the water flowing
between. People would marvel at the bumps on it and the
holes in it. They would marvel at the very thin layer of gas
surrounding it and the water suspended in the gas. The people
would marvel at all the creatures walking around the surface of
the ball and at the creatures in the water. The people would
declare it as sacred because it was the only one, and they would
protect it so that it would not be hurt. The ball would be the
greatest wonder known, and people would come to pray to
wonder how it could be. People would love it and defend
it with their lives because they would somehow
know that their lives could be nothing
without it. If the Earth were only
a few feet in diameter.*

Joe Miller, 1975.[*]

Globalisation combined with technology combined with social media and constant information have disrupted people's lives in very concrete ways… people are less certain of their national identities or their place in the world.' Barack Obama.[†]

---

[*] Joe Miller, 1975, *If the Earth were a Few Feet in Diameter*, by Joe Miller and Wilson McLean, Greenwich Press Ltd, 1998.
[†] Quote taken from Mark Odell, "Globalization and rapid change sparked populist backlash, says Obama," *Financial Times*, 15 Nov 2016.

WHERE ARE WE GOING?

There are two ways in which we seem to be approaching globalisation and working out what it means. The first is through a Western 'takeover.' The second is a cross-cultural phenomenon, which is genuinely more globalist in nature. Through these two approaches our modern idea of globalism is emerging, but there are key questions that we are beginning to ask about its nature and its future.

The Western takeover model comes from the 16th to 21st century European empires. It became a more interwoven control than had ever been known before. 'New world' colonies were set up largely by adventurers, followed by religious and then economic refugees as 19th century industrialisation took hold. Europe's power contained and subsequently overcame the increasingly inward-looking Muslim world, the civil service of a weak China, the Mughal and other kingdoms of the Indian subcontinent, destroyed the great Aztec and Inca empires of Central and South America, and nearly wiped out the Indigenous peoples of the Caribbean, North America, Australia, and New Zealand. Europe was not one nation but its white man's rule, similar monarchies, economic exploitation, and Christian missionary zeal were strong common identifiers, and transplanted wholesale. There were a whole array of consequences involving education, family life, public authority, livelihood, community, ownership of goods and land, indigenous self-confidence, and new perspectives on the world, as well as death and destruction. This is well documented across the continents in missionary schools, forced adoption, slave and indentured labour, land contracts, repression of traditional ritual and authority, etc. Western science became predominant and was seen as superior and often misused to justify superiority. Western finance and accounting dominated large-scale oceanic and land trade. Cash crops and industrialisation were imposed. Even rebellious groups within Europe who emigrated for a fresh start took European culture with them. An original thirteen licensed colonies developed the entitled superiority of 'Manifest Destiny' that enveloped the rest of the North American continent. The pursuit of European nations' own interests changed whole economies, landscapes, demographics, and settlements. Europeans in the Americas imported millions of people as goods from Africa. This exporting of its economic model placing ownership, competition, material wealth, and 'growth' at the heart of nationalism was as revolutionary as the governmental, educational, religious, and cultural changes that swept non-European societies. This Western global takeover had a depth, comprehensiveness, power, and speed that had never been seen before, justified by an arrogant European Enlightenment.

It is this model that has led to much of the modern globalism that we see today. Aspects of European domination have changed over time, becoming more secular for example, but this also raises the nature of different perceptions from a Western and non-Western view, for Christianity remains a force in many post-colonial nations. A liberal democratic style has replaced monarchy, although this has been difficult to replicate for many post-colonial nations lacking the required civic infrastructure. Economies remain structured and judged by Western ideas, frameworks, finance, and economic dominance. This is only just beginning to be challenged by China and the new-found voice of post-colonial nations. This is the globalism that has power, dominated by economics. On the international stage it is relatively mono-cultural, transactional, and materialistic. Nearly everyone wears the same clothes, Western ones.

The historic tragedies of the Western expansion and sense of superiority are now being understood better than ever: drowning islands because of climate change from industrialisation, plantation cash crop agriculture and lack of local land ownership, and collapsed indigenous confidence in identity, would be three widespread examples of ongoing consequences.

The Western dominance of globalism is now being challenged. This includes a more critical review of the Western economic model, of democratic government, and the concentration on individualism and personal liberal action. During the First World War when Europe again illustrated a lack of moral authority to lead, the Indian writer and philosopher Rabindranath Tagore wrote of the need to question European-style nationalism and what he called the organised selfishness of nations. He rejected the individual v State, labour v Capital, and the accepted inequality, transactional government, greed, and materialist practices of the European nations he saw. He rejected their conflict and competition, their use of science to promote position, and their exclusivity. He believed these things had brought world war, international slavery, colour-based racism and cultural discrimination, a never-ending treadmill of 'progress,' and a spiritual decline that reduced the purpose and fulfilment of people's lives. He knew that colonialism in Asia was not itself new, but he saw its combination with capitalism as much more destructively overpowering of local values and ways of life. Japan had recently beaten Russia in the first modern Asian triumph over Europe (the 1904–05 Russo–Japanese War), but he saw in the rise of Japan its transformation into a copy of European models. He wanted India to emphasise a 'gain not grow' approach. He wanted a resurrection of spiritual recognition, of social responsibility, of the Indian soul and identity, and a rejection as he saw it of the pursuit of European freedoms that he thought in practice meant slavery to them and of the nation. Such developments were essential requirements if nations were to be truly free, and moved on from Irish and central European nationalism that had taken root in the mid and late 19th century. His writing was an important contribution to the global development of the cultural awakening in colonial lands that would inform localised nationalism. Similar ideas were already out there forming alternative Islamic and Chinese nationalism, expressed by people such as Jamal al-din al-Afghani and Liang Qichao. Their intellectual arguments were not then seen as successful but after their death began to gain greater credit (with some criticism) for establishing the foundations of non-Western ways of thinking about the world and the West, and their ideas still have resonance. They did not reject modernity but struggled between a moderate cherry-picking of the best of the West allied to local nationalist characteristics, before gradually turning to a more anti-Western nationalism.

Over the last 100 years or so Marxism, Confucian principles, and Islamic fundamentalism are just three approaches that have tried to go beyond the global dominance of Western philosophical, governmental, and economic ideas. Fighting against the Western trend of globalism has not been easy. Specific examples of failure include Gandhian rural and subsistence Swadeshi and Swaraj based self-sufficiency and 'needs' not (Western) 'wants' in India; and a Nyerere-inspired Ujamaa socialism based on an African village-development economic model in post-independence Tanzania. Implanting it elsewhere has also not been easy, as evidenced by Sun Yat-sen's 1911 Chinese (democratic) Republic consumed by weakness of the centre, splits, warlord power and Western powers influence; and Japan's Meiji Restoration embracing Western modernity that turned to ultra-Imperialism.

Meanwhile our understanding of the global and historic nature of issues has developed. Health, pollution, climate and biodiversity, exploitation of the oceans and polar icecap changes, finance, security, inequality, and the physical and technological sciences all affect domestic politics and societies without purely or effective domestic solutions. Since a post-colonial Non-Aligned group first emerged non-Western individual nations have found the strength to have their voices heard on the international stage. Some smaller nations are finding a different way, individually or in combination, such as Bhutan with its Happiness Index, and the emerging Wellbeing Economy group including New Zealand, Scotland, and others. Furthermore, the international movements raising gender and minority equality are changing societies from within and across the globe. Since a Western globalism took root societies internally have changed, including Western ones, and international relations have been transformed. Globalism is now a social and cultural phenomenon as well as an economic and political one. No single nation can control trends that affect multiple aspects of life.

For some people digging out the roots of the superiority-based old Western Enlightenment globalism is a pre-requisite to something better. This is the revolutionary approach. For other people they are not roots, but too-dominant ingredients in a recipe that needs to be rebalanced for a more accommodating taste that appeals to, and will culturally and economically sustain, more and different people. This is the more moderate, gradualist, consensual approach. Both of these require a more globalist philosophy. While this cross-cultural dialogue may be expected to be a slow burner the more urgent nature of some global issues is making nations work together and peoples find their common humanity.

WHERE ARE WE GOING?

Climate Change

Man-made climate change is the most obvious and destructive of these global issues. Whereas poverty and inequality can be hidden from many, the nightmare potential of making whole areas inhospitable, if not uninhabitable, may affect well-developed nations not just remote poor ones. Climate change is also a more complex issue than any other. In effecting the interplay of the world's eco-systems it affects how we and other species may live, and how we interact with each other. Nor is this 'effect' just in liveability or migration, it is about food chains and life expectancy. It is also psychologically 'worrying' because we do not as a species like things that are not under our control. A young generation is growing up to believe with each new revelation or milestone that their personal opportunities, and even the existence of their generation itself, is being called into question; while often also believing that older generations do not care or understand, or do not do so enough.

Climate change is therefore also questioning some of our fundamental ideas about how we now live and 'make progress.' Even where there are known solutions and commitment we don't agree on emphasis, urgency, responsibility, or accountability. Timeframes, finance, aid, state or corporate action, voluntary or legislative compulsion, innovation or austerity, binding international agreements with monitoring and enforcement mechanisms, and the effectiveness of individual action are all hotly debated. We continue to look for blame and want to apportion responsibility for the whole sorry mess, to previous generations, to other nations, to the whole concept of economic growth, to materialism and selfishness in our nature or that has been nurtured, or to an obsession with science and technology. Multi-millions of people around the world lacking wealth and influence are in virtually no position to affect the outcome of debate or action, while at the same time seeking the gains others have already made, and we are also getting better at understanding that perspective. Climate change is therefore also a moral minefield of dizzying proportions. How does one generation carry the responsibility, or let go of the original sin? Where is the correct moral position discussing the limits of climate-related migration, exploitation of resources to alleviate poverty, or population control? Ecuador, in

2023, stopped an Amazonian oil exploration – as a result its credit rating fell and so it was forced to pay more on its interest rate for loans. Who pays for climate change solutions? One way to get through all this is to ignore it, or at least most of it. Concentrate on the positive and on what can be done. Don't let the perfect or entrenched principle be the enemy of action. Look to the future. Look for a diverse range of solutions. Call everyone to action and seek out what you can do personally and individually. Have a big plan and daily action. Be practical and visionary. Have a clear moral view and accommodate the views of others. In fact, there are almost as many clichés about dealing with climate change as there are books and plans. These clichés, of course, may not be wrong or unhelpful, but the devil is in the detail.

We should not underestimate how difficult global action is. Oil and gas companies are commonly five of the twenty largest in the world, whether measuring turnover, profits, employment, or political and geographical reach. This influence would also be found in the 'beef/meat' lobby, in terms of 'way of life' arguments. And where there are beef and fossil fuel lobbies, there are many others too.

The Beef

The consumption of meat, still increasing in Asia, is now considered one of the main drivers of climate change. It is conservatively estimated that raising livestock (for meat and dairy) accounts for nearly 15% of global greenhouse emissions each year, mostly methane, which is more dangerous than CO_2. Production, distribution, consumption, and animal feed production all contribute to the carbon footprint.* The consumption of beef has exploded with the increase of the fast-food burger outlet, which is seen as part of the American way of life, globally copied for that reason. It is an example of more affluent people having a bigger impact on resource exploitation than poorer people. The production of a beefburger may include clearing forest for pasture, water use, and transport, as well as the feed (and antibiotics) needed,

---

* Paul Hawken, 2017, 39. He also references a 'groundbreaking' study, completed in 2016, by Oxford University citing a worldwide transition to plant-based and vegetarian food by 2050 that could reduce global mortality by 6–10% and save $1 trillion in healthcare costs, with subsequent improvements in productivity.

and methane produced. While different studies can be slightly different 1kg of beef produces between 30 and 60kg of greenhouse emissions, twice as much as the next food, lamb; with rice less than 5kg; and one cheeseburger is responsible for about half a gallon of petrol. Alexandre Koberle from Imperial College, London, has said, 'Next to flying less, … as individuals, reducing beef consumption is the most significant contribution (to tackling climate change) directly under our own control.'*

However, if people cut beef from their diet tomorrow there would be a significant economic shock in major producers and consumers. In some parts of the USA this would be seen as an attack on people's way of life, whether that came from a 'traditional' or 'nostalgic' or 'anti-government' background. In the USA vegetarianism is already seen in some places as part of the 'culture wars.' In Texas in 2012 $10.5billion came from cattle production, half the state's commodities revenue, from 130million acres.† Texas, a growing state, has the second-highest number of representatives in the Electoral College who elect each American President. And what would happen to 130 million acres of landscape that are currently cattle ranches – perhaps turned into solar energy farms or re-wilded?

For many people such 'fast-food' is now their cheapest food, or a chosen regular spend, related to cooking ability, taste preference, or time, and presented as a sociable experience. These choices and behaviours are not so easy to change. If people give up beef one option is likely to be alternative meat sources, perhaps pork or chicken. Animal welfare standards for chickens – the majority of which are raised in factory farms – are often considered appalling. Increasing chicken consumption

---

* David Vetter, "Got beef? Here's what your hamburger is doing to the climate," *Forbes*, 5 October 2020. Koberle was research fellow at the Faculty of Natural Sciences at the Grantham Institute for Climate Change at Imperial College, London. See also, Jamais Cascio, "The Cheeseburger footprint," *Open the Future*, www.openthefuture.com, and *Carbon brief* a UK climate change website. Assessing the comprehensive carbon footprint of food is still a developing science, and there will always be individual variables such as transport, but these also include good explanations of assessment method.

† Amanda Carr, "The Texas Tradition of Cattle Ranching Began in Tejas," *Texas Historical Commission*, Dec 2, 2023, https://thc.texas.gov/blog/texas-tradition-cattle-ranching-began-tejas. Beef production can also be searched for on the *World Population Review* website, www.worldpopulationreview.com.

may therefore increase animal welfare concerns and become another moral minefield. Alternatives to beef often involve highly-processed plant-based materials and the use of chemical-based flavouring. For most people, there is still something weird about divorcing the food itself from any knowledge or recognition of its 'natural' production. 'Grown' meat is not yet on a large enough scale to be an alternative to 'real' meat, and to have its carbon emission footprint accurately assessed. But developing production techniques will likely improve its carbon footprint, food texture, look, and taste, and, essentially, costs and consumer price. And plant-based food still has the potential to provide a part of the solution to climate change. Either way, it seems possible that the traditional farming skills that have been part of the bedrock of human history will eventually go the way of old-fashioned weaving and spinning.

Meat consumption is only one part of the 'food' section in the debate on climate change. Changing what, where, and how we farm and distribute food from the land, are now seen as important as changes in our energy use. Live issues include sustainable or managed farming to protect the soil, environment, and habitats, maintaining biodiversity in the process; the overuse of fertilisers and antibiotics which build up in nature and the food chain; and genetically modified crops, with its philosophical argument about efficiency, resilience, and provision of amount versus long-term interference in nature. Then there are issues around farming the Oceans, intensive urban and even single building food production, and the moral problem or opportunity of eliminating the very idea of farming animals for slaughter. Strategies have consequences in economics, politics, science, social and cultural norms and expectations, affordability, building design and the urban landscape, the rural landscape, and people's identity. This is part of the complexity of tackling climate change. In asking about the beef, for example, cutting consumption in half is better than not tackling the issue, while still producing profound consequences.

WHERE ARE WE GOING?

Nuclear Energy

Virtually all nations have committed with various timeframes and transparency to cut fossil fuel carbon emissions and move towards sustainable or renewable energy. For many this includes using nuclear power. French electricity production is 70% nuclear. Neighbouring Germany had promised to decommission all its nuclear plants by 2023 although the war in Ukraine effects that timeline.* Nuclear power is not a solution without problems. Cost and production time seriously hinder development, and other non-climate change issues make it a very divisive policy to pursue. Newer plants are technically more reliable, work in different ways, and are less wasteful. Smaller-scale fixed design power plants are being explored to maximise these changes, reducing costs, and fit a potential future of more localised energy hubs, greater safety, and less environmental impact. Nuclear energy can be good for tackling climate change in comparison to coal- and gas-fired plants. There is also legitimacy in seeing the need for varied energy production methods to guarantee supply. So, nuclear energy overall?

A host of other issues call its use into question now and in the future. Some of these appear intuitive, some practical, some moral, and some certainly emotional. They show how suggested and now operable climate change solutions still need careful consideration in the round. It might be argued that logistical and technical problems of development may be neutralised by innovation. Safety and security may be more problematic. Three Mile Island in 1979, Fukushima in 2011, and especially Chernobyl in 1986 are the three, but not only, most destructive nuclear plant accidents. The Chernobyl reactor is expected to be dangerous for 20,000 years, an area of 45km around the site is considered uninhabitable (its 'exclusion zone') for a generation even though wildlife has returned, and altogether 150,000 sq. km across three countries were directly affected at the time, with approximately 350,000 people evacuated. Nuclear power is an energy source that can destroy so much of value so far away from its centre for so long, so immediately, and that needs future generations beyond

---

* Kerstine Appunn, "The history behind Germany's nuclear phase-out," *Clean Energy Wire,* 9 March 2021, https://www.cleanenergywire.org/factsheets/history-behind-germanys-nuclear-phase-out.

GLOBALISATION

our comprehension to be wary of it. A similar argument applies to the disposal of nuclear waste. Storing High-Level nuclear waste (about 4% of waste) requires security for periods ranging from tens of thousands to a million years; both infrastructural safety and physical security.* This has only begun to be addressed and is not with any consensus resolved. It may be that safety and waste disposal will be accommodated by technical advances – which may be pie-in-the-sky optimism – but this does not necessarily ensure security. Issues of nuclear material mining security, of theft and subsequent misuse for terrorism, and cyber security of nuclear plants, are major ongoing issues, as is a nuclear plant in a war zone. The development of nuclear power material for use in nuclear weapons by established states is also a credible concern. These security and safety issues, and potential nuclear weapon proliferation, are polarising views of the public. No-one wants a nuclear power plant in their backyard, except perhaps people who see their future working there. In some nations the public have no acknowledged influence. Plants, which need cooling water, in many countries, France, for example, cannot realistically be remote from population centres. After the ocean earthquake/tsunami-caused Fukushima meltdown it was clear that studies that portray resilience in the face of natural disaster are only as good as the information that humans choose to base them on. How often is 'a thousand year' natural disaster going to happen, because that does not mean it will only happen *after* a further thousand years. Some of these judgements depend on our evolving education about the definitiveness or interpretational nature of science itself.

Nuclear power can be important in our plans to tackle climate change, and the provision of power for continually developing economies and standards of living. It will benefit from future scientific and technological improvements. However, it can also cause unimaginable and 'permanent' damage, accidentally, or through an over-confident belief in human control, or through deliberate misuse. Nuclear power may be an example of a blinkered solution, a short-term perspective to fix a problem, ignoring its own moral debate, with such long-term

---

* See "Storage and disposal of radioactive waste," *World Nuclear Association*, 30 April 2024. www.world-nuclear.org. Also see The International Panel on Fissile Materials, an international panel of independent nuclear experts, formed in 2006.

consequences that it creates its own future nightmare, for which we are unprepared.

Population Control or Family Planning

Population control or family planning is another different type of climate change solution. In fact, the two different labels should denote a very different approach. Language is as important in discussing climate change as it is with other important issues. A few years ago many people in China and the West talked about population control. The global population was and is continuing to rise.* What was feared was the Malthusian idea that more resources would simply produce a higher population which would use up those resources rather than improve living standards.† This view still lingers partly because the reverse seems logical: less people use less. Population control therefore became a 'green' issue. The Malthusian view has been added to by the liberal view that one person in a developed nation must be equal to one in a less developed nation. However, wherever food has become more plentiful living standards have risen and birth rates have fallen. Furthermore, Western voices with media profile and power telling other nations to cut their population rise was seen as a privileged morality by the recipients of the message. It was. In a few nations without developing welfare systems and with relatively high child mortality more children mean more family earning power and elderly care, and the message is unrealistic. In many more developing nations figures show this to be the wrong or outdated message. Tamil Nadu State in India from 1971 to 2011 halved its population growth rate through increasing female education as well as increased food security. Iran and Bangladesh, not obvious examples to Western observers, have reduced their TFR, total fertility rate i.e., total births per woman in her lifetime, between 1960 and 2020 from 7 to 2.1 and 1.9 respectively. The birth rate is falling across the world. Only Central and West Africa currently have birth rates significantly

---

* See "Population," *United Nations*. https://www.un.org/en/global-issues/population.
The population reached 8 billion on 15 November 2022, and is estimated to level off at about 10.4 billion in 2080 where it will remain until 2100.
† Thomas Malthus was a British cleric and economist, whose key work "An Essay on the Principle of Population" was published in 1798.

beyond the 2.1 per woman to replace their own populations. In the most dramatic example of South Korea it is currently 1.1; in the UK it is 1.7. China at 1.7 will see its population fall by 2.7% by 2050 and its total has already been overtaken by India.* Even more relevantly, the idea of one person being equal to any other on the planet in relation to climate change and other resource-driven issues is also not true.

In the early 1970s Paul Ehrlich and John Holdren came up with a better approach and calculation: I = P x A x T, i.e., Impact = Population x Affluence x Technology. Population still mattered but combined with affluence and technology it mattered much more. Affluence meant access to healthcare, welfare, and family planning; and Technology meant developed transport and energy consumption. One person living a poor subsistence lifestyle would therefore have far less impact on the environment than one who lived longer with better health, took holidays by car or plane, commuted to work, and had ample electricity for their needs and their luxuries. The Total CO_2 output in 2020 of an average Kenyan for a year was equalled by an average Canadian in nine days. The USA had 13% of the world's total, China 30%, but Nigeria 0.26%. The contributary solution to climate change impact for *both* the high-energy-use developed world and developing world where birth rates are falling but actual population totals are still currently increasing, are energy efficiency and sustainability, and alternative behaviours like less meat consumption. However, no-one could expect a poor family, or nation, not to want better living standards from economic development; and, specifically in relation to family planning, success can only be achieved with developing infrastructure and health systems. It is the economic development in parallel with population in developing nations that is important. If they developed economically while still maintaining a larger family, then their impact would grow. In urban Nairobi families typically have three children, but in rural Kenya they have five who tend to both finish education and marry earlier.† Family planning not

---

* "World Population Prospects 2022," report by, *United Nations Department of Economic and Social Affairs*, https://www.un.org/development/desa/pd/sites/www.un.org.development.desa.pd/files/wpp2022_summary_of_results.pdf. "Fertility rate, total (births per woman)," *World Bank Group*, https://data.worldbank.org/indicator/SP.DYN.TFRT.IN?end=2022&start=1960.

† "The secret solution to climate change," *The Climate Questions* [podcast] BBC World

'population control' may become decisive in tackling global resource and environmental damage. There are, however, other serious obstacles to achieving the desired outcomes.

Population control is about authority-driven compulsion, but family planning is about a liberal-friendly choice that people make for their own circumstances. If family planning in principle is accepted, then access and acceptability are the issues. Access is a logistical problem of development and healthcare priority. That is not to say that it is unimportant or simple – it is neither of those – and access may be as large a problem as acceptability. Acceptability may be a cultural issue, primarily in nations (or within nations including developed ones) where societies hold back independent choices for women, or emphasise a religious restriction to birth control (although there are also plenty of examples where religious belief within a nation has not hindered the personal choice of a family's planning). Family planning is therefore intertwined with female education and freedoms. Education can teach the benefits and methods of family planning but these come to little if a married woman has no independence of action. Improving gender equality is therefore as important as economic development, and includes the education of boys in school and men in society. This is the revolutionary nature of gender equality. The falling birth rate would seem to show that nations across the globe are addressing this as well as those developmental issues that make a falling birth rate more likely. Then again, in 2020 4/160 national climate change plans mentioned women's rights, and 1/160 mentioned girl's education.*

Where family planning takes place in developed nations other issues emerge. The declining population of nations like Japan, Germany, and Hungary is good for climate change based on the $I = P \times A \times T$ calculation, but the result of this is labour shortages endangering economic growth and standard of living. Japan encourages a wider workforce from its established population, and the use of automotive and robotic development to improve productivity. Germany's response was to open its borders, resulting in one million immigrants over two

---

Service, 14 December 2020; "CO2 Emissions by Country," *World Population Review*, https://worldpopulationreview.com/country-rankings/co2-emissions-by-country.
* Jackson and Razzell, 14 December 2020.

years. Chancellor Merkel's policy was not driven by climate change, but a different and very liberal adjacent solution to population stagnation and refugee crisis. However, if climate change continues to produce more extreme weather it will produce more climate refugees. In Hungary the right-wing government of Victor Orbán has rejected immigration as a solution to a falling population, whatever the push or pull factors of the immigrants. Instead, his government has gone down the path of creating benefits and incentives for a home-grown rise in births. It is too early to judge its success. The population problem in relation to the carbon footprint may eventually take care of itself through falling global birth rates, albeit with serious effects on other areas of life. A few commentators even foresee the onset of a global population crisis within thirty years because birth rates are falling so dramatically.

It is now the scientific and political consensus that we need to drastically cut carbon emissions and maintain biodiversity to reduce or reverse very damaging man-made climate change. The authoritative Intergovernmental Panel on Climate Change (IPCC) in April 2022 stated that keeping global warming below the long-held target of 1.5°C was now not realistic, but that 2°C was possible, with emissions halved by 2030 at affordable costs of action taken 'across the board.' Yet the concern has been out there for a while: German scientist Alexander von Humboldt was the first to identify human-induced changes to the climate and the living environment, based on his early 19th-century travels. He specifically identified deforestation, extreme irrigation, and the 'great masses of steam and gas' being produced in industrial centres. In 1971 Pope Paul VI called ecological concern 'a tragic consequence' of unchecked human activity and the 'ill-considered exploitation of nature.' Pope Francis in his 2015 Encyclical *Laudato Si'* (Praise Be To You/On Care for Our Common Home), wrote of 'ecological sin,' the 'differentiated responsibilities' of nations, and the need to 'seek other ways of understanding the economy and progress.' However, plans internationally to reach 'net zero' emissions are still at early stages in terms of detailed international agreement, corporate change, infrastructural changes, and consumer impact. They are at an early stage of transparency, monitoring, accountability, and enforcement. They are at an early stage – compared to what is necessary – of investment, innovation, and government action. Many issues are only just beginning to reach public boiling point or serious international negotiating tables, such as Ocean exploitation and Off-setting (essentially paying someone to do something good in return for being able to do something still bad). Some required changes clearly have interactions with other major global trends such as addressing inequality and discrimination. Many solutions, like re-growing trees within parched farming land to rejuvenate soil, known as tree intercropping, part of 'farmer-managed regeneration,' are local and ancient skills. This is halting desertification in parts of West Africa. Not all solutions are based on modern science, large-scale, or even new. Some new technology is needed, such as new fuel or design for boats and aeroplanes. The current, as opposed to future, consequences of climate change are already causing major domestic disruption.

The examples of meat consumption, nuclear energy, and family planning show the complexities are political, economic, social, cultural, logistical, and even religious and linguistic. They illustrate how the moral imperative to act over climate change can produce other moral dilemmas, and even contradictions, as well as practical difficulties. Recognising the revolutionary nature of really tackling climate change is the point of fear as well as opportunity for those considering effective solutions. The questioning of the economic and political model of permanent industrialised growth that helped to produce it in the first place and helps to sustain it now, is still a radical concept. The very nature of a nation's wealth, or GDP, and how we compare one country to another may need redefinition. Questioning those models also means questioning how we as humanity intend to live, and what making progress really means; and this questions what sort of people we are. Tackling climate change may well need this level of transformation and this level of commitment. There is no point in tinkering with the edges of the issue even if we cannot change everything, or everything at once. Such a fundamentally profound discussion has barely started. Yet at the same time solutions are out there and there seem to be new developments every day. We should not be negative about what we can do.

Economic Inter-Dependence

Modern economic globalism can take different forms. International companies' resource, employ, manufacture, profit, and hopefully pay tax, in a variety of different countries and legal jurisdictions. There is also state-directed expansion of economic influence to further political influence, such as China's Belt and Road Initiative. This was adopted by the Chinese government in 2013 to directly invest or make loans in nearly seventy countries and international organisations through maritime and land trade routes, creating a new 'silk road.' These loans have led to a fear of 'debt trap diplomacy' i.e., loans resulting in debts that cannot be paid and therefore increased Chinese leverage. The USA's Marshall Plan to support Western European democracy after the Second World War comes to mind. Arguments can be made about the expansion of trade and bringing people out of poverty by raising living standards. They can also be seen as undue influence or unfair competition, or subtle 'soft colonialism.' Purely noble motives are rare.

Consequences of global economic development have become clearer for individuals and 'the workers,' and for the effective economic sovereignty of nations. The workings of international aid and trade and related international debt have also been questioned from both an effective altruism perspective and an effective national development one. The nature of free trade that the development of globalism is allegedly based on has been questioned as local accountability and national regulation struggle to become more responsive to more independent and democratic voices. International bodies have begun to be more internationally representative in their outlook. Authoritarian nations resist regulated free trade.

The extent and nature of global inequality is now more visible, causes consternation if not anger, and is linked by many to the internationalisation of 'free' trade. Poorer consumers in more independent (and at least mildly democratic) nations are now able to demand greater national regulation and protections from an international system and international companies they believe disadvantage them, economically and culturally. In fact, poverty is being eliminated at an historically fast rate and there is a question here of historical perspective.

International communications and cross-cultural morality promote the understandable impatience of people, in the developed and developing world, wanting greater change towards a fairer international system, and the apparent short-term fragility of progress towards eliminating poverty. This contributes to the promotion of such issues as women's rights and immigration. Economic globalism is personal. Governments themselves may lose economic power but maintain social and cultural influence. Economic globalism is also governmental. Another aspect being questioned is the assumption that prosperity from inter-dependent economic development would result in more democracy, and therefore more peace. Two examples show how this has foundered. The collapse of the Soviet Union after 1991 produced such an economic catastrophe that an emotional, nostalgic, nationalist, oligarchic, authoritarian state emerged from the ruins to take control of the chaos. Perhaps chiefly it has foundered on the success of the CCP. Both raise serious questions as to how much Western leaders and thinkers understand the rest of the world.

Additionally, questions have been raised by the practical difficulties experienced by global trade in recent years through financial collapse, Covid-19, and the war in Ukraine. These have disrupted supply chains and supplies themselves. They have raised prices, lowered living standards, and encouraged a feeling of fragility and powerlessness. Globalism appears to many people like a business-biased model, where the link between business and worker benefits has been broken. Current public demands may yet make for a better system of fair trade, a protection for development, and national governments that can be more responsive to national voices. This can be a populist or democratic-based questioning of the status quo and the political predominance of economic globalism, its consequences, and its future.

Inequality Between Nations

GDP per capita broadly measures economic performance and gives an idea of average economic wellbeing within nations, as does life expectancy at birth (though neither show domestic inequality). The variation between nations is stark:

GLOBALISATION

Country	GDP per capita (US $)*	Rank / 195	Life Expectancy (LE) (yrs.)†	LE Rank /200
Canada	54,870	15	83.18	24
Costa Rica	18,030	65	80.47	54
Indonesia	5,270	117	71.24	170
Italy	39,580	28	84.35	8
Lesotho	1,110	166	55.10	234
Peru	8,290	93	77.14	98
Tanzania	1,220	169	68.13	183
Thailand	7,810	85	80.13	58
World Average	13,840		73.67 (30 lowest all in Africa)	

Poverty is personal. If you are poor then you know it, and nowadays you are also far more likely to know how the other half live. While real poverty needs to be disentangled from a moving poverty line which is relative to others, and from changing expectations, these are also important. It is true that millions have been taken out of the worst poverty in recent decades, but it is also true that millions remain and that 'the richest' of the world continue to get richer. The Occupy Movement born from the 2008 financial crash became a worldwide vehicle for a debate about the increasing relative wealth of the top 1%.‡ The richest people have been able to build a resilience, often through diversified wealth and interests, into their livelihood and lifestyle. Accumulated, usable, wealth enables new investment opportunity and expertise

---

* "GDP per capita, current prices," *International Monetary Fund* (IMF) World Economic Outlook, https://www.imf.org/external/datamapper/NGDPDPC@WEO/OEMDC/ADVEC/WEOWORLD

† "List of countries by life expectancy," *Statistics Times* (Source: UN, World Population Prospects 2024), https://www.statisticstimes.com/demographics/countries-by-life-expectancy.php.

‡ Forbes' 2021 list of billionaires, accessed 3 May 2022, and Hurun Global Rich List, Hurun, 2 March 2021, show the wealth and location of the world's billionaires. NB. Wealth calculations are a snapshot, as often wealth is in shares that can change value significantly from time to time.

in accounting and other advisory roles and new technologies in the personal and business spheres. Their wealth allows them to have a buffer between a failed investment and becoming significantly poorer. They have invested in education. They are more likely to be born healthier and remain so. They have time, or employ people, to reflect on actions and changing circumstances, to be creative and visionary. They have bought governing influence either directly or through the importance of their economic power. They have tried, like all successful people before them, to entrench and future-proof their and their children's predominance. In our competitive economic model these all seem natural, maybe inevitable, things for people to do.

As within nations, so too between nations. Being able to invest in education, technology, health, and in physical and digital infrastructure, and have reasonably paid jobs, make and maintain a nation as 'developed' and 'rich' in our modern eyes, maintained by good governance. Like-minded successful nations can control the rules of the game by which the other nations are also trying to succeed. An economic interdependence becomes a power-play of unequal players. The rules of the game at 'best' involve the cost of trade and aid, allowance of technology transfer, enticing the best and brightest, deciding arbitration procedures, and controlling the governance of international bodies. The rules at 'worst' include the power to interfere in the stability and governance of other nations directly, to sanction, to 'regulate' out or simply buy out competition, and to pick and choose trading partners. International 'free trade' and 'the markets' are not benevolent fair exercises with a level playing field. Aid often becomes debt; loans may be dependent on spending less or raising taxes or opening domestic markets that then cripple local business, and so in practice reduce longer-term investment in health and infrastructure that would sustain development and rising living standards. Multinational corporations lobby for subsidised investment and light regulation. Everyone knows they are playing in a competitive system. In all these ways the inequality of nations is sustained. This is a depressing, pessimistic analysis. However, things can change.

The specific assistance of a more powerful partner, discovery of a new resource, exceptional governance around taxation, investment, and entrepreneurial encouragement, and the relative decline of others through mistake or disaster, are the things that can help a nation break through the glass ceiling of sustainable economic development. Compare North and South Korea. Gulf oil and gas-rich nations became important when oil and gas became important, and now have the money to diversify. Norway has built the world's largest self-sustaining sovereign wealth fund from oil and gas revenues for future investment. Mexico has become a rising economy by being monopoly-friendly. Just as China once developed manufacturing investment spurred by cheap labour so that mantle has been taken on by nations like Indonesia and Vietnam. Outsourcing of services where educational levels permit (and type, e.g., learning English or other languages in the education system) has allowed such as India to create these jobs. Sometimes pay seems low by Western standards, but this can be (not inevitably) a significant step to raising income, consumer spending, expectations, the tax base, and investment. Development becomes a possibility. The wider that opportunities for innovative and technological change, education, and entrepreneurship are spread then development moves away from being exploitive and extractive and becomes more sustainable and inclusive.

In March 2023 the Australian Strategic Policy Institute (ASPI) judged that China led the world's research in thirty-seven out of forty-four 'critical and emerging' technology fields.[*] However, it still seems unclear how much political inclusivity and civil society would be needed to sustain this. A phrase about not needing to be able to read a free press every day to design a phone would seem to be relevant here – but it may apply to design more than innovative content based on people's needs and wants. In contrast, while the USA has its issues it is clearly more inclusive and sustainable based on its more openly opportunity-driven society. Russia has gone down the path of state-approved oligarchy, with a key energy sector, but as an increasing authoritarian state would seem to be stuck as exploitive and extractive. India has a path to the third-largest economy in the world with a developing educated, civic, and entrepreneurial society. It needs to maintain these developments but does still then face significant hurdles: development of infrastructure,

---

[*] Daniel Hurst, "China leading US in technology race in all but a few fields, thinktank finds," *The Guardian*, 2 March 2023.

vulnerability to climate change, a long tail of educational catch-up required, and wide inequality. Additionally, educated and ambitious immigrants can add further talent to a nation's progress, and this helps the USA. China chooses to send students abroad who then return. The ASPI stated that one-fifth of Chinese high-impact research papers are being "authored by researchers with postgraduate training in a Five Eyes country [USA, Canada, UK, Australia, and New Zealand]."* In parts of Africa there is a drive towards more localised entrepreneurial encouragement enabled by mobile technology. Population increase can be an instability and a burden in needs, or an opportunity in talent, workers, and markets. Over the next thirty years Nigeria is expected to grow from about 200 million to 400 million people in probably the world's fastest-growing large population. Although few nations now have an increasing or sustaining birth rate many still have a young bulge of talent coming through to their prime.

More nations are in economic blocs intended to lessen trade costs and increase opportunities. More varied leadership of worldwide organisations like the World Bank, the International Monetary Fund, and World Trade Organization are inevitably following global institutions like the UN and movable organisations like Intergovernmental Climate Change Conferences. These changes can help to change the ideas, the direction, and the working of international rules around trade, aid, arbitration, investment, and regulation. The non-exclusively Western, more cross-cultural dialogue of new globalism is making an impact. The balance between 'free trade' and protection, including when the latter should be eased, remains a live debate. Treatment of multinationals in terms of regulation and taxable income is beginning to be addressed. Arbitration in economic disputes remains in dire need of reform, not least in its speed. Improvements are not inevitable, easy, or irreversible, but in an historical context it should be remembered that many nations are only a few decades old, and so the version of the global system that they can now take a part in shaping is still emerging. Logically it will take many more years for new consensus to emerge and reforms to appear and take root.

A major route to improving economies the world over is the

---

* Ibid.

development of the role of women. Childcare policies and work (and return to work) opportunities need to improve in many places, as well as maternity and paternity leave. Alleviation of rural poverty, where women work the family land too, also falls behind that of urban. In some places the concern is still the acceptability of women working, or the educational opportunities afforded. Here too there is progress: Iran became the first Middle Eastern country to have more women at university than men in 2001 reaching 60% in 2012. However, that is not to say there are not steps backwards or still to be made: in Iran a call for more 'Islamisation' of education in 2009 has since limited some aspects of education, e.g. denying access to particular university courses.* In Japan four times as many women as men were in part-time or temporary jobs; and in 2020 the USA was one of only three countries globally not to offer statutory paid maternity leave (it was offered by some states and private employers, and only four states offer paid paternity leave).† Fifty per cent of legislators being women in fully elected legislatures only occurs in Rwanda, Cuba, and Bolivia.‡ Change will continue to arrive: in 1970 UNESCO said girls on average spent only seven years in school, and by 2020 it was twelve years.§ This growth in girls' education is the fuel of increasing gender equality campaigns. Malala Yousafzai went from primary education under threat in rural Pakistan to Oxford University graduate in 2020.

Poor governance, conflict, and natural disaster can destroy progress. The American economist Douglass North, who specialised in developing economies in the mid-20th century, placed the development of institutions and related behaviour at the centre of economic development. Oil-rich but poorly governed Venezuela is such a modern warning. Good leadership and good law do not just establish the general peace and

---

* Fariba Sahraei, "Iranian university bans on women causes consternation," *BBC Persian*, updated 22 September 2012, which suggests increasing female voices in national protest may be one reason why.
† "Women in the workforce: Japan (QuickTake)," *Catalyst 60* (a global non-profit group helping to build workplaces that work for women), 24 November 2020.
‡ Inter-Parliamentary Union, based on information from national parliaments, 1 February 2019, www.archive.ipu.org.
§ Jackson and Razzell, *The Climate Question*. Also see "Education and gender equality," and "UNESCO strategy for gender equality in and through education 2019–25," 2019, *UNESCO*.

stability on which economies thrive. More specifically they minimise large- and small-scale corruption and develop trust in government, they develop an efficient and independent civil service, they enhance credit, insurance, and safety net provision making risk-taking possible, they collect taxes efficiently and distribute support, they make infrastructure reliable, patents accessible, normalise property rights, and enforce regulation. All these things are needed for 'development,' but the path of institutions can be a vicious as well as a virtuous circle if they are uncared for.

Both civil conflict and external-origin conflict changes government and business priorities, stability, efficiency, and therefore predictability. It disrupts the labour force, distribution of services and goods, availability of markets, and spendable income. It stress-tests leadership. Conflict is in large measure human behaviour, based on decisions made, even when these accumulate and interact unexpectedly. It is therefore always a tragedy, and we must do more to prevent it. Questions of identity, existence, or security may be at stake in the eyes of a nation or a leader, and the consequences for lives and livelihoods is about far more than economics, but conflict must always be the last resort. The duty of a nation to secure safety for its citizens is an economic as well as physical one. Enforced arbitration must become a development of the future to avoid conflict between nations.

Natural disaster can also destroy progress. While preparations can be made, from earthquake resistant buildings to post-event relief, often little can be done to prevent the disaster itself. We tend to think of natural disaster as sudden and immediate but two contemporary disasters provoke significant thought: Covid-19 and climate change. The true economic effects of Covid-19 are clearly complex and yet to be measured, if they can be. Climate change, as written about previously, will have unexpected, unpredictable effects across all sorts of nations regardless of their level of governance, cohesion, development, or wealth. For both Covid-19 and climate change it may be said that they were in some measure 'predictable,' certainly more than earthquake or tornado, and that all nations were unprepared.

One part of fighting the inequality of nations is the need for both a moral and self-interest acceptance of richer nations that they should live in a more equal world. This limits a purely competitive capitalist model although it can embrace permanent growth by encouraging, or even depending on, new entrepreneurial activity, new labour forces and new consumers. The better off new consumers are the more they will buy. Raising standards elsewhere can maintain living standards of those already in a good position. Incidentally, economic globalism is also currently, mostly, about goods rather than services, which present their own opportunities and dangers.

GDP is the current accepted method of measuring and comparing the wealth of nations: it measures the value of what is produced as determined by what people are prepared to buy and sell things for. There are other things now being spoken about to hold a nation to account for itself. One is the opportunities it gives people through the provision of services like housing and education, their safety, their health, and their satisfaction with governance. Another is a valuing of the natural resources held by a nation. The primary aim of this idea is to raise the level of importance and awareness of the natural world and resources we use or that we need. Wealth by this measure therefore demands sustainability of these resources. It moves us away from our current model of resource exploitation to produce permanent growth, and the idea that we must always have more. It recognises the planet that we have rather than just the one that we are making, and it may give a greater and better value to the primary resource providers. It would require some way of valuing those assets: put simply, what is the value of a few trees keeping soil together on a small farm to maintain an eco-system? Problems abound. For example, how does a nation conserve a glacier affected by global temperatures, or a river that flows through different countries, and can it be held responsible for doing so, and what value would this be given, and would it change over time? Natural resources may be divided into resources we keep and those to be used and replaced. Resources we use and replenish may be given a value based on their human and environmental use. That might be possible. Some natural resources can bring joy and fulfilment to lives but do not put bread on the table, is this measured through wellbeing? A carbon 'off-setting' model, or models of polluters paying for environmental clean-up, may provide incentives for behavioural or technological change, locally and internationally.* Investors, businesses, consumers, influencers, and political leaders can all be incentivised with a different vision. Engineering, invention, politics, and finance can all be brought to bear on developing this approach. What we value will help to (re)frame how we work. For some people readdressing how we measure ourselves is the greatest economic opportunity of our time and a key part of replacing the 'industrial revolution' with the 'sustainable revolution.' Philosophically it is still based on the idea that land and natural resources are possessions to be owned and that have a specific monetary value. We may have gone beyond being able to un-possess land, but there is surely mileage here in expressing different ways of judging the environment we live in and resources we use. It may help us to look at what is good for the planet. It can be part of the approach that helps us to readdress what sort of people we are and what we are trying to achieve.

More fundamental than reviewing the use of GDP, we must also acknowledge Indigenous peoples around the world who do not accept ownership and valuation in the same way. Their fate has been, and still is, tangled up with the European Enlightenment of free trade, competition, and superior science, industrialisation, and imperialism, followed by legalism, contracts, materialism, and questions of status, resulting in such as homesteader land takeover, cash crops, or 'gold rushes,' and in many places an attempt at what we would now call a cultural genocide. This could be written about in several different chapters. In Canada in 1857, for example, the *Gradual Civilisation* Act (my italics) was passed stating that an 'Indian' could become 'enfranchised' if deemed sufficiently educated. In practice this meant giving up links to their indigenous heritage and status, and their land and people, to qualify to vote and superficially be considered civilised. Canadian Chief Bob Joseph has written of livelihood and economic dislocation, enfranchisement-type laws, and residential schools as having 'the potential to be a slow dismemberment of land and culture.'† Economics was a key driver in

---

* Essentially, this means producing carbon dioxide emissions but doing something to compensate for them or paying someone else who contributes to carbon dioxide reduction, so the carbon footprint is 'off-set.' Typically, this may mean paying for planting (carbon-sucking) trees, or for renewable energy schemes.

† Bob Joseph, 2018, 27.

these attempts at cultural genocide. There must be lessons to be learnt from this.

Multinational Business

In the West people tend to think of multinational businesses as the American 'big five' tech companies Apple, Amazon, Google owned by Alphabet, Meta (previously Facebook), and Microsoft, lump them all together, and put a question mark over their reputation. By market value Apple was worth US$2.91 trillion in June 2023, followed by Microsoft; by earnings Saudi Aramco with $294 billion was the largest, then Apple; by revenue Walmart $622bn, then Saudi Aramco; and by employee numbers Walmart with 2.3m, then Amazon.* In the most profitable top 20 list in 2021 were nine American companies, seven Chinese, two Japanese, Samsung from South Korea, and Saudi Aramco from Saudi Arabia. It may not be that multinational companies are a problem to the world economy, it may only be the way some work, which ones we have, and how we define them. That they work across national boundaries has created regulatory inconsistency, new ways of conducting themselves, and highlighted intergovernmental difference and competition. They can choose their headquarters or nations to account themselves in, choosing one with low regulation and low corporate tax in preference to one where they may do more business. Opponents want more tax paid where profits are made, rather than products created. Large multinationals are large enough to demand preferential tax judgements, investment subsidies, planning and building preferences, and their preferred labour and operating regulations. Their success allows them to make good profits. Their size, wealth, reputations, and what they contribute to an economy directly in their chosen field gives them a voice and lobbying influence hitherto unknown since the East India Company equivalents and the Gilded Age of late 19th-century USA. These are the common perceptions of the largest multinationals.

Not all are the same, and there is nothing inevitable about any of this. Pressure for unionisation is slowly increasing, influenced by the prevailing national culture. Google workers, at least in mid-level

---

* www.companiesmarketcap.com, accessed 17 June 2023.

positions, have successfully and publicly made feelings known that are contrary to leading management or company policy, such as in response to engagement in China. Corporate tax and regulation are just beginning to be addressed internationally, aiming to produce fairer, more transparent, and enforceable rules. The extent of lobbying for influence – which most large companies do – is becoming clearer. Influential voices in the USA have begun to talk about monopoly influence, breaking up the largest and the non-economic influence of the 'big five.' Data protection has been readdressed, with the EU leading the way with General Data Protection Regulation (GDPR) in 2018. Whistleblowers have increasingly come forward to provide insights into the inner workings and decision-making of such companies and provide evidence of the difference between public standpoints and real practice. Multinational media research and reporting has increased. Enquiries and evidence within nations are increasingly co-ordinated or shared with other legislators elsewhere. Media exposés and political leadership have been shown to make a difference. Also too, at least some lessons are being learnt from previous battles, such as the decades-long denial by tobacco companies of cancer-inducing products. Currently big pharmaceutical companies, fossil fuel energy, banks, and social media are all experiencing these winds of change in relation to environmental impact, insufficiently tackling corrupt money, disinformation, effects on health, and personal digital data security. These are big juggernauts to turn around.

As expected, the companies themselves are fighting their corner. Alternative business models and corporate culture and ethics are likely to be more effective than constantly trying to catch out companies willing to stretch the boundaries of the acceptable. At the top of businesses are people. It is people that make decisions. The boss of a company can have a decisive say on a business model that allows unionisation, that enforces fair contracts with outsourcing or supply companies, that can open its algorithms to independent experts, that can decide to publish its lobbying efforts, etc. As much as the negative effects of multinationals are played out on an international stage so could these improvements be. There are several factors that can create a more virtuous circle of improvement: consumer awareness of company work, and willingness to press corporate or individual shareholders to act; political leadership; international co-operation; changes to business education, economics, and ethics so that different parameters are set of what is acceptable or is good practice; and best practice treatment of whistleblowers. There must be personal and professional morality as well as formal business practice for those in business.

We should not lose sight of the fact that these companies are successful because they have a successful product or service. Consumers have often benefitted through cheaper or more choice of products and services provided by global reach and scale. We must find a way to regulate without losing these benefits. We must find an acknowledgement and a way to allow a company to build on its success. It is not that these companies are big, or profit-making, or international, that are themselves the problem; it is how some work, knowing how they work, holding them accountable, and resistance to change, that are the problems. They work within the systems that they are allowed to work in. When outsourcing and zero-hour contracts without benefits are allowed then companies will use these strategies. Business will be business. This is also quite a Western perspective. The companies that come to mind in the above are Western, and primarily American, companies. This is where they get their economic model and business culture from, Western competitive capitalism. They may not be truly international companies, they are multinational, i.e., they are anchored within a particular nation or type of nation, with a particular American-style approach. If they were genuinely more global then they may have a quite different approach. The Renault-Nissan-Mitsubishi Alliance is an interesting example of how this might develop, and whether the model can weather the difficulties of different national business cultures. Energy companies and airline alliances are other examples of non-tech truly international global industrial or service sectors that could also develop in this way. This could yet be the future, as headquarters move to gain advantage, as workforces become more international, as education improves across the world to feed employment, as cross-cultural understanding takes shape. As international companies merge, truly globally independent ones may be born, with international leadership. This would make these companies harder to regulate, more politically powerful, perhaps more economically agile, because they would in fact be more independent. They would also face serious difficulties, such as the national origin of raw materials and national concerns about infrastructure and security. 'Control' of raw materials remains essential. Technology that reduces or re-shapes workforces is another element of change. Currently, workforces are moved from high pay to low pay nations. In some nations this has been an important factor in raising working standards, creating jobs, raising the tax base, allowing more investment – even when they must compete with others for provision of subsidies and allowance of influence. Not necessarily by design, multinationals have contributed to economic development globally. However, even this is subject to change, as automation reduces both unskilled and technical employment.

We know far less about non-Western origin multinationals, of which a growing body of Chinese companies would be the most obviously different. These companies are as likely to be susceptible to their home national government priorities and preferences.* There is the unpredictable context of a nation of one-party rule subjecting business to individual leadership whims and a specific ideological direction; but also professing to be developing regulation and enforcement, and coming to terms with international norms of accountancy, copyright, and patenting. Aside from higher political machinations, in society at large the Chinese government is clearly concerned about widening inequality, business power, and economic stability. The extent of integration of business with China's developing individual social control is yet to be seen. Clearly, business cannot openly question political leadership. An increasing trend of authoritarianism is oligarchical in nature, with big business hand in glove with government in mutual dependence, preservation, and enrichment. This is a suicide pact if one believes that eventually people will be free. Internationally this big business is holed under the water line in terms of trust when it is domestically subject to these pressures.

Nor should we take for granted that which may seem inevitable.

---

* Arjun Kharpal, "Huawei says it would never hand 5G data to China's government. Experts say it wouldn't have a choice," *CNBC*, 5 March 2019. Bonnie Girard, "The real danger of China's National Intelligence Law," *The Diplomat*, 23 February 2019.

The free movement of capital and investment is not inevitable if the economic blocs that nations belong to become ideologically and economically competitive with different views of what the world should be like. Just as the internet can become nationally ring-fenced, so can money and investment, movement of skilled and other workers, etc.

Western nations need to find democratic – law-based, transparent, consensus, broadly liberal – methods of regulating multinationals. It is vital that nations co-operate, and establish what level playing fields they can. True multinationals are likely to become more globally independent. Political leadership and civic society must be strong enough to uphold more elusive accountability. An increasing number of multinational businesses, and the increasing nature of business as multinational, will both play an important part in the development of globalism and economic inter-dependence. It is important that they continually earn an acceptable reputation.

Aid and Trade

According to OECD protocols, in 2017 the USA spent 0.18% of its Gross National Income (GNI) on aid (Official Development Assistance), several European nations about 0.7%, Japan 0.23%. The UAE (in 2015) spent 1.17%, the greatest percentage of GNI of any nation. China, which does not follow the OECD protocols, between 2000 and 2014 spent an estimated $75bn in aid and $275bn in some form of more commercial financial loan or grant (the USA about $424bn in that period). China does not characterise itself as a donor but as part of a South–South co-operative effort. India is in transition between recipient and donor and spent about 0.3%, mostly on regionally close nations. In many countries not all 'aid' is transparent, and other money may also be given through special projects or international organisations. The UK Foreign and Commonwealth Office states, like many nations, that ODA is to further its own interests as well as alleviate poverty, and achieve Millennium Goals. In 2015 it legislated for, and in 2017 was one of only five OECD DAC member nations that achieved, 0.7% of GDP spent on international aid, first voted for by the UN General Assembly in 1970. In many countries aid, as opposed to emergency disaster relief, continues to be relatively unpopular, is almost always greatly over-estimated by the public, and often seen as aid for 'poverty' given to nations with a 'more developed' profile.* Like many countries the UK signed up to the UN Millennium Development Goals from the year 2000 for achievement by 2015: to eradicate extreme poverty and hunger; access universal primary education; promote gender equality and empower women; reduce child mortality; improve maternal health; combat HIV/AIDS, malaria, and other diseases; ensure environmental sustainability; and to globally partner for development.

The moral stance is not so transparently seen in practice. Self-interest is certainly as important: to gain favour diplomatically, and prevent instability and emigration, by building health and welfare safety nets, infrastructure, and seeds of economic development. There is also the practical necessity of priority, so nations helped are usually the subject of emergency need, or longer standing relationship, or political choice, leading to accusations of short-termism, colonial attitude, and vanity projects (for both donor and receiver). It is surprising that this aid is never characterised as reparations for historic imperial destruction or control. It is also still recognised that much aid achieves minimal success through economic inefficiency, lack of infrastructure, corruption, or poor but well-intentioned governance. As domestic donor finances come under pressure so does the pressure to measure it more clearly and accurately. This is welcome. Money needs to be spent well to justify it to both the people of the donor and the recipient nation. This should not amount to a belief that 'efficiency' and 'effect' can ever be 100%. The UK spends about 50% of its ODA in Africa. From OECD

---

* "Financing for sustainable development including Aid at a glance charts for 2018–19/2019–20 data," *OECD*. I have deliberately chosen pre-pandemic figures. The pandemic in general reduced foreign aid given and made figures less clear. In 2021 the UK suspended its 0.7% commitment and reduced it to 0.5%. It is unclear how long such reductions will last. Also see (UK) www.gov.uk, (USA) www.usaid.gov; Michele Wheat, "Which countries provide and receive the most Foreign Aid," www.wristband.com; Chaorong, Wang, "Five countries that provide the largest foreign aid," *The Borgen Project* (independent non-profit based in USA to address world poverty) 14 March 2018; www.commonslibrary.parliament.uk; Naomi Larsson, "Foreign Aid: Which countries are the most generous?" *The Guardian*, 9 September 2015; and Daniel Martin, "Foreign Aid farce as Britain's aid to India RISES by a third, and UK will still send millions to China – despite foreign aid budget cuts," *The Daily Mail*, 24 September 2021, illustrates domestic disagreements on ODA.

DAC members (therefore not including China) the top recipient in 2017 was India, then Turkey with more than 50% from the EU, then more obviously Afghanistan, Syria, and Ethiopia; and then followed Bangladesh, Morocco, Vietnam, Iraq, and Indonesia for the rest of the 'top ten.'*

Effective Altruism is on the surface a statistical measure of QALY (Quality-adjusted Life Year) in relation to aid given: 20% improvement in the life of someone who can be expected to live to sixty years of age amounts to twelve QALYs. It may appear unemotional and to ignore individuals. It may appear to set up impossible moral choices. Give someone an expensive life-saving drug to extend their life by ten years or relatively cheaply cure someone's blindness to improve their own productivity and life expectancy every year for their lifetime?† On the other hand, it makes for a greater concentration on what success looks like. It compares usefulness to what would have happened otherwise. It encourages looking at root causes of problems not high-profile or dramatic suggestions, or headlines. It encourages comparison of low probability but high damage concerns with high probability but superficial or contained damage. It measures the effectiveness of giving the millionth £5 to an established project in comparison to the first £5. It addresses the individual actions of people in developed nations, illustrating that 1% salary donation from here can go much further than 1% from elsewhere.

The exercise of a different type of value decision is calling into question all but the most emergency aid: this is the 'Trade not Aid' debate. Fair trade is seen as a way of giving recipient nations more control. It removes the moral aspect of aid looking like rich nation condescending interference. It removes a possible 'handout' mentality in favour of available opportunity. It can be more effective and more long term. It can still satisfy the self-interest requirements of a donor nation. Trade not aid is about replacing all but emergency aid with a fairer international trading system. In practice this is not free trade each way. Not only can genuinely free trade be destructive as strong first

---

* OECD. See previous footnote.
† William Macaskill, *Doing Good Better*, 2015, Ch2 and Ch5. Macaskill is acknowledged as a co-founder of the Effective Altruism movement.

nation traders suffocate developing traders, but it often has conditions relating to what protections or subsidies or production standards, and sometimes social policy, there may be. Fairer trade does not mean all standards should be dispensed with by developing nations, it means a time-limited advantage with basic standards to give developing nations an opportunity. More important, limiting foreign trade through tax or regulation to allow domestic business to grow would become more common. This then puts a premium on good governance encouraging entrepreneurial activity to drive economic development domestically, raising domestic spending and saving, and raising the tax base for state investment. Individual governments can prioritise what type of economic, social, and cultural investment they prefer, and so keep the distinctiveness of their preferred approach. Furthermore, well managed domestic-driven success rather than foreign driven investment, increases national confidence and societal stability. While apparently being a repudiation of the sacrosanct free trade of post-Second World War international institutions, that was never the reality for developing nations. Nor would domestic protections last forever, as the wish to export and expand a successful domestic business then results in an easing of their protections in a quid pro quo for their international expansion.

Economic globalism is slowly reducing individual poverty and international inequality. Several different paths lie ahead. Developing nations and non-Western nations will have an increasing influence on international economic frameworks. Increasing global technologies, international leaderships, recognition of the need to manage dominant multinational companies, developing domestic governance, slowly improving international trade fairness and arbitration, and the developing cross-cultural dialogue and creativity between people can all raise the floor of living standards across the world. That can be done without being a move to the lowest common denominator. This is the optimistic, liberal, 'new-Western' view. Prevalence of authoritarian oligarchical regimes can choose to be isolationist or protectionist according to their political will, and in their number and co-ordination can shape the extent of globalist economics. China will soon be the world's largest economy and manufacturing nation, with high-level technology, and

Russa will remain a major oil and gas provider. Contradictions between business professing independent action on the international stage but having to conform to authoritarian regulations and decisions may limit their influence. Multinational or truly global independent companies with diversified interests may yet escape effective regulation and if they do will impact wealth, development, and inequality. Technology will also shape these unpredictably. The effects and solutions of climate change may destabilise some economies more than others. Communications seem irreversibly international, but communication technology can be managed, and a 'balkanisation' of the internet and other technologies cannot be ruled out. This would have a halting effect on the cross-cultural dialogue that a developing global economy needs. Education investment is vital as a knowledge economy, and services, become relatively more important. The value of natural wealth and its inclusion in international trade practices and economic comparisons will rise. None of these developments loosen the approach of ownership and growth as the foundation of an economy. They may soften the approach of a competitive lightly regulated capitalism, in favour of a more communal approach of self-interested nations. This compromise, however minimal the moral change, needs to be a deliberate choice. It may even be a grudging recognition that humanity is a co-operative species, or that it can make itself one.

Nationality

Modern Nationalism has been the driving force of international relations for at least 300 years, not globalism. Some nations emerge over a prolonged time, some appear natural, and others artificial. That makes it debatable whether nations are fixed entities. Globalists might even say they are out of date. Furthermore, origin stories, identities, and ownership are cultural, not just geographical. There is an argument that national governments have a greater influence on culture because they have decreasing control over economics, and that therefore 'culture wars' may be the battlegrounds of nationalism and globalism. Nationalism doesn't just face this challenge from within, but also an emerging challenge from without, of the world coming to, or directly through, uninvited, its front door. Multiculturalism mostly appears through immigration of people with different experience, that cannot be easily ignored. Substantial emigration also presents its own challenges. There is also cross-cultural dialogue and development of ideas which might be welcomed or might come through protests and campaigns being adopted across frontiers. Nationalism itself is still strong around the world. It can still be a strong shaper of the cross-cultural dialogue and new global philosophy. For some people a nation employs a social contract to bind its people together and globalism weakens the control a government can have over that contract and over national identity. For some a more widely shared or altered sovereign power is their future being lost and their history denied.

Nationalism: Ghost of the Past and the Future

The move from peoples to nations emerged in Europe from the 16th century. The idea became accepted that a nation should be fixed, but that has never been so. The United Kingdom is a unity of nations and peoples. Germany and Italy became modern nations in the 19th century. Yugoslavia was constructed artificially in 1918 and fell apart through war within the century. Czechoslovakia peacefully divided in 1993. Some of this has been to do with the fall of empire, some deliberative decision, some harks back to language and 'people's,' around which the narrative of common values are built. It is invariably defined in greater focus by a common enemy, and perhaps all national narratives involve the spilling of blood and martyrs.

Western nations primarily started as an accumulation of Tribal kingdoms and city-states, a common racial identity, and Christianity. Muslim invasion of Europe and the Crusades provided an external enemy. Roman trans-nationalism was conveniently forgotten about as was the contribution of Islam to the maintenance of Western thought in its 'Dark Ages.' Reformation and Renaissance nations reinvented themselves as reformist and then believers in freedom and liberty. Then came Western empire-building and the claiming of a superior Western 'civilisation,' misusing both Christianity and Enlightenment values.

GLOBALISATION

Then came worldwide conflict caused by European competition, twice. At which point, and with the development of a Cold War between different ideologies, there was another re-think. The Soviet Union wanted a community of nations under its own communist model. Western nations decided that sovereignty could be shared in self-interest, and both NATO and the European Union emerged to put this into practice. The West's culture has been summed up wittily as 'from Plato to NATO.'* The essential willingness to be bound together has brought benefits to those people; and those benefits have brought a deeper cultural binding that has formed into common identity and empathy. These are the stages of development of a successful 'nation,' but there is no fixed line here or definitive endpoint. New circumstances may call into question benefits and common values, some stories will be forgotten, new generations may need to re-learn or re-shape them, outside influences may present alternatives.

From an Indian perspective Rabindranath Tagore had seen European nations not merely as constructs but as bureaucratic ones without a soul. He saw them as soul-destroying money-making exercises, materialist and greedy. What he wanted to emphasise was the need for colonies to re-find their own culture and through that their own identity. The perversions of nationalism he saw included jingoism and xenophobia, expressed by a youthful exuberance of successful wider-franchise democracy that flexed its muscles in a populist and imperialist direction. These are the results of specific leadership to misuse nationalism for power. European nationalism has changed. It has adapted. It will continue to do so. It will have to, in a more globalist world. In population or geographical size Europe as an entity (without Russia) is one of the smaller blocs that might emerge across the world, and its 'mature' economy is being caught by others. Furthermore, what was once thought of as a strength of its nation's – the relative racial homogeneity – may in future be considered a weakness. Europe's nations may yet change this, but to do so from a position of weakness because of its history, reinforced by the mindset of imperialism that it must

---

* For example: Christopher Norris, From Plato to NATO, 1983; Brian Redhead, Political Thought from Plato to NATO, 1988; David Gress From Plato to NATO: The Idea of the West and Its Opponents, 1998.

reverse, is a big challenge. European nations are having to renew and re-set the make-up of their national identities and come to terms with a more global inclusiveness, while having less control over their own and everyone else's fate. This is why immigration and the multiculturism that follows are such fundamental aspects of that renewal, and for many so controversial. European nationalism shows the challenges facing many nations, but also shows that the idea of the nation state itself is not impervious to change. Most recently, history shows that nations can even make themselves individually weaker to become communally stronger, and that they can renew common values. This builds on self-confidence in their own nationhood and uses their wealth to adapt. In the democratic setting that they have set for themselves the most necessary pre-condition is a realisation that the core of national identity and culture that binds people together is a willingness to be bound, but that this can also apply to voluntary co-operation with others. Other nations will have similar challenges from globalism even if their national origin stories are different.

Israel is in a difficult position, the only openly and deliberately modern state founded on a specific religion, it is facing a crisis of identity as it struggles to cope with a large Muslim minority with historic and cultural roots within its territory. It is difficult to see how it can resist a more multi-cultural future, although its healthy birth rate is driven by its Orthodox religious groups. Japan remains a largely homogenous nation. It has internationally successful business but very little immigration. It has a long history of nationhood and embraces a mix of ancient and ultra-modern but has also followed the European path of imperialism and subsequent destruction. With a starkly falling birth rate it is unclear how Japan can withstand the forces of global change, but it may be ideas from abroad that change it rather than the arrival of new people. India is a modern invention and an ancient idea. Pre-British Mughals and the British worked across Muslim–Hindu divisions and only the India–Pakistan partition narrowed India. They were cultural and spiritual mixes, of varied kingdoms, ruled by a civil service 'efficiency' that epitomised the notion of exploitative colonialism. Independence brought Partition and a second aspect, the integration of these kingdoms and different histories and languages into a newly federal state. In recent years it has moved towards a more overtly Hindu state as a unifying factor. This may be a natural return to pre-colonialism but may be contradictory to the winds of change of globalism in terms of cross-cultural dialogue. How, for example, will it deal with caste inequality and women's rights in rural India? There is also the tension between increasing centralisation and strong regionalism. Pak-i-stan, the land of the pure, became overnight an almost wholly Muslim state. Pakistan's history (more than that of secessionist Bangladesh) and its globalist future appears as a struggle to find modernity within an Islamic context that is battered by external influences from Saudi Wahhabism to radical Taliban.

Between Japan and India lies China, a nation of increasing confidence, wealth, and influence, a global economy but with a distinctive and controlled domestic government that brooks no foreign influence. It has an ancient national narrative through historical events and Confucian philosophy, but espouses a One-China policy that will make it as much a multi-ethnic and multi-cultural nation as any in the world, unless it chooses a path of nationalistic replacement or apartheid. The latter may be the policy in Tibet and Xinjiang, while in Hong Kong it has confronted difference and opted for takeover rather than integration. China is now an avowedly nationalist nation, with a distinctly and overtly Han Chinese profile, and ethnic variation is not shared and displayed as it once was. It is susceptible, increasingly so, to the charge of empire-building. Its leadership continually says that the point about One China is that it has always been one nation and one indivisible people. This, and any global leadership, will be sorely tested both by the increasing independence of Taiwan, or by its inclusion into China by anything other than peaceful means. China's political change has long been hopelessly expected but it may find the intrusion of social and cultural globalist winds of change – more individual freedom, individual rights, materialism, campaigns for social equality and women's rights – harder to resist. Chinese leadership revels in playing the long game, and its wealth may shield its political distinctiveness for another generation or more, and bask in the success of achieving One China. But then what? It will be a mature economy, a multi-layered people of different religious, cultural, and political experiences, possibly with different but serious resentments. It will face the choice of external engagement to defend its actions and its wanted influence, especially if it continues domestic deliberate homogenisation; or an accommodation with its constituent parts within the rule of the CCP; or continued internal dissent answered by an increasingly repressive surveillance and enforcement state. One way or another its nationalism seems on a fractious course within the winds of global change. It may be the leader of a group of authoritarian nations able to be independent of Western ideas of society and government, but no nation with power, especially leading power, seeks to promote unpredictability.

The USA is a nation that wears its nationalism on its lapel and has a specifically written Constitution beginning 'We the people.' It is also a nation based on independent colonialists, European migration, Native American removal, slavery based on race, and the bloodshed of civil war fought between two opposing ideas of what the nation should be: federalist, or separatist states. Its self-professed 'Manifest Destiny' to cover coast to coast is a part of its identity. Like many nations it includes a narrative of being a beacon to others. It is not like traditional Europe in that it has also embraced 'give me your poor, your huddled masses' and is a racial and cultural, in 1960s terms, 'melting pot.' It willingly moved well beyond its east coast and north European foundations decades ago. It can be the most successful multi-racial nation on earth with high percentages of white European heritage, black/African American, and Latino-Hispanic communities, protection of varied Native American cultures, and high numbers who consider themselves of two heritages… German American, Cuban American etc. In 2021 California, its largest state and one of the top ten world economies, only 21% of public K-12 (primary and secondary) school children were classed as ethnically (and in traditional terms) white, with 56% Hispanic.* The USA will over time become increasingly mixed race ethnically and simply 'American' in self-identification. It is uniquely placed to be at the heart of the global cross-cultural dialogue with high levels of communication and emigration and with high levels (if inconsistent) of wealth. Yet within its borders it is easy to find division and doom. It proclaims its uniqueness

---

* "Share of students enrolled in K-12 public schools in the United States in 2021, by ethnicity and state," *Statista*, https://www.statista.com/statistics/236244/enrollment-in-public-schools-by-ethnicity-and-us-state/.

GLOBALISATION

to reinforce its national identity, but as elsewhere this is changing. The culture wars of globalism are on its screens every day. To outsiders it seems like it is buffeted by opposing views on almost everything, in principle. There is a real prospect that the nationalism of traditional America will be completely inconsistent with the ideas and identity of emerging America.

Within Africa there are nations that may yet have an emerging acceptance of the cross-cultural dialogue reminiscent of a new global philosophy every bit as valid as the USA. Migration is nothing new, nor is knowing Western systems of government. A cultural acknowledgement of the power of the natural world (rather than resource-driven exploitation) remains strong, as do strong societal attitudes that lay between Confucian East Asian emphasis on the order of society and Western Enlightenment's individual freedoms and liberties. Tribal heritage affiliations remain strong but for centuries 'Africa' has been multi-ethnic and multi-cultural. Nations are often struggling to have efficient governments that provide the benefits a strong national identity needs and that foster a national empathy. Nor are most in a wealthy position to adapt to the ever-changing winds of the world economy, with Africa having the highest and fastest-rising population in the world. Yet modernity and urbanisation stalk the land from Cairo to Lagos to Johannesburg. It is another stereotype and generality, with a large dose of optimism, but Africa may just be a place where a new global philosophy and cross-cultural dialogue can profitably take root within national identities. South Africa epitomises hopes and challenges.

The Misuse of Citizenship

Citizenship is a tool being used in some instances destructively and in others for selective benefit. One argument for denying it is often that those people have decided to forego the values that the nation represents. One example would be removing citizenship by European nations from those who went to fight for ISIS/Islamic State. It is defended by a government on the grounds that they are looking after the security of the majority of their citizens. It can be deliberately misused: Belarus currently proposes ending citizenship for 'extremists,' by which it means its democracy activists. Other examples illustrate the denial of citizenship being prosecuted around the world today. In Kuwait Bedouin have traditionally been loyal to their Sheikh, travelled across modern borders and saw no need for nationality papers. In an exercise of state power and modern officialdom, and a nod to the pre-eminence of 'security issues,' they are now denied Kuwaiti citizenship because they do not have the papers to prove their heritage is based on their connection to what is now – but historically wasn't – the State of Kuwait. In the Windrush community of the UK children born or brought up in the UK by immigrant parents in the 1950s and 1960s have had to officially prove or attain UK citizenship, despite knowing no other nation; and if they cannot do so, and while they cannot do so, have been denied access to employment, health services, state benefits, and other rights, placing them effectively in a legal limbo of statelessness. In the Dominican Republic of the Caribbean since 2013 200,000 people have been denied access to education, health insurance, official marriage certificates, etc because they are of Haitian heritage, and although may have been born in the Dominican Republic have not officially attained its citizenship.*

Citizenship is about the right to have rights and is arguably even more important to one's life chances than class or wealth. It is a legal identity, and fundamental to democracy and engagement in society. Often, denying it is a legal and practical exile from the nation of one's birth. Citizenship should be a right given by the nation of one's or one's parents' birth. There should also be a scheme towards attaining citizenship through naturalisation. Some nations also allow dual citizenship, others do not, but it should not simply reflect the power of government. To want to define a nation is perfectly legitimate, but to do so on a hostile and exclusive basis rather than a reasonable inclusive one is neither acceptable nor appropriate for an increasingly globalised world, where mobility is far more common, through both choice and necessity, and where mixed heritage is increasing in almost every nation in the world.

First-generation immigrants often find integration difficult, second generation often struggle with having a foot in two sometimes

---

* "The price of citizenship," *The Documentary* [podcast] BBC World Service, 14 January 2023.

contrasting or competing cultures. However, there is lots of evidence to suggest that second- and third-generation immigrants are relatively more successful, socially and economically, and often change to fit in, even in language, name, or religion. Indeed, it is an acknowledgement but subversion of the potential success of this fluid nationality that is the origin and reason for the right-wing idea of 'great replacement' – the replacement of the 'native people' by others, therefore leading to a very different nation. However, most people want to fit in, do want to find out how to be successful, and very rarely are such a number as to threaten those already there. Multi-cultural societies can be shaped by those already there too, and the state can forge common ground. The difficulties for all those real people involved on both sides of the change should not be underestimated, and a transition for individuals is inevitable, but significant immigration, as opposed to mass uncontrolled immigration, in a more globalised world, need not mean everything changes. If societies are to develop in such a way then citizenship itself must be accessible. The movement of peoples is, after all, older than the nation state.

Elsewhere citizenship can be bought at the cost of investment in a country. This has happened in such as Cyprus and Malta, within the EU. This is citizenship for convenience and benefit, for the rich and connected, not by right of birth, settlement, or commitment. In 2022 a staggering 43% of the income of the Caribbean island state of St. Kitts came through its citizenship scheme. This is a sort of nationality haven like the idea of tax havens.

Migration

Migration clearly relates to economics, politics, population, international relations, the state of individual states, and discrimination, and is therefore complex, and a key part of nationality and globalisation. Economically, the accepted norm is that growth requires stable or increasing population. Multiculturalism in Western nations is the effect of the larger-scale immigration that the world has seen over the last seventy years. In a time of falling birth rates but continuing expectations of prosperity, and international immigration, nations have three choices. They may want to concentrate on boosting the traditional nation without immigration; or to maintain its traditional essence but cautiously manage significant immigration; or to allow whatever change new people may bring with more open borders.

Victor Orbán's anti-immigration leadership in Hungary is generally considered xenophobic and therefore not a good example for others to follow, but there will be elements in many countries sympathetic to that approach. Japan, a better example, is also closely guarding its Japanese-ness. In Tokyo only 4% of its population is foreign-born, about twice the national average and in line with most of East Asia; but this compares to New York and London at about 35%.* Japan's solution to falling birth rates is limited immigration (without strident nationalism), encouraging more women into work, older workers, and the use of technology. It may successfully reject larger-scale immigration, but like Hungary it will not be able to reject the winds of globalisation and cross-cultural ideas. More women in work are already changing the attitudes within family life and the voice of women in Japanese society. The use of technology will inevitably engage it in discussions about the social and cultural consequences for society. In the UK, immigration was a major issue in the Brexit vote to leave the European Union, and subject to widely different and controversial political opinion and interpretation. Across the UK and the EU, the issue of immigration remains highly politically charged.

In 2015 German Chancellor Angela Merkel reacted to German labour shortages and Syrian refugee problems from civil war by deciding to open Germany's borders. Turkish heritage people were already a significant minority. Merkel promised an 'unlimited' number of asylum applications. Over two years, before the policy was stopped, one million people were accepted. Five years later over half are in employment and the number with 'good or very good' language skills has risen from 1% to 44%. Worker shortages have eased. Most were young, educated, unemployed, ambitious, and determined. It was a policy with effects on attitudes to immigration, discrimination, and national identity,

---

* Hannah Beech and Hikari Hida, "Japan's diverse Olympic stars reflect a country that's changing (slowly)," *New York Times*, 24 July 2021. "In major shift Japan looks to allow more foreign workers to stay indefinitely," *Japan Times*, 18 November 2021.

themselves deep cultural issues. There have been problems of integration, but a similar proportion of the German population continue to support immigration as before, although a higher number than before think integration cannot be achieved. Four years after the policy immigration stood at about double what it had been four years before it. People questioned Merkel's political future because of this one decision alone. Consequences remain, including its exploitation politically by far-right political groups that continue to find more support among Germans uncomfortable with accepting refugees from a different religious-cultural background and political experience.[*] No nation supports unlimited immigration.

Large-scale immigration from Latin America, the Pacific, and from the Indian subcontinent, is one of the USA's most controversial issues. Rising domestic multiculturalism, changing power balances and power holders, and social attitudes, and the effects of a more diverse electorate on foreign policy may all be consequences. Currently about 15% of the population of the USA was born outside its borders, roughly 50 million people. Many believe that it cannot cope with its current and expected number of immigrants. The day-to-day working, identity, and nationalism of the USA, the UK and other European nations in the face of globalised immigration will continue to change.

Invited migrant labour is one aspect of immigration. According to the World Migration Report of 2022, international migrant labour in 2020 made up 3.6% of the world's population, 281m people, up from 173m in 2000. India, China, Philippines, Mexico, Egypt, Bangladesh and Pakistan have long been leaders in supplying 'temporary' labour. In terms of money sent home, leading sources were the USA, UAE and Saudi Arabia, with total global remittances of US$702billion in 2020. In Arab States migrant workers comprised 41% of the entire working population. In UAE, Qatar, and Kuwait numbers of migrants (not just workers) are higher than a 70% share of the national population, i.e., outnumbering citizens. In these cases, immigrants often work in developing infrastructure projects, as domestic servants, or middle managers. The highest actual number is in Saudi Arabia. Migrant

---

[*] Sekou Keita and Helen Dempster, "Five years later one million refugees are thriving in Germany," [blog] *Center for Global Development*, 4 December 2020.

worker status rarely leads to citizenship. Rights for migrant labour are very varied between different nations, but are frequently limited in terms of movement, housing, and labour rights; in terms of national identity and culture they are often unacknowledged.* They are often accused of lowering wages in developed nations, but fill labour shortages, and contribute to rising living standards, through consequences for economic development and demographics. It is important to note that the definition of key terms can vary between nations, and also that Covid-19 does not seem to have caused long term changes in migration and migrant labour.

Accepted immigration and multiculturalism presume that new arrivals will be given a chance to maintain their own cultural experiences and beliefs, as they integrate with the culture they come into. It needs some understanding of and respect for each culture. It presumes that living separate lives within their new nation is not an option. It is surely immoral as well as impractical to expect new immigrants to give up their previous lives. Empathy is essential. That empathy also needs some self-confidence on the part of the welcoming authority. The intellectual, practical, and emotional difficulty of moving to another country should not be underestimated: the journey itself, learning a new language, following unfamiliar laws, leaving family or friends behind, and numerous instances of adapting to unwritten cultural rules about behaviour and relationships. It may also involve coping with another layer of resentment or discrimination individually, by accident or design, in legislation or institutions. One might ask why migrants would be prepared to face those challenges. For some it is desperation as they immediately flee war or disaster zones no longer inhabitable, others flee persecution for their political or personal beliefs and for their safety, or they seek to move away from a life they believe offers few opportunities to improve. Moving the ground underneath your feet is neither easy nor an easy decision to make. This is the explanation of why immigrants are either the most desperate of any age; or the most

---

* "World Migration Report, 2022," *IOM UN Migration*, p. 3 (for key statistics), p. 23 (for overall global numbers and percent of global population, p.25 (for top destinations and origins), p.41 (for receiving / sending remittances), p.75 (for migrant percentages of national populations), https://publications.iom.int/books/world-migration-report-2022.

ambitious, determined and maybe idealistic, and often younger. The desperate need the most help, emotionally wracked by the decision they have had to make. The latter need opportunity to make their wishes of a more productive and successful life come true. They wish to contribute, know that they will have to work hard, and often possess the skills and/or personal character that can make them and their children successful. These are the reasons for migration that have always been true and remain true today, from mass 19th century European migration to contemporary global migration. This is half the context in which a nation must decide whether to accept immigrants or asylum seekers and how to treat them.

The other half of the context is what they come into. It is immoral to deny new immigrants the opportunity to be a part of a nation that they have volunteered to go to or been offered shelter by. There needs to be a willingness to sacrifice a little of one's own, a willingness to be patient, and to use the skills of new arrivals. Language lessons may take years for confident fluency. Availability of health, welfare, housing, and work support are needed. These types of support may take a generation, and so need leadership, institutional and individual positive engagement, and patience from each of these. History is littered with need but lack of support, and this is the breeding ground of discrimination and isolation. How long the support takes is a question that determines not just how long that discrimination and isolation last, but how long it takes for immigrants to become taxpayers, members of civic groups, and positive messengers for the society they have joined. These can be the great rewards of immigration, but how long it takes for an immigrant to be seen as 'one of us' is individual, variable, not predictable, and increasingly political.

For many people even the Japanese example is fighting against the tide of the inevitable. There is a positive entrepreneurial model which acknowledges that new ideas, new workers, and new markets can reinvigorate an economy. It can still acknowledge that for some people they fear 'losing' too much too quickly, whether this is perception or reality, whether this is about job competition, political power, or social and cultural tradition. Making it work is usually presented as the maintenance of 'traditional' values while on some point of a spectrum fitting in, tolerating, respecting, or embracing the new. Some of the culture of immigrant communities can therefore be chosen to be accepted and some rejected. This is the approach of most nations. It can also result in a softening of the conflictual new ideas of elsewhere, as links with other places, traditions, and beliefs around the world allow elements of understanding and empathy to pass *both ways*. Accepting 'the desperate forced' asylum seeker but rejecting the economic young ambitious migrant would rarely be a good balance, limiting the chances of immigration paying for itself or positively contributing to development. According to the World Bank, if rich nations let in 3% more migrants, then the world's poor would have $305 billion more to spend, which is roughly three times the size of the current world aid budget.*

The world must come to terms with migration as it is now and as it may yet become. Leadership can negate culture wars over immigration and multiculturalism by the deployment of vision, empathy, explanation, and resources, employing both moral and self-interest arguments to both protect the existing and to manage change. Emigration of the young, educated and ambitious from nations with a severe shortage of jobs and hope produces instability on a national and international scale. There must be a greater accommodation to be had. The domestic cannot be separated from the international, and both need better management than we currently employ. As the birth rate around the world continues to fall, and developing nations continue to make economic progress, immigration itself will be a less available solution for some nation's problems.

A New Culturalism through Global Dialogue

The cultural expression of the negative consequences of globalism is becoming a driving force of politics in the developed world. Politics is also making this a driving force of attitudes towards globalism. This

---

* Bregman, 2018, 230, citing the World Bank. T.L. Walmsley, L.A. Winters, S.A. Ahmed, C.R. Parsons, "Measuring the impact of the movement of labour using a model of bilateral migration flow," *Global Trade Analysis Project*, www.gtap.agecon.purdue.edu/resources/download/2398.pdf. These sorts of figures depend on many factors, e.g., productivity of migrants through age and health, amount sent home, etc.

was part of the concern expressed by President Obama. The genuine concerns of those that feel left behind are being elevated above the economic gains and emphasis previously thought of as globalism, and sometimes manipulated. Without good leadership it is difficult to imagine this not producing more division, both within and between nations. Developing nations have for some time experienced this tension of global economic development that has not always been in their best interests economically or socially. Politics trumps economics, and culture trumps politics, everywhere, but culture can also be the solution, if not an easy one.

Cultural dialogue strengthens bonds between people and nations by improving empathy and understanding. It happens and is strengthened by practical ties. Dialogue includes sharing lives, and listening to concerns and fears, and being prepared to debate them, find compromise, and find win-win solutions. One criterion for success must be, and can be, not leaving people behind. This empathy must surface between people in different regions, and not just in and for developing or poor nations but in developed nations too. Understanding requires more specific knowledge and depends upon education from school systems and civic society.* Real stories and visual impact can create the mood and possibility for understanding and compromise. When Pacific Islanders can visually show the existential threat of rising ocean levels comfortable Westerners can understand the value of encouraging wind farms or solar energy. Empathy kicks in. Policy can follow. Understanding does not need to be unrealistically all-encompassing but can be exemplar. Practical ties include things that so many already take for granted: music, fashion, food, sport, and art are all multinational enterprises, from English Premier League footballers kneeling against racism seen around the world, to rap lyrics sung about social injustice and inequality and poverty. Practical ties include collaborative newspaper investigations on corruption or lifestyle, collaborative television and film for message-driven fiction or illustrative documentary about everything from

---

* *Dollar Street* is a website set up as a Gapminder project in 2016, featuring 431 families in 66 countries using photos and video, founded by Anna Rosling Ronnlund, that visually shows the housing and lifestyle of people from around the world and of different incomes, side by side. Gapminder is an independent Swedish foundation that seeks to use reliable data to address misconceptions in global trends, www.gapminder.org/dollar-street.

leadership to the natural world.

All these ties come with values, from showing the positivity of individual or collective freedom to act, to the worth of education, to learning how not being the victor can still mean not being the loser, to learning the value of a different perspective or timeframe. These connections are hard to resist and to shut down. The consequences of such dialogue can be a way forward on the international issues that face us by establishing a consensus of key values that can lead to progress in action. This is different to a respectful multiculturalism. It is a new global culturalism of its own, a new globalist philosophy. Pope Francis, in Chapter 5 of his 2020 *Fratelli Tutti* Encyclical wrote that global society needs 'fundamental reform and major renewal.' It begins with people from whatever perspective and experience they start from being willing to consider whether they themselves currently, really, see other individuals and cultures as equally worthy of consideration, or engage judgement without bias. Can we, as philosopher J.S. Mill expounded the need to do in the 19th century, debate our most fundamental and accepted assumptions? Can we reassess our self-image, our virtues, and our experiences? Only then, with a balanced self-assessment, can we move towards that new globalist philosophy. If we do all that it is likely that we will have reassessed what we as individuals and as humanity are trying to achieve.

A key aspect of this dialogue is the phenomenon of international common protest. Independence movements have always inspired and learnt from each other, as have women's and civil rights movements. The Occupy Movement after the financial crash of 2008 had tents in 951 cities in 82 nations across the world discussing the culpability of finance, the wealth of the top 1% and inequality. The Black Lives Matter movement has been adopted not just in relation to black lives in the West but also in India and Australia and other places in relation to caste and Muslim minority or Aboriginal treatment. Climate change has been a great international movement. As well as common aims, common language, tactics and strategy emerge. There are directly political campaigns that also begin to resemble this international campaigning style: the anti-Vax movement against Covid-19 vaccines became international. It may have been the Arab Spring of 2010–12 that first drew the world's attention to the use of modern communication in the organic development of a national and then international political movement. The ease, directness, and encryption of such communication between individuals could produce a rapidity and agility previously unknown, an immediate creativity in communication, and a transparency to events reaching into people's hands or hearts unknown at least since American TV naively filmed the Vietnam War live. Naturally, authorities of all sorts have learnt, and blocking digital communication has become commonplace, from democratic India doing so to hide its actions and protests in Kashmir in 2019–20, to authoritarian governments like China routinely blocking the use of certain words or phrases, and Russia blocking all but its own controlled digital communication in its invasion of Ukraine in 2022. The development of technology to create and spread false or misleading information, i.e., rumour and propaganda, also continues to develop at an alarming pace. The tension between nations learning how to block and control, and individuals finding ways to bypass such censorship, propaganda, or surveillance, looks set to be a continuing struggle. However, it is also true that people will educate themselves into the digital world and will learn to look at sources and data in a different way that allows them to develop their own judgements on its authenticity. This is a learning process.

The movement of people is cultural dialogue's strongest root, whether through migration, leisure and temporary movement, business, or wider culture. All these add emotive and experiential aspects to any message that makes it harder to ignore, and perhaps easier to judge the authenticity of when transmitted face-to-face. People will learn that no single source is enough, that a statement sincerely made is not the same as it being true, and that motivation may inform credibility. When we can do that, even amid disruptive technology and old-fashioned propaganda, cross-cultural dialogue can thrive, and a common philosophy can emerge.

Dialogue across frontiers, whether direct, planned, structured, creative, personal, technological, or institutional, will be very hard to resist. A country seeking isolation from world movements will need to be very isolated indeed, so isolated that people will notice and wonder why, especially if that is not working out for them. Globalisation is the emerging force of government, economics, and culture, even as nationalism and self-interest continue to drive politics. Issues like the Covid-19 pandemic, climate change, multinational corporate power, ethics for new disruptive technology, and migration, are increasingly encouraging nations to work together, and to see the necessity to do so. They are beginning, in practice, to share their sovereignty in their own as well as the common interest. International frameworks are taking shape, slowly, to deal with a whole range of international issues. Often far too slowly. Few countries now see themselves as individuals alone in the world. It is harder for anyone to be truly alone.

Nations will continue to rise and fall. New leaderships are a constant and can go wrong. Internationally there still needs to be much greater focus on the prevention of the deepest inequality. The morality of intervention in failing states, whether failing through poor governance, civil conflict, or specific events, remains a hotly debated topic, with many still denying the principle, in case it comes around to look at them. Deliberate conflict between nations is still a threat to any progress being made. Ensuring military and economic security are underestimated at a nation's peril, as is shown again by the invasion of Ukraine. 'Smaller' nations still require guarantees of security from larger ones or effective organisations. The agreed criteria with which to measure intervention and the nature or extent of a 'failing state' is not there yet. This should be a priority of the international community, but to be so it also needs to be a priority of the people. A global public opinion has not yet emerged in establishing principles of international relations. A globalist mentality is different to the current competitive one. It requires more give-and-take, more compromise, more recognition that one view may not be right or agreed with, and yet also a determination to make sure that agreed international norms are meaningful, not meaningless rhetoric open to wide interpretation. Nor can they be win-lose scenarios. This is another aspect of the cross-cultural dialogue that must form the new global philosophy that we need.

Douglass North wrote that previous explanations of economic development missed out 'the nature of human co-ordination and co-operation.'* Part of any global philosophy must be a standard

---

* Linda Yueh, 2019, 243, quoted in Douglass North's *Institutions, Institutional Change*

of morality that is inclusive, that allows fair opportunity, that has a longer-term perspective. Trade not just aid, dealing with international corporations, how we intend to use AI, etc, all require moral or ethical decisions or judgements. Authoritarian governments must decide how much they need to be, and can afford for their regimes to be, involved in international dialogues. I expect more protest movements to be international just as much as I expect more fashion and food to be so. Whether people choose to reflect and gain or scoff and denigrate with their new knowledge is a matter of individual moral choice, informed by personal and emotional connection, or not, and media presentation, and leadership. It is something that we can be deliberate about, and deliberately positive about. Being a digitally responsible and critical news watcher is therefore also more essential than ever before. Emotions can be manipulated but it may be that the more we know and can see for ourselves from a wider range of places then the more light has a chance to seep through, as much as the risk of being overwhelmed by, and shrinking away from, the effort of independent thought.

A global philosophy most of all must be positive engagement on a grander scale than we have previously been prepared to entertain. We need to think internationally, as well as nationally, locally, and personally. If we update our view of humanity and what we are trying to do we may find new opportunities in, and different solutions to, the developments of globalism. There is a view that the accumulation of international events, communication, social movements, and dangers makes our time now a generational tipping point. This is a time when we need to, and can, think differently about what is happening, and make a course correction. There is also a view that humanity is inevitably on a path to unification, but that is not inevitable. We may establish space travel to look for other planets to conquer, or accidentally destroy each other, before we solve the problems that we have between ourselves, or before we magically merge into uniform global citizens. Thomas More believed that 'Humanity itself is a Treaty' and believed that mankind is a moral being, and that materialism, individually and societally, is temporary. On a global scale that is what we need to find, or re-find, and put into practice.

---

and Economic Performance, Cambridge University Press, 1990, 11–12.

WHERE ARE WE GOING?

Frameworks for Progress

The non-governmental practical ties creating dialogue are supremely important, but even these at some point require some form of framework. There will not be one all-encompassing organisation, and nor should there be. Any form of 'global government' would be thought of as an elite, out-of-touch, unresponsive 'organisation.' Instead, we are slowly formalising individual aims, and how we achieve and measure them. This requires patience and urgency. An interesting comparison is the 100 years it took the first industrial nation, the UK, to adapt to its revolutionary new industrial condition.

The world has made strides in enunciating the basic human rights and opportunities that everyone should have. We have done this before: witchcraft, cannibalism, and girls' infanticide are almost a thing of the past. The Universal Declaration of Human Rights (UDHR) originally adopted by the UN in 1948 includes the right to life, freedom of movement, of religion and thought, rights to an education and healthcare, and notes areas where individuals have a responsibility to society or when individual rights cannot be applied. It has formed the basis of human rights law the world over and many other treaties and agreements since its adoption.[*] Eight UN Millennium Development Goals from 2000 address social, economic, and environmental standards. The UN now offers an umbrella framework for issues stretching from cultural protection to refugee support, but not everything is done under its guidance or control. Nuclear non-proliferation treaties to international sporting bodies, Interpol to the World Bank, the International Federation of Journalists to the Red Cross and Red Crescent, represent a whole range of non-governmental, non-(directly) political and charitable organisations. They are establishing a generally accepted international baseline of standards and services, if always capable of improvement.

Transforming our world: the 2030 Agenda for Sustainable Development

---

[*] Forty-eight of the fifty-eight members of the UN General Assembly at the time voted for its adoption, none voted against but eight abstained (Saudi Arabia worried about freedom to change religion, South Africa about 'dignity of the individual' having just introduced apartheid, five communist nations and Yugoslavia possibly worried about freedom of movement or wanting stronger anti-fascist wording), and two did not vote (Honduras and Yemen).

GLOBALISATION

(2016–2030) is another example of the developing manifesto.* It states: 'Sustainable development recognises that eradicating poverty[1]in all its forms and dimensions[2]. combatting inequality within and among countries[3], preserving the planet[4], creating sustained, inclusive and sustainable economic growth[5] and fostering social inclusion[6] are linked to each other[7] and are interdependent[8].' That's a lot! What does it really mean? 1 is ambitious, it does not say tackle or minimise poverty; 2 acknowledges this is about more than income and wealth, and suggests tackling the gradient of poverty not just the extreme; 3 understands the often great disparity within nations often hidden by national figures and comparisons, as well as the international inequality on a national level; 4 could not be more ambitious, and acknowledges the new environmentalism of climate change, biodiversity degradation and environmental pollution, but also recognises the planet itself as an entity; 5 is no less than suggesting the need for a new economic model based on sustainability not exploitation, although still focussing on 'growth'; 6 addresses discrimination and disengagement; 7 links all these issues and acknowledges the need for the comprehensive nature of plans; while both 7 and 8 hint at the required global partnership in order to achieve those plans. This is therefore a radical statement, written as a moral imperative, while still being a statement of its time when climate change was becoming a catch-all for comprehensive change. Like all such statements, the statement itself is open to interpretation and the devil is in the agreed detail to follow.

Major geographic blocs with varying depth of integration are now also established around the world. The European Union has integrated economics, political structures, social programmes, and a range of cultural and scientific links, and 'free movement.' Each continent has its sometimes cross-over groups, such as the Economic Community of West African States (ECOWAS) although there is also the African Union.† Their different economic and diplomatic power currently prevent these pitting themselves against each other directly. Nor, since the Sino–

---

* Adopted by the UN in 2015 it has 17 Sustainable Development Goals (SDGs) and is part of the UN Development Programme, www.undp.org.

† ECOWAS has fifteen members, began in 1975, and seeks economic integration and regional security, www.ecowas.int.

WHERE ARE WE GOING?

Russian split in the 1960s has there been an authoritarian 'club' of nations, despite a 2022 Sino–Russian agreement. 'Friendship between the two Sates has no limits' said the agreement, which appeared to fall short of a formal alliance but nevertheless was their most detailed and elaborate agreement to date.* In the future there is a risk of a dystopian George Orwell *1984* scenario of breakdown between blocs that carve out distinctive identities for themselves. Geographically unrelated groups can engender significant cross-cultural diplomatic, educational, social, scientific, and entrepreneurial links, and can reinforce the cross-cultural dialogue of an emerging global philosophy if they remain inclusive, not exclusive, in nature. Nor is the original Non-Aligned Movement dead.†

The Covid-19 pandemic is itself a lesson in the reality of where we still are in the sense of having a 'global community' and 'global dialogue.' Genuine international co-operation among researchers and scientists from China to the USA to Europe and South Africa produced virus understanding and vaccines in record times. However, the labelling of it as the 'China virus' by President Trump, lack of transparency by Chinese authorities in the WHO investigation of its origins, and most of all the buying up of global stockpiles of vaccines, and occasional use of them as political bargaining chips too, have illustrated a clear 'us first' approach from many (richer) nations. While to some extent this is inevitable and is what electorates or domestic audiences have usually demanded, and governments would see as their foremost duty, the scientific appeal to spread vaccine up-take more globally to prevent mutations and the continued spread of variants that might make those vaccines less effective, was generally a voice ignored by legislators. There needs to be a better way forward.

---

* Robin Wright, "Russia and China unveil a pact against America and the West," *The New Yorker*, 7 February 2022.

† Rishabh Pratap, Larry Register, Heather Chen, "Indian leader Narendra Modi tells Putin: Now is not the time for war," *CNN*, 17 September 2022. At the Shanghai Cooperation Organization summit in Uzbekistan, Modi, face-to-face, said, 'I know that today's era is not of war and we have talked to you many times over the phone on the subject that democracy and diplomacy and dialogue are all these things that touch the world.' India has since been seen to have a relatively neutral and nuanced position in the Russia–Ukraine war.

VII

RELIGION

If God did not exist, it would be necessary to invent him.
Voltaire, 1769.*

We know ... that religion is the basis of civil society, and the source of all good and of all comfort.
Edmund Burke, 1790.†

Christianity should make a difference to the way you hold your knife and fork.
Toyohiko Kagawa.‡

Since the Enlightenment began religion has been seen by many people in the West as the opposite of rational, and of individual rights and freedoms. Its relevance, coherence, and honesty have all been called into question, and in many Western nations its influence often appears peripheral. Often those with an overt religious faith are seen as out of date or unrealistic or other-worldly, and sometimes all of these, and maybe dangerous too, to others, or to 'progress.' In many places religion has been officially separated from the functions of government. The

---
* Voltaire, *Épîtres*, 1769.
† Edmund Burke, Reflections on the Revolution in France, 1790.
‡ Toyohiko Kagawa, a Japanese Christian, 1888-1960, quote taken from Chris Wright, *Religions in the World,* Oxford University Press, 2002, 67.

less overt and less confident faith of a much larger group is generally ignored. The 2021 Census of the UK showed that in England and Wales 37% said they had no religion – 63% therefore, may still say they do.

The judgemental perspective on religion needs to be a long one. Religions can change, and have changed, often substantially. Arguably, they toggle between being open to different interpretation and consolidating fixed beliefs, rules, and rituals. Then there is the greater menu of religions now available for people. People can choose a different religion to the one they grew up in. They can choose an aspect of a different religion to integrate with the hand they hold already to suit themselves, even perhaps changing its meaning when taken out of its original network of a religion's concepts. In the West at least, the very notion of what religion is, is being subject to comparison and to the secular perspective of rationality and 'scientific' analysis now becoming dominant. This includes whether religion is specific with hard expectations, is 'truth' or faith, can be proved, is an historical narrative, or is an individual or mass psychological phenomena. The extent and purpose of free will in relation to God-decided predestination itself remains a fundamentally challenging question. However, we must remember that more people in the world express faith in a religion than do not, not just in terms of general principles but in ritual and authority. We must include it in our debates about the future of humanity and the world.

A part of whether our current religions need to significantly change themselves is whether they need to, and can, change their outlook on the world. This is in relation to specific issues like conflict, inequality, climate change, gender issues, sanctity of life, quality of life, and scientific and technological development at the life-forming and human decision-making level. It also means religion must deal with the globalisation of ideas as well as the individualism of mind. It is often thought that spirituality itself is on the decline. There is no inevitability that religion becomes less important, but nor that current specific religions remain dominant or the same. In making changes religion itself may change. Religion should have a positive contribution to offer in how the future should or could be shaped. To explore these issues we must first, however, be clear what we mean by 'Religion.'

RELIGION

The Religion We Have

Some Indigenous groups have no word for religion. For many people it is such an essential part of their living culture that the two are thought the same. Religion is inextricably linked with the human character, how to interpret it and control or shape it, as well as trying to divine a larger picture, including a more powerful and usually comforting presence that can explain what humanity cannot. It may form a link with past generations and be intended to be fulfilling in this one. Many people in a more secular place pay lip service to it at traditional times: naming ceremonies, marriage, and death. This is as much tradition as belief, which may be seldom thought about.

What Do We Mean By Religion?

Religion in this book means beliefs that have established themselves from time to time among a significant number of people and that have stories of some permanence, coherence, and compelling ideas. They seek to answer the 'big' questions that have occurred to humanity through its existence: the origins and purpose of human and other life; of the planets and stars we see; the determinants of the path of life we take including fate or divine intervention, and free will; and how we know what we think we know. Such religion is voluntary but there is a necessity to have faith.

As well as philosophy and faith, they also employ ritual and rules. Religions are seen as a way of life by their stricter adherents, giving guidance about everything from food and clothing to new life and burial, and relationships with others. They establish traditions that make people familiar, and communal, and that seek to give comfort and security. They establish what we like to call morality. They usually employ leadership and structure for decision-making. Some religion's specific guidance comes from what they see as the Word of God. Religions tend to add new rules over time, some to address new circumstances, some to reinterpret less clear-cut beliefs, some at the request of specific leaders from their own interpretations of belief or for power, or to make their communities more distinctive. Traditions can change but they sometimes get set 'in writing,' an apt phrase that signifies the modern importance of the development of writing (and then printing) in fixing the ideology of a religion. 'Fundamentalists' are not quite precisely that – they are usually believers who accept the written word of their scripture as unarguable, although from when that written word was established may be more problematic. There is schism – division – in most religions, caused by an application of real-world power which people disagree with, or over a different attitude to the interpretable nature of scripture, core belief, or important ritual. The power and brand of our modern religions have largely eclipsed spirits, ancestors and guidance. Modern religions tend to keep their communities in line in a way that was not used before, with the fear of eternal damnation or some form of lower status in the next world. Heaven is a good incentive, but Hell is an effective 'stick.' Furthermore, if a God is permanent and everywhere then there is no escaping from its judgement. With a permanent and watchful divinity, a religion can become a way of life that must be upheld.

Before our modern monotheistic religions one could choose which Gods to pray to or influence. They were often protectors and guides, or punishers, but they were not determinants of everlasting punishment or reward. These ancient 'gods' or spirits were usually based on nature and objects (totemic, animistic, or primal beliefs) or personified human characteristics. In some places ancestors took centre stage. Calling them belief systems or simply traditions is often intended as a secondary recognition, whether the intention is discriminatory or not, but they continue to be followed by millions of people around the globe. Buddhism is unique in its concentration on the individual believer's search for enlightenment, although still in relation to community. Both it and Hinduism have a sense of life cycles different to monotheistic religion. All belief systems include the idea of human conscience and soul, separate from mind and physical body. Ritual and tradition then train the believer to use, or accept, or confirm, their belief in the guiding principles. Acceptance of these is Faith.

Religion actively promotes community, for distinctiveness, recognition, and strength of faith, supporting each other in difficult times, and keeping fellow adherents in check or on watch. Community, ritual, and higher ideals provide anchors that can give meaning to lives and events. Community also means social order through 'moral values.' Religions almost always have leaders, hierarchies, and specialists to interpret for, communicate with, and represent, believers and the divine. Leadership is likely to come from individuals but may be through scripture. These elements have in combination given successful religions a stake and power in the world at large. Religions have used that 'political' power in their development, and to develop further resources to defend and maintain themselves. However, religions reasonably profess not to be cults or gangs that compel membership and directly punish waywardness – an ideal not always adhered to in their histories.

Religions' rituals and traditions must be appealing, even if their philosophical beliefs are based on faith or fantastical narrative. They address and tap into the character of human nature, both its virtues and vices. They must serve to keep a community together. Religion must give a person a sense of fulfilment or happiness. Within religions are the virtues one would hope to find: compassion with varying degrees of forgiveness, charity in recognition of mutual support, and 'honest' family values to sustain it. Some form of custodianship of the environment is common too, recognising the world we live in, and depend upon, and therefore have some responsibility for. Loyalty is prized, and this is seen as Faith, to cope with unknowns or the unexplainable, from the death of a loved one to the position of the stars. Co-operation makes individuals happier, more resilient, and less questioning, and make communities stronger, richer, and more powerful, and therefore also safer. Arguably, religion as we know it in most cases today is the best argument for the success of humanity as a co-operative species.

Yet many think of religion as divisive. Individual religions have fought each other, often literally, to prosper. Religion is also co-opted alongside other causes of war. Much of the restriction within a religion comes from its need to better face internal doubt or an external threat. Rituals and beliefs become totems of loyalty. Alliance with political power for protection has often been sought. It is one reason why Western religion is often associated around the world with colonialism. How religions that claim they are exclusively the 'truth' relate to each other in an increasingly global world is one of their challenges, and reflects the debate about whether humanity is co-operative or conflictual.

We must also recognise some pitfalls in discussion. There is always a triple danger as explained by Baggini: Ideas may be 'domesticated,' namely translated into something familiar so that we understand, but losing some of their meaning. They may be 'exoticised,' the opposite, making something so alien it is 'unknowable,' resulting in platitudes like 'Native Americans are so spiritual.' Thirdly, 'essentialising,' namely being too broad about traditions or beliefs or specific concepts, for which he gives the example of a general misunderstanding that 'harmony' in Confucian belief is just about conformity. These dangers also remind us that religion has been portrayed in different ways, for different reasons, just as other concepts are: conforming harmony can be taken up by the CCP in China as a route to control, but harmony through diversity, Baggini's 'traditional' interpretation, less so.

Where Does Our Religion Come From?

To know the development and ebb and flow of our religion is to understand better the role of religion and its potential future; and the potential future of specific religions; and even the potential development of new ones. Logically, humanity has been curious about the world it inhabits, from the stars to the earth beneath our feet. We have sought understanding of the things we cannot control or predict that affect our lives, the dramatic storms and the everyday miracles of day and night, of rain and sunshine, that have made lives difficult or allowed them to blossom. These are the 'big questions.' Explanation has been found in the things around us, objects both permanent and temporary. We have weaved stories that personify what we wish for, seek to avoid, or that personify the characteristics we think of as human. These became familiar, ritual, tradition, and faith. This was, or is, an ongoing process over thousands of years. First, these were totemic, or animistic-based, and ancestor-related faiths.

General religious practice was organised, then codified, and social order, or morality, became a key aspect of religious belief, promoting safety and community into the bargain, bolstered then by political alliance. Philosophies could be developed, which also bolstered the religion itself. Writing helped to standardise and spread ideas. Across

RELIGION

the globe different circumstances, lifestyles, and continuing strength of specific stories, produced a diverse global picture. Personified gods developed, whether of ancient Vedic or 'Hindu' origins, or Ancient Egyptian, or of the Ancient Greeks. In other places fundamentally different ideas concentrating on the character of humanity and communal life became more predominant, hence the duty, harmony, and order of Eastern thought. While not wanting to exaggerate this, this thousands-year-old division may be one of the subtle causes of our current global individualism v communal debate, and more than hints at the momentous difficulty of bridging that gap. Between the sixth and fourth centuries BCE began the modern age as we would recognise our philosophy and belief systems now. This was the age of Socrates, Confucius, and Buddha, promoting, arguably, our three greatest philosophical traditions: personified gods, communal emphasis, and individual enlightenment. Localised, climate, landscape, and ancestor-based beliefs, often more flexible and individual, were in decline.

The vastness of Africa to some extent bucked this trend, and that is one reason why until recently Western historians often thought of it as a set of backward tribal societies. This is an historic prejudice and misunderstanding that must be addressed if we are to have a truly global dialogue. African, and indigenous religious beliefs from elsewhere, such as those of the Pacific peoples, must be thought of as another strand in our idea of global tradition. This does not mean we need to accept everything. There is no moral equivalence between, or acceptability of, every tradition. Cannibalism and the putting to death of wives and slaves with the burial of a male are no longer acceptable, just as the wine of Catholic communion is not the actual blood of Christ. In time religious practice that denies the equality of males and females may become equally unacceptable.

The development of specific religion across the world can be instructive even now. Chinese Confucianism is not specifically considered here. In a strict sense it is more a cultural and ethical system. Within China, Taoism, or Daoism, does add a religious element to Confucianism with its emphasis on the balance of nature and life cycles, and use of yin and yang; but it is Buddhism that has generally been thought of as predominant in China aside from Confucian ethics.

WHERE ARE WE GOING?

The indigenous belief systems of Native Americans, including Inuit, of Australian Aboriginals, Melanesian, Polynesian and Indonesian peoples across the Pacific, of Amazonians and African origin beliefs are the oldest descendants of totemic and spirit or supernatural-based beliefs, and many have ancestor aspects. Some may effectively be from the dawn of humanity. There are some key things in common. Traditions are often cross tribal, over thousands of years of influence. Rituals and magic in places as varied as Africa and Melanesia are often about influencing ancestors or spirits to act favourably, and warding off evil. Some form of Shaman – in Western mythology often simplified as medicine-man or witchdoctor – is often employed for these purposes. Spirits may be personifications of humanity's characteristics as well as natural elements, such the Inca sun god *Inti* and rain god *Apu Illapu*. Nature-centred beliefs are not just about working with nature, but that nature is the place where life-force is found. Another common characteristic is belief in a soul, but there are various life cycle or other-world ideas about life after death. Many Australian Aboriginals believe that the soul returns to the land, from where it came. There are varied creation stories such as Aboriginal *Dream Time*, thought of as at least 65,000 years old, often a creator god or supreme being like *Io* of New Zealand Maori and other Polynesian peoples, and often an overarching 'great spirit' such as *Wakan Tanka* of the Sioux of the North American Plains. There is often creative power and taboo, or unwanted power, such as Maori have *mana* and *tapu*, respectively. As with newer religions, beliefs and traditions are usually a part of the cultural and political structures of societies.

We must also remember that often these groups have been interpreted through external eyes, whether for entertainment, denigration, exoticism, simplification, or through simple misunderstanding, and a Western language applied that may not do justice to an 'alien' concept. Discovered by Western explorers in 1974 the Korowai tribe of the Indonesian province of Papua on the island of New Guinea became famous as being perhaps the last tribe anywhere known to participate in cannibalism, but this is misleading. People were killed and eaten – cannibalism – but only if they were deemed to have been possessed (and hence eaten from the inside) by a demon – so in their view the demon was killed and eaten, not a human person. The Korowai rejected the idea of cannibalism towards enemies. External influences are also likely to have made a difference to indigenous beliefs and sometimes this will be subtle rather than specific. So, for example, the idea of a creator God, as opposed to spirit or story, may have been adopted or acquiesced in by Indigenous believers to satisfy external missionary religions. A short paragraph here can barely begin to do justice to the ideas, differences, and commonalities in these belief systems, but they are the origins of what we think of as religion. They all engage human virtues and characteristics to explain the world around them. They try to answer the 'big questions.' They are communal and co-operative. There is much we do not understand and cannot know about them, but they have the criteria that we think of when we think of religion and religious beliefs. Whether these are inevitable and natural, or learnt, these characteristics were continued as religion developed through the ages. They are of their cultural, communal, social, and political contexts, but they may also show us how we have complicated our current religions, placing layer upon layer of structure and developed stories. This possibility of learning from them goes far beyond the most obvious current idea of learning about their management of the relationship between people and their natural surroundings, although that may be the most substantial specific reference-point we have between their world and ours.

For most people cultural references such as re-naming Ayers Rock as Uluru, the Maori Haka, the 'Day of the Dead' in Mexico, and Disney-part-mis-presented Pacific Ocean heroic demi-god Maui in the film *Moana*, are the extent of their knowledge. Japanese Shintoism and African/Caribbean Voodoo may be the most high-profile contemporary authentic manifestations of these religious origins. Voodoo is seen in the West as dark magic. In modern terms it derives from West African Vodun beliefs and was transported to the Caribbean and southern USA with slavery. It still has traces in West Africa but is most associated with Haitian culture. Taking on aspects of Roman Catholicism, voodoo generally believe in one God but spirits that may interfere. Voodoo 'magic,' spells, rituals, charms, etc aim to influence those spirits, often to do good rather than to do harm. Shintoism is still the state religion of Japan. It is based on calling upon ancestors and divine beings, or *kami*, to act in one's favour. Many households in Japan will still have these beliefs coexisting with Buddhism, although in the 1868 Restoration of Japanese authority Buddhism was officially downgraded as an imported religion. Only as recently as in 1945 did the Japanese Emperor cease to be considered a divine presence. Shinto rituals are still important in public and private.

At some point, in many places, these spirits became 'gods' within polytheistic belief systems, living fantastical lives. Human characteristics often remained, some form of spirit influence too, rituals were still needed, and explanatory stories multiplied. What we think of as Hinduism was an evolution in the subcontinent between the sixth and second centuries BCE from ancient Vedic religious beginnings. One example is the battle between King Passion and King Reason from the Vedas, the most ancient religious writings from the subcontinent. The spirit of Brahman evolved, so too the eternal soul of *atman*, sin and merit in *papa* and *punya*, a *samsara* cycle of life-death-rebirth, and the development of castes. At the first World Parliament of Religions in 1893 in Chicago Narendra Datta introduced the *sanatan dharma* 'eternal laws of nature' i.e., Hinduism, as a world religion, and the label, an external rather than an internal one, allowed an engagement with the world it had not previously had. Jainism, as far as we know, was the first major offshoot of Hinduism, pre-dating Buddha. Its cyclical and eternal nature of the universe and time on a cosmic scale, and the idea that a person could escape physical existence, were important contributions. Jainism reached a high point of influence between the fifth and tenth centuries CE before succumbing to Hindu and Islamic political dominance.

In the mid-sixth century BCE Buddha learnt from his life to reimagine his Hindu faith. Buddhism shares many of the facets of Hinduism, including the cycle of life and lives, but its development was revolutionary. It imagined a way to find the fulfilment of *nirvana*, of enlightenment, through personalised responsibility for *karma*. It is a personal search and an attitude, with 'right' guidance for the right 'path.' Ritual and festival still play a role. It does not promote one single god or multiple gods. It does promote moderation, and the non-violence and compassion of *ahimsa*. Buddhism is one of the great philosophical strands of humanity. In the West it has often been seen as more psychological than theological or an 'organised' religion. There are different variations, most notably Theravada and Mahayana Buddhism with different geographical centres, and monks and monasteries, but is also sometimes divided into Theravada, Zen (eastern), and Tibetan Buddhism, the latter led by the Dalai Lama. Buddhism may envelop individualism, yet it remains anchored in how people treat others. It is not a solitary experience. It has frequently coexisted with other religions, and 50% of the world's population lies in areas where it has at some point been dominant and left an influential legacy.

Successful monotheistic – one God – religion began with Judaism in the Middle East. The Torah, its key scripture (and first five books of the Christian Bible), places the beginning of Judaism in the life of Abraham about 4,000 years ago, and it believes its origins are from the Word of God. God is all-powerful, permanent, and everywhere. God is moralistic, and Judaism has a version of a heaven and a hell. Judaism has developed rituals and rules to make it a way of life, *halakhah*, with things forbidden, *kashrut*, and things expected or permitted, generally *kosher*. It is often seen as a religion of law. There are many sects based on different Rabbinical histories or leaders, and general divisions including Orthodox, Conservative, Liberal, and Reform Judaism.

We tend to think of religions as forever. That is not accurate. They can succeed and then fall away. Some we 'just' think of as historical items, like the Ancient Egyptian gods, and Greek and Roman Gods, which themselves show how one belief system can be commandeered or assimilated by another, with a change of language and names, based on cultural and political power. Beliefs of the Maya across Central America or Norse Gods of the Vikings are more recent examples. We have pieces of a jigsaw we put together historically to try to understand them, although they flourished after all except one of the six major current religions had become established (not Sikhism). Names like Thor and Odin and the 'paradise' for fallen fighters of Valhalla were known across Europe from Kyiv in Ukraine to Ireland. Some pieces we dismiss out of hand as 'barbarian,' emphasising ghoulish elements, like human sacrifice thought to be employed by several Pre-Columbian civilisations in the central and southern Americas including the Maya, Aztec, and Inca. These belief systems maintain a modern trace, whether

WHERE ARE WE GOING?

in historical and anti-colonial national identity, artistic imagination and creativity, architectural heritage, or language. Alexander the Great in the fourth century BCE and Mughal Emperor Akbar in late 16th-century northern India, are two rulers who tried to create hybrid or 'new' religions for their empires which could not survive their deaths. Ashoka, Emperor of the Mauryan Empire in northern India in the third century BCE, tried adopting Buddhist teaching wholesale and by decree ending slavery, abolishing animal sacrifice and protecting many animal species, abolishing the death penalty, renouncing war, and setting up free hospitals. Twenty *Pillars of Ashoka* survive in the subcontinent exhibiting his laws, and he did much to internationalise the teachings of Buddha. Again, however, his government-by-decree religion could not stand on its own feet after his rule.

The Parsi, most frequently now found in the Mumbai region of India, are the remnants of one of the great religions: Zoroastrianism. This was perhaps the second great monotheistic religion, centred in Persia, dating originally from about 1300 BCE, official religion of the expansive empire of Cyrus the Great in the sixth century BCE, persecuted by Alexander the Great two centuries later. Zoroastrianism promotes one eternal, but not all-powerful, God based on the teachings of Zoroaster, with a heaven and hell based on Man's judgements in life, belief in a saviour, equal access for women, and prayer five times a day in the presence of 'righteous' fire. It therefore has similarities with religions that pre-date it and others that post-date its height. On the surface it shows us how different ideas may cross-pollinate between beliefs. As a major religion with significant reach and influence it lasted for about as long as Christianity has lasted so far and longer than Islam so far. It was eventually pushed to the margins by the spread and conversion of Islam across the Middle East, Persia, and the northern Indian plains. Historically it struggled to 'modernise,' being seen from a Western perspective as largely cut off from changes to learning and science from the ninth to nineteenth centuries CE, and most notably only beginning to use written language rather than oral tradition to record its beliefs from the 14th century.

Christianity has been the most successful modern religion. Originating from the teachings of Jesus born into a Jewish culture, it is the second of the monotheist religions originating with Abraham and believing in the same god. Over several centuries it revised and defined its beliefs, scripture, and rituals beyond the essential core message of love, compassion, and forgiveness for all, seen as more welcoming than the Judaism of law. It became established as a major faith with its adoption by the Roman Empire in the fourth century CE, and from that time allied itself to political power, a relationship that has been struggled over ever since. From a Western perspective its universality was previously unknown. It spread with expanding European power, converting (sometimes forcibly) and overwhelming indigenous beliefs around the globe. From a non-European perspective its association with colonialism is an historic fact, leaving a destructive legacy to ancient cultures. Around the globe Christianity has struggled to face this, as well as adapting or adopting indigenous traditions within the Christian practices of each locality.

From the regional birthplace of Judaism and Christianity came the third great Abrahamic monotheist religion of our age: Islam. From the seventh century CE Islam quickly spread across the Middle East and North Africa, and then further afield, reaching into south-west and south-east Europe and across Asia. It also quickly split, mostly over religious authority, into majority Sunni believing in a consensus of religious authority, and minority but significant Shia or Shi'ite believing in the leadership of an infallible Imam descended from Muhammed (now centred in Iran and for whom an Ayatollah is a 'caretaker' of his authority). Within these there are now many significant groups, from strict Wahhabism to mystical Sufism allowing music, dance, and saints. Like Christianity Islam has successfully spread globally in modern times, and there are Muslim communities around the globe among different racial and ethnic groups. Like its Abrahamic monotheist forebears Islam established rules and rituals that make it a way of life, and sacred scripture fixed as the Word of God, *Allah*, given to the prophet and founder Muhammed ('peace be upon him,' as Muslims would say). Allah is also an ever-present, watchful, and all-knowing God, nominally the same God as in Judaism and Christianity. It also shares a sense of heaven and hell; sin or *haram*; a soul; both free will and predestination, or fate, determined by God; compassion; and the sense of 'fighting for one's religion,' *jihad*.

The most distinctive offshoot from Islam has been Baha'ism, emerging from Shia Islam in the mid-19th century. It was the first religion to set itself up as a world faith, in the West promoting tolerance, gender equality, and harmony with science, under one God. However, it did not envisage separation of Church and State, and over the last century has seemed more socially and politically conservative. It remains a relatively small group. Much larger is Sikhism, now counted as the sixth major world religion. Set up in the 15th century from a fusion of Islamic and Hindu beliefs and practices at a time of conflict between the two in south Asia, Sikhism has successfully carved a distinctive identity for itself, although some Hindus will consider it a part of their faith. With teachings from the Gurus and its sacred scripture, the Guru Granth Sahib, clearer gender equality, strong community, and God constantly in mind to guide honest, moderate, and compassionate living, Sikh communities can be found all over the world.

All religions at least begin as products of their time, and go through phases of growth, consolidation, return to founding principles, confidence, and needing to re-justify themselves. Divisions are almost inevitable, and over authority need not be fatal, although over core beliefs probably would be for a common label to survive. Complacency in the face of criticism may fatally separate religious authority from its flock. They all have potentially eternal basic commonalities, and any prospective new religion will need to include and maintain these. Most profoundly, they must give a coherent and compelling answer to the big questions of how we got here, who we are, and what we are here for. Like any believable and inspirational narrative they must support the virtues of humanity. There must be a sense of community and rituals, festivals and celebrations, that keep that community together, mark milestones, create shared experiences, offer mutual support and a bulwark against bad times. They do not have to be monotheistic. Any new religion will need the fundamentals of business: distinctive brand, investment, raw materials (scripture, leadership), and a market (a willing membership). Any new religion can be expected to face active opposition from current market leaders. Current and new religions will have to be adaptable in two specific ways: they must have an 'answer' for the current challenges of humanity, including lifestyle stress and manmade destruction; and they must be flexible enough for individualism to thrive in a global world of many different historic and cultural traditions and individual rights, while, perhaps contradictorily, building its own community cohesion. Our currently successful religions have so far proved themselves adaptable, but can they continue to be so?

Adapt, Be Marginalised, or Perish?

'God moves in mysterious ways' is a Christian phrase which essentially means that we cannot always understand God's motives and reasoning for why things happen. It applies to miracles, but especially when 'bad' things happen, which may be a 'test of our faith.' These phrases infer that God does know what He is doing. This also gives religion an adaptability to change in different circumstances, and so more resilience. Some do not adapt well enough and fade away. Those that adapt while maintaining consistency with their core beliefs and manage to take their followers with them, either through following them or leading them, are likely to last longest.

The required interpretation comes from our humanity. Schopenhauer, writing about the 'horrors and absurdities' of religion in the 19th century, thought that humanity was moving beyond religion. It may be that religion was a good starting point only. And so, in these ways the positive, and perhaps some negative, characteristics or virtues of humanity have come to bear on the interpretation of religious belief and religious instruction, even on allegedly fixed sacred texts, and religions have adapted. And yet ... if the belief of humanity as a conflictual species is maintained there may remain a role and need for the idealistic moderation of religion and religious morality, however artificially constructed that may be deemed to be.

WHERE ARE WE GOING?

The Adaptability of Religion

The historical path of a religion includes change. The books of the Christian New Testament are usually thought to have been written in the 100 years after the death of Jesus but were not officially fixed as such until the Council of Hippo in 393 CE. There remains serious discussion about the role of Mary Magdalene in Christianity and the possibility of her written story having once stood alongside that of Matthew, Mark, Luke, and John. In the sixth century CE Pope Gregory combined three Biblical characters of Mary into one, a division not reversed until 1969. This shows how religions clarify even their written narratives. There were specific discussions and decisions made about the date and importance of Christ's birth and resurrection, i.e., Christmas and Easter; and Orthodox Christians still celebrate these on a different day and in a different way to Roman Catholics and Protestants. The 'immortal soul,' originally from Plato, was only imported into Christianity 200–400 years after Jesus. It is not in the Old Testament and only entered Judaism in the first century BCE. Free will was only introduced into Christianity in the fourth century CE.

Biblical passages have been reinterpreted, downgraded, classified as 'early' or 'historic' or 'developmental' according to the changing cultural norms of different ages. The story of Ham, used by slave traders and owners to justify slavery, can be excused by Christians as being in the Old Testament, but Judaism also no longer accepts slavery, nor the death by stoning for adultery and other Old Testament or Torah punishments. As one's faith is challenged, perhaps by outside influences, then practices can change and become more defined to define its distinctiveness, as well as confirm it. Sometimes it may seek to envelop and include the influence of other ideas and so it is that pagan rituals were accommodated within Christianity, that the Day of the Dead festival in Mexico sits within a strongly Roman Catholic nation, and that African Christianity often includes a greater use of spirit healing and mediums and the exorcism of evil. Division of authority within a religion is a clear point when this may happen. Charles Darwin's Theory of Evolution pitted science and Church against each other and there has not yet been an accommodation aside from some form of interpretation of Genesis as allegorical. The maleness of the twelve disciples, and the original sin of Eve, are the biblically justified reasons for the maleness of authority in the Christian Church. The relatively recent acceptance, after and still with struggle, of female authority in elements (only) of the Protestant Church in Christianity might also show the historical timeline needed for important change. For some these changes and interpretations will be marks of struggled-for maturity, for others simply historical development and definition, for others practical change, and for others self-serving changes to keep power and relevance, or that lack requisite faith in the Word of God. Whatever the reason, they show that Christianity has adapted.

Even the sanctity of life itself remains interpretable. Thou shalt not 'murder' (often replaced by 'kill') is the Sixth Commandment in Judaism and Christianity, and in other religions in slightly different forms. Yet all religions believe in fighting for themselves in self-defence. Christianity sings of 'onward Christian soldiers' and has justifications for a 'Just war.' Jihad in Islam means standing up for one's religion, not specifically physical fighting, but can be interpreted that way. Only in recent times have we largely, not entirely, dispensed with outright religious conflict. We kill – murder? – domesticated animals in their millions in farming for food, even breeding them for that purpose, allowable across religions. Around the world there also remains the death penalty. Authorities take it upon themselves to administer extreme justice to people that in religious belief are also the work of God. For some people deliberate termination of a pregnancy is also murder. Not to kill is a key part of most religions, yet interpretable in completely different ways according to our own judgement of circumstances. The words kill and murder can mean different things, illustrating that even in the use and interpretation of single words religions can find room for adaptability, or inconsistency. 'An eye for an eye,' known from Hammurabi's written laws of the Babylonian Empire in the eighteenth century BCE appears in the Torah, the Bible, and the Quran, and remains as strong in many people's consciousness as the modern religious doctrine of non-violence.

Islam is a younger religion, and is often seen by the West as inflexible. The words of the Quran are said to be the words of God. It was not always so. Between the 9th and 11th centuries key Arab scholars offered a more liberal path to the then 300–500-year-old religion. Al Kindi, Al Farabi, and Ibn Sina (known in the West as Avicenna, possibly the greatest of Arab scholars), encouraged revelation and reasoning as well as scripture, i.e., not just the literal Quran. In adopting free will, with Allah's guidance, they promoted individual freedom of action, seeing the Quran as a product of its time and place. Al Gazzali in the 12th century produced a philosophy that is the origin of the 'moderate' Islam of much of the world.

From the invasion of Egypt by Napoleon in 1798 Islam began a more recent century of modernisation. In the 19th century Middle Eastern Islamic scholars could discuss the merits of Evolutionary Darwinism, individual liberty, and democracy. In 1876 Ottoman Turkey gained its first written constitution, and a constitutional revolution followed in Iran in 1905–06. Ameer Ali's *The Spirit of Islam* written from an Indian Shia perspective and published from 1891 had a widespread impact on contemporary Muslim life, including its arguments for the abolition of slavery and polygamy, both common in the 19th-century Middle East, in favour of modern social values; and its belief that Islam and science could go hand in hand. There was also a backlash. Jamal al-Afghani from Persia moved from a modernising stance to an anti-Western politicisation of Islam that is frequently cited today. It was this thinking that promoted the Salafists, conservative Sunni reformers, afraid that Islam was losing out to Western values. This led to the establishment of the Muslim Brotherhood in 1928, arguing for the dominance of Islam in government, law, and social life. This was Islam as a religious-social-political movement. Those that were to become the Saudi royal family had already adopted the stricter Wahhabi Salafist form of Sunni Islam. These views were a mainstay of popular Arab nationalism, both Sunni and Shia, underlying or running alongside an urban and eventually authoritarian Baathist political secularism, most successful in the 1950s and 1960s. Political Islam was again reinforced by the anti-colonial and anti-Western revolution in Shia Iran, the temporary seizure by extremists of the Grand Mosque in Mecca, and Soviet communist invasion of Afghanistan, all in the same year of 1979, which radicalised a generation, and the expanding financial influence of Saudi Wahhabism. These 19th- and 20th-century ideas and events are the milestones of the

RELIGION

Islam that we recognise across the Middle East today.

While we should be careful about using Western terms we can say that there have been periods of liberalisation and stricter orthodoxy, as well as the divisions of authority and emphasis that we see around the world now. The politicisation of Middle Eastern, Afghan, and Persian/Iranian Islam may blind us to its variety and complexity, and to its potential for change. Indonesia is the most populous Islamic majority nation, holding 13% of all those in the faith. Egypt, the most populous Middle Eastern/Arab/Persian Muslim nation is sixth. India holds the largest national group of Muslims. In Western, Christian-lite, secularist, humanist, and Enlightenment nations, Muslim communities largely coexist peacefully as minority groups with other cultures, adopt greater individual freedom, and partake in secular-based democracy. It is not widespread but female Imam's leading women's prayers is growing and is now not unknown in varied Muslim nations including Iran, Lebanon, and Sudan. At the time of writing Iran's women-led protests for freedom may be the greatest threat to the theocracy in its nearly 45-year history; and the Saudi government professes a long-term wish to separate Wahhabi religious authority from the running of the Kingdom, and to moderate it, introducing limited social reform. Contrarily, in some places, such as in Indonesia since the early 2000s there has gradually been an increase in Sharia law. The *Charter of Makkah*, endorsed in 2019, largely conceived by the Muslim World League, was signed by about 1200 prominent Muslim figures from 139 nations including Saudi Arabia, from 27 different denominations of Islam. It creates a pan-Islamic set of principles supporting religious and cultural diversity and cross-denominational communication, countering hate, violence, and extremism. More needs to be done on its profile, but its Articles are a progressive and wide-ranging document, clear in promoting tolerant and diverse Islam.* All of this shows the crosswinds of Islam flow in all directions, and that Islam is also capable of quite different interpretation.† As a percentage of the world's population Christianity is

---

* For a copy of the Charter and analysis, see "Readings of the 'Makkah Charter' – ISESCO," The Islamic Educational, Scientific and Cultural Organisation. https://charterofmakkah.org/index.php/en/home/research.

† Kenan Malik, "An art treasure long cherished by Muslims is deemed offensive. But to whom?" *The Guardian*, 8 January 2023, with reference to depictions of the prophet

expected to remain at 31% to 2050 (with 4/10 in Africa), but Islam to rise from 23% in 2015 to 29%.

We should not underestimate the depth of the religious tradition at the heart of our current lives, but religions can also adapt to specific issues, to subtle changes in their role and influence within society, and to cross-cultural influence. That religions have adapted in the past is encouraging for believers too, whose lives continue to change. This leads to the next questions, how serious are the challenges they face now, and how much do they need to adapt? They need to adapt to a whole variety of specific 'hard' issues, and to use their 'soft influence' to maintain their integral part in the narratives of nations and individual lives. They also need to continually recalibrate their relationship with government and power.

Hard Issues

Religions are naturally protective of their belief and if this is seen as an exclusive way of life then they can certainly seem restrictive to the idea of freedom, especially if allied to a political power – compulsory attendance at church being a case in point in the past, and Iranian compulsory hijab another case now. A blanket denial of scientific discovery can do so too. As political freedom has multiplied so has religious tolerance, although there remains a societal prejudice of 'foreign' religion in many places. We should still recognise the religious faith of many people today, especially those facing uncertain 'modernistic' change in their lives, but we should also recognise that government and religion promoting each other in partnership is the misuse of both, and needs to be combatted.

The global rise of individual freedoms challenges organised religion. A confident individual in a free society can choose their religion to suit themselves, and then adapt again, and reinterpret what they choose, taking several steps away from the original. Hierarchical, fixed religions will find this difficult. This is part of the idea that Hinduism in south Asia gradually envelops all those that seek to challenge it, adapting itself to integrate or overcome its challengers. Buddhism may be in an even

---

Mohammed causing 'offence or harm,' and endangering freedom within Islamic communities.

better position to do so. This is increased by the real-world changing profile of communities through increased migration. Migrants bring different ways and interpretations of the established religion, or may feel, as minorities, the need to adapt their own to new environments. Community can be harder in such circumstances.

Two more specific societal changes stand out: Women's equality, and Climate/Natural World/Biodiversity changes, although gender choice may become another in time. All the main religions maintain rhetoric of respect and equal status in daily life for women, but in different ways they express 'difference,' a difference that is sometimes, not always, used to prevent equality or freedom or both. This may be in the name of reverence, modesty, or protection. Difference and secondary roles are at the heart of their historical narratives in the authority and role of women. Even on the everyday level mixed gender worship and marriage of clergy or having female clergy are far from being established around the world. In the long term this is simply unsustainable, but changing how a religion and religious authority works after centuries of development is an historically difficult change to make. Religions around the world do recognise this, and change has begun, and a tipping point may be reached sooner than ever predicted with the generational expanse of female education, but make no mistake, the idea of a female Pope or Ayatollah is truly a revolutionary thought.

Schopenhauer also said that Christianity had made what he called a 'fundamental error' in separating humanity from the natural world. The predominant attitude has been one of superiority and stewardship of something under their control, not one of equality or inter-dependence. We are now being forced to appreciate our inter-dependence through exploitation of resources, what many scientists call an extinction level period for biodiversity, or the crossing of disease between species. This is going hand in hand with a renewed idea of humanity as 'another' species of animal, not a separated superior being. While we currently focus on the economic and climactic consequences of humanity's development these fundamental revisions of humanity's place on the planet are waiting impatiently in the wings for reassessment. Some religions and beliefs are certainly better placed than others to accommodate new thinking in these areas, and it might be said that old totemic religions, and those like Jainism and Buddhism, never took part in the 'man as superior to nature' belief of the West. Humanity knows it is not God, and that the earth was here before us, whether scientifically or religiously measured. If nature is part of God's work we owe God to look after it. If we are unique then we have a unique responsibility towards it – but not from a 'might is right' or a 'we can so we will' perspective.

This relates to another area of challenge for religion: religious truth. Is 'faith' incompatible with 'knowledge,' is religion incompatible with science? This is not about keeping up with modern ways of doing things, even religious fundamentalists use modern weapons and television and encrypted social media for communication and propaganda. This is about the fundamental idea of a religious truth. Religious belief, and religious authorities, need to grapple with the idea that it is becoming a belief in the public consciousness that science may eventually be able to explain 'everything.' We are increasingly being drawn into the belief that science is an infallible creed. In other words, at some point religion may face the possibility of being 'proved' or 'disproved,' or of having to 'prove' itself. If the latter becomes the only way to maintain its credibility in a science-based culture, it will struggle. This is at the same time as understanding that science is interpretable, and that it can recognise mistakes and move forward to develop alternative theories and 'latest' knowledge. Religion does adapt but it struggles to admit mistakes. As science explains distant galaxies, develops an artificial brain, manipulates people's emotions, and understands the ability to change gender physically or emotionally, then what price the idea, the faith, that humanity is made in God's image, or that God is within each of us? The philosophical development in Christianity of First Cause by Thomas Aquinas in the 13th century is one religion's counterattack against the march of science, the idea that before the first scientifically provable sign of life there was something, with the religious-philosophical question of where or who that something came from. This has been complemented by Intelligent Design, that the complexity of the world that we discover 'must have had' a guiding hand. Is this a fundamental accommodation of science by religion, even a 'maturity' of religion?

The extent of 'free will' will be tested in humanity's willingness to try to explain everything, to explore everything, to make everything, to set no boundaries on its curiosity. The meaning of free will may be tested by the ability of science to explain emotions and manipulate thought. As free will – or individual choice – may be explained, and as humanity is more critical of its decisions, then how do people judge things like divine fate or heaven and hell? One possibility is an allegorical or metaphorical belief in psychological torment or reward of the soul, or of consciousness. This is psychological religion. That way may lie different Hindu-Buddhist ideas of enlightenment, and perhaps even cycles of life and rebirth – although scientific explanation of death will challenge those too. The development of science will test our core religious beliefs, our faith in them, and in religion itself.

Fortunately, there is Pascales Wager. This is that God may not exist, but we should believe just in case he does. If he doesn't exist then you lose nothing; if he does then you can only gain. Of course, one problem is that a true God will know when belief is manufactured, so the only way this works is if the belief is a real commitment. Another antidote to the science bug may be the idea of a utopian journey, rather than the destination itself. For religious faith it would be the lessons learnt on the journey about ourselves that would be important, undertaken within the guidelines of religious morality or belief. Hopefully we would recognise our utopia – or enlightenment? – when we reach it!

An increasing global dialogue also highlights difference and inequality. Minorities can usually be accommodated because they are not perceived as a 'threat,' until they grow. Nations may then put more consideration into understanding and tolerance of difference in general, into integration into national and daily life, and into toleration of different specific beliefs that may seem to jar with the established view. In practice this means things like whether to allow a loud call to prayer from Muslims in a non-Muslim nation, protection of minorities where there is a more radical anti-minority group, and education or allowance for non- or misunderstanding of blasphemy laws. Differences then may shine a spotlight on discrimination. In majority Christian Europe the higher profile of minorities clashes with a European sense of individualism and freedom, and with historic intolerance and misunderstanding. For newcomers there is usually a natural desire to maintain religious belief and cultural heritage, and community links, for that is one aspect of their feeling of security. Some nations have passed laws which try to balance tolerance and security. Some try to force integration in the name of a majority culture, which is quite different. In the latter, contradictions of disallowing individual choice in the name of maintaining liberalism are easy charges to make. None of this is new, as with English intolerance of the Irish Roman Catholic migration in the 19th century, or American of southern European Catholic migration, or historic treatment of Jewish minorities. It is mirrored around the world. Aside from real security issues, in both directions, religions that see themselves as tolerant need to be speaking out against these intolerances. To do that they will need to be confident in themselves; an intolerance often portrays a lack of that confidence. Multi-cultural societies are here to stay. Neither should anyone be trying to determine the changing path of another religion from the outside. That would be the sort of colonial arrogance we should have put behind us. Change needs to be organic not imposed. Outsiders may ask questions, but they must be confident and show enough of a perspective of change to believe that core principles of humanity will win out in the end. In a world of increasing migration, temporary and permanent, forced by circumstances and voluntary, the need for religious neighbourliness, understanding, and tolerance even amid disagreement, becomes more important than ever before to individual nations and to the world at large. The need for religious followers to respect the cultural norms of the nation, a nation that shows respect for minorities, diversity, and equality of opportunity and in law, is essential. This applies even if minorities peacefully take part in trying to influence or change the norm. The common good needs to be interpreted for all.

A global humanity adds another dimension to considerations of welfare and aid. Domestically within nations religious provision of welfare has largely been taken over by the state, and religious leaders seem to have often abdicated willingness to speak out on welfare issues, although that will seem a harsh judgement for some. Part of this is a reluctance to criticise legitimate or allied political authorities, but one must wonder if this lack of willingness to publicly show moral leadership, again perhaps a harsh judgement, has been a factor in the rise of inequality. There must be a way to express moral positions based on religious principles which are deep-seated in public consciousness without alienating those who feel non-committal or even hostile to organised religion. In Europe in recent years this may have begun to change. Various religious figures including the Pope have spoken out about economic inequality, poverty, and the treatment of migrants. Surely this should be a key part of a religion's mission in the world if they are to put into practice their religious faith. For those worried about 'interference,' religion cannot be seen as being a part of society and yet not have a valid voice. Internationally, religions face similar issues, and are making similar statements. They must speak out about international inequalities, but they also need to do so consistently, not purely from a national perspective, and arguably, not only from their own religion's perspective.

Part of that, whether Christian or Islamic or other, needs to be a genuine recognition of their own histories and parts they may have played in the development of inequalities, just as they need to recognise parts played in colonialism, discrimination, child abuse, or acquiescence in authoritarian rule. Some of this is about separating themselves from governmental perspective, not just influence. A history that can be criticised should not prevent a role, just as being a victim of history also does not denote a new superior view that automatically has greater credence. A genuinely global view, within religions that have diversity and between religions across the world, needs to be part of the global dialogue. In recent years leaders of the world's religions have attempted more co-operation and agreement to promote tolerance, and common statements on international issues, such as conflict, climate change, natural disaster, and terrorism. This is an historic change of relationships between religions which should not be minimised, will take much longer to be natural and frequent, and is encouraging for the world.

One of the hardest specific issues for religion is the question of life itself. Aside from the idea of taking life as punishment or in war mentioned earlier there is a host of issues involved including abortion, artificial IVF, assisted suicide, and quality of life. These are difficult because they go to the core of religious belief and engage the most emotional practical dilemmas in real life. There are also issues of individualism, community duty and values, and the march of science. Fundamental beliefs are involved, like whether only God should create life 'naturally' and a belief in life cycles, determined by a combination of free will and fate predetermined by God. Added to that is the toxic politicisation of issues, notably abortion and contraception, including population management as a way of dealing with climate change. We have barely begun to deal with the idea of animals feeling emotions being used and abused by humanity. Religion needs to find a way through these that maintain its principles and that are practical for most of its prospective believers. If abortion is against the fundamental sanctity of life there must still be room for the practical implementation of such belief: When does life begin in the womb and when do we know that, at what point can a life support itself, what about the rights of the woman carrying a potential life through a pregnancy to birth, especially if they are the subject of coercion or in some form not in control of their life or the conception? These are the matters of science, of individual rights, of female equality, that religions must find a moderate and perhaps messy accommodation with. If they do not, they will not carry with them the mass of people who want the support of their faith but who are faced with such an issue sometime in their life for themselves or someone else they care about. To politicise these issues does them a great disservice and makes the real-life judgements of ordinary people harder. Religious beliefs may influence their judgement, but they should not feel coerced by peer pressure. That is not a voluntary religion. Religions need to move with their believers – within the fundamental ideas of the club, namely, in this case, if a 'life' can be preserved and then led without additional harm then it should be. That harm is a judgement for individuals to make, after guidance has been offered or sought. If life is to have a sanctity, a sacredness, to it, then it must also be a life with quality. That quality should include spiritual and mental wellbeing not just, but not ignoring, a minimum available level of materialistic comfort and physical independence, which perhaps can be supplemented by support. Religious advice and guidance must take place within the humanity that religions profess to have and promote. Similarly, the 'artificial' creation of life through IVF. Like advocates of same-sex marriage concentrating on supporting the institution of marriage itself, here the greater point is the wish to create life within a loving relationship. There are moral positions in a modern context that religions can genuinely justify that are not 'traditional.'

Assisted suicide is about quality of life. Someone with a terminal illness or such poor quality of life now or in the foreseeable future may wish to maintain some control over that future and the manner of their death. It is the ultimate in individualism, or some might even say selfishness, but all religions have a quality-of-life indicator in their beliefs. As the world's population gets older, and much of it not necessarily richer or more in control of their lives, assisted suicide will become a larger profile issue. God is surely not about allowing suffering on anything other than a temporary 'test of faith' basis. The religious guidance must be based on a humaneness within humanity. That God may work in mysterious ways may be true, but it supposes no intervention in any specific part of the human decision-making process. There will be religious arguments on both sides: no-one has the right to take a life created by God, yet people have free will given by God. For a religion to maintain its relevance it must find a practical balance between its core faith and the realities of the believers it seeks to represent and protect. It can independently seek to lead, but like all leaders must find consistency in its mission. Allying to political power directly does not help either religious resilience or the individual believer.

Surging individualism, changing social values especially in respect of gender, reassessment of the inter-dependence of ourselves and the natural world, and the rising 'belief' in science as the source of our knowledge and our 'truth,' are a formidable array of 'hard issues' for religion in general, and for specific religions. Religion's credibility and power in and for people must be stronger than relying on a wager or undefined journey to utopia. Like any leadership or brand, clarity, co-operation, and consistency are needed, and humility.

Soft Influence

As religious belief becomes more individualised it may be that its soft influence is entrenched. Opposition to ritual may weaken organised religion but remove some of the opposition to religion itself. People making individual decisions will still maintain their core individual morality as at least partly informed by their own confident journey of 'religious-like principles,' even if they do not call it religious belief and it is not part of politically aligned religious power.

Confucius, Buddha, and Socrates led the way globally towards making individuals responsible for their moral choices. At this point the fate of Fate hung in the balance. When a single God became a lawgiver, and humanity believed it knew the views of God in detail – in food, clothes, sex, marriage, naming, and burial rites, etc – then the morality of God became ever-present and all-powerful. The parallel adoption of free will allowed the explanation of evil and of bad decisions, a space between a Just God and humanity, and a sense of how humanity could make progress by measuring the reach of religious morality.

This has led to some version of 'do unto others as you would have done to you' as the 'golden rule' of religion. It informs attitudes towards equality and inequality, charity and welfare, and discrimination and prejudice, or at least it could and should. The Sermon on the Mount from Jesus and the Parable of the Good Samaritan are examples of this. More specifically so is Zakat, defined as almsgiving and important enough to be one of the five Pillars of Islam, and generally the idea of *Umma*, the full community of Islam. So too *Mitzvah*, the 'good deeds' of Judaism, and Sikhism's *Sewa*, serving others. It might be said that everything else in terms of religion's influence on daily life is 'mechanical,' the 'how' of making religious faith work in practice. To their credit religions have aided and abetted the rise of rules, or laws, to contain anger and discrimination, and to define justice; and an essential core purpose of religion has been charity, real-world help as well as spiritual welfare, compassion, and solidarity. There is strong soft influence through religion on these issues in every country on the planet.

This influence has changed over time, but it has been one of the key influential aspects of religion on the foundations of human society. Even if the development of a communal morality was inevitable from humanity's characteristics – which it may not have been – religious belief has still given us the foundations of the framework we use. Former Archbishop of Canterbury Rowan Williams said in a BBC Reith Lecture *The Four Freedoms: Freedom of Worship* in 2022 that freedom of religious worship – the freedom to express, conduct, and portray oneself – was the basis of freedom of speech. Whether you agree or not it is a sign of the part that religions believe they can play in contemporary society, as well as a plea for that freedom of religion. Whether religion continues to get credit for this soft influence may depend on how clearly it can maintain a voice in society and the consistency of its morality. Religion must therefore accommodate itself to the ideas of the more truthful or purer, and global, Enlightenment now developing, and be critical of its own inconsistency. If it can do that then it can still provide the foundations of human morality and be respected for doing so. That applies to individual organised religions and individual religious belief. If it can be consistent in its morality then it can reasonably claim to be in favour of, and to promote, the genuine 'common good' of societies. This then, is a key part of its future voice and its influence. This is a way of negating the idea that religion is a conversion to closed thought. It can encourage living one's religious values and maintain a relevant voice and profile in society. If religious leaders feel the need to comment on individual, often politicised, policy issues then at least it can give such comments a clear foundation. It can also use consistency in its application of morality to find a way through the hard issues of individualism and scientific discovery, etc discussed above. If religions across the world can work together, or international religions can take a global perspective on the common good and morality, then that would also enhance religion in its entirety.

Government and the Power of Religion

Religions became associated with, sought the protection of, or were co-opted by, rulers, empires, and specific peoples. It was often seen by political rulers as both a necessary and useful ally, and a 'fifth column' with divided loyalty within its borders and with foreign support or leadership. Arguably this applies less to Hinduism and Buddhism. In Europe the Renaissance and Reformation, which between them can claim to be the beginnings of European modernism and the Enlightenment, began to separate Church and State. Henry VIII's divorce of England and Wales from Papal authority was truly revolutionary. Christian authority became more separated from political, but often with the concession that it became the 'established' religion of a nation with preferential treatment. This often therefore gave it an association with nationalism and 'national values,' and the national heritage. Christianity was also a religion of conversion, and so an alliance with political power also meant missionaries with expeditions sent for trade, exploration, and conquest. This made it a global religion after about 1500CE, as well as a cause of its poorer reputation in places around the world. Islam similarly allied religion and state from its earliest days. In more modern times religion has found competitors in secularism, agnosticism, atheism, humanism, democracy, communism, individualism, materialism, and science. These are overlapping and different types of competitors, or simply that take people's attention away from religion. Religion has also found urbanisation and secularist mass education have played a part in loosening its communal strength.

This separation of Church and State is much healthier. For very strong adherents this may be unwanted. It may be that one has a religious belief in one's Faith as a way of life but that now, especially in Western societies, this means a choice between adapting one's faith or an increasing isolation. Religion must now stand on its own principles for its profile, support, influence, and power. It has something to work with. In most places there remain physical structures, resources of money and people, historical sympathy, soft influence, and willing accommodation with religion – which includes recognition on coinage, teaching in education, representation at national events, financial power, established charitable work, and local community links. It still has enough in its favour to enable addressing new issues and circumstances. It must do so with confidence. There are so many 'hard' issues that make this a moment of danger for religious cohesion and influence, but also give Christianity in Western societies, and other religions elsewhere, an historic chance to redefine themselves with modern relevance as independent institutions.

In 2021 the about-to-be appointed Archbishop of York Stephen Cottrell said: 'There's (been) a loss of vision about what the world could be like' and 'I don't accept a separation between the Church and politics, faith and politics' and that 'Loving your neighbour is a profoundly political statement.'* This is also surely a recognition of a religion

---

* Harriet Sherwood, "Britain must reset its compass, from housing to wages, says archbishop of York," *The Observer*, 28 February 2021.

RELIGION

needing to have confidence in itself even in the context of declining membership. It echoed comments in recent years from varying religious leaders in and beyond Europe, in and beyond Christianity. He was, importantly, talking about Church and politics, not the organs of the State itself, or party politics. He was saying that religious principles had a relevance and should have a voice in society, something which his ancient forebears would have taken for granted.

Islam is much more varied in its association with political power around the world than most in the West are given to believe from the daily news. The original Sunni–Shia split was about the exercise of religious authority, and different political authorities arose in parallel to that split. Now, Islam in places from Indonesia to West African nations is in a similar position to Christianity. Its ties with government are loose. Its strength, aside from that of its belief and peoples' faith, is social and cultural, communal, and historic. Between Pakistan and North Africa it is also on a journey, much as Christianity has been, even if comparisons should be tentative. In places it is entwined with government authority, most notably in the Kingdom of Saudi Arabia, the Islamic Republic of Iran, and in an even more fundamentalist way in the Taliban of Afghanistan. Elsewhere different types of governments and rulers adopt and protect it, use it as a shield of rule, or of national symbolism, or allow an influence on policy, and this includes Egypt, Turkey, Morocco, Iraq, and other places, a variety of monarchist, authoritarian, or democracy-light governments. In most places in this region Islam will remain at the core of social systems, the law, communal and personal relationships, and be representative or symbolic of national values, for some time to come. Nevertheless, it will be challenged by democracy or by the individual whims of monarchs and authoritarians shaping or misusing, denigrating, or associating with it. It will be challenged by materialism and by the global dialogue in social issues such as women's rights and individual privacy. It would be foolhardy, and wrong, from an outside perspective, to make pronouncements or assumptions as to how Islamic authority and the power of Islam will change in its relationship with political power, but change it will do, in the face of such globally powerful forces.

Intriguing and important is the moderation and potential separation of Wahhabism from the political authority and state institutions (including education and law) of the Kingdom of Saudi Arabia. This is presented as modernism and moderation to allow globally recognisable and acceptable constitutional, political, economic, and social progress. It is presented as taking the Kingdom back to a more original tolerant Islam. Whether it is intended as an eventual separation of religion and state power is unknown. In many ways reforms mirror Ottoman and Egyptian ones of a century ago. Religious authority is being bypassed and remodelled, removing religious officials from being state officials. Whether moderation can happen by state diktat is another question, whether it would happen without it in the Kingdom is another. There remains a danger that separation means a loss of control over religious authorities and their pronouncements before moderation takes place, and that more independent religious authority is less supportive. Religious authority may resist the loss of its direct political influence; or its independence in moderate or less moderate form may 'need' to be squashed by the political authority. It may or may not take its traditional-religious support with it, or indeed may choose to leave it behind in favour of taking a younger more globally minded, but still strongly Islamic, sector of the population with it instead. The consequences of any of these routes are likely to be profound for the religious-political power dynamic in Saudi society. Over the last ten years change has been and still is incremental, and reversible, but cumulatively significant. This will have an influence on Sunni Islam the world over, but we should understand that the Kingdom is not aiming to become more 'Western.'

The religious-political enmeshment is even more true when considering Iran. As a theocracy the religious is in control of the political. Yet the influences of the world cannot and are not being negated. Democracy, already claimed within a restrictive Islamic guidance, individual freedom's especially for women and of privacy, and materialism, are having huge effects on Iranian society. A society suffering hardship through sanctions and relative international isolation, yet historically cosmopolitan in its cities, now with a young but well-educated population requiring entrepreneurial and personal life opportunities to make their way, unable to be cut off from international communication, is a society at a crossroads. No-one is suggesting that suddenly or any time soon Islam will cease to be important and a bedrock of Iranian society and values, but a non-engagement of an older religious leadership, seen as having misrepresented the original 1979 causes of revolution, undoubtedly make that crossroads conflictual. This may be the irresistible force of 'progress' coming up against the immovable ideology of the theocratic – but now also paramilitary and inflexible – power of the state. The journeys of Iran and Saudi Arabia will be historic, whether peaceful or violent, and will have serious consequences for the rest of the world, and for Islam itself. Any domestic or religious influence of the beginnings of a surprising but welcome diplomatic rapprochement between the two states in 2023 is yet to be seen.

Elsewhere two other nations present interesting studies in the religious-political dynamic: Israel and India. Israel was created as a Jewish State after the horror of the Holocaust to protect those of the Jewish faith. It is buttressed by the history of Judaism and the 'next year in Jerusalem' saying during Passover, and since its inception Jewish people have emigrated to it in significant numbers. It was created by largely Western powers through the United Nations. However, although there are religious claims to the land it is also the land of Arab Palestine, mostly Muslim with a small Christian community. Israel is a Jewish state where internally Jews have lived with non-Jews, and with hostile or unsupportive neighbours, for all its existence so far. The external threat is not over but as time has passed the internal nature of its divisions is coming into focus as equally hard to reconcile, and many of these are about, or have an identifier of, religion. Politically socialist, Kibbutzim, fervent settler, socially conservative, Orthodox and Reform, liberal Western, and strongly traditional, are all elements represented in Israeli society. Israel may choose to be a Western-style democracy, tolerant of minorities who have equal rights under the law, and who need – for its own safety and success – to be integrated into its economic, cultural, and political life. Or it can go down the more religious route giving preference to its Jewish population. Such is the nature of its politics that religion-centred parties have a significant and apparently growing influence, often in multi-party coalition governments, still restricted by a security situation of non-peace with its neighbours and the difficult occupation of, and responsibility for, the West Bank and Gaza (and the Golan Heights) in which some want to project a Greater Israel. In 2023 Israel's government became its most nationalist and religious yet seen. Notably, it is also Orthodox families that are the main source of the increasing Jewish population. For those concentrating on the development of the Jewish nature of the state its minorities are objects of concern, or even 'fifth column' potential enemies. Israel, such a mix of a jigsaw, may face a reckoning of whether it moves towards a religious state or a democratic one, and it may not achieve both. Peace with its neighbours and the creation of a peaceful Palestinian State will not settle this question but may be needed to allow Israel the deep breath necessary to decide what sort of state it wants to be. The Israel–Hamas Gaza war from 2023 seems to make peace more distant, and yet may draw this question into even sharper focus. Israel is light years away from being a religious state in the manner of Iran or Saudi Arabia but there is a path leading in that direction. Judaism is at its everyday, social, political, constitutional, and foreign-relations core in a way that a religion is not at the core of most nations today. Making this work is Judaism's greatest challenge.

India has similarities and differences. Its government since 2014, the Bharatiya Janata Party (BJP – Indian People's Party), is a clearly Hindu nationalist one. Politically it may be seen as populist but what characterises, or first characterised it, is that it is not the Congress Party that led India in the early decades of independence. As India has slowly thrown off its post-colonial hangover and become internationally independent and confident, a growing economy in world terms, and more electorally mature, it has chosen a ruling party that has deliberately sown its Hinduism into its nationalism. It has not appeared out of nowhere, nor is it the most extreme of Hindu parties, and therefore can present itself as moderate and reasonable. Nevertheless, its policies have enabled campaigns and enacted laws to give committed Hindus a more prominent position in society, and to do so partly by negating the role of others, most notably the largest minority Muslim community. With the confidence of renewed power it has also become more authoritarian-minded, or at least arrogant in its power with greater intolerance. In practice this means ending quotas and positive discrimination, acquiescing in the unequal treatment of Muslims in law enforcement, intolerant treatment of critical media, looking for ancient Hindu land rights, and proposals that appear to make Muslim migrants second-class and less likely to be accepted in India. Hinduism may be in danger of becoming party-politicised and subject to the whims or propaganda of government in shaping it in the public consciousness. India must avoid a situation where to be seen as a loyal Hindu means voting in a particular way, or where within that vote there is an appeal to 'the most Hindu.' Democrats within the nation trying to make the economic and cultural most of, and safety for, all its talents would constrain the BJP on the path it is taking their nation. India, of course, is not just the BJP. Hinduism is familial in a million different ways in the homes, shrines, and temples of India, and there is still a strong civic society and media, within a nation that still takes democracy seriously. Aside from its politicisation, the major challenge to Hinduism is, like other religions, individualism, promoting a weakening of the caste system that buttresses its traditions. Its flexibility can take it into the global future through variation in belief and ritual, a lack of fixed single leadership, no fixed scripture but sacred writings, and a history of slow evolution. However, India must not become a one-party democracy, such as Mexico or Japan were for long periods of time. If it does so there is a peril to Hinduism as well as to India, at the very least in international reputation. The elections of 2024 showed a welcome but not yet decisive return to less religious politics.

Israel and India are not theocratic states in any sense. However, theocratic states reach credibility step by step via adoption of identity based on religion. Most nations have separated 'Church' and State, even when the former remains preferred as the 'established' or state religion. Those states, and leaders, that do not, risk the independence of the state, and the independence of the religion. Both religion and state are altered by the closeness of the relationship between the two. When the only opposition is within a religious-centred dominant single party then follows a willingness by some to be 'more' religious than another to gain support, and that leads to an activist-led inflating of religious importance and power. That is one way a religious-dominated state emerges. Another way is the use of religious belief by leaders that emerge with their own arrogance or agenda, or who are bound by the religious activists that support them. That is what arguably happened in

Iran in 1979. That 'use' may be for personalised power or a nationalist cause – just as communism was used as a vehicle for nationalism during the anti-colonial independence movements of the Cold War. Religions used in these ways are likely to be themselves altered without beneficial long-term consequences. The same might be said of Xi Jinping's attempt to make the 'faith' of the CCP inseparable from the Chinese state.

The Long-Term Choices for the Future that are Beginning Now

Whether God, religion, and organised religion each have a future are not the same things. There are different possible futures: religion concentrating on the cosmic and human mysteries; one of the everyday lawgiver in people's lives which will maintain the importance of 'fixed' or interpretable scripture and leadership; one of spirituality or 'internal enlightenment' which is very personal and Buddhism-like or Buddhism-lite; and a fourth as a cultural and community-supportive backdrop. Or some combination of these. Then there is the question of whether differences in faith and ritual will, over a long period, be maintained, or whether they will matter as much. Christianity's and Islam's globalism remains one of their major challenges, internally and externally, in global leadership, and cultural compromise, including major division between Roman Catholicism, Orthodox, and Protestant churches, and between Sunni and Shia. If spirituality or individuality is what is to remain then these become less important. As does the challenge of politicisation faced by all major religions. If distinctive ways of life remain important then reaction to social change and continuing global inequality – across gender, race, and class – will remain serious challenges for all religions. Morality itself will be a source of more debate as AI makers have influence over algorithms and robotics that can decide people's lives, but morality will have a foundation in both secular reasoning and religious faith.

We have seen that religions adapt over time, and that they can fade away too and others rise in their place. In a more global world there must be considered the possibility of the rise of a more deliberately global faith. Baha'ism does not seem fit to fulfil that role. A new religion may arise organically across the globe in a patchwork way that we may not recognise at first as a religion in the traditionally accepted sense. Could the Enlightenment be the new religion, or creed, of the modern age? Enlightenment's colonial-era introduction to others and politicisation may have hindered its acceptance globally but it has shown the ability to change, to shape people's psychology, to be communal, to give people purpose, to address morality, and through its Reason and Science to give some possible explanation to the future and the currently unknown. The last 100 years may be seen as the American Century and the spread of 'life, liberty, and the pursuit of happiness' i.e., individual freedom is sloganizing for the Enlightenment, but it needs to be the 'new' version that is more global, more consistent, more honest, than the one associated with the colonial era. Currently it seems doubtful that this is enough to replace the alluring mystery, comfort, and compelling stories of religion as we know them now. It may exist in parallel. So too the narrower idea of Science as a defining creed to live by. We know enough to understand that 'Science' is of vast variation, interpretable, changes, can lead us to mistakes, and it can be both definitive and open-ended. Most of all we understand that science needs to be 'controlled' and is a tool of humanity that may help shape it but is not the choice-maker of what happens to humanity. Science, could, however, make religion redefine itself. There will be increasing discussion about the meaning and role of fate and free will, just as there has needed to be a revolution in the idea of heaven and hell above and below the world we live in. The Chinese idea of heaven – *tian* – is of a power rather than a place. There will be re-evaluation of how the human body is made up as we unravel its complexity – atoms were once thought indivisible. As we explore more of the universe we will need to re-examine religious explanations for it. More knowledge may only increase the awe and wonder of creation. Meeting alien life of bacterial or intelligent form would be a whole new dimension to consider. Neither have Science or the Enlightenment marginalised the idea of a soul.

The influence of religion and specific religions are qualified by the situation they are in. People are by nature intuitive about them. They must involve and be relevant to human nature. Judgements and decisions on the issues of the day from free speech, ethical science, issues of life and death, gender identity, discrimination, welfare, etc must chime with the reality of people's lives and the cultural flow that people are experiencing as their lives change. At the same time, religion and religious authorities must appear consistent and clear, and exhibit qualities like honesty and transparency expected of any organisation. Religions can lead as well as be led. We have seen that religions and people do adapt. Fixed scriptural religions will find this harder, but not impossible. All religions must move away from competition with others and concentrate on coexistence and confidence in themselves. To some extent this is happening already. Religions that willingly entwine themselves with government directly must also understand that they will be changed by that, and will be associated with, and must take some responsibility for, what that government does. Activists should not determine such a power dynamic without the constraining legitimacy of the continuing consensus of the majority. Religions in or out of government cannot dissociate themselves from the practicality and reality of the people they represent and serve.

Another accommodation may need to be made with the linked specific ideas of progress and stewardship, perhaps through the linked eyes of economic inequality and climate change / environmentalism. Climate and environmental change can alter the idea of what progress is and how we achieve it. Inequality, and at least life chance fragility, is expected to get worse through climate change, but is on a medium-term negative path already. All religions accept some form of stewardship of the earth, and respect for others based upon a human equality, but there is needed a more overt inclusive and global perspective of quality of life – mental and spiritual as well as physical and economic, and that addresses discriminations. This may call into question the current economic model of 'progress' accepted around the world. That is a major shift. It may be helped by a declining rate of population rise, and eventually decline or at least stability. Cross-religious co-operation will help, and greater solidarity or compassion for those in need through no fault of their own. Addressing stewardship and inequality could, or would need us to, lean towards more practical action, moving the emphasis away from ritual, tradition, strict 'scriptural determinism,' and fixed 'correct' belief. They might also lead to a more diverse religious leadership.

If religions accept a global world and want peace, and believe in an unknowable God, then they must tolerate all other voluntary religions. Religions must become a peace-activist coalition. This is risky because coexistence may help a global dialogue to flourish and further the prospect of individuals choosing their individual beliefs rather than communal and structured religion. It may lead to a virtuous cycle of realising the commonalities between, and minimising the distinctiveness of, religions. Inter-marriage in multi-cultural societies, mixed or multiple heritages, and co-work, all encourage a fluidity and increased understanding of religious experience, as they do of lifestyle and other culture. However, peacefully coexisting distinct religions and blurred boundaries would be long historic trends. Let us also remember that if we are social beings we want to be part of a recognisable community for support, and that becomes more elusive with more familial or individually based beliefs. Humans do, however, manage multiple identities and communities in our daily lives. Humans can chew gum and walk at the same time, while holding two thoughts in their heads. If we are conflictual then religions will find ways to remain distinctive. If we are both then the conflict or/and co-operation may simply be cyclical, or perhaps at the mercy of how quickly we can expand our idea of familiarity with other people we do not know. It may be that 'religious man' can work out and follow Faith whether conflictual or co-operative, and that religions show these are methods of what we do, to be changed according to circumstances, not determinants of what we do.

Another challenge to the core of religion and religious experience and belief may in time be specific disruptive technology. Long gone are the idealistic hopes of the internet and social media producing peace and harmony. The development of machine learning, the acceleration of discovery and invention that may bring, and use of AI to reproduce the human body or create new life are deeper longer-term challenges. If humans can be augmented intellectually and physically, or if there is an emergence of non-organic life through the creation of AI, then religion will be forced to have a view on these. Clear co-operative views not just on quality of life and the equality of life, but on the nature and value of life itself will be needed. God working in mysterious ways will not be a good enough answer for many people. Is there a heaven and hell for new life-forms, is God within them too, is God still in control as some of us assume enhanced powers or life expectancy…? Our ethics and narratives of life will be questioned. The Enlightenment and Science bring us a feeling of reason or logic, of exactitude or measurability. AI or biotech revolution coming out of this may still be difficult opposition for religion.

As China and India become ever larger in profile around the world, and in an age of greater migration, and given their numbers, their predominant cultures will also have an influence. It may be that Hinduism, in different forms, becomes less India-centred, and core beliefs like karma and rebirth become more global. It may be that Confucian ethics and duty become more popular as people look for ways to maintain community in the face of 'extreme' individualism; or seek an order they can see as non-religious in a Western sense. In that case the politicisation of Confucian traditions by Chinese authorities, and maybe even Hindu ones by Indian nationalist governments, may be laid bare for all to see. This could lead to rejection, or to these beliefs re-finding themselves, or to a 'usefulness' of pick and mix ideas by more secular or Enlightenment-based societies. This might also be said for African beliefs even further into the future. It is impossible to know accurately how many Africans merge traditional and Abrahamic religious practice, but a generally accepted figure is that in 2002 about 100 million Africans, or just over 10% of the then population, took part in traditional African religion outside Islam and Christianity. It has been resilient under the surface and can be expected to continue to be so, despite its lack of obvious political affiliation.

In facing some very hard specific and conceptual issues leadership is needed, especially in two respects: coexistence and reinterpretation. A religion that allows only the legitimacy of their own faith cannot lead or take part in coexistence. That was the path of Islam in the 7th and 8th centuries, the Crusades, Christianity in Central and South America in the 16th century, and of ISIS and the Taliban today. Leadership is needed in a global world with an inevitable global dialogue. Reason may establish economic or judicial equality and stability, but tolerance or fraternity is more moral-based, and in a global world they are needed for that dialogue to be productive, and for religions themselves to flourish together and within themselves. For that, a good level of peace and harmony is needed. The alternative is believing that one religion will eventually 'win' and overcome all others. Those leaderships that can bring people together, that can admit mistakes – such as ditching the Papal Infallibility of previous times – have more of a chance of taking people with them in a path of coexistence, and in any necessary reinterpretation of their stories. The most important reinterpretation required is that of religious truth. In the face of continuing discovery of new knowledge and continuing individual and individualistic self-discovery religions may need to be more guiding and advisory institutions than ones that purport to continually tell 'the truth,' especially in lifestyle.

God is likely to have a future, some form of religion too. Whether, or what sort of, organised religion has a long-term future depends upon how it handles the present and up-coming challenges. As we have seen, religions can adapt, so there should be hope as well as concern for them all.

VIII

SCIENCE AND TECHNOLOGY

An automobile does not create freedom of movement... it is a mere machine.
Rabindranath Tagore, 1917.[*]

Science is a magnificent force, but it is not a teacher of morals.
William Jennings Bryan, 1925.[†]

The search for human happiness, fulfilment, and improvement continues through science. Even physical science is moving into the areas of creativity and emotions. We tend to have a view of what science is, but think less about what it is for. The science we think of now is one of reason, experimentation, proof, and of data, and both physical and social sciences are multi-disciplinary. Many discoveries and consequences are 'accidental' or unexpected, even when there is a specific purpose of research. The modern world has been laid at the door of the humble plough, from nutritional changes, population increase, diversification of human behaviour, land ownership, hierarchical government, and urbanisation, but obviously there were many steps to get to these consequences. No discovery can be treated as if in a world of its own. It always has a context. It always has influences and

---

[*] Rabindranath Tagore. *Nationalism*. 1917. Penguin Books, 2010, 84.
[†] William Jennings Bryan at the Scopes Monkey Trial, 1925, quote taken from Julian Baggini, *How the World Thinks*, 78.

factors in its development, use, success, and failure. We need to think about the impact of human decision-making before we 'blame' science and technology for its uses. Science may be inevitable in the sense that curiosity is a core human virtue, but its uses are choices. It is knowledge rather than wisdom, and needs interpretation. As Enlightenment principles have been used to re-model our social affairs, we have also used science to justify all sorts of 'developments' in the life we lead, with winners and losers. Some of these are justified individually, some as for the good of groups or nations.

Science is still, philosophically, a work in progress, mirroring the application of the original and fundamental Enlightenment principles. It has a specific purpose of improving our current life, our health and our happiness. This is directed purpose, and for many is narrow-minded. It also has a purpose of helping to understand humanity itself, and individual humanity, what sort of people we are, how we evolved, how we work, and what we are capable of. Some will say, science is about helping us to understand or discover our place within the natural world and the cosmos, seeing humanity as part of something greater, and understanding ourselves better because of the journey it takes us on.

Early Enlightenment science was used to openly question or deliberately discredit religion. Accommodation between the two is not, and maybe cannot be, settled. Many scientists, of different faiths, remain religious. Many hold on to the idea of a greater power working in mysterious ways, to explain the things that we cannot explain; that humanity has been given a 'free will' to live by; and that at the beginning of the beginning there must have been something. Doctors the world over take an oath to 'do no harm' and to treat all patients before them, but while scientists are assumed to work to improve life there is no such public universal confirmation. Science has also made its fair share of mistakes and U-turns. The knowledge it gives us does nothing on its own, except perhaps give us a sense of awe and wonder, which may itself have led us into a reverence for it that we should not have. It is one input into life and wisdom.

In the 13th century Roger Bacon wrote about theories requiring proof, and the progress of an enquiry. William Ockham fused Ancient Greek, Roman, and Arab writings to forge a general theory of logic, encouraging efficient and simplified reasoning. Galileo worked on laws of motion, gravity, and astronomy, at the expense of being placed under house arrest by the Church for the last ten years of his life. The Reformation questioned the power of the Roman Catholic Church, and the Renaissance turned into an Age of Reason questioning its core beliefs. In 1687 Newton published *The Mathematical Principles of Natural Philosophy*, connecting what was still often known as 'natural philosophy' to modern science, and exploding the connection between the laws of nature and the laws of the heavens and supernaturalism. The idea of science as neutral and objective was being established, capable of understanding the natural world, while, ironically, confirming the Christian religious idea that humanity was in charge of, and superior to it. This was all part of the arrogance of the 'old' or original Enlightenment. This is only now being questioned. Science now explores the complexity of biodiversity and climate change, investigates the origins of space, and of *Homo sapiens*, and delves into the atoms and neural pathways of the human body. Science has become 'professional,' mathematical, the product of teams, and egalitarian. It has also, in some measure, become popularised. The place of science in society, the reach of its work, and the fundamental nature of much of that work may mean that science itself is at a critical point.

Origins and Nature

Over an industrial period that has led us to think of 'nature' as sacred or in a nostalgic way, and to lose our personally dependent obligation to care for, and respect it, for its use, the natural world became a commodity. The rapidly changing profile of the climate is now making us reassess its fragility, complexity, opportunities, and dangers. This requires operational, moral, and philosophical changes. We are understanding more about the building blocks of life from quarks to proteins and expanding our horizons beyond the stars we can see to peer into the past and the future. These are challenging science's certainties, its capacity to use complex data, and its ability to predict. As Darwin's Theory of Evolution challenged and dismayed those of a strong religious faith, the science of climate change challenges our idea of progress. Continual discovery is also placing the evolution of our version of humanity within its original family tree; and making us reassess how it is that 'we' became predominant, with consequential discussion about what makes up our 'human character.' The non-human life of the planet is not only being understood better but given more credit for what humanity can learn from it, reversing centuries-old assumptions of human superiority and uniqueness. We are gaining knowledge of the origins of the universe, including our own planet, and how we might travel through and beyond our own solar system, perhaps even forcing religion to re-frame the work, its scale, and the purpose, of divine power within their faith.

We are beginning to reach the maturity of understanding that not everything can be predicted, we are not in control of all that we survey, and that artificial science and technology can have unexpected consequences for humanity and in nature. One of the best-known examples of this is the use of DDT insecticide from the 1950s, the development of which earnt a Nobel Prize. With the laudable intention of improving crop yields it has now been shown to build up through the food chain to become toxic to birds, animals, and marine life, and is widely found in humans. In water it has a half-life of 150 years, and in the human metabolism up to 6 years. It is now almost entirely banned globally. Concerns about genetic modification in plant, animal, and human life are largely based on this idea of unexpected and accumulative consequences. There is now recognised to be an overuse of antibiotics, especially in animals, an economic and medical choice. Views on plastic may be on the same path. Social science has its equivalence. In the UK there are proposals to trial lie-detector tests for various serious crimes, on the proviso that such a test is a guide not to be relied on solely. However, how long will that withstand the pressure of harassed staff and an overburdened criminal justice system. What effect it may have on the tester as well as the tested is unknown. It may reinforce discrimination, as current facial recognition appears to do, and in so doing achieve the opposite of its stated intention. Other misguided ideas can fill the vacuum when we do not understand – HIV/AIDS as a punishment from God or a 'targeted' medical affliction comes to mind. We do not yet fully understand all or even most of the consequences of interventions we have already made through science, physical or social. Another of the greatest misuse stories still playing out shows that sometimes we do know, but commercial or political interest prevents that knowledge being widely understood and acted on. Fifty years ago oil industry scientists were telling their executives that continued fossil fuel use was already triggering a change in the climate through increasing greenhouse gases, and would continue to do so. By 1980 most research into alternatives was stopped on non-competitive grounds and the research on climate change suppressed. Genuinely 'honest' scientists usually welcome and expect accountability through peer review and debate. This needs to be allowed to flourish whether in business, in academic institutions, in government, or in society at large. Climate scientists have also learnt lessons from their work, including the need to clearly state their uncertainties, not to over-hype based on their evidence, to widely peer-review to achieve consensus and credibility, and to explain and debate publicly in accessible language. People have, as a result, learnt that science cannot tell us everything and may not always give us clear 'answers' to the problems it raises, but understand that the way that scientists work and publish gives them credibility. The climate change debate may have been a precursor to our more mature understanding of the findings of science in relation to Covid-19 (although its political spin remained). The understanding, credibility, and popularity of science go hand in hand.

A Reassessment of the Natural World

In the mid-17th century Antoine van Leeuwenhoek developed a microscope and saw microbes (or 'animalcules'), and Robert Hooke coined the idea of 'cells' and saw living micro-organisms. Three hundred and fifty years later large translucent and bioluminescent species are still being discovered in the deepest ocean on a regular basis. We think we know 'wildlife' or 'the natural world' but we have only gone through an immature adolescence of thinking we know everything and can do anything, to understanding that there is still so much out there that we do not know, and that what is out there is far more complex than we originally thought. We are beginning to reassess nature, and what we learn from it, rather than simply how we can control or improve it.

The use of plants and animals in many cultures remains a basic and common form of medicinal help. The art of Acupuncture is worthy of considerably more discussion than possible here. It is still widely used in east Asia, primarily for pain relief, often in conjunction with other natural treatments. Ginseng root has long been used in Eastern medicine and has been shown to have various pharmaceutical properties easing inflammation and stress, and promoting immune and antioxidant activity, with research ongoing into its apparently positive effects in relation to diabetes, cancer, and neuro-degenerative diseases. The venom of poisonous Conus Snails has been shown to give pain relief by inhibiting parts of the nervous system. This 'new learning' is being researched to see if it may be adapted as a painkiller, and for use in addiction and withdrawal treatment as an alternative to opioids. This was also an example of accidental or secondary research, resulting from investigation into how Conus Snails hunt and capture their prey.

Applications relating to biodiversity and engineering are the most common indication after medicine of our renewed interest in nature. In July 2022 wild Bison were reintroduced into a part of the county of Kent in the UK. Their closest relative species had not existed in the UK for 6,000 years. Like almost all landscapes in the UK Kent is 'managed' land parcelled out between industrial and residential areas, farming is extensive and valuable, and its seas are fished or part of extensive traffic flows. The Bison are expected to encourage a mixed woodland, scrub, and glades area to flourish, boosting insect, bird, and plant life. They are a 'keystone' species, i.e., one that by its natural actions is at the centre of a naturally maintaining habitat. This is going backwards to go forwards, and is one of many such examples around the world. India's Ministry of Environment, Forest and Climate Change said, of re-introducing the (African) Cheetah to India in the same year, that 'bringing back a top predator restores historic evolutionary balance.' Bats have an echolocation system for 'sight' that is being investigated for visually impaired or completely blind humans. Bats send out a sound that bounces off objects, and its returning sound allows them to build up a picture of the objects around them. The Rose Butterfly has cells on its black wings that can collect light at any angle. Their structure has been copied in a new generation of thin film solar cells twice as efficient as previous ones. The detail of nature is important. This whole new discipline of using nature to find sustainable solutions to human problems and challenges, or just luxury improvements, is called biomimicry. The extent of plastic use in the 20th and 21st centuries may be comparable to the use of iron in the 19th century. We now know that micro-plastic is prevalent throughout the food chain, in every ocean, and on both Poles. Roughly two-thirds of all plastics ever produced remain in the environment. Their toxic constituent parts are believed to affect hormones and damage DNA, as well as being surfaces on which pathogens can accumulate. In 2016 Japanese scientists discovered a bacterium, *Ideonella sakaiensis*, that seemed to decompose, or 'eat,' a particular type of plastic. Other bacteria have since been observed 'eating' other types of plastic. The enzymes produced by the bacteria are now in widespread lab testing to see if they can be replicated on a large scale, to work at speed, widely. They may need to be genetically modified. This may have its own unexpected dangers – the evolution of these enzymes and these bacteria in ways we cannot predict. Research may lead nowhere – another lesson. However, this may be another example of how nature may be used, and may evolve, to help solve even some of the bigger problems that we have created for ourselves and the planet.

In 1979 James Lovelock coined the idea of the planet as an interconnected self-regulatory system, which he named Gaia, although this remains a theory not approved of by many evolutionary biologists. We recognise danger through change in the world's eco-systems, and perhaps now the extent of that danger to life on the planet, but not yet the complex nature of all the interactions between them. We extrapolate theories related to known timelines of change. An important lesson from climate change study has been that we know we must act even though we do not yet understand absolutely everything; and even while we know we may act in ways with unexpected consequences it has still put us on the path of improvement, or rather repair. Science is teaching us about the workings of the planet we inhabit, but it is also teaching us about the nature and place of science.

WHERE ARE WE GOING?

Homo sapiens, **Then and Now**

Even a book written 20 years ago is likely to be out of date in expressing the timeline and physical development of *Homo sapiens*, our distinct race of humanity. There was a time when we knew of Neanderthals and 'original' skeletons in the Rift Valley of east Africa and believed that *Homo sapiens* were simply a physical development, with Neanderthals being the 'brutes' that developed from primates. Now we know that there has been a whole family tree of human species development, spread around the globe, overlapping in time over many thousands of years. Some of these developments seem to have been isolated 'dead ends' in evolutionary terms. The 'hobbit man' species *Homo floresiensis* of Indonesia discovered in 2003 is one example, a specific strand notable for their shortness in height. We now understand that there was no single replacement of one early species by another but a mixing and slow development. Our study of DNA offers us, in evolutionary terms, a modern picture of how we are linked to each other. This goes to the core of understanding not just our origins and development but also how we may wish to see our identity, here and now, and our attitude in the future to each other and those that we have always considered 'other' or unfamiliar. As we understand the DNA of our ancestors one possibility is that a widespread perception of 'original' co-operation could transform our view of humanity's future and how we can shape it.[*]

We have laboured under various assumptions for many years. These include the notion that *Homo sapiens* must have physically outfought their ancestors, and that our species is a continual progressive development. As we learn and understand more about DNA, the physical development of the human body itself, and the way we believe our ancestors lived, we are asking new questions. A multiplicity of human strands of development should make us question the permanent uniqueness of our species. The overlapping of different strands should make us think about how that

---

[*] E.g.: Kristina Killgrove, "50,000-year-old DNA reveals the first-ever look at a Neanderthal family," *LIVESCIENCE*, 23 October 2022; Elizabeth Sawchuk, Jessica Thompson, and Mary Prendergast, "50,000-year-old DNA reveals a critical shift in ancient human history," *INVERSE*, 28 February 2022.

happened, and continued, for probably thousands of years. We know now that some species existed for many thousands of years longer than previously thought, often in isolation, but how isolated could they have been? If different species mixed as people migrated across the globe in waves of evolution, and there was no single or forced replacement, then are we a conflictual and competitive species or one that found a peaceful accommodation with new migrants, who may or may not have looked different? If we talk about 'stone age instincts' in terms of physical or physiological attributes, like the instinct to judge leaders on appearance of strength or the instinct to store fat and seek sugar, then should we also look to those Stone Age instincts in terms of relationships with each other. If we understand that even the physical development of humanity was not one straight line of progress, then we must reject the comforting notion that things will always and inevitably get better. Then there is the size of our brain, and our 'brainpower.' We are moving towards theories related to psychology and skills, and *Homo sapiens* being those that developed and survived because we were cleverer than the rest, especially in terms of social co-operation. We must be as careful here as at any other time not to look for a timeline that justifies what we want to believe and fortifies our species arrogance of superiority. It may be that cleverness was the decisive factor, but if so we need to understand why. In any other field we would be looking for a multiplicity of factors and circumstances. The acceptance of luck, circumstances beyond our control, and a unique timeframe are key ideas that we should embrace in considering our future development as well as our past.

The controversy of Darwin's Theory of Evolution in terms of questioning religious faith was substantial, and of physical development revolutionary, but logic of anthropological psychology may be just as earth-shattering. We are embarking on a search for the logic and evidence of a more complex multi-level selection within evolution that might explain why we are all different, with, on the face of it, different instincts, and different talents. We also continue to explore the associated idea of cultural evolution, although the 'evolution' label here is a little misleading. Cultural evolution would seem to currently have few defined parameters scientifically, including any sense of time-defined 'evolutionary change.' However, in recognising the development of behavioural change in relationships that determine how we live together we are adding yet another perspective to our past and future development.

We may never be confident that we have revealed our full 'family tree' and how it came to exist. The idea that Dinosaurs, a whole plethora of different species, were effectively made extinct as the result of a meteor hitting the earth, was once fantastical. Now we are sure it happened, have a reasonable idea how, and can even, relatively, pinpoint the time when it happened with physical evidence. We also realise that we may have no way of preventing a similar event ending mammalian life in the future.

Our Planet and its Place, Now and into the Past

Another strand of science investigating our origins concentrates on the origins of the planet itself, and its relation to the rest of the universe. Life-forms with eyes will at some point have all looked up to the sky and wondered what was there, and where it came from. Over time humanity associated stories of the sky's power and influence with their own origins, and interweaved those stories with other aspects of the natural world it did not control or understand. In different forms some idea of the heavens (and hell) formed, and these provided a faith-based understandability to the limits of humanity, both physically and in relation to the power of a creator. Our current understanding of the heavens has changed from times past, without definitively proving or disproving a divine existence. As with the study of our physical origins, we are inching closer to knowing the origins and place of our planet without knowing the endpoint of that study.

What we know includes the processes and physical evolution of the planet and what is on the surface. We understand our planet's core, moving tectonic plates, and have a theoretical understanding of how gases came together to form some coherence recognisable as a planet. The oldest material yet discovered on earth are pre-solar dust grains (from exploded stars) within the Murchison meteorite found in Australia dated at 7.5 billion years ago (byo), in comparison to the age of the Sun at 4.6 byo and the Earth at 4.5 byo. The study of meteors and other planets and moons is providing further clues about this process. We know a lot about how the Earth's climate, land masses, and oceans have changed. We therefore know how our current continents and oceans were formed and have plotted the scientific evolutionary path of life, including different extinction events. We also see that the natural world is in continual long-term evolution and short-term change, and know that the continents continue to move, in which direction, and the processes that explain how they do so. We know, for example, that Antarctica and Australia were once together but separated, and how that changed their climate and therefore their natural life, and that the latter is moving towards Asia.

The Hubble telescope and now the James Webb telescope have enlarged the scale of what we can see. We believe that the universe is expanding, and because of that, what we see on the outer edges of the universe is getting further away. It may be that we are in a race to see more and look further back to the origins of spatial phenomena before it goes beyond our 'sight.' That is a lesson itself, that science, however good we may become, may have its limits in what we can learn. Nor are we neglecting non-planetary phenomena: black holes, comets, and asteroids. Incidentally, NASA estimates that asteroid Bennu has a 1 in 2,700 chance of collision with Earth between the years 2175 and 2199 causing 'continent-wide disruption' making it the most dangerous asteroid we currently know! In 2021 a probe led NASA to claim that it could determine the internal structure of Mars. Our understanding of the planet Mercury from 'radar mapping' leads us to believe that there may be deposits of ice at its poles. We have sent probes out beyond our solar system, from which we are beginning to recognise thousands of planets and moons and what makes them inhospitable or with potential for life. However, humanity may only return to landing on the Moon in the mid-2020s, putting the notion of space exploration in perspective.

So much of this may be natural curiosity. It may also be foolhardy arrogance. How will we alter these places – planets and space itself – by our very existence there? I do not think that we are ready to begin tackling any more than the most fundamental questions. Are we clear why we are doing this? To say curiosity alone is not a sufficient answer considering the potential effects, even if we truly believe that the pursuit of science and exploration itself is likely to have unexpected beneficial consequences. We know we should not be exporting bacteria and we know that we must not be reckless. However, are we at risk of being hypocritical in diminishing exploitation and establishing the sustainability of how we live on our own planet only to ignore that principle elsewhere? Is part of our future the exploitation of space to sustain our own planet? That too would be a sign of the arrogance of humanity. Our persistent world population rise has always provided a positive answer to settlement, but the rate of increase of global population rise is now slowing, it will level off, and demographists already anticipate future decline. It may not be impossible that space will be explored or colonised by our machines, but it is still unlikely that humanity itself could resist the temptation to make that leap, whether to learn more science or more about ourselves. Our motivation may have multiple causes, but we need both clarity and consensus, and not just from scientists but from society. Such huge endeavours must have societal support and understanding, otherwise they become one person's vanity project resented by others with competing priorities. Science in that scenario is misunderstood and resented by the very society it sets out to serve.

All that is in the future. Even more fundamental is that we achieve clarity and consensus for the science we are pursuing now and how we are doing it. The International Space Station (ISS) was one terrific antidote to the 'space race' of the Cold War between the USA and USSR. It was both a technological and a political achievement, and expanded alliances. The ISS needs replacing technologically, but the key part of the alliance is now also falling apart politically. Furthermore, China has committed itself to the status, pride, and technology of establishing its own lunar and deep space achievements. UAE, India, and other nations are developing space orbiting or exploration programmes. Then there is the curse of imagining space itself as a theatre of war. The disunity of resources and purpose does not bode well for the future. There is also the potential privatisation of space. It may be that space is legitimate tourism, and that just like airlines, travel, and airspace will include leisure, research, military, commercial, and governmental spheres which can coexist. However, there are clearly dangers. We have in the past expressed a desire to own everything, to parcel it out between interested parties. These are major ethical issues that are coming into focus through the scientific and physical exploration of space. Why do we think we have a right to explore space when we cannot agree among ourselves what sort of people we are, or what type of society we are coming from or moving towards. We must understand and act on the principle that scientific discovery, like physical or digital technology, will be used in a way that reflects on ourselves.

Opportunities and Threats

The current pace of modern scientific change and discovery seems rapid if not bewildering. We are manipulating materials, and life-forms, and creating scale and complexities of data individual humans can barely comprehend. How our brain and the processes of our body work can be monitored, stimulated, and manipulated. There are almost no boundaries to communication with people across the globe and across perspective. There are clear dangers, but tremendous opportunities are being developed to improve life for individuals and the global population. We are continuing to be more scientific in our outlook, in our dependencies, and in our hopes and ambitions. Biotechnology, nanotechnology, the expansion and access of digital information, the potential of Machine Learning (ML) through big data, algorithms and AI, and the development of Virtual Reality may all be affected by, and effect, how we see ourselves as a species, what we think we can do, our relationship with this planet and the universe, and our beliefs in a divine presence.

Bioscience and Biotechnology

In March 2022 scientists announced the completion of the full human genome sequence in the journal *Science*, thirty-two years after the Human Genome Project launched. It had taken more than two decades for the last 8% of the roughly 3 billion paired letter sequence. This gives us a full view of the hereditary material of humans. This was about 160 years after the discovery of DNA, and about 70 after its structure became known. This should in time lead to the identification of variants in people's DNA that cause disease, and therefore result in better healthcare. It should also help us identify the previous evolutionary path of humanity. Gene-editing is possible, to replace or add DNA, with the CRISPR technique developed since 2000 now widely used in labs and animal models, but this is not yet in regular medicine. Nor is it used yet in embryo cells which would make the changed DNA a part of someone's heredity, i.e., permanent through following generations. This is partly because we do not yet fully understand the interaction between genes and the way in which replacing or repairing multiple genes would work.

Genetic Modification (GM) is more widely and generally understood in crops such as tomatoes and grains to make them more disease resistant, improving harvests, to change their appearance, and reduce pesticide use, but is not approved everywhere. This may maintain food production in more difficult and changing conditions and for a growing population. GM is subject to the same type of ethical debate as gene-editing in humanity: worries over 'changing nature,' and long-term unexpected consequences through the build-up of GM modified material.

Editing genes to eliminate some diseases may soon be possible, but is it wise? At present the technical difficulty of doing so in a generational, or 'germline,' way is a challenge not yet met. When it is, what power would humanity hold? We could potentially eliminate a disease for ever, but ethically there are questions that would be asked. Would such a power, or opportunity, be equally accessible or affordable, or become such a basic discrimination that it results in a physical superiority and an underclass, dividing humanity in two. Eliminating single-cell diseases is a likely first step. Such 'healthy' gene-editing could be voluntary or compulsory, for sale, or seen as a public health issue, saving healthcare resources, and affecting insurance. The Navajo Nation agreed to a limited study of genetic markers among its people, but scientists took more data (such as markers for alcoholism), published the findings without permission, and as a result the Navajo banned any further DNA-genetic tests on tribal lands. This was not done in some distant pre-ethics time but occurred in 2002. This is about trust in science, participation, and avoiding holes in research that would affect those who might benefit most. What if current debate about whether regular smokers or the obese should have full access to healthcare if they refuse to moderate their behaviour, while often misunderstanding the causes of their behaviour or condition, were applied to those that refused gene-editing to eliminate the chance of developing disease? Who gets to decide what is a liveable condition and what should not be? Is a two-generation trial acceptable or feasible? We have made important strides in understanding and accepting many forms of disability in recent years, and we may put all that at risk. We currently see eugenics as unacceptable and it is generally a taboo topic, equated by most with murder, but gene-editing may be a scientifically 'cold' way of achieving the same ends of shaping humanity in a particular form, especially when it can be done in embryonic cells for generational change. Many societies still prefer male children and that too may come to be involved in this question. We have not sorted out our own ethics on these issues yet, and avoiding them or bypassing them would be a mistake. In what ways may the empathy of humanity be changed if we have the power to 'perfect' ourselves?

The potential misuses are obvious. International scientific and government statements since 2015 have stressed the need for public engagement and scientific and governmental regulation and transparency but have also promoted the potential of germline technology to tackle complex and entrenched disease. Gene-editing in human embryos up to fourteen days after fertilisation for research only, was allowed from January 2017 in the UK, Sweden, and China. Embryonic research in the USA is a mainstream and controversial moral and political debate.

Dolly the Sheep became the first cloned mammal from a single adult cell in 1996. Despite extravagant predictions cloning has not taken off, yet. Cloning a person is seen as technically unfeasible with a realisation that a cloned person would still be shaped differently by their environment. Cloning animals may be quietly growing in that of livestock embryos for breeding, and of rare plants. In 2006 the USA said there was no discernible difference between various cloned and non-cloned farmed livestock, but in 2015 the EU banned cloning animals for food. Cloning has, however, led to stem cell research which is showing

WHERE ARE WE GOING?

enormous scientific and medical potential. Stem cells are cells capable of developing into specialised cells for different parts of the body and different functions. Stem cells can be taken from an embryo, which, like embryonic gene-editing, is controversial. However, as induced Pluripotent Stem cells (commonly known as IPS cells), they can also be taken from adults, which won a Nobel Prize in 2012, and these are now most used. We are therefore on the cusp – still measured in decades before general availability – of being able to replace damaged cells. This could be done for individual patients. In theory any cells can be replaced, those damaged through cancer treatment's chemo- or radiation therapy, in a damaged spinal cord that has resulted in paralysis, cells of a muscular degenerative disease such as Motor Neurone Disease, those of a neuro-degenerative disease such as Parkinson's, in cases of Multiple Sclerosis (MS), type 1 Diabetes, and more. Stem cells could also be used to grow organs for transplant, supplementing an acute shortage. The medical revolution resulting from stem cell research will be seismic enough to gain the attention of those with ethical questions about how 'natural' a human being, or an animal, should be, whatever its 'flaws,' and whether we have the right to 'play God,' and alter our development.

Research into the brain is another aspect making rapid and wondrous strides, with an equal rush of oncoming ethical questions. We have learnt how to pair a mapping of the brain's structure with a functional mapping. With the quality of visual image now available we can see individual neurons and brain speed. This was done in 2020 by MIT for the visual aspects of the brain but is a technique applicable to all areas. Computer power will only increase the clarity and scope or scale of what we can now do. Seeing the function of the brain allows us to begin seeing the difference between healthy and less healthy brains and allows us to see how brain function is affected by environmental and other outside stimulation. More complex decision-making can now also be seen across the cerebral cortex. The ethical questions, as often, do not so much relate to honourable and perfect but more to dishonourable or flawed use. If we can see the brain at work we will study emotions and thinking as 'objective science.' We may be able to alter or train parts of the brain related to addiction, but also see when someone is angry or confused. It may become possible to deliberately stimulate brain function

SCIENCE AND TECHNOLOGY

for specific purposes of medical intervention or social manipulation. Is it possible that, maybe along with losing outward physical privacy through constant societal surveillance, and losing digital privacy, that we might even lose the privacy of our thoughts and emotions? ML AI will only quicken the pace of this scientific development, which outpaces societal and governmental understanding and regulation.

Positive brain-related developments in recent years also include the implanting of a device, done using keyhole not invasive surgery, and using wireless technology, that allows a paralysed patient to use a computer.[*] Patients with paralysis are not yet speaking, but with further synthetic voice projection development they may. Effective micro neurotechnology may in time be on a par with physical prosthetics in the potential transformative effect on people's lives. On the science-fiction style flipside, when we dream the neural patterns continue – so could such technology translate or verbalise our dreams? Understanding of the brain has developed so much that we can now use stem cells to grow limited three-dimensional 'mini brains' with complex neural activity that allow us to study isolated aspects of, and effects on, brain function or misfunction down to individual cells. Neuroscience remains one of the fastest developing areas of bioscience and biotechnology.

We can already transplant a human heart. In 2022 polymers were used for the first time to create human heart tissue. A 3-D printed full-size heart has been created with soft polymer to train surgeons and understand how structure helps function. This moves us a little closer to creating an artificial human heart.

Similarly, developments in understanding and measuring blood flow, breathing, metabolic rates, and chemical balances, and how these are affected by outside influences from drugs, stress, or exercise, can be beneficial and mis-usable. We can already take drugs to keep us awake or induce sleep, and wear a watch that tells us our heart rate, and we understand body language more than ever before. We need to start addressing questions of artificial physical inequality. We need to be addressing the idea of people buying physical and intellectual superiority, and the notion of individual biological manipulation. People

---

[*] Margaret Osborne, "Brain implants allow paralyzed man to communicate using his thoughts," *Smithsonian Magazine*, 25 March 2022.

will be tempted to work out how they can biologically stimulate, train, and develop to give them or their children or their class or their allies an advantage. A personal tutor, inspiring cultural visit, visualisation, plastic surgery, or family network, may be supplemented by buying into stimulative psychological or physiological activities and techniques: a drug that enhances the cerebral cortex and can be commercialised and monetised; or one that regulates metabolism to enhance training or competitive performance. If physical development, then why not intellectual development? Where do we draw the line in terms of ethics in a race that has already started? Sport is struggling to grapple with the individualised biological and technological interventions possible within the body and external to the body. These questions will come to apply to education and intellectual performance. What parents do not want the best for their children, what students do not already know they face a very competitive job market where not just qualifications but also looks and style matter. What price would people pay for intellectual enhancement? We already have different life expectancy, with unequal access to good health, environment, and nutrition. This is a dystopian nightmare and in the not-too-distant future perfectly feasible. We are capable now, already, of creating biological superiority.

What price the creation of watches that detect raised stress levels and chemicals that recognise depression or happiness, that monitor for illegal drugs (which can already be done from sweat) and neurodegenerative breakdown, as a matter of preventative and public health. These, or an implanted version, are the biosensors of the future. A good thing? Again, privacy, access, and accountability are key. Maybe stress will in time be considered a contagious public health emergency requiring medical intervention. What chance a sensor that releases a drug automatically to counteract the 'problem.' Is the principle of a contraceptive implant working for a specific period any different? What price a sensor that interprets brain activity to 'reveal' sexual preference or psychopathic tendencies or 'risk-taking' or whatever other form of categorisation or discrimination is chosen to be highlighted? This is bioscience that knows us better than we know ourselves, and with big data can spot patterns and symptoms well before we feel ill or rebellious. This is the *Brave New World* of bioscience, and it is not all good. How safe would people's biodata be, how much would privacy be interpreted as secrecy with something to hide, how much right would an insurance company have to such information, or an employer. Many might question the efficiency of any government to regulate and enforce well enough, but perhaps decide that this is the realistic and beneficial option.

However, the bioscience that can make people's lives better may also be what makes others, or you, inferior or powerless: the prospect of physical, social, and emotional isolation for the rejected or unable-to-access, with lower life chances and life expectancy, all on an individual basis. It is easy to be dystopian. In practice few people try to cheat at exams, few sportspeople use performance enhancing drugs, few have cosmetic surgery to look better for a job. A current consensus of ethics includes societies against eugenics and euthanasia. However, we should not be complacent. How many people with physical, biological, or intellectual superiority does it take to change the trajectory of the community we live in? Biological changes would be difficult to overthrow in a revolution. When everyone obeys the rules and the consensus is widespread most things are fine, most of the planning for any event is for when things go wrong, when people disagree, when things don't work out, when something unexpected happens. We are nowhere near that planning when it comes to the development of bioscience and biotechnology for human enhancement.

Perhaps we will go on to screen people for suitable enhancement, falling into a prioritising model. Maybe there will be a military use or use with violent convicts, or after pre-school assessment. If privatised, commercial, bought use effectively promotes superiority what would be the psychology of such a person? This is a whole new dimension to debates about equality/inequality. Is this all bad and is it possible to regulate this development, and is its 'success' dependent on values like equal opportunity, or 'just' logistics like cost, if we can define success. What individual decision-makers do might depend on their view of humanity as a conflictual or co-operative species. What we decide, or don't decide, in the realm of bioscience, can shape humanity. The biotechnology route to super-powers may at least be more evolutionary than the strictly computer-built version, but perhaps that is just a different complacency.

New Material: Nanotechnology

'Nanotechnology,' a term first used in 1974 by Norio Taniguchi, was popularised by K. Eric Drexler in his 1986 book *Engines of Creation: The Coming era of Nanotechnology*. The 2000s saw the development of government funding and commercial interest. Nanotechnology is the use of matter on an atomic, molecular, or supramolecular scale. One nanometre is one billionth of a metre. Material on this scale can change its properties, such as altering its conductivity, strength, colour, and temperature. Chemical processes can happen faster and more efficiently because of the increased surface area. This gives nanotechnology the potential to make, for example, faster and more efficient computers, power sources, and life-saving treatments. *Nanoscience and nanotechnologies: opportunities and uncertainties* published in 2004 by the Royal Society and Royal Academy of Engineers in the UK is seen as a landmark report into the possibilities and dangers of nanotechnology. One of its conclusions then was that due to needs of scale, manufacturing development, demand requirements, safety research, and the multi-disciplinary skills needed, the creation of nanomaterials with specific properties for applications (rather than the easier use of current materials) 'will take decades to mature.'

Graphene, perhaps the most well-known nanostructure, is a material made of two layers of carbon atoms in a honeycomb pattern, ten times harder and six times lighter than steel. China is currently making about 70% of the world's graphene, but it is still hard to mass-produce and potentially toxic. There are currently at least 800 nanotechnology products on the market, but much more research needs to be done. Nanotechnology in general use includes nano sensors in food packaging that can detect food contaminants. Medical research includes the creation of nanocages in 2014 to contain a drug, with a view to developing drug delivery systems into the body at a molecular level. Textiles can be made stain or bacteria resistant. Screens can now be made with nano structured polymers for better light and picture quality. In theory nanotechnology can restructure items at a molecular level and is therefore both revolutionary and fundamental to anything that we call material.

The 2004 report also stated in its conclusion: 'There is speculation that a possible future convergence of nanotechnologies with biotechnology, information and cognitive sciences could be used for radical human enhancement' but that this was 'currently... far future or science-fiction... but [may raise] fundamental and possibly unique social and ethical issues.' It noted the essential importance of public knowledge and attitudes, referencing the controversy of GM crops, and the need to adapt regulation. We now know that some nanomaterials can affect protein combinations in the body and may be toxic. Carbon nanotubes have been shown to cause cancer in some animal testing, and some resemble the shape and size of asbestos fibres. Research continues on long-term accumulative effects, and interaction with other natural materials. These are serious concerns but let us also remember that 'nanomaterials' means a very wide range of different material, which will have different properties. Aside from these practical matters nanotechnology is susceptible to the same general concerns as biotechnology: access, equality, self-replication, and weaponisation. The ability to turn anything into a different substance remains theoretically possible but closer in practice to medieval alchemy. Nanotechnology may be a major part of the future, but like all science and technology its future cannot be so confidently predicted in either its developmental timeline or uses.

Internet and Digital Access

Most people who have easy access to digital technology and regularly use the internet take them for granted. The other half of the world do not. About 600 million people in Africa do not even have regular electricity. The internet has been likened in consequences and importance to the development of printing, and yet also been described as of little economic benefit. It has been thought of as a connector between generations, the lifeblood of the young, and liberator of information; but the 'rabbit hole' of conspiracies and isolation that threaten democracy, social cohesion, and sanity, is a technological one. The internet is the place to find out about the contents of a museum a thousand miles away, the place to order a local pizza, and the place to attain life-enhancing qualifications. It is also the place of pornography, finding out how to commit suicide or murder, and deliberate lies to undermine individuals or whole nations; inside or outside of its shadow, the 'dark web.' People rail against it, and its destruction of privacy, but it can be part of the solution. One example of this might be *Remojo* which for a small fee blocks access to sexual content on multiple devices and offers advice. It is not anti-pornography, therefore not 'anti-free speech,' but it is anti-addiction; it is technology-based, and commercial in origin. There is also the internet of the economy, now lauded as indispensable for economic communication and a key to global trade, allowing a one-person business in rural Cornwall or sub-Saharan Africa to sell to a customer in New York City or outback Australia. Then there is the 'internet of everything' whereby household goods are linked up, so that the empty fridge can lead to an order for goods to fill it again, or so that you can switch on the heating before you get home. All this is a revolution of communication, with consequences for security, privacy, relationships, the spread of ideas, the psychology of people, and social globalisation.

It remains to be seen in the long term how beneficial all of this will be, and how the dangers we know about now will play out. This is all still up for grabs amid debate about education of the next generation, continuing expansion beyond original heartlands of use, individual government and international regulation, competition between key corporations, and whether companies are publishers with responsibility or platforms for free speech. The internet is no longer a new toy, but it is still in the hands of people i.e., us, getting used to what it can do, should do, and how we want it to work. 'Us' being people of varied motivations and skills. The internet in general looks set to remain a wide marketplace to pick and choose from for some time yet.

Tim Berners-Lee, widely acknowledged as a key founder of the World Wide Web, has spoken in recent times of two more fundamental problems of digitisation. The first remains a problem of access. Even in the USA many people lack digital access, namely the poorest and in minorities, and this applies around the world. This is a division, an inequality, in relation to something that others are beginning to see as a human right or an essential service. Government and services are increasingly online. This is happening in 'developed' nations more frequently, and it is leaving behind and disengaging a minority of unknown number. Some of this is about being able to pay for services. Some of the issue is technically about digital access, to be solved by innovations of satellites and servers. These are important but solvable problems.

Berners-Lee's second problem was more fundamental. He wants an open internet, accessible to all for all its benefits: social, cultural, economic, and political. His fear is that other internets will develop, or be on offer. He worries about the future of truth, equality, and diversity on the internet as it is operated around the globe. Different futures for the internet are now visible. There is the free-flowing internet with little regulation and open to all for all their purposes. Secondly, there is the internet controlled by few geographically and culturally similar corporations, a corporate version for money-making, based on money-making models, controlled by isolated executives with little transparency, often with its working not generally understood. There is an EU-style regulated internet, with the Wild West or the childlike version gradually brought under governmental and societal accountability, with more transparency and accountability, with personal data being more genuinely private. In this scenario it matures, becomes more responsible, more globally aware, and more of an enabler of global dialogue than a divider, people trusting it as a force for good in their communities and in society in general. Discussion of the acceptability of its content would be permanent, changing with the times as society's norms change. Now we have the technology to stop information at the border and the evidence that some regimes want to do that. Their power lies not in openness, opportunity, and independent regulation, but in control. This fourth type of internet – that is already emerging – is a walled web. In a walled web regimes control the flow of data, control access, secretly monitor, promote propaganda, and prevent organic relationships and protest from emerging. This is all now technically possible, and when the subtleties are not or do not work then it can just be switched off. This is becoming increasingly common and is possible in every country in the world. The reasons will be the same reasons as always: national security, social order, maintenance of traditional or national values, and the prevention of foreign influence. These reasons are of course legitimate – if they are developed through consensus, informed consent, a legal, regulatory, and governmental framework that is transparent, accountable, and accepted, with individuals' rights respected and without discrimination to individuals or groups. Innovatory, monetised, and regulated internets can be reconciled with a general freedom, but this combination is not possible with a vision of an isolated and state-controlled enterprise. Division would be a sad demise to the internet proposed and given birth to by its founders, and this may be a part of the anti-democratic populist backlash to negative economic and cultural aspects of globalisation. It is part of the debate about whether global dialogue is inevitable and an unstoppable social force, and whether globalisation will only happen as the result of the deliberate and positive decision-making of nations.

Algorithms, Machine Learning, and Artificial Intelligence

AI, a wide-ranging term, is essentially the use of written algorithms to pick out pattens from data and do something with them. There is 'weak' AI and 'strong' AI. Natural Language Processing (NLP) is an algorithm understanding a task from the natural or real language of a person, and is the way that Siri or Alexa would understand you asking 'What day is it today?'. Then there is supervised ML, i.e., inputting supervised data for specific outputs, such as finding disease risk factors or predicting prices. ML may also be unsupervised, where algorithms have a wider remit to make conclusions or predictive models, i.e., if X is done then Y is likely. A third aspect of ML is 'reinforcement learning': the algorithm learning from itself through a multi-layered level of data. This needs more computer power and is also thought of as 'deep learning.' ML in this instance may use billions of data inputs to recognise a more complex structure in a specific location. The algorithm learns from itself through trial and error and reward to make its own decisions. These forms of AI should not be seen in isolation, and are increasingly used together, to supplement or enhance and confirm each other.

SCIENCE AND TECHNOLOGY

Each of these forms of AI are in use today, often behind the scenes of common actions. They produce the personalised recommendations for social media and entertainment streaming services. Search engines use ML. Route-finding, airline reservations, spam filters, automatic logistics, and credit card fraud detection all use ML. Industrial robotics and medical decision-support use it. So too image, facial, and speech recognition; and automatic language translation including chatbot and speech-to-text services. This is not an exhaustive list. Nor does it mean that all these uses are perfectly delivered or accurate, but they will become better. The machines *DeepMind* and *AlphaGo* learnt from historical games and then trial and error with themselves for 'reinforcement learning' to become better than any human player at Chess and Go. Machine translation for communication is now being developed into the ability to summarise, and then analyse text, and moving onto analysing sentiment. In 2021 MIT scientists announced that a computer model had taught itself to smell in just a few minutes with a similar strategy to that of the brain using a built neural network. AI ML may be most 'obvious' and most beneficial in medicine. In 2021 the AI program *AlphaFold* completed its prediction for the structure of virtually all known 20,000 human proteins, the building blocks of life. Of predictions tested so far 95% have proven correct, and all data was placed online for the free use of other researchers. Free data, peer review, potential benefits for disease or fraud prevention and much more are all very good and far-reaching.

However, there are all sorts of dangers in adopting ML. These relate to objectives, operation, and power. The key operational point is that if the inputted data at the beginning is 'off' then the foundations of its work can be wrong and the end results questionable or worse. Put simply, if all data input related to facial recognition (FR) is of white people then the algorithm will not recognise black people. Law enforcement across the world is using FR, with various degrees of accountability and transparency, and an uncertain effect on criminal justice. In 2020 IBM withdrew from the FR market citing concerns about its responsible use, specifically mentioning racial equity, mass surveillance, and training needs for those employing it. Discrimination can be not only continued but embedded. People's and societies' biases are simply expressed more efficiently. The real problem here is the lack of acknowledgement of flawed input, but the impatience to use it anyway. This is a problem that can be addressed, but also one that risks bringing ML into disrepute first. If it is not addressed then its inaccuracies, complex decisions, and recommendations, to institutions and governments, will simply reinforce prejudices of the original data – denying educational opportunity or appointment or promotion, criminalising others, denying insurance or mortgage based on false risk etc. The reverse would also apply: promoting the less deserved, who may make poor decisions, or that do not understand the systems they are employing, but feel a sense of unwarranted superiority anyway. Algorithms as we are already using them can give power to some and deny power from others, across all aspects of society. A community deprived of insurance or targeted for more law enforcement surveillance or denied job opportunities becomes a resentful community; and one given advantage comes to feel superior. If designers, operators, and decision-makers maintain a belief in the infallibility of 'tech,' and of the algorithms themselves, with inadequate transparency for accountability, then ML will be discredited, and reinforce the status quo, but at the same time harder to oppose or hold to account. All of this is made worse if we are not aware of when ML is being used and how it works. This is why AI engineers and others need ethics training and a sense of the world they and others live in, why education needs to include an understanding of AI and ML, why the sources of research need to be global and globally peer-reviewed, and why those in charge are always the ones that need most accountability.

The use of personal data is also an issue – who is in control of it, who is responsible for it, and who 'owns' it. You may be OK with anonymised health-related information that might include records of sexual history or your lifestyle being used for research, but the profile included (age, sex etc) may make you identifiable. If you buy one item, perhaps something personal and private, do you want that to inform less private recommendations you get to buy other things? If a photo of you is posted by someone else on social media and is tagged, in other words you are named, are you happy for both your name and photo to be harvested in a FR programme sold to institutions or governments?

Harvesting copyrighted material – that may provide someone's livelihood – for AI to learn from and re-use, without permission or acknowledgement, is a current debate. Would you be OK with news recommendations based on what you already think, depriving you without you even knowing, of more objective, or just other, points of view? All these things are already possible. Conspiracy theories about all this abound, and it is also a citizen's duty to understand more. ML makes the use and dissemination of this information more valuable, and much harder to change if it's wrong, if you ever find out. There are many, many benefits to ML, but we must be aware of the dangers of its uses too in all areas of life.

Users' data being pored over by social media and shopping platforms to identify and profile, to make recommendations, and to promote specific content, is now commonplace. The result is news feeds that narrow access to different opinions and do not have objective or verified truth at their core. User data, as we now know, may also be sold on to others, perhaps for a benign advertising campaign, perhaps to a political party now able to target thousands of more individualised ads that may even be contradictory when viewed together, although people only see the ones sent to them, based on their profile. Now we are beginning to understand how this can be dangerous to democracy and a sense of shared communal truth upon which societal norms are based. Equally true is the almost complete openness of social media platforms that frequently include all sorts of controversial material, from suicide or self-harm instructions to easily accessible sexually explicit content. Whether these are platforms or 'publishers,' which denotes more responsibility to regulate their content, is a key point still not yet settled. Whether data about a person in one country can be held offshore and not therefore subject to that person's national regulations is another point still in question. How much a company or its CEO can be held to account by different countries' regulators and legislators is only just beginning to be explored. This mirrors questions about the tax responsibilities of multinational manufacturing. The role of social media and multinational digital commercial services continues to grow, and the trails they leave and how they are dealt with in terms of transparency, accountability, regulation, tax, and national values and

WHERE ARE WE GOING?

priorities, are experiences we must learn from.

The philosophical dangers come into even sharper focus when we specifically consider deep learning, and its next steps. ML does not have to be perfect to be accepted; it must only be as good as human decision-making. At that point its accuracy is bolstered by its speed and scale and possible value-for-money, to make it the superior or just commercially viable decision-making process, bolstered again by possible misguided thoughts ('it's the new and improved version' etc) of its 'objectiveness' or 'independence.' As deep learning builds on multi-layered inputs, and works across subject boundaries including, for example, behavioural and biological and financial models, it will reach a point of Human Level Machine Intelligence (HLMI). The forecasting timeline of experts in this field is not great – driverless cars are still trying to negotiate older road networks – but Nick Bostrom in his book *Superintelligence* surveyed 'experts' whose median prediction was a 50% chance of HLMI by 2050 and 90% chance by 2070–90. At which point ML will be able to do things like recognise changes in any location in the world from satellite imagery, and be able to auto-translate any language in real time with a spoken voice. That may be great for communication, mapping purposes, or showing the damage of war or natural disaster. Will it be fine when it recommends financial investments, based on people's previous actions, their lifestyles, and identified social trends; or advising government on the necessity of taxes or borrowing or paying off the national debt? How much will 'lower level' modelling provide faith in its accuracy – for experts or the public? After HLMI, working more efficiently than a human brain, will come 'superintelligence,' a next step that could take weeks or years. A superintelligence would be able to strategise, learning from itself at exponential speed. While the computer power needed would be enormous only one superintelligence would make a difference. Theoretically, the speed and scale of HLMI is just coding, elaborate inputs, physics, and computer infrastructure.

HLMI and superintelligence could therefore, according to these experts, become a reality in people's current lifetime. Such machines could test flaws in security systems, create new robotics, and develop sustainable materials saving us from climate change. At what point would such self-learning machines be taking the decisions determining our lives away from humanity? Decision-making itself is at the core of what it is to be human, with its hesitancy, inconsistency, caution, risk, relationships to others, psychology, physiological effects, and potential for considered reflection, satisfaction, guilt, and shame. This is why we elect leaders and have governments. Bostrom gives the example of asking superintelligence to 'make humans smile' and gives two levels of response: level one is things it would 'do' like tell jokes; level 2 is changing the world in which people live. The latter might be giving suggestions to eradicate poverty, but it might also be introducing a drug into the monitored water system to change the chemical balance of the brain to make people 'happier.' Objectives and access are important. A superintelligence might also create ways of increasing its own data power.

This leads us to the necessity of creating ML that places the care and safety of humanity at its core. This might mean the creation of AI that understands the feelings and emotions of others, and models or replicates them. At which point we may have created new life, one beyond the control of humanity, even intellectually superior, at least less moody and inconsistent. In nightmare futures this is AI capable of limiting the actions of humanity 'for its own good.' Are we prepared for these fundamental changes and this potential competition, or partnership? To be prepared now is unrealistic and unnecessary, but we should not assume that we are in complete control of the timeline of a machine that learns from itself. The simplest solution may be to pull the plug on it. However, it may be that by then we are dependent on its use for the lifestyle that we have become accustomed to. We need to deliberately build in the requisite values of humanity – human rights – if we have set a task where efficient options ignore them for some, or in some circumstances, or temporarily; and can this translate into plans to deal with the unexpected? These issues may seem a century away, but those born now may have to face them. What groundwork is being done, how are we educating people, how are we globally co-operating in regulation and transparency, in objectives and common values; and in the commercial and governmental international competition, and military ambition, that is already driving the development of deep learning, and will do so for HLMI, and superintelligence?

WHERE ARE WE GOING?

Data related to individuals should only be collected for their own or their relevant community's direct benefit, not third parties. Such data must be challengeable and correctable, by ethical and enforceable legislative right. Not too much data should be kept in one place. This is not only about security or power, but about trust and explainability. The technology industries need to pay far more attention to these. There needs to be some level of accepted and enforceable standard for algorithms, their creation, their creators, their transparency, and their uses. Routine mass surveillance should be banned. AI 'engineers' could do with an equivalent of a doctor's Hippocratic oath, starting with 'do no harm' and including the promotion of equalities of respect, treatment, and opportunity in their work. Algorithms can have such an impact on people's lives that accountability must include some form of provenance trail. Most of all we need a much clearer philosophical foundation for using algorithms that change people's lives – are they the best way to do so, who is in control, and what does both expected success and damage look like? Agreeing on protocols and their practical enforcement, domestically or between nations that have different outlooks of government, economic purpose and management, and different communal norms of social interaction and behaviours, is a mammoth task.

On 29 March 2023 more than 1,000 leading digital scientists, researchers, owners, and academics signed a published letter calling for a pause in the development of 'giant AI.'* It came barely two weeks after the company OpenAI released GPT-4, a Large Language Model (LLM) 'chatbox' aspect of AI, that, after having 'learnt' from billions of word sources can write text based on predicting the next word. It came one week after a group of Microsoft researchers (which has a stake in OpenAI) claimed that GPT-4 showed 'sparks of artificial general intelligence.' (It also has competitors now being released.) Its new abilities are being quickly discovered, including how it can write for different audiences. Its quality will improve, but already OpenAI claims that it is at the level of the top few per cent of humans in passing

---

* Alex Hern, "Elon Musk joins calls for pause in creation of giant AI 'digital minds'," *The Guardian*, 29 March 2023. Stuart Russell, "AI has much to offer humanity. It could also wreak terrible harm. It must be controlled," *The Guardian*, 2 April 2023.

postgraduate exams. Arguably, anyone whose career is about using language may soon be in a career-, and credibility-threatened, position, including journalists and academics.* However, LLMs 'are notorious' in generating false answers, with fictitious sources. This is a recipe for convincing false or misleading information, deliberately or accidentally. OpenAI's own tests showed that GPT-4 'could deliberately lie to a human ("No, I am not a robot, I have a vision impairment that makes it hard for me to see the images") to get help solving a captcha test designed to block non-humans.' Sometimes it simply does not make sense – perhaps a temporary flaw as it learns more. The letter stated that: 'Recent months have seen AI labs locked in an out-of-control race to develop and deploy ever more powerful digital minds that no-one – not even their creators – can understand, predict, or reliably control.' The letter judged it unlikely that tech companies themselves would pause their development, and called upon governments to take urgent action, internationally. On 2 May 2023 Geoffrey Hinton, 'godfather' of AI at Google, announced his resignation/retirement. He said that GPT-4, and competitors, eclipsed the amount of general knowledge a human could hold, and although their level of reasoning was limited, he expected it would quickly improve. He said that he 'now regretted his work' and that, 'Right now, [GPT-4 and others are] not more intelligent than us, as far as I can tell. But I think they soon may be.'† History is littered with commercialism outpacing public debate and governmental regulation. When those at the heart of developments warn seriously of its dangers, then it is indeed worrying. Caution needs to permeate all aspects of AI, including facial and voice recognition, and cultural creativity, for example, not just language prediction and formulation. Less than a year later Google is advertising a mobile phone that can completely manipulate a photographic image instantly.

Virtual Reality

Virtual Reality (VR) is another technology, or use of technology,

---

* Emily Bell, "A fake news frenzy: Why Chat GPT could be disastrous for truth in journalism," *The Guardian*, 3 March 2023.
† Zoe Kleinman and Chris Vallance, "AI 'godfather' Geoffrey Hinton warns of dangers as he quits Google," *BBC News*, 2 May 2023.

for the future. It is more specific, in that it is based solely on bringing a different reality to people, but its uses may be multiple. Its first use is in terms of entertainment. It can make game-playing more realistic in constructed 'reality.' While seemingly less serious this poses an example of potential unexpected, and wider, consequences. The neuroscientist Susan Greenfield wrote some time ago of the dangers of addiction to realistic game-playing changing the way the brain works. To some this is fanciful but as the reality does indeed get more realistic, as it is more accessible, as the whole e-sports phenomenon continues to grow, this will come into focus for debate much more. Such game-playing is an 'opium of the masses' scenario, making people less sociable in real life and affecting their ability to form and develop real relationships. We are already seeing both game-playing addiction and other people making new connections to others, including less able-bodied people taking part in an activity where their disability is not a factor and may not even be known. There is also an argument that war-based games continue to push physical conflict away from humanity, as people's urges are satisfied by the reality of the game – although it is just as likely that the game is a learning or training tool, a simulation, giving some people the probably misplaced confidence that they have the fighting skills of a soldier. One albeit adjacent comparison is the preponderance of online pornography changing the way that people view what is acceptable or expected in real sexual behaviour and relationships.

VR could in theory kill tourism, an important aspect of many economies. If immersion in VR gives you the full 360-degree view, the closeness, the scale, proportion, and perspective of really being in the Louvre or at Angkor Wat then why pay the expense of travelling there, dealing with visas and airports in the process, and the crowds. The virtual journey too, and even auto-language conversation, may really feel like a holiday. Touch and smell are the two senses that need to be developed by VR to give this all-round persuasion. We are more aware now of real-world and environmental tourist damage inflicted on the destinations themselves, disruption of ordinary life in overcrowding or price rises, or damage to natural or man-made physical infrastructure – Venice would be a clear example, with its big cruise ships – aeroplane pollution, and the direct human footprint requiring more water resources etc. VR can address these, but maybe at the cost of employment – how are these locations to be maintained if people do not visit? Some hybrid is likely, an economic balance between VR program development costs and consumer prices, with lottery style or elite access. VR can also change some of the heritage and conservation debates currently taking place: Should the Elgin/Parthenon Marbles be in the British Museum or in Greece etc? If a VR user can truly get a close-up sense of them from sitting at home, then the location of the original physical objects matters less. VR presentation of rare artefacts would make them accessible to many more people to admire or to study. VR could also be used in the 'tourism' of rare wildlife, and even extinct life for which we have fossils and DNA – the Serengeti tour, or Jurassic World, anyone? Yet this may also, however, threaten to make us complacent about these objects, locations, and issues of conservation. Within entertainment, leisure, and tourism there are potentially serious repercussions of VR as well as serious potential benefits. And it can do much more.

VR is already being used in a variety of training purposes. It may explore more than any real training may ethically allow. More realism in the setting, such as showing the effects of natural disaster or terrorist incident, or just awkward customer, make for better training, better real actions under pressure, and better appointments and promotions in jobs. In a health context VR is already being used to help people overcome their phobias such as a fear of heights, by providing gradually changing realistic situations that help to train the brain to cope with the fear. This is VR as accessible, relatively cheap, clinical benefit, combining neuroscientific knowledge with technology. On 1 August 2022 it was reported that VR was used to successfully separate conjoined twins in Brazil who underwent several operations to separate them in Rio de Janeiro with direction from surgeons at Great Ormond Street Hospital in London, operating in the same 'virtual reality room' together.[*] The benefits here are clear, and the potential damage thankfully less obvious.

---

[*] Shiona McCallum, "Conjoined twins separated with the help of virtual reality," *BBC News*, 1 August 2022.

WHERE ARE WE GOING?

The Scope and Importance of Science and Technology

Science fiction has long been an expression for our hopes and nightmares, from time travel in *Doctor Who* to the details of replicating food in *Star Trek*, and mechanical enemies like the 'replicators' of *Stargate*. It has often been based on real science, but often not, creating new myths and new narratives. The popular view of alien life in its physical forms and its peacefulness or violence comes from fiction. *Inside Out* gave us the picture of emotions within us, *Brave New World* gives us docile control of humanity, *I, Robot* gives us our creations turned against us, *1984* our worst instincts, *The Expanse* our perpetual division, *The Circle* gives us tech companies control, etc. They give us a sense of the scope and importance of our current thinking, which is more often based on dangers and division than opportunity or utopia.

We may never be able to predict with accuracy, or ever know if we have discovered everything: at one time atoms were the smallest imaginable matter. It may be that some things are too complex, such as the integrated nature of biodiversity on earth: at one time we could not even see bacteria. Some things may not ever be provable in scientific terms: we may yet understand the full workings of the human brain but not the idea of individual consciousness. Some things may become harder to know, as the universe expands and its edges become more distant. We will never know the limits of superintelligence. There will always be a place for logic and philosophy too. In thinking about what we may never know we may also think about what we want to know.

To make specific predictions about the advancement of science and technology beyond a short timeframe is therefore a fool's errand, but to reach general conclusions and make general guiding comment less so. Indeed, it is a responsibility to do so. The pace of change, what discovery and invention may mean for lifestyle, relationships between people, and for the human character itself, are all legitimate areas of discussion. As, therefore, is our understanding of science itself, and the place and importance of it in society, and in relation to the natural world.

SCIENCE AND TECHNOLOGY

The People Factor

Forbes Business Insights predict that the 'ML' market will rise in value from $21bn in 2022 to $209bn by 2029. The World Economic Forum *Future of Jobs Report 2020* predicted that AI including ML will generate 97 million jobs by 2025. In the USA an AI Engineer may well have a starting annual salary now of $100,000. These jobs are often not unionised, and while pay and conditions may be good, they are often not protected. The bigger problem is the unknown number who lose their job – driverless vehicles at the expense of drivers, auto-translate algorithms at the expense of call centre operators etc. Training for a new job based on a known foundation may be manageable, training for something new, even every ten years, less so, not to mention the loss of accumulated skills. People's work activities are often seen as an important part of their identity, and this would also have to change, although perhaps losing that labelling of people would be no bad thing. Such renewal will certainly have a psychological edge. It involves strain as well as opportunity. It requires self-confidence to be seen and judged in a different light, to find personal satisfaction and identity in something different, and make new relationships. That may be refreshing once or twice, but the third and fourth time may well be damaging. None of this is impossible but transition to automation currently has little analysis on a personal level and will be difficult for many people.

It was long thought that automation would make life easier and we could bask in a three-day week. However, the reality from our current perspective is different. One problem is that people will still need income. In a monetised economy everything will still cost money. If repetitive jobs are done by machine, if high-skill jobs and decisions are taken by AI, then what is left – will everyone be a technician, or a soldier, or in the creative industries, or service industries satisfying our every need during someone else's time off? Automation and AI must not become rampantly capitalist in a 'completely free market' sense, everything bought and sold to those who can afford it, including education and training, and second-class citizenry for the rest. There is a scenario here of governments having to be much more interventionist and pro-active, and of more services being provided through necessity. Lifelong education and training may need to be a right, a basic income guaranteed, and retirement age ideas reconsidered. Currently pensions are getting progressively later, more work is more fragile, and many still depend on the hidden or 'family' economy. What numbers make this acceptable or manageable, in economic, social, or political terms? A less interventionist approach trusts markets and competition and self-regulation more than we should be prepared to do so, and assumes that people, or 'enough' people, will have the skills to thrive in an ever-changing set of economic circumstances and skills.

A second problem, or future stage, is that humans might just become productively useless. In that case where does a nation get its tax base from for investment in services and defence? Corporate tax may be less dependable as big companies go genuinely international and are harder to regulate, especially in an internationally competitive model and where their economic power is bigger than some of the nations on the other side of the negotiating table. With a more limited income base what chance is there of a catch-up, or keep-up, with other communities – and on a community trajectory so may go whole nations too, ones without essential raw materials, without the science and technological education and research, and unable to offer tax incentives for entrepreneurial development. This is a nightmarish scenario resulting in disorder, governmental mistrust, mass migration, and plummeting community self-belief, poorer mental health, and an identity crisis. Historical comparisons, such as the fate of the Aboriginal peoples of Australia or Native/First Nation peoples of America do not augur well for how we cope with transformational and sudden change in the core aspects of our life. That may not be a perfect analogy but if we think of them as 'not modern,' 'resisting the march of change,' or even 'relatively unintelligent,' then apart from showing our prejudice it would also show our complacency.

'Humanity' has been said to be the drama of decision-making. If decision-making is gradually taken away, then how would what it means to be human change? Would they really be taken away, however, is the first question. Biosensors that spot symptoms of illness with automatic health intervention may take some decisions away from us. Whether to go and visit a coffee shop is not the preserve of AI – although it may advise based on sociability and calorific intake! Autoordering the weekly grocery list and energy management may be one-and-only decisions we take and then leave to the algorithms regulating our house. Whether to have cereals or porridge and wear bright pink or black will still be up to us, and the recommendation of adding vitamins or wearing a 'more professional' pastel shade are ones we may choose to ignore, even if they have consequences for our health and likeability ratings. What job we choose may be guided heavily by AI-based personality and skills tests but if we are meeting people we will always have the option of how we relate to them – until we get fired or dumped. Our pay may be determined by algorithm that considers the pay of others and other economic conditions, but we may still have the right to protest, and good management may still include the necessity of personalised communication, maybe even negotiation – or is that really an auto-language vocalisation and hologram? There are many things we may still do in a highly monitored, robotic, and AI-led world. However, if we have 'faith' in AI, if we think we have tested it, consulted about it, regulated it, then the gradualism of handing over decisions to ML AI will become more and more tempting for those big, difficult, and communal decisions. Gradualism will become a problem. Future generations born into such a world will have different parameters for decision-making, perhaps accepting the maxim that it is up to AI to make the complex decisions 'fairly.' Whatever sort of job we may hold, and being a parent, a partner, and a citizen, will all involve decisions too, but there is a danger that over time we will outsource the risk-taking of our lives: do we meet the love of our life by going to a bar or by an algorithmic assessment of uploaded profiles? To what extent changed decision-making may affect the maturity and social skills of individuals is another unanswerable question until it happens. Our faith in AI and our dependence on it may erode our human resilience when things go wrong. Who or what would we blame, and why, is a significant psychological state to consider, a lack of which leads to disengagement and powerlessness. What is the psychological impact on individuals and on a civilisation? Remember that AI does not need to be perfect to be used, it merely needs to be as good as, and cheaper or easier than, human decision-making or actions.

Human Rights

In an AI world ML will go beyond ordering airline tickets and recommending a date. It will also recommend decisions – perhaps through prominent think tanks or for a technocratic government – on political, economic, and social action, as it is programmed 'for the benefit of as many people as possible' or 'for the nation's wellbeing' or 'to promote economic growth through sustainability.' Whether AI will increase or decrease inequality may be a question of the inputs and aims it is set. We currently have little global consensus beyond broad brushstrokes of the value-laden parameters we may set it. How much will individuals be prepared, in faith, psychological and practical senses, to ignore these recommendations by the 'new and improved' DeepMind-like models on offer, and think for themselves?

Why become a musician or artist when robotic AI can create an original masterpiece? What faith will religion hold when AI performs complex surgery, writes its own philosophy, goes deeper and deeper into space, or says that the idea of a God is unprovable? AI may free us for another golden age of human philosophy and creativity, but it may take that away from us too. These are dystopian visions that need not come true, but they do illustrate the dangers in the long term and of gradualism. They illustrate the dangers of accepting AI, or science in general, as a new creed in which to have ultimate faith. They demonstrate the absolute need to be clear-sighted about the aims, limits, and inputs that we give machines that can learn from themselves. Will we programme a driverless car to avoid a 75% chance of hitting one child crossing the road or the 50% chance of killing two people in an oncoming car it may hit if it swerves, or an 85% chance of serious injury to its own film-watching occupant, owner, and bill-payer if it stops so suddenly or swerves the other way and mounts the pavement? How are we training and monitoring those in charge of writing the algorithms? Perhaps 'the car' will decide that some people are more economically relevant than others, perhaps it will decide that surgery can save the lives of whomever it hits.

The price of the practical maintenance and use of our free will may well be tested in complex and everyday scenarios. At which point, how might human psychology and character change? There will be those that say that most of humanity is already dependent for their life chances on others, which is true, but people still have the ability, to some extent or other, to protest, to hold others accountable, and to at least influence change. How do they hold a secretive computer server accountable, in a distant country or 'the cloud,' controlled by a person they never see or hear from, who lives a completely different lifestyle, and has widespread political influence? These are dangers. They are not inevitable. There is a very long way to go before we reach the future of humans giving up their free will, but we must also consider it a possibility. We should begin to consider what happens when AI makes better decisions than we do. And we so frequently misjudge the timeframe as well as the consequences of change.

Experience tells us that prevention through clarity and planning is always less costly than dealing with it afterwards. That does not mean that we must have a dystopian view of the potential dangers and challenges of the future. It should help us have more confidence in being able to face the future positively. Some of the planning is obvious, such as internationally enforceable frameworks for ethics and testing, and education in how to think about and judge AI. We may need to clarify or add a different dimension to what we mean by 'human rights.' Science writer Stuart Russell proposes two new human rights: banning machines that can decide to kill or harm humans, and the right to know if we are engaging with a real person or a machine. *I, Robot* used laws devised by writer Isaac Asimov for the robots themselves, which included the do not kill/harm law, and that a robot must obey human orders, and must protect its own existence, with the first law taking precedence, the contradictions of which in the film were their Achilles heel with the robots deciding to help humanity by taking full control. Autocratic regimes will deny these human rights and stretch the use of AI for their own ends. Even technocratic ones may decide on balance that AI freedoms should be allowable in certain circumstances or for certain reasons – after all, if machines fight wars, will that make humans less subject to the trauma of war and of having to kill others, and would defence be more cost-effective; or would robots make health and social care more efficient and affordable? Even real democracies embracing new human rights and AI limits would face the context of a competitive 'race' to the lowest common denominator with less ethical or more 'efficient' regimes.

We also need to do a better job ourselves of caring about individual people, and their rights. To be called a Luddite is generally meant as an insult, implying someone that does not embrace new ways of doing things because they don't understand or stubbornly stick to 'old-fashioned' ways that are by implication inefficient or in some other way 'not as good.' Gradualism may overcome us in the end, but Luddites should make us think about 'what is happening,' not just about 'what we are doing.' Disruptive technologies will have, or have now, the power to change individual people's lives in direct ways: they may predict which children are at risk of abuse, exam results, insurance levels, promotion, successful surgery, and much more. People's own perception of these circumstances or powers are also important in themselves. Leaving people behind comes primarily from a lack of transparency, explanation, and education, listening, and persuasion. Honesty and engagement are crucial. If we ignore the Luddites, or those with caution and questions, we will be not only be disenfranchising their views but creating a group of resentful people isolated by others, not just disengaged by their own actions and opinions. This is the opening for inequality, disorder, and populism, and these people will not be powerless, but their power will not be in writing letters or 'pointless' voting; it will be in disruptive actions they take or non-engagement. They may be seen as inferior by the rest of us, an action that will imperil our desired progress, shape our own actions towards them, and shape what sort of people we ourselves are. We ignore Luddites at our own peril as well as at theirs. Luddites are born when their standard of life falls or their opportunities fade, without them understanding why, and when they feel powerless to influence change; and when leaders are not open, honest, and realistic. Being a Luddite is rarely a position that someone wants to be in, and a Luddite may be any age, not just someone older. Avoiding a Luddite-style backlash to the predominance of technology needs to be given much more thought, especially in the evolution of frameworks in law and psychology that will aid understanding and opportunity.

Furthermore, what will be our view of people who make a

principled and informed decision to step outside the mainstream of society, perhaps going as far as to live 'off-grid' but maybe being selective in participation, doing no harm to anyone else? If our belief and faith in the scientific age that we are hurtling towards are strong, will we maintain enough empathy with others to acknowledge a validity to their point of view? Vaccinations are generally voluntary, but in the post, or next, Covid-19 age can you be off-grid with vaccinations, whatever reason you may have? What about smoking, or, in the future, fossil fuel use, or actions seen as physically dangerous like personally driving a motorcycle, or a car? This is a matter of culture. In fifty years' time we may all be carbon neutral and vegan as well as non-smoking and avoiding obesity, but these must be voluntary decisions for individuals. We must make sure that if science is the new creed we can maintain our own individualism and our ability to allow others to swim against the tide. Belief in scientific and technological development must avoid a puritanical streak that mainstream religions have all had in the past.

Our Place in a Scientific Age

Religions used to justify their control as maintenance of 'the truth.' Supposing a nation has a different sort of truth and wishes to go its own way. What if they have a different attitude to the community/individual balance of freedoms, or to the sanctity of life? China is an obvious example but not the only one. Supposing a religion rejects technology, or Japan goes down the route of mechanised and robotic solutions? If we are to maintain our humanity with its relationships and mistakes and individual decision-making and belief systems, then logically some will be ahead of or divergent to others in that thinking. How does one nation keeping scientific and technological advancement in its place – banning machines that can kill humans, limiting the use of personal data, banning compulsory biosensor implants, etc – deal with another that takes the opposite view?

International frameworks, research teams, peer review, and monitoring and enforcement, are obvious parts of an answer, based on an agreed set of principles. Given the current nature of international affairs it is difficult not to be pessimistic. This is often exacerbated by the speed of new discoveries and inventions. With climate change there is emerging the understanding that all nations are affected by the issue, and that national sovereignty and nationalism itself is best served by international co-operation. However, there are major elements of scientific and technological advancement that are nowhere near this public consensus: military-related development, societal surveillance, biotechnological human enhancement, individual privacy, depth of government regulation, and extent of commercialisation, all show little sign of international agreement, and often little sign of domestic consensus. Space may be an area where agreement is being lost. In a few individual instances there seems to be some agreement, not cloning humans seems to be one. It can be done. The wide-ranging global dialogue emerging is sorely needed in the world of science and technology. Perhaps digital technologies will be able to break away from their current control from a very small number of nations – but we do not know if that is diversity or division. Social science needs to get rid of its WEIRD problem – research being in Western, educated, industrialised, richer democracies. Consensus forming from the ground up is positive, especially if connected to legislative processes and accountability, but it is no substitute for governmental and international action. The importance of the global dialogue in establishing a consensus of basic values cannot be overstated. Otherwise, there will be an arms race of scientific and technological advancement based on national competition. At the very least this will increase global inequality. At the very worst it will lead to a divergence of lifestyles and a fragmentation of higher and lower levels of humanity itself. Perhaps that is how a new or adapted version of *Homo sapiens* will emerge.

We are also reassessing our idea of nature. As a species we have lived in, adapted, used, explained, and felt superior to it. We continue to learn, and are finding a new language for it: climate, biodiversity, biomimicry etc. We continue to categorise it, and be scientific about it. Part of us still wants to use it for our own ends and believes we can explain all its current mysteries. One strand of 'sustainability' continues to be destruction and replacement or substitution, which continue our idea of control and exploitation. This continues the pre-eminence of science as an objective search for ultimate knowledge and use by a dominant and superior species i.e., humanity. In other words, as our new creed, without a moral or spiritual backbone or context, science may again place us in the danger zone of thinking that we are and should be masters of all we survey. This danger emphasises the necessity of a philosophical change or renewed clarity to the sort of species that we want to be and our relationship with the natural world – and that applies to any future hospitable planet too, or else we are doomed to repeat elsewhere the mistakes of here and the past.

One fundamental theory related to science and technology is 'the entanglement of things.' For thousands of years humankind was nomadic and could not accumulate things – and then farming and settlement came, and the ability to accumulate through invention and discovery. Despite benefits the new ways of doing things could still be improved, or had other effects that needed mitigating, and these were done with other new inventions etc. Things have needed other things to work, and this entanglement of things and humans has become a dependency, affecting how humans live, think, our idea of progress, what we do, and how we relate to each other. We judge progress, wealth, and success by how much we accumulate and the importance we give it – and so inequality is magnified in this way too. Ian Hodder gives several examples in *Where are We Heading?: The Evolution of Humans and Things*, one simpler one being the spindle, leading to an industrialisation of cotton production, part of the descending web of which is T-shirt production, with one T-shirt requiring hundreds of gallons of water for its production.* The dependency of entanglement has mushroomed as people accumulate, and in the example of cotton has contributed to industrialisation, slavery, child labour, imperialism, and exponential use of natural resources. Such entanglements are now complex and global, central to how our economies work and planetary exploitation. Human-Things entanglement has led to webs of dependencies that have changed us. This is a portrayal of science and technology as an addiction, and while we cannot and should not simply ignore or eradicate humanity's achievements, it must make us think about the human factor determining it, not just the human factor within it.

Covid-19 science was good at identifying problems and contributed

---

* Hodder, 2018, 17, 62–63.

massively to what we now accept are the solutions, but with interpretation not all the solutions were scientific. Many democracies were not good at matching the speed of action required to the situation, but a learning process was taking place that solidified the foundations and consensus for the action that then took place. The most effective governments and actions were explanatory, and in nations with trusted governments or still reasonably deferential or dutiful citizens 'learning to live with' Covid-19, although controversial, which kept us on our toes, became a realistic option. In democracies people learnt what that meant. In other regimes this took far longer because there was not the open societal learning process. Less democratic regimes had an unwillingness to let their people debate and learn because that would or might make them as rulers seem weak, and indecisive, and to lack control, not just of the disease but of people's opinions and ideas. That could not be countenanced, because where would it end? To what other issues might that freedom to have and debate different reactions or even emotions be applied? Where authoritarian regimes acted like this over Covid-19 they are doing so with algorithms, AI, and other disruptive technologies. Cnut knew when he told the waves to turn that they would not. The lesson was to his people that even a king does not have complete power. Any authoritarian regime that gives the impression it has complete power is destined in the end to fail. If the lack of power, or mistakes made, are not enough, then the cover-up will be. The cries of the people from Wuhan and across China as the Covid-19 outbreak spread were as much about the treatment of whistleblowers like Dr Li Wenliang as the disease itself. They were calls for freedom of information and truth, and messages about trust in government. In China, the CCP managed to shut these down, as far as we can tell, but another generation learnt about the necessity of government with integrity. Arguably, the attempted denial and cover-up of the Chernobyl nuclear disaster was a key reason for the *perestroika* (reform) and *glasnost* (openness) of the Gorbachev regime that led to the rapid collapse of the Soviet Union. Repetition may be wishful thinking as authoritarian regimes also use science and technology to tighten their grip, but setting aside the real-world experience of people is always the countermeasure, the secondary action, after the real-world experience has happened.

SCIENCE AND TECHNOLOGY

Whether we are yet in an Age of Science is related to all these questions. The maturity that we have to recognise its weaknesses, its dangers, unknowns, and mis-directions, at the same time as exploit the knowledge it gives us, is very debatable. We have also not worked out how the constant development of a scientific age relates to our spirituality and to nature. How do we place science within the big questions of where we come from, what sort of people we are, and how we are changing?. We may still be distracted or overwhelmed by the excitement of potential awe and wonder of science, and this is not necessarily progress. When we have a mature reflection on these questions, both embracing science and able to regulate its place in society and within ourselves, then we may be in a Scientific Age. We are not there yet. Our immaturity may yet lead to new benefits of equality and freedom and happiness but may also lead to unwanted transformation or annihilation, of ourselves and our planet.

Over the course of human history – the last few minutes of our planet's life in a 24-hour version – it may be that the science and technology-led industrialisation of the planet is an aberration, temporarily distracting us with shiny things, a short-term vehicle for human progress or human destruction. Our philosophical attitude to ourselves and our relationships with other people, those we know and those we do not, and with the external world, has been changed, but we are in no position yet to say that it has changed these things permanently. As we have explored already, there are fundamental aspects of humanity that we have not yet understood, especially our balance of conflict and competition. The trends of history that form its direction remain of unknown length. Most people in the world maintain a religious faith, perhaps that will trump or determine the nature and uses of scientific and technological advancement. It is not yet impossible that we shall regain a more spiritual focus. As India and China as recently as 1,000 years ago were the predominant economies of the world, perhaps in a short time, when they are again, we will be looking at their social and cultural norms to see whether those ideas and values should be more global. Rabindranath Tagore rejected the imposition in his native India of a Western industrial-led materialism and individualism which he viewed as competitive and conflictual and bound up with the evils of imperialism and slavery. He wanted Indian nationalists to learn from their past and project a modernised or new 'moral' man with a focus on humanity 'growing' not just 'gaining.' He argued that humanity needed to examine the core of who we wanted to be and what we should be striving to achieve.

There is no reason why the philosophy of humanity cannot change, or return, whether in the direction Tagore would wish or in a different way. There are key conditions and changes taking place that may make us think that it will, including exploration of space, climate, and planetary reassessment of resources, re-thinking our economic objectives and relationships, a 'new' Enlightenment of genuine equality of respect for all, and a reassessment of our origins. Such philosophical change will trump the scientific and technological, and re-focus or confirm them as tools to be shaped not as the tail wagging the dog, not as humanity's status quo but as knowledge and training. It may even be that our better understanding of the interpretative nature of scientific 'truth' will itself encourage the resurgence of a more philosophical wisdom, if we do not make ourselves extinct in the meantime. At that point we may be able to maturely consider if we want to be in a Scientific Age.

IX

UNTHINKABLE

I am urging that we extend to other species the basic principle of equality that most of us recognise should be extended to all members of our own species.
Peter Singer.*

Sometimes I think we are alone in the universe and sometimes I think we're not. In either case the idea is quite staggering.
Arthur C. Clarke.†

In the chapters of this book there are reasonably predictable themes and events, ideas and movements, and possibilities for future action. There are, however, other issues that need to be addressed. These could reshape the world across all walks of life and possibilities of progress. They would test our virtues and vices and what we think of as our human character. They have some connection with what is happening now but get little attention beyond specific expertise and opinion. They are 'known unknowns,' but their consequences are not general matters of public discussion.

---

* Peter Singer, *Animal Liberation*, 1975.
† Quote taken from Brian Cox and Andrew Cohen. *The Human Universe*, 2020, 63.

WHERE ARE WE GOING?

Speciesism

Dutch primatologist Frans de Waal has asked which is the greater problem – that we do not see the 'animal' in ourselves, or that we do not see ourselves in other animals? Peter Singer is acknowledged in the West as the modern founder of animal rights, with his 1975 book *Animal Liberation*. He argued in favour of animal rights (as I will simplistically refer to non-human life from here on) through equal moral consideration of any being that is capable of suffering. Writing amid the 'liberation' and 'rights' movements of the 1960s and 1970s, his point was that anatomical or character differences, or those related to intelligence or personal morality, should not prevent different people being treated with equal consideration. For Singer, it was an extension of this argument to write that other animals should be treated with equal consideration to the animal that is humanity. Equivalent to the terms 'racism' and 'sexism' he used the term 'speciesism' (first used in 1970 by Richard Ryder) to denote the common human attitude to animals. At the time of his book animals were seen as lacking specific or controlled emotion and feelings, and 'animalistic' in the sense of being non-thinking, learning skills by intuition or repetition. It was only at about this time that Jane Goodall and then others were beginning to demonstrate the complex social structures of animals and the ability of 'higher' and related animal species to learn and use tools, and to compare these with human behaviours.

Singer traced the speciesism of humanity to the Ancient Greeks and Aristotle, who wrote of plants existing for the sake of animals, and animals for the sake of Man; and to Judaism and Christianity whose verses in Genesis spoke of Man's dominion over the animal kingdom, and that Man not animals had been created in the image of God. Francis is the first Pope to publicly move away from the traditional philosophy in Christianity, in the context of environmental damage, biodiversity, and climate change. The original European Enlightenment allowed the idea of animals as property with neither feelings nor intelligence. French revolutionaries raised the idea of any person, including women, not having to be rational to still be considered worthy of moral consideration. This was the logic followed by Singer. The 'old'

Enlightenment and Christian view predominant in the West should not be considered global. In more ancient traditions other living beings may be guardian spirits, go-betweens with divine power, and omens of good or bad luck. East Asian life cycles present another view. Yet it is also true that despite cultural and religious tradition the non-human world has been traditionally and globally considered second-class. We have moved on, but the nature of Singer's animal liberation is still revolutionary. We still breed for farming and food, and eat and lab test animals, and the acceptance of speciesism is not yet an accepted part of philosophy or the public norm.

There has been progress since 1975 through conservation, with political, violent, and non-violent campaigns, and individual laws relating to animal welfare and trade. There is far greater understanding than there was in 1975 of social structures, species-wide and individually different behaviours, the use of tools, and interaction between individual animals and family groups, in marine and insect life as well as mammals. High-profile ambassadors have used widespread communication to explain the animal world, and developments in technology have shown wild and animal behaviours never before seen in public. We have far greater scientific knowledge of anatomy, and physical, biological, and chemical processes across a wide array of species. We are using some of this knowledge directly, and some indirectly, in biomimicry projects to improve our own lives in areas as varied as medicine and building infrastructure and engineering. New knowledge is helping us to find scientific proof of the intelligence of species such as bees and cuttlefish and leading us to see how animals sense danger and show emotions, including pain. We know that different parts of at least certain animals' brains light up when faced with different situations, emotions, or actions, just as human brains do. Cephalopods (squid, octopus, etc) are now thought to have less centralised brains and relatively independent thinking tentacles. This may even lead us to ask whether there are different levels of conscious awareness, or the ability to 'feel' (sentience), not just different levels of intelligence. Animals may be as likely as humans to instinctively sense danger and experience joy when they see predators or a food source. The project Foundations of Animal Sentience, ASENT, set up in the LSE in 2020 for five years and led by Jonathan Birch, is making headway in precisely this type of research.

While once we viewed equating human and animal behaviour as being insulting to Man, we have now moved to a phase in which animal behaviours are often seen through a human-equivalent lens. We should move through this phase towards a real understanding of animals as different to humans with similarities, species as different to each other, and individual beings showing individual character, feelings, and intelligence. When we can do this we will be able to fully acknowledge and consider Singer's idea of treating animals, collectively and individually, with equal moral consideration. We will have moved from stewardship through recognition of inter-dependence, to coexistence by design. This will be revolutionary. We are currently a long way from that, but the 2022 Animal Welfare Sentient Act in the UK was world-leading in saying that those working with or effecting non-human animals should 'pay due regard to animals as sentient beings.'

We are moving towards a greater understanding and appreciation of the inter-dependence of different human/animal species, and the sociology and psychology of complex eco-systems. This would be a whole new dimension to us understanding the world that we as humanity live in, how it works for us, and the threat we pose to it. It would probably open new possibilities in biomimicry and sustainability benefitting humanity. We can get to this path alongside, and supplemented by, our increasing understanding, appreciation, and mitigating actions in relation to the environment, biodiversity, and climate change, and how these are affecting each other. These issues are binding us to the natural world in a way that we have not understood before. They are pushing us to further our moral consideration of the non-human world.

There is a chance we will stop reassessing our relations with the natural world at the point that we feel we have 'conquered' or 'mitigated' climate change, environmental pollution and destruction, and narrowing biodiversity. This would be maintaining the predominance of our interests over following the philosophy of Singer towards its natural conclusion. The natural world would remain a commodity. This would be much easier for humanity and may negate the need for religious review or economic re-modelling, or other more fundamental reviews of the lifestyle of humanity that come from a philosophical reassessment.

We should be able to get past the idea of animals as existing for our own interests. Another limiting danger to a radical reassessment would be that humanity gets stuck on transposing human characteristics onto what we discover about the natural or non-human animal world (anthropomorphism). This would surely lead to a misunderstanding, and limiting misuse, of new knowledge, with a predominance of those self-perceived human characteristics above all else.

Farming, by definition, sees animals (and plants) as food, for our benefit. Replacing our current farm food from the natural world is, however, a huge challenge. Globally, in most countries an average of 5%–10% of people identify as vegetarian or vegan, only three nations count over 15%, including India, which might be expected to be very high but is between 20% and 40%. In the UK about 8% currently identify as vegetarian. It is not all or nothing, however, and in the UK 31% of people say that in recent times they have reduced the amount of meat they eat. Globally, those nations with a Buddhist influence tend to eat less meat, but in China the figure is thought to be about 5% vegetarian.* There may also be a gender difference to consider here in people's attitudes. Eating habits are often ingrained through cultural or social and family traditions. This gives us a clue as to the size of the task of changing them. Nor must farming go the way of coalmines – scrapped without replacement, without social and economic compensatory strategies, without empathy for the people affected. Farming remains a major industry and forms part of the culture of most nations. With that identity and historic role also comes a respect for nature from that significant part of the population. If that is lost through the loss, or denigration, or downsizing, of farming, then all sorts of countryside and landscape will be changed, unless replaced by a different vehicle to maintain them, a nostalgia or rewilding or repurposing which may not itself allow those attitudes and skills to survive. One stage post will be whether 'free roaming' bred animals for food will be as practical on the scale necessary, and as philosophically acceptable as our interests will let us go. At some point we may decide that farm-bred animals are different to those in the wild and are therefore 'second class' in any moral

---

* These figures are from various public survey sources generally using self-identification, over the 2018–22 period. Definitions are not all the same across the world.

consideration of their lives. We could in theory clone and lab-create animal protein-based food or animal organs and meat. If, or when, the last farmed cattle, pigs, chickens, goats, etc are left may we set them free as wild animals, or deliberately 'conserve' them, or may we be thinking that they are not 'natural' and have served their purpose entirely, to be allowed to die off? The place of agriculture in the development of humanity, its relation to peacefulness, development of community and societal structure, and spur to urbanisation, are cemented in history. We have now left that behind, but the deconstruction of agriculture and food supply chains as we know them would be every bit as fundamental, if not even more so, than the deconstruction of the largely industrial exploitative economic model currently driving our idea of progress and driving climate change.

Should we also consider 'animal rights' for specific wild animals and natural eco-systems? Zoo's may be dying out but are all animals equal? Do natural predators have the right to hunt, and their prey the right to protection? To interfere in this process would be a blatant interference in natural biodiversity and coexistence. This would itself be a supreme arrogance of humanity, a stewardship gone wrong. Humankind's introduction of non-natural species, and predators, to different regions of the world is an added complication. To try to reverse this or let nature re-balance itself is another moral as well as practical conundrum.

Around the world there have been and are different historical attitudes to animals from the predominant Western view, but the picture is still mixed. As well as increasing meat-eating across the developing world, continued wild animal markets and land clearance for farming from Brazil to Indonesia, should all be antidotes to our complacency. This increase is related to Western-style ideas of progress and wealth. Yet it is also true that older groups have had a greater harmony with nature. We are beginning to appreciate those views more, from Australian Aboriginals to Native Americans/First Peoples. We know that animals were exploited – the most famous example in the West being the Great Plains Native American use of the buffalo. However, we now understand that there was an efficiency of use and a 'don't kill more-than-needed' attitude that exemplified what we would now call replenishment, conservation, and consideration. Accepting speciesism philosophically affects how we live, and what we think of ourselves, as well as our relationship with the world around us. By learning from the past and being armed with new scientific knowledge, irrespective of or helped by population changes, we can design, or re-design, a new relationship with the natural world that could lead to the moral consideration for which Singer argues. If we want to. This should not be beyond the horizon of our imagination. The logical end point of re-evaluation may never be reached, but there are many significant milestones along the way that will themselves be profound for what humanity thinks of itself.

Eliminating Suffering, Illness, and Disease

Well beyond the horizon of our current abilities is the elimination of illness and disease. This endeavour would be on most people's wish lists and is assumed to be 'a good thing.' But is it? We understand far more about, though not completely, the decline and regeneration of cells, repairing and re-growing or replacing human bones, our immune and metabolic systems, and artificial, environmental, and externally manufactured ways to improve physical performance. We see before us an extending life expectancy, and that is what eliminating disease means in the first instance. In mere decades the life expectancy of a human across the world has risen from 50.87 years in 1960, to 72.27 in 2020.[*] It may be that there is a 'natural' limit to life expectancy, but we have not accepted that concept. If these words are read by a middle-class young reader in a 'developed' nation, then that reader may have an expectation rather than just a hope of living to the age of 100. However, the journey to eliminate disease is problematic. Even considering the search is problematic. The practicalities are well beyond scientific. If we live longer in good health, the life span of work will increase. If we live longer in ill-health the problem becomes more acute. It becomes a major economic, social, and state issue relating to how older people connect to each other in their generation, to other generations, how they continue to access services, how they are paid for and by whom, and the balance

---

[*] Figures provided by the World Bank and found at www.datacommons.org, accessed 27 January 2023.

sheet of state expenditure at the expense of other areas. Living longer is as likely as other forms of progress to become a commodity. That means something to be bought, or influenced, by the highest bidder and the wealthy through biotechnology, healthcare access, non-discrimination, better environmental and general living conditions, including personal and digital safety, and access to education. To a certain extent this is already happening, and always has, whatever form of government is the context. As inequality continues to extend, so life expectancy for some will continue to reach unprecedented levels. Even a slight increase in life expectancy for the poorer could mean an unhealthier, more financially and socially insecure, more isolated, and more politically and societally powerless life. The conditions in which most people live are as essential to life expectancy and quality as scientific advancement. Extra living time as a commodity would be a monumental human folly that must be avoided. This is the pessimistic future that follows eliminating disease without tackling poverty, or conflict. Progress *could* be made through both co-operation and war but not for most people.

For religion the aim may be noble but near-immortality could be a game-changer if not a death knell. Religious belief across the world places its ultimate faith in an external power over humanity. How could any of this have meaning if there is no foreseeable and ultimate influence on life by God, if the prospect of going to heaven or hell is always pushed further away, if life loses its human fragility? However, it is also conceivable that if the most likely way to die early is by committing immoral/criminal acts then perhaps the balance sheet of one's life may come into even sharper focus. It may make no difference to the philosophy of religion if a person lives for 75 years or 150 years, because in such an instance humanity's own understanding and perspective of time would surely change and adapt to the new reality. Anything short of actual immortality keeps humanity in a position of inferiority in comparison to the idea of God.

The required new perspective on the passing of time if we are to live much longer may also encourage us to adapt our day-to-day lives and decision-making, perhaps in unexpected ways. We have no idea if such qualities as patience and tolerance would be extended or their onset delayed with an extended life span, let alone our mental and intellectual health. Would partnership and childbirth be delayed? If inheritance and differences in education and health continue to fuel inequality, then what dislocated and divided state would any nation be in if this began at birth, was supplemented artificially, and were to last over a life span of 110 years or more? One result may be less short-termism. To take a major example: if the life span of the average human born in 1850 had been 150 years would the alarm bells of climate change through industrial changes to our environment have been recognised sooner and dealt with? Or are they seen better through the fresher eyes of a younger generation? If you were to live longer and always see a scientific solution to the consequences you experience early on, then perhaps you might become more and not less complacent about the dangers and those unintended consequences. This would surely be a danger in a species that lived substantially longer but that had become more materialistic, more individualistic, more about short-term gratification, more unequal, and had not found a unifying vision of humanity with some form of civic morality at its core. The psychology of expecting to live longer and planning for it is also quite different to it being unplanned and unexpected, although we know now that wealth predicts life expectancy so perhaps there would be more predictability than randomness.

We can move towards societies that minimise illness and disease by addressing discriminatory effects that we know about now, with political willpower and motivations of citizenship. We can engage in a greater global dialogue that clarifies our own self-interest through the helping of others. We could make this a priority of science. In this scenario there are still issues to be addressed. If we use gene-editing, end birth defects, and 'solve' disability, are we dismissing the value of non-able-bodied lives, which in turn may affect the diversity of the human species and the empathetic character of humanity? Will we review our opinions of suicide and assisted dying? Elimination of the suffering, illness and disease that we know we can address now is itself a mammoth task with society-changing requirements and repercussions, the motivations for which can only come from a more positive interpretation of our human nature. Nevertheless, the journey, like other life-affirming journeys, would itself be worth the effort, and that is the reason it is a noble aim of humanity, even if it may never be achieved or be achievable.

WHERE ARE WE GOING?

Lunar Exploration, Deep Space, and Aliens

We have landed on the Moon, are actively spending billions on deep space exploration, and some discussion of alien life has always been a part of the human imagination. Education, science, and enough peacefulness are allowing us these luxuries. Competition, pride, and ego have played a part, as well as the human characteristic of exploration. We have learnt from our scientific progress and been able to adapt some of that to improve life on Earth. Studies by leading economic forecasting company Chase Econometrics estimated that for every $1 spent on the Apollo missions there have been $6 or $7 of increased GDP. We have learnt more about ourselves, what we can physically and mentally endure, and stretched our ambition and vision of what humanity is or might become. The bright lights of space are as enticing as the bright lights of the city have historically been.

Neil Armstrong placing the first human foot on the Moon in 1969 was Cold War political imperative, technological challenge, and human endeavour. Only three years later humanity decided it was no longer worth it to do so again. Until now. In 2023 the USA began the first of the Artemis missions to establish a new method of lunar orbit and in 2025 or 2026 land on the Moon again, and eventually establish a permanent lunar base. That would use a SpaceX *Starship* – SpaceX being the private company vision of Elon Musk, developing reusable craft. China, in 2024 having landed on the dark side of the Moon, says it is working towards a joint lunar base with Russia by 2035. China already has Tiangong, its own space station orbiting Earth, as a 'rival' to the ISS set up by the USA, Russia, and other nations, and which is now beginning to wind down in use.

There has emerged in the West a belief that few states can justify the enormous expense alone, are often seen as less likely to be 'efficient,' and more political in oversight and mission choice. Private companies do not have so many restrictions and may not be political, but they may be equally ideological, and are also about commercial exploitation. To some this is an inevitable and natural development, and an encouragement of science and entrepreneurial activity. For others this is exporting the economic competitiveness of capitalism into space, akin to the Wild

West of initial industrial development and leading to the same inequality and exploitation, with businesses too big to regulate. The trick will be to maintain regulation, public good or benefit, and ethical values. Do we have the willpower, the political will in the sight of the bright lights, to avoid that fate in space, or have we already started on a long path of exporting private greed and inequality beyond our own frontiers? There is also the fear that lunar exploration serves to distract attention, money, and even ambition, public or private, from solving our own problems here on Earth, and this is a criticism of all nations, but especially where less transparency exists. There are also concerns that the Moon may be effectively divided up into spheres of influence by different nations. The use of private or state-sponsored companies is just another way of expanding and projecting individual national power. The Moon may provide minerals, opportunities for scientific development, and even a launch pad for missions further afield, such as to Mars.

There is no inevitability about lunar exploration being completely commercialised or driven by national aspirations of power. We can develop multi-corporate alliances, and multinational missions, that better reflect a more co-operative human race. This is a choice that we can make. What it requires most of all is a common vision of humanity and of benefit for the common good. What it is all too susceptible to is short-termism of political interests and commercial competition, of ideology and ego, a short-termism that currently seems overwhelmingly likely to predominate.

Mars is the stated intended target for several nations. It may once have had water, meaning that it may once have had life. It may tell us something about the nature of our own planet and the origins of other planets. There is currently an American 'rover' collecting samples from Mars, and from 2021 an experiment called MOXIE has successfully been producing oxygen from Mars' CO_2-rich atmosphere. Mirroring the lunar race, but with bigger risks and political, social, and cultural ramifications, both the USA and China have plans to land humans on Mars in the late 2030s. It is 'practice' for deep space exploration, and an idea of colonisation remains in the public perception. All the fears about commercialisation and exclusivity that apply to discussions about lunar exploration and permanent bases also apply to the exploration of Mars.

WHERE ARE WE GOING?

It is impossible to separate motives, just as it is impossible to deny the inspiration of human curiosity. The European Space Agency plans to go 'beyond' Mars to Europa, one of the moons of Jupiter, with the Jupiter Icy Moon Explorer – JUICE for short. Jupiter is strongly believed to hold iced water under the surface of its poles, and JUICE would take between 5 to 7 years of travel to get to its destination.

The highest profile of about 200 craft exploring our solar system or beyond are Voyager 1 and Voyager 2, both launched in 1977. They carry the Voyager Golden Record – written, diagrammatic and visual images, and sound recordings giving an impression of life on Earth, the place of Earth in the stars, scientific knowledge and human anatomy, and a recording of fifty-five human languages. The James Webb Space Telescope gives us unprecedented clarity over much further distances, even picking up evidence of clouds and unusual molecular formations on distant planets. The first exoplanet – a planet outside our solar system – named *Poltergeist*, was identified in 1992. Now we believe there are 5,000 and counting. We know that our galaxy, the Milky Way, is 105,000 light years wide and holds at least 100 billion stars, and that there are many other galaxies. (A light year is the distance light travels in one year, being about 9.46 trillion kms or 5.88 trillion miles.) We can judge with increasing confidence which of these exoplanets are in the 'goldilocks zone,' i.e., not too hot and not too cold, and therefore potentially able to support life. Mars is inside our goldilocks zone, and Venus is on the edge. Many other factors would, of course, contribute to the potential of life, including planetary mass, geology, atmosphere, and the nature of the central star. We know that our Sun is one billion years younger than other parts of the galaxy, and so any living neighbours may be 'older.' We understand that a 'natural' frequency through the hydrogen of space (which makes up 74% of matter of the universe by mass) is 1420 MHz, and we believe that this is therefore the most likely frequency to hear any form of alien sound. The only non-natural transmission we have heard was on 15 August 1977, but the technology used to record it at the time makes it almost impossible to study now. Since the beginning of the USA's Spaceguard Survey from 1992 (which promotes the detection of objects that are potentially a threat to Earth) one known object from outside our solar system has been detected. This occurred on 19 October 2017 and was observed relatively close to the Sun. It was half a mile long, ten times longer than it was broad, and changed in brightness as it moved, which means that there was another force acting on it to move it. It appeared to rotate and 'shudder,' with no sound detected. It was named (in Hawaiian language) 'Oumuamua.' Origin and purpose unknown, it may have been a deliberate object, or debris, or yet unknown phenomena. Since 2015, ATLAS (the Asteroid Territorial Impact Last Alert System) was formed as part of Spaceguard. The aim of ATLAS is to give a (reassuring?!) three-week warning of significant impacts with Earth. In 2022 the USA Congress held its first public hearings on Unidentified Aerial Phenomena (UAP has generally replaced the abbreviation UFO) and published the material it had on such UAPs. In an era of conspiracy theories and 'controlling the narrative' this was a bold move. We also know the universe is stretching apart, a theory from Edwin Hubble in 1929 and supported by the finding of the afterglow of the Big Bang in 1964, which means it has 'energy.' All the motives, concerns, dangers, and potential rewards for lunar and solar system exploration apply to deep space, and more.

The most important 'and more' relates of course to the possibility of alien life. Science fiction has educated us to think that life may come in any form of energy, of no fixed shape or form. NASA simply notes any entity that can reproduce itself. It looks for any combination of molecules or chemicals that could be considered complex, i.e., not naturally producing, such as phosphene, of which there would seem to be traces on Venus, which has therefore become a test case for such an approach. The definition of life that we accept has repercussions for the future of what we may produce on Earth as well as anything found elsewhere.

The chance for us to find recognisable life, or life sufficiently advanced to recognise us, depends on the duration of our progress. We have been building spacecraft for less than a century of *Homo sapiens*' 200,000 years, and of the 13 billion years of the universe, and, pessimistically, the thought of our civilisation lasting another 10,000 years is beyond most people's comprehension. The discovery of any biological or chemical, or technological, signature of life, present or past, would probably be the greatest discovery of humanity and would profoundly affect us –

even if communication is one-way. It would mean that we would need to characterise the universe as biological. For humanity's religious faith it may simply mean that God has a finger in more than one pie, even more wondrously; and perhaps that could be psychologically 'reasoned.' It would also, however, influence our psychology. We may no longer see ourselves as unique or exceptional, or bound to continue on and on, and perhaps not as the original life-form, whether created by chemicals or by God. We may realise that we are not in control of all that we survey and that we still have lessons to learn. The prospect of discovering even the debris of simple alien life is profound, and we should be acutely aware of our biases in understanding such civilisation. If we discover contemporary life we believe to be intellectually inferior to our own we must then also remember humanity's arrogance in its superiority. If alien life were to be seen as technologically superior to us, or if it discovered us, then these dangers could be multiplied but in 'reverse,' and we could face our own crisis of confidence.

The United Nations has a division devoted to space exploration, and an agreement that space is the common province of all humanity. It has a protocol of UN agreement for any reaction should an alien signal be received.* The success of the UN in other spheres does not inspire confidence. Nor would we want a private company on the frontiers of space to represent humanity in its entirety, or to give that impression. Perhaps this is one of the few scenarios that would bring people together. However, while the historic fact that danger tends to bring a community together in common defence may have positives, it is also a recipe for distrust and suspicion of what is then frequently characterised as a common enemy, or intruder, or competitor – hardly a good foundation for friendly relationships. Ask Indigenous Peoples the world over what their perspective would be. Caution and defensiveness are almost certainly inevitable, and necessary to some degree, but humanity must do better than this. The establishment of a communicative common language could be a civilisation-long enterprise. That we are not alone in the universe might be the only known. Would there be

---

* The UN Office for Outer Space Affairs (www.unoosa.org) has a Committee on the Uses of Outer Space, and what are known as the Five UN Treaties on Outer Space, created between 1963 and 1996.

transparency to the Earth's population, or government secrecy, and how could that be kept globally? To what extent would people feel they had to 'do something' – which could range from prayer, religious conversion or questioning, and celebration, to gun sales, panic-buying, and governmental mistrust. There would be an individual and a group mentality to these reactions. The prospect of meeting intelligent alien life with a disunited and unclear intent is potentially disastrous for us as well as whatever we may meet. We are just as woefully unprepared for that scenario as others.

The prospect of humanity itself settling elsewhere mirrors many of these concerns. Would we regard ourselves as alien visitors, or would we think of ownership of new lands? Have we settled the moral issues of how we treat our own planet and organise our own society in such a way as to be confident of our righteous treatment of another planet and of how people settling on it would develop their own community, from one generation to the next? The current state of global division gives little confidence that we would not simply export our intellectual prejudices and our mistakes, and while a dystopian view may be survivalist caution it may also be self-fulling psychology. Settled bases on the surface of our closest and most familiar entity, the Moon, will set our precedent. Understanding that a lack of perfection on Earth should not close off other opportunities will trump the idea of whether we should settle anywhere else at all.

Lunar and deep space exploration, and consideration of alien life, are not new but they all still require thinking 'outside the box' of our current experience as a species. Our journey into the stars has the possibility and opportunity to teach us more about ourselves, and shape who we want to be, in a more profound way than perhaps anything except a consideration of our species life expectancy on this planet itself.

There are other issues we might yet need to consider too, just as 'unthinkable,' such as the decline of human fertility, or extinction level disaster. Motives and reactions can easily be considered well-meaning and beneficial, but any boxer knows that the plan goes out the window after the first punch has been thrown. These issues can affect every aspect of human life. They all involve potentially changing emphasis or clarity of the human character. However much we try to think through our actions, we will not be completely risk-averse, and nor should we be. As a species we must remain adaptable and resilient. We need to remain ambitious and outward in our expectations and hopes. Therefore, while the issues in this chapter will be beyond the daily grind of most people's lives, within a new-found global dialogue we should have the bandwidth to consider them, and we should do so.

CONCLUSION

The cosmopolitan impulse that draws on our common humanity is no longer a luxury, it has become a necessity.
Kwame Anthony Appiah, 2018.*

…each individual is for his own part called upon by nature itself to contribute to this progress [of humanity] to the best of [their] ability.'
Immanuel Kant, c.1784.†

If we believe that the world can be improved we either have a blind faith and optimism, or a belief that it can do so if we work at it. Most people would say that the former is trusting to luck or a sign of childlike immaturity. Where people despair surely there is a reason, or someone or something that is fairly or unfairly to blame – which also means things can change, and it is the method and effort and power dynamic and scale of change which is too daunting. For some there is such a need for concentration on survival in their own lives that they have no capacity for reflection or forward planning. If things positively change for them then the possibility of further change becomes inescapable.

Human Nature

If we are not willing to see that over the course of the human timeline

---

* Kwame Anthony Appiah, *The Lies that Bind: Rethinking Identity*, 2018, 129.
† Immanuel Kant, *Conjectural Beginning of Human History*, 1786.

there has been change then not only are we being completely illogical, but we are denying the very point of having a mind, consciousness, and a soul. What is the point of these things if we are oblivious to the world we live in and have no interest, even self-interest, in how it may change for us, or how we might be changed by it, or how we might improve our lives? We should ask ourselves why and how change has occurred. The doubling of human life expectancy – through lower child mortality and record longevity – over the relatively very recent last 200 years may itself be the most substantial change in humanity's history. If we conclude that these changes were not entirely down to luck or natural processes outside any influence of humanity, then we could say that humanity can effect change. A refusal to accept this is indeed very fatalistic and gives us no agency or role in determining our future. Currently, it is commonly and logically seen as an indicator of the uniqueness of humanity as a species that we can consciously and deliberately reflect on the past and can plan beyond our known surroundings, people, and circumstances, or easily foreseeable timeline of necessary actions. This is part of what it is to be human, and to be judged as reaching 'maturity.' This is part intuition, part experience, and part specific strategies that we learn. Descartes' method breaks down a problem into its smallest pieces, seeking the simplest truth, and building on that, while seeing the whole problem. We deal with addiction by saying that we must overcome denial, recognise reality, recognise triggers to unwanted behaviours, and take small steps, supported by others. We understand 'trial and error,' and scientifically we theorise, experiment, and assess, trying to be objective. Daily we 'do what we can do' – a definition of the balance between need, realism, and positivity.

Character and Change

If it is a logical and evidentiary conclusion to believe that humanity has had some influence on its past and present, it is therefore only logical to believe that it can influence its future too. It will be influence not control, at least for all those who do not believe in the supreme all-encompassing abilities of humankind to do precisely and successfully whatever it wants. Nor does it make any difference whether one is religious or not if there is a belief in free will. Free will is, by definition, there to be used, and infers that judgement is made by God only after the decisions of humanity, not before. If there is no free will then we are mere puppets of a higher being with no self-conscience or meaningful lives, and that is no way to consider a life or to live. The emotional meaning of the word humanity does itself signify a conscious being with values that we recognise as individual to each person. If we understand our human nature, in any way like this, whether positively or negatively according to our character, then we have some belief that we can effect change.

There remain unanswerable questions, most notably two: the relative importance of nature or nurture in the development of our values and character, and whether we are at our core a co-operative or conflictual species. These two questions are important for understanding our past, present, and future. Yet they need not determine the latter. As we understand them, and whether we believe those answers will be permanent, may simply reflect our understanding of ourselves and our consideration of how we make change, rather than the specific ability to make change itself. We have changed our lives either because we are co-operative, or because we are conflictual, or because of whatever balance we have attained or may naturally have between the two. Change has nevertheless happened, *much of it positive*. Nor does it matter whether nature or nurture is more important. We can influence nurture most clearly, but we have shown that we have changed, and whether our 'automatic' nature is being suppressed, or adapted, or learning, is neither here nor there. These questions may be interesting, and it may be useful to better understand them, but they are therefore not determinants of whether there will be change, or whether we can effect change and influence our future. Either it has benefitted us to combat conflict, or conflict is in fact not natural, or is secondary to a predisposition to co-operation, or is in some way in a 'proper' balance with it. Change only through conflict is surely destructive, even to the 'winners,' and, by definition, not inclusive. A balance of opposing forces may be within each of us individually even if it is to be struggled for. A balance may make up the overall nature of what we call humanity, or maturity. To consider a third unknowable, the individual's, or society's, balance of optimism and pessimism is also neither here nor there. It does not negate the idea that humanity has changed, and can change, but only influences the method of change – with caution, with safeguards, being risk-averse, or with soaring ambition, or somewhere in between. It is a balance of some sort that would seem most likely to have contributed to humanity's survival – we have logically been neither reckless in our ambition nor so pessimistic as to be completely risk-averse, even from the first hunter-gatherers who recognised the need and benefits of going into the world, but also sensed its dangers.

Maturity

What follows from this is that humanity is neither at the beginning or the end of its development. It is still maturing, making mistakes, and still learning. It is still learning an understanding of itself, how it thinks, and achieves, and how things can go wrong. At times, like an adolescent, our civilisations have seemed arrogant, self-conscious, or moody, acting unpredictably or illogically. As a young adult we can still find idealism while struggling with the realities of life. Through middle age we can forge a new-found approach to address our challenges. Disasters will leave memories and experiences to learn from, and scars. Humanity may not entirely understand the world it is moving into, but it is a world that it wants to shape and believes that it can.

We live our own lives individually, with varying amounts of control, making individual decisions every day that affect what we do next. Yet we also know that our individuality is bound by a community of others. Most decisions we make affect others, and others affect the decisions we make. Those others include people familiar and close, and unknown and distant. The latter is more and more evident as humanity has developed. That there is a balance is logical, but its precise weighting seems unknowable and ever-changing. Ethics, or morals, are the vehicle we use to achieve some form of acceptable balance, and so relationships with others include rights and responsibilities. These give us freedoms that allow us some space for our own creativity, ambitions, opinions, and lifestyles, and we have space to form the specific individual morality that forms part of our individual character. A meaning and purpose of

CONCLUSION

life emerges. This means that our individual-civic balance is capable of change, and is likely to continue to be a daily struggle for individuals. We learn (whether the right or wrong lessons), another cause of change – whether in completely new directions or in a cyclical way. The timeline of change depends on the change, and clearly individuals can change much quicker than communities.

People realise that they need a story to make sense of their world, and that they need to feel a sense of belonging and worth within it, or them. For some people this highlights individual ambition, for others it may be 'simply' trying to make their own or family lives better, and for others a matter of developing a 'philosophy' or accepting a religious narrative to live by. Sometimes that story, or narrative, must be shaped to fit their own reality to make sense of, or to justify, their place and their actions. For most people that narrative involves the acceptance of morals or ethics that make their lives easier, with an empathy towards others, because they know that also makes their lives easier. Empathy is an important factor in the development of humanity as we know it. Our empathy means that we can live in different communities, in families, local neighbourhoods, nations, cultural groups, etc. Whether any of this comes from a 'soul,' or 'consciousness,' is less knowable and less important than knowing and understanding how we think, and how we can apply that to our lives. If we accept empathy, understand how we think, understand that we construct the narratives we live by, realise that life is never fixed even if it is because of things beyond our control, and know that we have individualism and yet must also live within community, then we have the ingredients for positive change.

The confidence to change is the confidence to make different decisions. Pessimism or optimism may affect how you make those decisions – planned, thought-through, risk-averse, cautious, 'plan for the worst but hope for the best,' being ambitious beyond the evidence, etc- but it is less relevant than being evidentiary. Nor is his limited to one strand of political thought, and making new decisions can benefit from both optimism and pessimism!

WHERE ARE WE GOING?

The Challenges We Must Face

So, what change do we need? Realising and accepting a need for and possibility of change in how we live comes from three sources: Firstly, the acceptance that the natural world we live in is not fixed, and therefore needs different responses and reactions as it changes. Secondly, that how the world works does not benefit as many people as it should or could. Thirdly, a belief that 'making progress' is a human ambition, whether a survival technique or one driven by curiosity. Only one of these needs to be believed in for an individual to engage in change. We must also, and can, think individually, locally, and with and for those we do not know or are familiar with. These different levels inform and reinforce each other, and to think only on one level, or even two, is self-defeating. It is, indeed, like the child or adolescent who has no or little awareness of the larger and greater world around them and how it impacts what they do and how they impact it. We now understand that so much of what we experience has a global perspective. This is the next stage of how we must view change. The need for such a global perspective is one of the themes of this book, and I believe one of the inescapable consequences of our experiential and intellectual development, individually and communally.

A Global Perspective

We traditionally identify with what is familiar and reject what is unfamiliar. This is a survivalist technique. We are now gaining far more knowledge of people we have never met and will never meet. We are developing a wider empathy and wider perspective. Many of our challenges are multi-layered in how they affect different people according to circumstances and place. That therefore must apply to any effective solutions too – multi-layered and connected. This is an encouragement to think globally.

The global dialogue is also about the bandwidth available to meet those challenges, fundamentally based on the idea that several heads are better than one in finding workable solutions. The most appropriate solutions for globally interconnected challenges need to benefit all of those effected i.e., be on a globally beneficial scale. That includes the 'buy-in' to solutions to make them effective. All of that is daunting but does not mean that individual actions do not count. To repeat the point, we need to think on an individual/family, and local scale as well as on a multinational level. As in any sports team we need to be 'a team of leaders,' which means as many people as possible accepting responsibility for what they can do. Leaders are also educators and communicators.

There are various subject-specific global surveys and polls, and a few global-oriented more general ones, and these are increasing in number. In time these will proliferate, from different sources, including, importantly, different nations, but with consistent, explained, and rigorous methodology. They will be able to reach representative groups, minorities, and the 'silent majority' in nations. They will gain in importance and use for opinion formers, followers, and policymakers, and enhance a global dialogue between nations and peoples. They have shown already, for example, that most people across international frontiers do not believe in radical solutions, and that perceived identity often divides people more than policy.

How We Measure Ourselves: The Economy into Government

Economically and governmentally are two of the most direct ways that many people feel the world is not working for them or helping them. In the 'developed' world many 'middle income' people have seen their standard of living stagnate for a generation. Lower-income groups see an increasingly fragile chance of 'social mobility' through education and the professionalisation of qualifications. Both interpret what they see as the rich getting richer, being more socially and economically separated, and therefore more resilient to potentially negative change. Widening inequality is seen to be one of the most troubling aspects of economies across the developed world. It is seen to be exacerbated by decaying public services and lowering safety nets to help when things go wrong. Another factor shining a light on these inequalities is an increased recognition of discriminatory factors. Add to that the increasing generational gap of opportunity, and the growing importance of inherited wealth. Part of this interpretation is to do with the expectation that there will always be economic progress and growth, and this has become a fixed cultural norm, and that if it does not happen then things have 'gone wrong.' Now, in developed nations, democratic participation is seen as not bringing the benefits that it should. Government and economic management are currently perceived as unresponsive. The economic and political models that the developed world has relied on for generations now seem to need significant change, or replacement. This is despite the fact that many more people compared to previous generations are 'doing OK,' and we should not lose sight of that. Education, health, and personal safety, while always subject to short-term ups and downs, are at historic highs.

In the less or later developing world the challenges are being felt at least, if not more, acutely. The multi-generational nature of social, educational, health, living infrastructure, work, and personal and public safety improvements, are often not yet embedded. Legal structures, regulatory frameworks for business, the sustainable tax base to afford public services, and media freedoms, remain fragile in these nations. This has meant that civic society is fragile. This in turn means that democracy is fragile, and sometimes not established. Power may be in the hands of the few. Authoritarian regimes have become economic, elitist, surveillance states not ideological ones – and the economic and political models they employ are not working for most people under them. Even China, having taken hundreds of millions out of poverty, is now at that crossroads.

Inequality itself is obviously not new. The modern problem is this sense of widening and not-before-recognised or acknowledged inequality. Let us also be clear, again, that over recent decades, a miniscule amount of time in the modern human condition, hundreds of millions of people globally have been lifted out of deep poverty despite a rising population. Let us be clear that the Malthusian idea that rising wealth or comfort would lead to a rising population and a cyclical return to poverty has not been proved. The competitive economic model we have developed in the West and now exported globally has encouraged creativity and entrepreneurship to take advantage of its benefits, and many people have found both material benefit and self-fulfilment in what they have been able to achieve. We cannot know if a less competitive model would have also allowed creativity to flourish.

CONCLUSION

However, we must now face up to its profound consequences. In direct broadbrush terms: a fight and grab for resources that produced slavery, colonialism, worldwide war; a culture of progress measured by and dependent on competitive nations; a planet being physically affected by a depletion of its resources; and a resulting subversion of a European Enlightenment about individual freedoms. Seen daily: an entrenched superior attitude through direct and less direct racism that is taking generations to reverse and ignores older traditional philosophies; entrenched inequality; climate change and a potential new age of extinction of non-human species; a particular Western view of education, science, and permanent progress that does not promote wellbeing and philosophy but promotes measurable 'value'; a rebalancing of the older individual/community balance of power, with corroding relationships; a short-termism of thought and perspective; and declining power of religion and religious community. This also means separated elites, and democratic disengagement, with still active discriminations; mental anxiety; loss of a sense of beneficial self-interest; consumer-driven exploitation of resources including people; increased extreme weather events that threaten to destabilise whole governments and regions; and potential generational fracture. These can be seen locally, nationally, and globally, across cultures and nations and types of government. Specific policies, or human actions, range from manufacturing goods with an artificially short shelf life; self-reinforcing social media algorithms; competitive tendering for government contracts (corruptly or not); the preference for paying off 'third world debt' over a preference for good governance; particular generation-focussed policies; a decline in business regulation and worker rights; international agreements with insufficient enforcement; and a lack of co-ordinated response to clear international rule-breaking. The consequences of our economic model built up from even before the industrial revolution, but certainly exacerbated by it on a global scale, go to the core of many of the world's problems, including but not limited to its politics and leadership.

Not absolutely everything can be laid at its door. Again, it is worth repeating that millions have been taken out of absolute poverty in a very short time. Our scientific and communications revolutions, partly a result of this freedom, mean that we know so much more about the immediate landscape and life around us and about people far away that we have never met, and about our own planet in the solar system. We are far more aware of how we think and feel and treat others, and arguably it is the Enlightenment's emphasis on reason and freedoms that have led to the historic and monumental tasks of eliminating gender and racial and other discriminations. We cannot go back to what there was before, some mythical golden age. That would not only be delusional and completely unrealistic but would negate and diminish the enormous benefits our developments have brought. We have had centuries of elitism, famine, early death, exploitation, war, fragile survival, powerlessness over our individual lives, and an inability to give our own creativity and problem-solving a meaningful voice.

Nevertheless, we need to move on. Our economic model has lost its soul, and its character has therefore been subverted. We must re-find its mission. We must do so optimistically and strategise how co-operation can lead to more progress than conflict. We need to confirm a global dialogue that would include a New Enlightenment of genuine individual freedoms and liberties, and yet remember that this is still only a vehicle for addressing the local, national, and international issues that we face. This may sound philosophical, but it is applicable to, and indeed should be at the core of, an economic system that moves on from the competitive-driven and resource-driven one that we have now. The change is both historic and can be done at the flick of a switch. It is an attitude as well as a policy. Specific solutions need the time for development, agreement, and implementation, but once the attitudinal corner has been turned there will be a momentum that increases. We will learn how to think with that philosophy. In fact, many of the solutions are common sense and are already happening or tried in individual places, and ad hoc ways, and can provide our initial momentum, and confidence: the Norwegian prison system, Chicago's library lending policy, Wikipedia's democratic and free knowledge, UBI trials, worker representation in company boardrooms, 'blind' appointment systems, co-operative and open-source research and entrepreneurship, etc. Nor must the consideration of change be subject to ideas of perfection. A changed attitude and a changed economic direction would not be a utopia of perfectionism, nor remotely easy, but it would be an irresistible hope to individuals all around the world.

The Future of Democracy and Non-Democracy

Those that see human history and progress as being defined by struggle and conflict aim to win or balance interests, and may accept compromise or alliance only in self-interest, not purposely for the common good. Decisions are transactional and based on power, even if making their choices for their own group may be a justification that one can have sympathy with. The global dialogue that we see and must encourage is characterised by this view as a weak or unrealistic response to the challenges we all face, and too often presented as threatening to domestic self-interest. Social and 'rights' movements may not be well supported by democratic governments but they are fundamentally at odds with authoritarian ones. Such regimes are limited in how they can change, who can rise to leadership or influence, who controls the interests of the state, and how they can allow people to think creatively or independently. They are limited whether they are purely self-interest, individually based, or ideologically certain of their own approach. None of the freedoms and liberties that inform individual morality and action, creativity, and entrepreneurship, can be entertained in an authoritarian state. Ethics are not organic and consensual but fixed until a ruler changes and everyone changes to follow, whatever their belief. The most likely authoritarian regimes to survive will be those that are technocratic, that allow limited change as a 'safety valve,' and that control expectations and knowledge of alternatives from the past or present or possible in the future.

Yet even this requires such a complete sense of control that democrats must, while having strategies to oppose, be ultimately confident that individual freedom will find a way, brick by brick, to put holes in the walls of such regimes. One of those strategies should be constructive critical engagement, even if that seems like talking to a wall, or to a sloth moving at one mile per hour, or even at a barking enemy. The crossroads that China faces is indicative of confronting this choice between a technocratic, surveillance, repressive, perhaps economically working, but intellectually, emotionally, and psychologically hollowed-out state, or a more creative and fulfilling one.

Non-authoritarian regimes must have the courage and consistency of their convictions, and look for what they can do – without ignoring the dangers and always being prepared to defend their core principles. Kang Kyung-wha, then Foreign Minister of South Korea – a country with an unpredictable authoritarian state on its own border – said during Covid-19 that the way through the dilemma of individual freedom of choice or government-imposed action was not less democracy but more, not repressive withdrawal of rights but more accountability and transparency. This is how the democratic leaning nations of the world must act in facing both the domestic and international dimensions of their challenges.

Democracies, and people within them, need a longer-term perspective on the issues they face. This is key in facing up to authoritarian regimes that may last decades. To achieve this, democracies need more openness and honesty, more participation of a wider population, and the establishment of more consensus. This leads to more understanding of issues and the democratic process, and more tolerance. It is these that promote trust in, and the resilience of, that democracy. It is these that promote a greater perspective and effectiveness. Those that oppose the system itself must be opposed, however that is consensually agreed. There is a premium on engaging the electorate, not sections of it, nor engaging it sometimes. The essence of democracy is participation, and the greatest threat to it is therefore non-participation, and in many Western nations where electoral turnout is less than 70%, allied to a sense of powerlessness in other areas of people's lives, this is a real threat. Where democrats do not engage others will – conspiracy theorists, dystopians, selfish leaders, any group of lobbyists or 'activists' with the confidence that they are right or must be heard, that have their own sectional interests, and learn how to identify and work the levers of power. In such a scenario democracy is in real danger even if it has the trappings of regular elections with a vociferous media, and even an independent judiciary. The façade of these things can indeed cover up a corrupt and corrupting democracy. Many Western democracies may be in this state.

CONCLUSION

The historic campaigns for gender and racial equality, justice, and respect, need to be heard among politicians and political parties as much as, or maybe more than, in other walks of life. If they are not, then changes in rights will always be because they become strategies used by others. This is not about culture wars and raising others as 'more than' or requiring special powers for a group. It is going back to the original idea of identity politics, indeed of democracy itself, – making people, whoever they are, more visible and more equal. Such campaigns will ultimately succeed not when specific genders or races are represented in proportion but when the principle of looking at people as individuals through their talent and character and individual need is applied to everyone. The art and structures of democracy have been neglected and need renewal, and the inequalities of society cannot be changed with a firm foundation unless this happens. There are ways, from citizens' assemblies, proportional representation, citizenship education in schools, and varied independent regulated media. There will be no single template for different nations. Politicians and their parties must not be in denial, must have the willpower to make changes, be prepared to listen to people's ideas about how to do so, and compromise, agree, explain, and persuade. Democracy on such a footing can be different in different places, can be local and national, and will always outperform and outlast an authoritarian state.

The Equality of Women

Women have not been written about in a separate section anywhere in this book. It is accepted that they are a part of this entire body of work. It is recognised almost everywhere around the world that women are 'equal' to men – but is not yet true in practice, on which part there is still much to do. Gender equality remains an historic task. Whether women and men are the 'same' or 'different' is room for some people to still think of unequal approaches, unequal characteristics, and unequal treatment. We need to get beyond this whether we solve it or not. The rights revolutions that began in modern terms in the 1950s have had side editions of ideas about positive discrimination and identity politics, but their end point remains to treat people as individuals worthy of equal respect and consideration. No-one is the same, but everyone can and should be treated fairly. The New Enlightenment is about individual liberties and freedoms. Whether women make different leaders, or are more 'natural' raisers of children, etc is irrelevant. Their talents and characteristics will be on a spectrum, the same as that of men. Like men, women will adapt to the culture – the nurture of society – and learn what works for them and how to succeed. An outlook of gender neutrality can change that culture for both men and women, and allow people to be themselves. That is what we should be aiming for. That neutrality is true to the original aims of the rights revolutions. It is also an answer to a perceived search for a new male role. Allegedly, masculinity is in crisis. The reality is that many males around the world are making a genuine attempt to change their behaviour compared to their grandfathers or fathers, and this is helping to put dominating masculinity into decline, not masculinity or maleness itself. Men themselves need to be nurtured – in a non-patronising way! – to be supporters of gender equality and gender neutrality. In many places men are helping to change the dynamic. Equality needs to have a buy-in contribution from men, as well as there be confidence-building, success, and leadership, from women. There is still a long way to go but there are many reasons for hope. New Enlightenment men do realise that exercising power is no longer a preserve only of males or dominating masculinity.

We are searching and aiming for a permanent change in values towards greater co-operation for effectiveness based on equal respect and fair opportunity between two parts of the same species. Victories for women should not be celebrated as defeats for men (and they usually aren't). They are victories for women. We know that an indigenous culture that loses its sense of identity and purpose falls into crisis, and the parallel to maleness is not the same but the psychology may be. We need to get past male or female roles. This is what needs to be informing our thinking. This is a gender-neutral outlook. It does not negate the continuing establishment of female role models that are still needed in many areas and situations. I am also confident that the ultimate unnecessary use of men, as opposed to sperm, to produce babies will remain a niche market. Emotional connection goes to the core of us as humans. Real relationships must still count. One parent *is* better than two *if* the two are a toxic mix for themselves or for the child, as role models and teachers, but two well-adjusted, different but co-operative, parents are better; and the same principle applies in same-sex parenting.

Three elements of modern life give cause for optimism about the equality of women: in many places around the world girls' and women's educational performance now matches or surpasses that of men; the knowledge-economy industries are surpassing the manual power industries; and there are more women legislators around the world. At the same time, it remains true that there is still a long way to go on more than one track – girls institutionally deprived of education because of politics or poverty, preference for male births, disproportionate lack of personal safety for girls and women across the world, lack of financial independence, less women in IT, science, and engineering, and unequal pay or promotional prospects, etc. There remains much to do, and our aims and perseverance must remain clear.

How We Measure Ourselves: Philosophically, Psychologically, Emotionally

There will always be individuals with a clear and satisfying approach to life, but philosophically, psychologically, and emotionally there are also many people and many communities that are not in a good place. Not all people or communities are the same across the globe. There are different levels of anxiety and lack of fulfilment, and different balances of causes, just as different places and individuals are at different levels of 'progress,' or comfort in their economic lives, and believe in different things. One aspect of this is whether resources can or will be shared in a beneficial way, with a finite amount of money. Yet at the same time as this competition and comparison, we think, even contradictorily, that we can always produce more. This anxiety drives competition between nations and between people. This consumes not just resources but ourselves. Our energy is spent on working ever harder to be able to afford more, to be able to compete with others or against a 'measure' of success, in employment, or for status or greater comfort. This is an anxiety that on one level is natural, for we all seek a level of comfort in our lives that makes things easier, and we all make judgements. Twentieth-century

WHERE ARE WE GOING?

French philosopher Michael Foucault has written that humans divide and label themselves and can become the self-fulfilling objects of their own perceived limitations through their labels.

It is inescapably true that nothing material is unlimited. There are very few, if any, nations that see themselves as developed that have not in some way become colonialist, either externally like the great empires of Britain and France, or internally where they have grabbed land and resources from indigenous communities. Nations measure themselves against each other in material terms far more than they do in the health, education, peacefulness, and contentment of their people. Many people remain allied to a religious purpose and community – remember, more people profess faith than do not – and people individually may well place their family above all else, but the context in which even these people live is the materialist and competitive model. Materialism has also exacerbated the movement towards individualism, often in a discordant tune with civic or established society. This is a phenomenon that has expanded to cover the globe. Of course, in many places by no means everyone has the material comfort that makes their life safe, or can plan a reasonable future. People still suffer from parasites in water, are unable to get a simple cataract operation to restore sight, live in makeshift housing subject to landslide or eviction, cannot send children to school or a doctor, etc. It is still true that these people need 'more' and are having to compete for it. Nevertheless, across the globe the mindset of materialism as a mark of progress and 'development' are clear. The root causes of a mental anxiety sweeping the globe are, to a large extent, due to this materialism, with secondary impacts on relationships and physical health. This anxiety is seen directly in addiction, youth self-image issues, educational stress, partnership breakdown, the loneliness or isolation of older age, economic expectation, and a sense of political powerlessness that is seen across all age groups and all nations. We know medically that stress affects decision-making, reinforcing this anxiety and fragility. Philosophically, psychologically, and emotionally, so many individuals, societies, and we in general as 'humanity,' are putting ourselves under pressure.

CONCLUSION

The New Enlightenment

It is the individual liberty and freedoms of a New globalised Enlightenment which remain firmly on the march. Overall, this is no bad thing, for history is full of powerless groups and individuals, ignored or repressed, that have not been allowed to fulfil their talents, express their opinions, in general contribute to the communities they are in (or that they have been excluded from), and have not had enough influence over the direction of their own lives. As the new, or back-to-basics, Enlightenment has spread, colonialism is now judged a 'bad thing' and eugenics discredited, and the widening of participation in government and 'rights' campaigns that we experience now are mainstream struggles. Religion and government across the world are still having to accommodate this. That the 'original' European or Western Enlightenment was misused to promote division, superiority, and exploitation cannot be seriously argued against. That is why 'Western values' are still not seen as universal ones around the globe. The global nature of a new, truer, Enlightenment can win out over these obstacles, but there is so much more persuasion required and benefit to be shown if it is to do so, and it must face up to its misuses.

Its benefits must be universal in nature, applicable to all peoples and communities. It cannot fulfil its destiny without a more global dialogue. This requires its further maturing. Such a maturity of its individual freedoms and liberties means an acceptance of other views. It is a vehicle for progress not the determinant of what that specific progress should be. A true Enlightenment allows religion to flourish alongside science, allows more than one form of democratic process, a variety of individual and civic balance in communities, and more than one economic model. Its strength is its investment in education, and in providing the possibility for individuals to communicate and learn and decide for themselves. Its only non-negotiable is that any decisions people make they make freely. There is no room here for undemocratic nations.

There is also a danger of heightened individualism within this New Enlightenment approach. Communication, tolerance, and empathy are essential. We as individuals need to recognise that we cannot always get what we want, that there is a self-interest in self-sacrifice, that provision for others (of material goods or power) is also in our self-interest, that we are not always right – at the same time as always feeling that we are listened to and appreciated for the arguments we put forward. A New Enlightenment approach like this may be the only way to resurrect the power that many people feel they have lost or never had, and to maintain the identities that are part of their core meaningfulness of life, and their communal tradition that binds people together. This is part of a realistic democratic approach being effective. This demands the greatest historic development of the peoples of the planet. It requires us to be nicer to our neighbours, prepared to shoulder a fairer burden if we have more, to measure our nation's success in more than material wealth but also in wellbeing, to be less nationally competitive, and to look more widely across the globe for ideas and good practice. And it requires the 'winners' of life to recognise that this is good, and good for them. It requires us in these ways to address both economic and social discrimination and inequality, to broaden our ideas and acceptance of identity and community, and to reassess our outlook on the rest of the world, which includes dispatching national wars to the dustbin of history. And then we all live happily ever after... which of course is itself a dream.

The New Enlightenment does not solve everything. It does, however, remain a vehicle by which we can work through challenges. It requires its own muscular defence against the tyranny of majorities or minorities, against individual opportunistic leaders, and against those who do not buy into the essential core principles of individual choice and informed representation. It needs to always be aware of new elites, new arrogance, new inequalities, which in any real world are almost by definition permanent possibilities. Furthermore, we must not be afraid to show our confidence that it can work, and to shape our education of children and society in this form. We must ensure a freedom of opinion only with such basic prerequisites as not allowing the harm of others or the dismantling of the beliefs that we hold most dear. To offend is not the same as to harm, but to incite is beyond causing offence. Built into this education and this confidence will always remain the notion of the minority view to be respected, and of accountability, and through those, of review and continual reaffirmation or change. A part of that will always, in turn, be the ability to react to new circumstances and challenges. A part of it will also be the recognition that beyond the borders of core principles so many decisions are not black and white, are not easy to make, or have negative as well as positive consequences. This is the application, and responsibility, of individual freedom and liberty, within a communal context that we all live in.

Science and Technology: Its Range

Science and technology offer fantastic opportunities and pose very significant dangers. We have been on the cusp – perhaps since the Renaissance – of a great scientific, including digital, age. We do not yet understand or accept any limits to what these advances might be capable of. Each invention and discovery is accepted for its intended use and secondarily thought about for its dangers, or possible misuses, or unintended uses. We are just beginning to understand as a general populace that much of science needs interpretation, and that we sometimes skew our research to justify what we already think or expect to find out. The changing and reinterpretation of Covid-19 and its interpretable consequences across a range of other areas beyond the purely medical has been another lesson.

We often remain blinded by the excitement of scientific discovery. We are currently blinded by the scale and apparent inevitability of algorithms and ML in digital technology, something that is seen as 'better' than a human, sometimes discriminatory, judgement. There are many warning signs in this already, from algorithm-based news feeds that close off varied debate to facial and voice recognition based on subjective or misunderstood inputs. Science and technology, including digital, is a vast area and we have clearly benefitted in all sorts of ways, whether in medicine, in disaster modelling, in fraud prevention, in understanding how the brain works, and hopefully, increasingly in climate change mitigation, alternative materials, and strategy. There is often great discovery by accident or as a by-product of an intended outcome, and this open-ended science should not be denigrated.

However, wherever we can, we need more public knowledge

of possible consequences, limits, interpretation, and sometimes its irreversibility. We must also engage with the ideas that not all solutions are technological, and understand the deep web of new entangled dependencies that technology can bring. We are not yet in a truly scientific age because we do not yet have that public framework and regularity and understanding. There are some aspects of science that pose real dangers to the sort of people we are or may want to be. Biotechnology is beginning to thrive as we understand the workings of the body and the brain more than ever, and how we think and make decisions. This can move forward our positive decision-making as a species and as individuals enormously, helping us to understand leadership, discrimination, creativity, and how we learn, to name just four areas, but it is open to incredible potential misuse. Legal frameworks, nationally or internationally, do sometimes exist but in many areas do not. Science in many areas has become dependent on commercial exploitation, with commercial direction. Revolutionary communications technology, once seen as an unstoppable force for freedom, is now mired the world over in controversy over its transparency, ownership, data collection, regulation, and use for surveillance and control by authority. Good scientists remain ones that show their methods, are transparent in what they do, how they do it and their results, allow peer review, and accept accountability. What must be avoided is an international race to control science and technology, or to exploit it for military means that affect the nature of war itself, or to use it to control without consensus, governmentally or commercially, rather than as an understood public good. These are big issues, and they make science and technology, especially digital technology through AI and ML development, one of the great challenges of the modern era. We must ensure that science remains a tool for our use, not a creed to be followed, and that its use is bound within the human character and ambitions that we want to exemplify.

CONCLUSION

Changing Ourselves

Individualism and materialism are influencing the way we live, what we learn, how we teach our next generation, and how we relate to each other. They are influencing the relationships and individual character of people. They are determining the narratives we live by, and some of those narratives have become simplistic.

Can we design a safe, not naïve, cohesive society that expects the best of people rather than assumes the worst? In saying that we can free ourselves from our prejudices, from our fixed narratives of history, and enable a new era of co-operation and creativity, we must understand that we need to be willing to reassess ourselves. We still cannot decide if we are co-operative or conflictual, but we know enough to negate what we do not want and to amplify what we do. This includes understanding that we are social and political animals, and that we need to look inwards to improve ourselves to promote good relations with others. As citizens we need to be active participants and independent thinkers, and our thinking must apply at an individual, family, community, or national level, and an international or global one. We need to know how to interpret different media. We need to appreciate and know how to think about creative solutions from science or technology, or other new strategies and new leaders, understanding what is missed out, not said, unintended (where possible), or open to misuse or abuse. We can do this, but we must do so before it is too late, before we end ourselves through pandemic or nuclear disaster or AI or digital breakdown/overload/mismanagement, or self-imposed isolation, or before climate change consumes the life we want to lead. Or before we are irreversibly altered or controlled by these changes or the way that these changes are used by a controlling commercial interest, social elite, governmental authority, or technocracy.

At the core of this is a need to communicate with each other. The division of 'identity politics,' a newish and Western term that belies the fact that in some form we have always had identity politics, or the 'interests' that the founding fathers of the USA were so intent on avoiding 250 years ago, is a 'pull' of influence on many people. We need to make sure that we do not just listen or talk only to those that agree with us. We need to maintain or re-learn the art of compromise. That also means we need to maintain and renew the sense of sacrifice for others, and of seeing our self-interest in the benefits of others. The will and determination to counter inequality and discrimination, to make changes in lifestyle over climate change, to avoid the addictions and impulses of life, are within each of us but we cannot be effective alone. This may sound remarkably difficult, if not patronising or unreal if we are struggling to heat a home or educate our children or look after elderly parents, but there are times every day when we make decisions that we can make in better ways with better results. This includes at voting time, school choice, commercial transaction, or what we do in our job, by knowing more about how we and others think. There are times when we can listen better, engage others in or for our support, or simply reaffirm positive behaviour and relationships – and that includes a smile or a 'thank you' or a little more patience. We can decide for ourselves how we treat ourselves and other people, and the planet that we live on. Many people do make such good decisions every day. This is the key human characteristic that we must protect and maintain against all malign influences. The ability to make our own decisions is what makes us human, and those decisions can be positive, practical, and resilient, and still within the context of ambition to make the world better. A new opportunity and ability to incorporate a global perspective, within ourselves and outwardly, can help to solve the challenges of humanity that we now understand are global. We can be in control of our own morality, values, and character. This is the ultimate prize of a globally influenced New Enlightenment, the prize of its struggle for individual freedom and liberty. It demands a lot of us. It demands that we question some of our most fundamental narratives about why we do what we do. In the changes we decide are needed what we cannot do individually others may do, and the whole can be greater than the sum of its parts, but we should all have a part to play.

CONCLUSION

To Be More Specific...

There are certain issues that the fundamentals of democratic principles, greater economic fairness and sustainability, and individual freedoms, need to deliver on. These issues are seen in Western nations, across the globe, across cultures, political styles, levels of economic progress or wealth, and historical background.

Urban Living

We need to make sure that urbanisation is subject to, not determining, the lifestyle that we want. Urbanisation has been a trend for 2,000 years or more. It has historically provided freedom from feudal-type relationships or back-breaking subsistence, and therefore offered more chances for individualism and creativity to flourish. It provided a greater array of job prospects to use a greater variety of skills that suited a greater number of people, although they depended on farmers' output and trade, and still do. Cities raised people's standard of living, especially of those that had become the labourers not the landowners. Cities also produced a different sort of connected community. They still offer this, but they need to be 'managed.' Industry has changed them, and the modern city is characterised by density of population, less community, and authority management. They may have only changed the style, not prospect, of controlling people. Inequality may now not be improved by city life. It is just as easy to slip into anonymity and isolation. Physical access to education, health, and other services are now less relevant, though not completely. New work patterns and work and other technologies do not negate the benefits of a city life and are just as likely to reinvigorate it. We need to ask ourselves what purpose cities now serve, while also still remembering that money helps lifestyle whether in an urban or rural area.

Meeting places are still required, from a working, social, and even psychological point of view. One only needs to think of isolated new mothers craving adult conversation; the euphoria of a crowd or audience at an entertainment venue that cannot be replicated individually; and lack of body language in a Zoom call. Nor is it easy in any way to completely rebuild cities or build new ones, even with the prospect of sea level rise and other climate change consequences as an incentive. We can do more of that with a greater imagination, and at a financial cost, but the short- and mid-term future is adaptation and renewal. We are now giving design and planning a greater importance to focus on living: less pollution, more personal safety, fulfilling public and green spaces, adaptable and 'breathable' housing, integrated transport systems, sustainable community planning, more localised work as creative and service sectors become more important, and public art. This is not just a case of allowing more home delivery, 'greening' cities and digital updating. The differentiation between city and rural life is likely to become more blurred. Megacities will include large green and blue spaces, may include food production, and accept the generational changing of land use between residential, 'industrial,' public facility, and natural or free space. This does not preclude building higher or deeper. Nor does it preclude cities being built with more control of the population in mind, such as closable sections and a lack of meeting or shareable spaces – as opposed to management of facilities and services – and we must be wary of this too. All this must apply to the budding megacities of developing nations as well as the established ones of more developed nations. New design and planning, and engagement with communities, can ally with re-prioritised government to bring about this reimagining of our urban spaces. New cities will be rare, but our existing ones can work much better for us as our working lives and personal expectations of both standards of living and wellbeing change.

Religion

Religion is not a thing of the past, and has shown the capacity to change. There will also always be a variety of religion available. Religions can still be representative of specific peoples and continue an entwinement with national governments to maintain their identity and influence through their 'establishment.' However, with this comes the dangers of governments being in fashion or not, and religion more prone to that influence, and less adaptable. More likely is the increasing independence of religion and specific religion from government. Religion will also

CONCLUSION

have to face up to the communications revolution, increasing global dialogue, and predominance of individualism. These all lead to a more varied set of religious options, in ritual and belief, and therefore a less fixed religious experience for individuals is more likely. Finding renewed ways to appeal may be a return to 'basics,' not in the form of a distinctive fundamentalism that competes, but in the form of general principles that relate to a more diverse society that people will be living in with ever more distractions.

These general principles will revolve around a version of the 'golden rule' of 'do unto others as you would have done unto you.' Religious belief may become more of a mosaic of philosophies. We should probably be using the term 'belief system' more than religion. Such beliefs will also remain relevant because they can weave a narrative that explains new circumstances, the position or cycle of life and death, how humanity can seemingly display love and hate through free will with divine final judgement, project a vision for the purpose of life, and promote daily beneficial actions. Religion can give people a solace they cannot get from 'liberty' and science, and maintain a sense of community in an individualistic world. Experience – or 'purpose' – could be within a Buddhist style search for personal enlightenment, or in the form of traditional religion that offers authority, structure, discipline, ritual, and celebration, or even a Confucian emphasis on duty towards oneself and community. It may serve to foster a sense of identity and place among a minority group. It could, with independence and clarity of purpose, find new respect and a new role in forging a better balance between individualism and community. There can be pursued a new-found co-operation between religions that enhance their mainstream reputation, marginalise their more extreme fundamentalist elements, and could encompass a more fluid membership. 'Extremists,' 'fundamentalists,' or 'radicals' are always likely to remain in some form. Genuine Confucian principles may yet overcome Communist Party interpretation. These are ideas of belief that allow religion to embrace the fundamental Enlightenment ideas of individual liberty and free-thinking, i.e., the ability to make one's own choices – up to a point.

Anything we call a religion is and always will be by definition a club of members, even if with different levels of welcome for those that act as self-invited but uncommitted guests. The maintenance of the community will be maintained by a daily practical contribution to society in word and deed, as well as ritual. These must continue for a religion's relevance, its brand recognition, and its continual self-reaffirmation. Religious principles that have historically formed the basis of societies in most places will remain respected, with or without that label. Individual religions will change. Some of those changes will be a return, such as a return to the greater profile of a harmony with nature. Some will meet new challenges, such as gender choice, but perhaps most notably scientific discovery about the origins of life and its workings, and how humanity itself may be able to change or create life. If religions cannot meet these challenges with believable narratives that chime with people's real experiences and give them hope for the future, then some beliefs may fade away.

Science and Technology: Its Development

Science, i.e., study, and Technology, i.e., its application, is certainly a challenge and an opportunity, and an ever-increasing field and connection. If we are in a Scientific Age we are near the beginning because there is so much more obviously on the horizon. That Age would need to include a study of science itself not just an acceptance of its results. We should already have some healthy scepticism towards science as an explanation of everything.

Such is the impact of digital technologies now that we often use the term 'disruptive technology.' We are also making great strides in other areas of science where this term is generally not used, understanding how we think and act, in terms of individual and group psychology and behavioural 'science,' and neuroscience. There is a saying that new discoveries cannot be unlearnt. but what we can do is get better at their peer review, at working out the pros and cons of discoveries we make, at public explanation, and regulation. Not all unintended consequences are unforeseeable. In these ways we can make more certain than we are now that science remains a tool for use, rather than a director of what we do.

Ethics needs to have a higher profile in science, and be more public,

CONCLUSION

even if we accept that most scientists now are 'ethical' in their intentions. This is not easy. 'Social Darwinism,' for example, still plays a part in some people's thoughts in relation to race, welfare, psychology, and emotion, and eugenics itself is returning in debates about gene-editing. There is also a global dimension to this: techniques and communications are now available globally to a larger range of people with different backgrounds, values, motivations, and under varying amounts of regulation. This was seen in the completely surprising announcement by He Jiankui and two colleagues in China in November 2018 that they had gene-edited embryos in then-born babies to make them resistant from birth to HIV, cholera and smallpox. In a sign taken as genuine unease by the Chinese government about precedence and lack of oversight they were each sentenced to various terms of imprisonment. The variation of perspective can be great for scientific development and may make it more 'democratic,' more creative, and is likely to make it collectively more accurate. However, it is also easier to attain the knowledge and technology and remain hidden from regulation; and that will be just as true of a billionaire's pipe dream as the creative genius of a poor boy or girl from the Brazilian favella, neither of whose character and motivations are known. The overwhelmingly negative reaction to He's embryo-changing work was encouraging, but there will be others in the future. Arguably Oppenheimer's nuclear bomb was an earlier such 'mistake' – which exemplifies the need for, and difficulty of, regulation, of both individual ethics and national motivation, especially in time of conflict – remembering that research was happening on both sides. Nevertheless, overall science has undoubtedly been a boon to humanity's progress, and it is accepted that it is better to know more about the world around us and ourselves, and how these things work, than it is simply to accept many things as they are. Science and technology can contribute to solving many of our problems.

Specific science and technologies are cause for concern. Around the world people will be putting effort into developing biotechnology – in closed, open, academic, and military contexts. The potential for biotechnology for disease prevention and surgery is enormous. Yet so too is its potential through such as gene-editing and stem cell use to make irreversible changes in the human body through succeeding generations. The varied consequences may range from attitudinal changes to disability, changes to demographic development, and constant biomonitoring of individuals. These may be some peoples' greatest fears, but others will consider them opportunities. It has taken 150 years so far for electricity to move from its first household to be available to almost everyone on the planet. Such a multi-generational time span for the spread of enhanced humanity through pills and procedures that enhance intellectual development, gene-editing to prevent hereditary disease, or augmentations to strengthen the human anatomy, gives worrying scope for the development of superior attitudes of one human towards another, the heightened physical prowess of one human compared to another, and their actual life expectancy. With superior attitudes also come the inferior attitudes of others, powerlessness, and decline. This is a recipe for a two-tier humanity, an augmented or half artificial humanity, and even a controllable humanity. It could yet happen, and reach a tipping point, without most of us realising, within the lifetime of people born already. There will be similar concerns soon about bioscience/biotechnology as are now being expressed about AI: accessibility, affordability, technical knowledge, accountability, speed of change, and control. However, it is the idea or variation of people's motivations, and their accidental or deliberate lack of transparency that should concern us most. Yuval Noah Harari writes about a 'hacked' humanity whereby the character of humanity changes, and where individual humans and humanity collectively are not in real control of their decision-making.

Just as capable of taking decisions away from humanity may be the disruptive digital technologies of Machine Learning (ML) Artificial Intelligence. As it deals with more 'big data' at greater speed, there will come a time when the human brain cannot understand the complexities of how ML recommendations or actions are made. At which point the human has a choice of faith – faith in what it has built and in its inputted boundaries and principles, or suddenly a lack of faith in what it has done. How to hold AI and ML accountable and accessible when you can't understand what it is doing is a pivotal moment that humans will have to address. The calls to pause AI development in 2023 are as concerning as Oppenheimer's reflections and regrets. Then there is the next stage: moving from being given the task of suggesting solutions to being enabled to make them through access to other systems is the definition of humans sharing decision-making power. Humans must understand and control the inputted data, and make sure that we have moved beyond our deliberate or unintentional discriminations. Then, there is the idea of how AI can learn perspective when it may clash with logic. Humans are inherently contradictory, and that is part of their experiential learning and character. Eventually, who is to say that an AI given the power of decision-making, including self-replicability, is not sufficiently different as to be a new life-form. Ethics specialists cannot afford to be separate from the creators, manufacturers, or policymakers, especially in a profit- or ideologically driven sphere. And ethicists' power must come from the informed consensus of the societies they are in. Nor can one nation afford to be naïve about the intentions of another. Trying to have a co-operative disposition or default must not mean naivete. We will all need to be ethically literate in a scientific age, and this must be on a global scale.

International Relations

A global dialogue can take place without formal international co-operation. It can take place as long as there is communication – formal, informal, frowned upon, illegal, individual, business or group focussed, or governmental. At its most basic influential core it is seeing and hearing other people doing or saying something different, and this will be extraordinarily difficult to stop, from migration to international styles of music and fashion. The social aspects of a global dialogue are powerful and reach deeper than the intended political or governmental ones. International relations form only a part of the global dialogue as written about on these pages. Nor do international relations necessarily bear a direct relation to what happens domestically, especially when, with new technologies, governments can effectively give entirely different messages to domestic and international audiences.

China has not become more democratic and open with more trade, and has become more nationalistic, domestically controlled, and less diverse. Yet it has not only traded, but takes part, to varying degrees, in a whole host of international agreements. We do not yet understand how it will develop its international relations, beyond its wish for unification, when it has a stronger position economically and militarily. However, that may also be a fleeting moment as India and the continent of Africa rise in power and profile, China's population begins to fall, and more is demanded of it as a responsible and powerful contributor to solutions of global problems. It may yet become more isolated, temporarily, after unification, especially if that is by force. It may lead a bloc of nations that reject New Enlightenment ideas of individual freedoms and liberties in favour of state-directed societies. It may capitalise on a lack of colonial baggage in relation to other nations, until its own ambitions are seen as colonial. That starting point will have undoubtedly helped it to mediate between Iran and Saudi Arabia in 2023 to trigger the beginning of a surprise rapprochement between those two nations – an enticing possibility of a world with a choice of mediators for different situations.

Democratic nations – increasingly domestically diverse – do need to engage with others. If the world separates out into blocs that have clearly different values it becomes too easy to blame 'the other side' for everything. This is a lose-lose scenario domestically and internationally for democratic nations, as well as in the long term for others too. There is also the possibility of non-national groups disrupting nations domestically and internationally, and themselves working together or with disruptive national leaderships. Such disruption could have every chance of becoming an entrenched element in international relations. Democratic nations need confidence and robust defence of their values but must learn from the past. At the end of the Cold War Western liberal competitive capitalism claimed victory and moved on, sweeping aside not just the politics of communism but the governmental and social structures that held people together and whole swathes of education, training, and health sectors, allowing a 'Wild West' of economic power grabbing and a demoralising national pride feeling betrayed. Years later the elimination of Saddam Hussein's regime in Iraq and Libya's Colonel Gaddafi had no effective post-regime planning. The benefits were huge, but the downsides huge too. Individual nations, and international groupings from the UN to regional economic blocs and military alliances, must learn to be more pro-active, clearer, decisive, and consensus based, in the addressing of conflict and its consequences.

From climate change to organised crime and much else there needs to be co-operation. The key areas of improvement for international bodies are threefold: dealing with and supporting failed states, effectively isolating states that are illegitimately aggressive to others, and continually improving the standard of governance to allow domestic development. International frameworks need strengthening, arbitration, and enforcement developing. The biggest stumbling block is the notion of interference in a failing state. The West needs to recognise its past mistakes and be realistic about how they have shaped opinions of them held by others. Such past injustices may need to be challenged, but they also cannot afford to drive the dialogue that those previously victim nations engage in, and they too must act on their principles rather than their history. Most authoritarian regimes will not contribute leadership to solve the problem of failing states. They may spy an opportunity for new influence, and would not risk accepting the principle of intervention – there by the grace of God they may also fall some day in a process started by their own domestic protests and dissidence.

There will not be a 'world government' in people's current lifetimes nor probably their children's, but we should be in a period of self-interest where international agreement on a range of issues is of benefit to almost everyone. As Africa's varied nations and India become more powerful there may become more room outside the traditional power blocs to forge an independent 'swing vote' voice on international issues. There is already much more room for the United Nations and its General Assembly to voice a more powerful and independent role in world affairs. Greater independent confidence from the GA nations, rebalancing UN contributions of all types, and a willingness of veto-wielding major nations to give up some power will be tremendously hard to achieve, but room must be found to move away from structure and workings that were set out in 1945 when most of the world was ruled by a small number of imperial nations, one and then two opposing nuclear powers emerged, and much of the world had the scars of battle and death. There can then emerge a more independent UN and international agreements with arbitration and enforcement; and if not, a clearer idea of who is blocking progress towards this, and why, which itself would forge new positive alliances. A New Enlightenment attitude from the West means a recognition that they cannot control the global dialogue, only influence it, and that the solutions that arise will not only be theirs and will be stronger for that. Then we can achieve a tipping point of effective global consensus, and can begin to pre-empt crises rather than act afterwards. This is almost utopian, but if we believe in a co-operative world, that the self-interests within a group can produce agreement and trust through accountability, that this can then breed further trust and agreement, then we must show the courage of our convictions. If we are less optimistic about utopian motivation we must ask how self-interest can be used better to solve increasingly global problems. The alternative is a dereliction of our duty to solving the challenges we face, and preventing new ones, whether we live internationally or in unfeasible isolation.

Future Government

The purpose of the state needs a reaffirming review: to protect and support all its citizens, with responsibility for all those that reside within its borders. To protect, most directly, means internal personal safety, and protection from external threat. In some form a nation must always be prepared to call upon an army to defend it, and the more successful we are at co-operation then the harder it becomes to justify that emotionally or financially, but not to have the ability to defend oneself is a dereliction of duty. In this context it might equally be argued that most states' apparent failure to adequately protect the personal safety of women is a similarly fundamental dereliction of duty. To protect means much more than that though. More attention needs to be paid to the quality of people's lives and the idea of 'gain' rather than material-driven growth. Protection also means support. The young, the old, and disabled people, and the most vulnerable socially, politically, and economically, all have the right to expect a level of protection that allows them to live a life of some fulfilment and quality and safety. The wayward, the free thinkers, and the whistleblowers also need society's protections. If we believe in individual liberty we must protect the practice of it and protect those

CONCLUSION

that do not cope with its mixture of rights and responsibilities, and that seek to hold it accountable. Reasonable equality must also be able to live with creativity and entrepreneurship, for the wealth creators need encouragement too. The limit is drawn at those that seek to overthrow the fundamental tenets of the social contract: that there needs to be a government based on the consensus of the people that can be held accountable.

The world also faces the connected and unprecedented issue of climate change. This itself requires major economic, behavioural, and philosophical changes. We need a new stewardship between people and planet, probably one that considers a new attitude towards non-human life and certainly one that embeds sustainability over exploitation. Then there is the apparently 'permanent' revolution of scientific and technological development.

All these add up to much more than a generational turning point. Each of them individually can permanently change the way we live. Some of them in the extreme can change the nature of humanity itself. Each of them can do that globally. The extent and depth of the challenges we face make this a turning point of several generations.

Within any contract – enabled by fixed constitution or custom – rights and responsibilities need to be understood and accepted by both citizens and government. Political systems need elections, term limits, public politics, clarity in the development of laws to be passed, etc. Nor does co-operation, whether through genuine solidarity or in self-interest, rule out competition, which is not the same as conflict. The dividing line between individual and community may need arbitration, and sometimes even preference towards one side at a particular time. That would be a balance achieved by independent judiciary and by the accountability of government. Both must consistently and robustly defend the freedoms of the individual: to think, speak, and act how they wish if that does not cause harm to others. The definition of harm is decided by the expression of the people in a civically strong society. Society must also be allowed to change its mind, just as government must be allowed to defend the more vulnerable. This is neither a government diktat nor a tyranny of the majority, nor a tyranny of a protected minority, whether by cultural, religious, social, or political group. Furthermore, the government has a responsibility to promote both an evidentiary and a public debate approach to its actions, not act subjectively. Any good government will acknowledge that its subsequently informed actions will be more effective and command more support. This is not technocratic government. There is a role for persuasion and opposition, and the humility of admitting mistakes, and decision-makers themselves cannot be expected to live in or come from a value-free vacuum. Accountability is the key to disagreement, the key to making 'party politics' work. Accountability comes through attitudes and structures. Leadership that lacks humility or shame, or hides personal motives, can be constrained by structures; and those structures can themselves create a virtuous cycle of action and attitude. Sustained and successful assault on those structures calls into question the successful development of the attitudes within a society that have been nurtured to protect it. Those that believe in any form of democratic government must make an active attempt to create the conditions for it to thrive, and to be prepared, as J.S. Mill wrote, to reaffirm even basic and accepted principles in debate.

An independent judiciary is an essential, one with neither fear of nor favour towards authority, one that is transparent and informed, one that either through structure or its participants, or both, is aware of the public and minority views of society when its interpretation is needed. This is not a Law that may arbitrarily overturn the laws of an elected government, but one that can uphold fixed constitutional law, interpret it for changing circumstances, support consistency of both law and interpretation, and therefore of government action, and prevent over-reach of that power. It follows that for such a judiciary to be accepted, and supported by and supportive of, a civil and criminal justice system, it must be understood by its potential participants, the public.

Future Citizen

Education stands with Law as a fundamental responsibility of a government to promote, and of a citizen to partake in. Education of the young in any society is investing in its future, and liberal societies should not shy away from that. What makes us a liberal society are the

CONCLUSION

opportunities that we are prepared to build into education so that it is inclusive and effective. In a world of rapidly developing knowledge that section of education concerned with rights and responsibilities, with law, ethics, understanding government, and accountability, how we think, and how to debate, is just as important as the knowledge of health, personal safety, understanding data, privacy, and relationships, maturity, and one's own character. And each of these are just as important as the development of specific 'subject based' skills, knowledge, and understanding. Good education systems do all these things, but we have reached a point where the first two sections of this education should be as officially important as the third.

Adult 'education' comes in four forms: job-specific training, education for interest and leisure, contemporary news delivered largely through the media, and the work of non-governmental organisations (NGOs) on more specific issues. The latter two are essential prerequisites for citizens to hold authority to account. We must take far more care than we do at present that we understand objectivity and subjectivity, and have access to free and fair media, and a variety of media. It is a citizen's responsibility to do their best to achieve these understandings and take advantage of such access. There has always been censorship and propaganda, but its elusive forms still make it hard to counter as a citizen. It is therefore a governmental responsibility to ensure that media sources and ownership promote good practice, and work within the values of society; and to minimise its own 'spin.' Our current social media can still be 'tamed' by public education and effective governmental regulation. Governmental regulation is clearly needed in a host of other areas too: only governments can enable copyright to be accessible and enforceable for new entrepreneurs to succeed, pass protective whistleblower legislation, work against organised corruption, and regulate business, private organisations, and public NGOs to make sure that they are accountable and follow the law of the land.

To believe that the authority of regulation is not needed is a belief in the law of the jungle or an idealistic delusion that everyone can always look after themselves, or that if they cannot then under some social Darwinism principle they should be allowed to die away. Even the completely isolationist person needs something to build their shelter from and the place and the right to be undisturbed and to find or grow their own food – they need rules to exist about land ownership and access, the right to privacy, and the right to defend themselves – unless their sole right is through the barrel of gun, which only works until someone brings a bigger gun. It is not just that a completely libertarian life is not beneficial to them; it is that it does not and cannot work. As liberal writer Rawls argued, in terms of a moral argument against inequality, we must still agree to share one another's common fate.

All of this can only work in a democratic-style society. All of this needs an active citizen. An individual citizen cannot be expected to do everything, but a community can be greater than the sum of its parts, provide encouragement and support within it, can educate and debate itself, and its members take turns in the participation and regulation of itself and its government. The trend of revolutions since 1789 have been largely social and economic and against governments not following Enlightenment principles. Nationalism has not hindered these and probably helped them, for nationalism beyond the short term has been about self-determination to improve more lives not just changing controlling groups. Communist revolutions and independence movements extended these globally. The advancement of this improving-lives agenda has been relentless. The world can remain a mosaic of different philosophies under these guiding principles.

Individual morality will always develop because it comes from the lived experiences of people. From that morality comes a sense of one's values, one's self, one's character, and one's creativity. These are human characteristics. Inevitable change through time or circumstances beyond an authoritarian's control – individually in such as age, or collectively through such as natural disaster - will always be a threat to that rule, because at those times people will need to do something different This is why modern authoritarian regimes crave isolation or contact only under their rules, and seek to change not just the actions of their population but their thoughts and ambitions, and perhaps even re-mould the memories of their experiences. This is why understanding how we think may be the greatest progress that humanity can make, and in its manipulation the greatest danger it may face.

Generally, Eastern values that should lead to more harmonic

inter-dependence, responsiveness to others, and sensitivity to context, have led, or been steered, towards deference, duty, belonging, and less individual expression. These, in a global philosophy, need to readdress the idea that an individual needs to understand themselves to be harmonious, and to understand the individual rights which follow from that. However, a Western universalist individualism with independence and primary responsibility for oneself, may be said to have developed materialism, competition, and less community sense of belonging and security. It needs to readdress the need for communal living. Reason and Science may need to pay more attention to the possible impossibilities of complete objectivity and of comprehensive 'truth.'

Logic tells us that human actions have changed humanity and the way we live, and therefore can do so again. To think that we cannot or should not even fight for improvement is a pessimism that legitimises bad behaviour and negates learning from mistakes, and needs to be rejected, even if only for our own personal development. Surely both nurture and nature contribute to the human condition. As a result, there is developing, globally, a further 'right and responsibility' of individuals and governments: the furtherance of wellbeing and fulfilment. This is the reward of progress and relative peace. In Pinker's terms, the 'better angels of our nature' have been given a greater chance to show themselves, and they can be self-reinforcing. They will need to be defended robustly. The difference now is that a balance of humanity can experience this relative peace and relative wealth, and yet still have a recent collective memory of the alternative that recognises danger signals and prevents complacency.

This is globalisation, New Enlightenment, and progress, in action. It is far more than economic money-making and the travel of people, lifestyle, or fashion. We may soon be in a position, perhaps by the end of this century, when the price of nation-v-nation war is irredeemably too high. This is not inevitable, just as the character of people can be bitten by various vices, so can nations, and so nations and the people in them will continue to make mistakes. 'Interests' will rise and fall. Humans will still struggle in and for the expression of their virtues, but as the balance of power shifts towards 'the people,' people the world over can choose co-operation rather than conflict. Success will depend on the character of individuals, of you and me. Yet there is urgency too. Time is our most precious resource, and we need to use it wisely. We must recognise that right now we have a unique opportunity to determine our own future. Our choices may bring us significantly closer to the knowledge and opportunity to live the 'considered life' that Socrates called for, or the reflective and contemplative enlightenment of Buddha, or indeed pursue the reciprocal free and fair duty to themselves, their families, and their communities, of Confucius, with a modern equality thrown in.

Bibliography

Appiah, Kwame Anthony. The Lies that Bind: Rethinking Identity. Profile Books Ltd., 2018.

Aurelius, Marcus. Meditations. Second Century CE. Penguin Books, 2004.

Bellaigue, Christopher de. "The Islamic Enlightenment," DU Center for Middle East Studies. YouTube, 5 Jun 2017.

Bhambra, Gurminder K. "Edward Said On Orientalism," *Palestinian Diary*. YouTube, 28 Oct 2012.

Bostrom, Nick. "Nick Bostrom on Superintelligence: Paths, Dangers, Strategies," *RSA,* YouTube, 11 Sept 2014.

Bostrom, Nick. "What happens when computers get smarter than we are?" *TED*, YouTube, 27 April 2015.

Baggini, Julian. *How the World Thinks: A Global History of Philosophy*. Granta Publications, 2018.

Big Oil v the World. BBC TV, 2022.

Bregman, Rutger. *Humankind: A Hopeful History*. Translated by Elizabeth Manton and Erica Moore. Bloomsbury, 2020.

Bregman, Rutger. *Utopia For Realists - And How We Can Get There*. Translated from Dutch by Elizabeth Manton. Bloomsbury, 2018.

Burke, Edmund. *The Evils of Revolution*. 1790. Penguin Books, 2008.

Capital in the Twenty-First Century. Directed by Justin Pemberton, Kino Lorber, 2020.

Carney, Mark. "From Moral to Market Sentiment / Credit Crunch to Resilience / Covid Crisis to Renaissance / From Climate Crisis to Real Prosperity," *Reith Lectures*. BBC, 2020.

Chang, Ha Joon. *23 Things They Don't Tell You About Capitalism.* Penguin, 2020.

Coman, Julian. "Julian Rawls: can liberalism's great philosopher [John Rawls] ride to the west's rescue again?" *The Observer*, 20 Dec 2020.

Cowen, Tyler. "Tyler Cowen on Inequality, the Future, and Average is Over 09/30/2013," *Econ Talk*, YouTube, 27 Jan 2020.

Cox, Brian, and Andrew Cohen. *The Human Universe.* William Collins, 2020.

Dworkin, Ronald. "How Universal is Liberalism," *2012 Ralf Dahrendorf Memorial Lecture,* European Studies Centre, University of Oxford Podcasts, 30 May 2012.

Engels and Marx, Karl. *The Communist Manifesto.* 1848. Penguin Books, 2004.

Epictetus. *Of Human Freedom.* Penguin Books, 2010.

Fernbach, Philip. "Prof Philip Fernbach – The Knowledge Illusion," *Ralph Shnelvar*, YouTube, 4 Oct 2017.

Gladwell, Malcolm. "Outliers: Why some people succeed and some don't," *Microsoft Research*, YouTube, 6 Sept 2016.

Gladwell, Malcolm. "Malcolm Gladwell on 'Talking to Strangers: What We Should Know about the People We Don't Know,'" *Rotman School of Management*, YouTube, 1 Oct 2019.

Grayling, A.C. "A. C. Grayling: Democracy and its Crisis," *Carnegie Council for Ethics in International Affairs*, YouTube, 27 Oct 2017.

Grayling, A.C. "Professor A.C. Grayling: Knowledge, Truth and Wisdom | University of Lincoln," 8 Dec 2017, *University of Lincoln*. YouTube, 21 Nov 2019.

Grayling, A.C. "A.C. Grayling: The Origins and Future of Humanism," *Wheeler Centre*, YouTube, 16 April 2017.

Greene, Robert. "Robert Greene | The Laws of Human Nature | Talks at Google," *Talks at Google*, YouTube, 8 July 2019.

Hariri, Yuval Noah. *21 Lessons for the 21st Century.* Vintage, 2019.

Hariri, Yuval Noah. "Yuval Harari – Sapiens: A Brief History of Humankind," *Mr, Todd*. YouTube, 11 May 2017.

BIBLIOGRAPHY

Hariri, Yuval Noah, and Daniel Kahneman. "Daniel Kahneman & Yuval Noah Harari in conversation." *Yuval Noah Harari*, YouTube, 13 April 2021.

Hallsworth, Michael, and Kirkman, Elspeth. *Behavioural Insights*. Essential Knowledge Series, MIT, 2020.

Hawken, Paul. *Drawdown*. Penguin Books, 2017.

Heller, Martin, contributing editor. "What is Machine Learning? Intelligence derived from data," *InfoWorld*, 15 May 2019, www.infoworld.com.

Hinnels, John. R., ed., *Handbook of Living Religions*. Penguin Books / Pelican Books, 1984.

Hodder, Ian. *Where Are We Heading? The Evolution of Humans and Things*. Yale University Press, 2018.

Ivereigh, Austen, and Pope Francis. *Let Us Dream: The Path to a Better Future*. Simon and Schuster UK, 2020.

Jenkins, Joe. *Introducing Moral Issues*. Heineman Educational, 1994.

Johnson, Noel. "Douglass North and the Hard Problems of Institutions – Noel Johnson," *Institute for Humane Studies*, YouTube, 29 June 2020.

Joseph, Bob. *21 Things You May Not Know About The Indian Act*. Indigenous Relations Press (Canada), 2018.

Kahneman, Daniel. "Psychologist Daniel Kahneman – Noise. Why We Make Bad Decisions and How To Avoid Them | Lecture," *Radboud Reflects*. YouTube, 2 March 2022.

Kahneman, Daniel. "Thinking, Fast and Slow | Daniel Kahneman | Talks at Google," *Talks at Google*, YouTube, 11 Nov 2011.

Kant, Immanuel. *An answer to the question 'What is Enlightenment?'* 1784, Penguin Books, 2009.

Keltner, Dacher. "Dacher Keltner, Ph.D. – 'The Power Paradox: How We Gain and Lose Influence' (05/19/16)," *Family Action Network*, 23 May 2016.

Klaas, Brian. *Corruptible: Who Gets Power and How It Changes Us*. John Murray (UK), 2021.

Krotoski, Aleks. *The Digital Human*. Series 26 Centenary series, BBC

Podcast, 2022.

Levitsky, Steven and Ziblatt, Daniel. *How Democracies Die: What History Reveals About Our Future*. Random House (U.S.A.), 2018.

Macaskill, William. *Doing Good Better – Effective Altruism And How You Can Make A Difference*. Random House, 2015.

Macaskill, William. *What We Owe The Future*. Oneworld, 2023.

Machiavelli. *Prince*. *Il Principe* 1531-2. Penguin Books, 2004.

Malik, Nesrine. *We Need Stories: Challenging the Toxic Myths Behind Our Age of Discontent*. Weidenfield and Nicholson, 2019.

Marmot, Richard. *Marmot Report. Fair Society, Healthy Lives, The Marmot Review into health inequalities in England*. 2010.

McRae, Hamish. *The World in 2050 – How to think about the future*. Bloomsbury, 2022.

Mill, J.S. *On Liberty*. 1859. Penguin Books, 2010.

Mishra, Pankaj. *From the Ruins of Empire: The Revolt Against the West and the Remaking of Asia*. Allen Lane, 2012.

Modern Conflict and Artificial Intelligence. A CIGI Essay Series. Centre for International Governance Innovation. 23 Nov 2020. https://www.cigionline.org/publications/modern-conflict-and-artificial-intelligence/

More, Thomas. *Utopia*. 1516. Penguin Books, 2009.

Morland, Paul. "229. Demography: A Window into History feat. Paul Morland," *unSILOed Podcast with Greg LaBlanc*, YouTube, 3 Jan 2023.

Morland, Paul. "The future of race relations: Demography and migration," *Institute of Art and Ideas*, IAI, Issue 89, 11 June 2020.

Morland, Paul. *Tomorrow's People: The Future of Humanity in Ten Numbers*. Pan MacMillan, 2023.

Mounck, Yascha. "Yascha Mounk: The Great Experiment," *The John Adams Institute*. YouTube, 14 April 2022.

"Nanoscience and nanotechnologies: opportunities and uncertainties," Joint Report by The Royal Society and The Royal Academy of Engineering, 30 July 2004.

Norenzayan, Ara. "Researching Religion and Prosociality | Dr Ara

Norenzayan | CERC Plenary Meeting 4 May 2013 Part 1," *Centre for Human Evolution, Cognition, and Culture.* YouTube, 31 July 2013.

Paine, Thomas. *Common Sense.* 1776. Penguin Books, 2004.

Pinker, Steven. *Enlightenment Now.* Penguin Books / Viking, 2018.

Pinker, Steven. *Think with Pinker.* BBC Podcast. BBC, 2021-2.

Pope Francis. *Encyclical Letter Fratelli Tutti of the Holy Father Frances on Fraternity and Social Friendship.* Vatican. 3 October 2020.

Pope Francis. *Encyclical Letter Laudato Si' of the Holy Father Francis on Care for our Common Home.* Vatican. 24 May 2015.

"P&P Live! Tom Burgis | Keptopia with Jennifer Taub and Bradley Hope," *Politics and Prose,* YouTube, 19 Nov 2020.

Rajan, Amol, ed., *Rethink: Leading Voices on What's Next and What's Possible.* Penguin Random House, 2022.

Robinson, James A. "Why Nations Fail | James Robinson | Talks at Google," *Talks at Google,* YouTube, 5 Nov 2015.

Robson, David. *The Expectation Effect: How Your Mindset Can Transform Your Life.* BBC Podcast, 2022.

Rousseau, Jean-Jacques. *The Social Contract. Le Contrat Social* 1762. Penguin Books, 2004.

Schopenhauer, Arthur. *The Horrors and Absurdities of Religion.* 1859. Penguin Books, 2009.

Sellers, John. *Lessons in Stoicism – What Ancient Philosophers Teach Us About How To Live.* Penguin Books, 2020.

Seneca. *On the Shortness of Life. Life is long if you know how to use it.* First Century CE. Penguin Books, 2004.

Singer, Peter. *Animal Liberation,* Random House, 1975.

Singer, Peter. "Peter Singer: Animal Liberation, Forty Years On," *Rotman Institute of Philosophy,* YouTube, 30 Sept 2015.

Singer, Peter. "Peter Singer – Meet the World's Most Influential Living Philosopher | Perspectives Podcast," *Remi (Sharon) Pearson.* YouTube. 16 July 2021.

Smith, Adam. *The Invisible Hand.* 1759. Penguin Books, 2008.

Strittmatter, Kai. *We have been harmonised: Life in China's Surveillance*

State. Old Street Publishing, 2020.

Tagore, Rabindranath. *Nationalism*. 1917. Penguin Books, 2010.

The Climate Question. BBC Podcast. 2020-1.

"3 Types of Machine Learning You Should Know About," *Coursera*. Updated 3 April 2024.

Turchin, Peter. "This View of History: A Conversation With Peter Turchin," *The Evolution Institute*, YouTube, 10 July 2018.

Turda, Marius. "Looking at Racism, Eugenics, and Biopolitics in Europe Historically: An Interview with Marius Turda," *Europe Now*, 6 Oct 2020.

Vugt, Mark van. "Selected: Why some people lead, others follow and why it matters," *RSA*, YouTube, 7 Sept 2010.

Waal, Frans de. "Frans De Waal: What Can Apes Teach Us About Politics and Society," *Room for Discussion*. YouTube, 6 June 2020.

Yueh, Linda. *The Great Economists: How their Ideas Can Help Us Today*. Penguin Books, 2019.

Index

Addiction 15, 70, 113, 148, 188, 194, 213-4, **221-3**, 372, 382, 388, 398, 409, 430, 444, 450
    Illegal Drugs 69, 114, 188, 195, 206, 211, 220-1, 224, 267, 384-5
    Legal / Future 301, 383-4, 386, 395

Afghanistan / Afghan 44, 103, 301, 342-3, 355

Africa / African *(see individual nations separately)* 83, 229, 265, 284, 287, 290, 374, 458-9
    Beliefs 82, 333-5, 339, 342, 346, 357, 366
    Colonialism and its Legacy 105, 270
    Family, Women 53, 56, 280
    Government, Economic Development 106, 115, 191, 244, 246, 252, 267, 272, 300, 309, 323, 387-8
    Tribe 225, 227-8

Agriculture, incl. Farming / farmers 43, 124, 157, 199, 271, 341, 372, 381, 415, 417-8, 451
    Beef / Meat industry 86, **275-7**, 281, 284, 417-9
    Climate 276-7, 284, 293, 317, 409
    Origins, Development, and Relation to Government 6, 94, 92-5, 207, 409

Aid (International / ODA) 86-7, 105, 180, 253, 274, 285, 288, 290, **299-302**, 321, 348

Algorithms 53, 86, 118-20, 182, 267, 296, 360, 379, 390-2, 396, 401, 403-4, 410, 437, 447

Ancient Greek 5, 9, 13, 16, 34, 36-7, 75, 98-9, 351, 368, 414
    Aristotle 13-14, 98, 208, 414
    Plato 13, 98-9, 305, 340
    Socrates 5, 11, 12-3, 80, 98, 331, 352

WHERE ARE WE GOING?

Ancient Roman 12-13, 16, 36, 304, 335, 337, 340, 368

Animal Welfare 276-7, 415-6

Artificial Intelligence (AI) 120, 180, 321, 360, 379, 383, **390-7**, 404-5, 410, 448-9, 457
    HLMI 394-5
    Regulation 179, 392, 396-7, 405, 456
    Uses 133, 179, 182, 363-4, 390-1, 393, 395, 401-6

Australia 115, 211, 289-90, 376-7, 388
    Aboriginal 249, 270, 318, 351, 402, 418

Authoritarianism 31, 88, 101, 208, 258, 264, 298, 436, 440-1, 459
    Citizens / Society 39, 41-2, 61, 77, 85, 88, 118, 185, 192, 223, 410, 439, 464
    Crime and Justice 129, 211, 225, 319
    Economy 285, 289, 302-3
    Leadership 93, 140, 179, 243, 245-6, 250
    Regimes 82, 104, 252, 262, 286, 308, 321, 324, 357, 360 342, 349, 355, 358

Baha'ism 338, 361

Biodiversity 4, 150, 178, 256, 273, 277, 283, 323, 345, 369, 372, 400, 408, 414, 416, 418

Bioscience / Biotechnology 46, 52, 66, 87, 364, **379-86**, 387, 408, 420, 448, 455-6

Black Lives Matter (BLM) 111, 127, 215, 237, 318

Brazil 5, 104, 187, 187, 249, 399, 418, 455

Bregman, Rutger 18, 70, 72, 188, 193, 205, 207, 214-5, 218, 316

Buddhism 10, 12, 15, 35-6, 82, 95, 221, 263, 331, 334-6, 344, 346-7, 353, 360, 417, 453
    Buddha 36-7, 81, 331, 334, 336, 352, 466

Capitalism 36, 71-3, 100, 118, 131, 154, 158, 160, **198-203**, 207, 239, 250, 272, 293, 297, 303, 401, 422, 458
    Capital 158-9, 176, 178, 198, 201-2, 271, 299
    Adam Smith 153 156, 158, 198

Carbon Footprint 275-7, 283, 294

China 1, 30, 114, **130-8**, 225, 244-6, 257, 307, 324, 360, 381, 407, 410, 417, 455

INDEX

Chinese Communist Party (CCP) 35, 41, 130-1, 133-5, 137, 228, 286, 308, 330, 360, 410
    Demographics / Population 51, 54, 57, 57, 280-1
    Economy 94, 110, 118, 154, 159-60, 247, 271, 285, 289-90, 295-6, 298-9, 301-2, 313, 386, 436
    Foreign Policy, incl. 'One China' 115, 245, 250-2, 307, 324, 458
    Government 82, 92, 104, 115, 128-9, 263, 319, 439, 457
    History (pre-1949) 130, 251, 245-6, 270, 272-3, 411
    Space 378, 422-3
    Xi Jinping 30, 131-3, 135, 138, 228, 360
Christian / ity 17, 22, 32, 36, 205, 231, 258, 326, 343, 355, 357
    Beliefs 9, 14, 17, 40, 206, 224-5, 339, 341, 346, 369
    (Roman) Catholic 54, 331, 333, 340, 348, 360, 369,
    Current and Future Challenges 32-4, 55, 232-3, 345, 347, 354-5, 360, 364, 414-5
    and European Empire 16, 250, 270-1, 349
    Origins / Change / Development 15, 304, 335-7, 340-1, 353-4
    Orthodox 33, 340, 360
    Papacy 1, 1̵, 15, 17, 32-4, 145, 283, 318, 340, 345, 349, 414
    Protestant 28, 340-1, 360
Citizenship 67, **75-89**, 110, 123, 212, 259, **309-11**, 314, 421, 441
Class 11, 18, 35, 43,-4, 53, 60, 93, 159, 176, 212, 225-7, 229, **237-9**, 240, 259, 310, 359-60, 380, 384, 401, 415, 417
    Middle class 2, 23-4, 44, 64, 110, 193, 203, 227, 419
Climate Change 29, 32, 34, 86-7, 115, 162, 172, 201, 246, 268, 271, **274-84**, 290, 292, 303, 369-73, 396, 416, 418, 421, 437, 447, 452
    Environmental and Resource Sustainability 3, 64, 155, 162, 178, 277-8, 281, 293-4, 300, 322-3, 323, 373, 378, 394, 404, 408, 416, 452, 461
    Global Co-operation 82, 137, 147, 162, 246, 290, 318, 320, 408, 449-50, 459, 461
    and Religion 326, 349-50, 362, 414
Cold War 70, 105, 154, 202, 250, 260, 305, 360, 378, 422, 458
Colonialism (/Imperialism) 24, 31, 35, 92, 105, 111, 137, 206, 234, 247, 249-51, 257, 273, 285, 294, 300, 305-8, 336-7, 342, 348, 360, 409, 411, 444, 458-9
    Effects of 29, 225, 231-2, 242, 249, 258, 272, 329, 349, 437

475

and the Enlightenment 16, 31, 101, 361, 445
Post-colonial 75, 105, 107, 115, 128, 244, 248, 250, 271, 273, 300, 358
Communism 22, 81-2, 106, 136, 156, 159, 202, 238, 250-1, 305, 322, 342, 354, 360, 458, 464
Confucianism 9, 136, 272, 307, 309, 331
and CCP 35, 130, 364, 453
Confucius 34-5, 37, 81, 94, 98, 130, 352, 464
Principles 34-6, 82, 130, 212, 223, 330, 453
Consumerism 24, 101, 118, 121, 127, 161
Covid-19 4, 28, 32, 161-2, 188, 191, 197, 200, 203, 227, 286, 292, 314, 320,
China 132-4, 136
Response to 27, 77, 108-9, 122, 134, 137, 167-9, 245, 318, 324, 407, 410, 440
Science 116, 186, 371, 409, 447

DNA 68, 134, 142, 168, 240, 257, 261, 275, 374, 380, 399
Darwin/ism 11, 19, 231, 342, 344, 371, 377, 455, 463
Eugenics 19, 231-2, 381, 385, 445, 455

Employment 78, 87, 121, 162, 176, 181, 184, 184, 189, 218, 225, 227.275. 297-8, 310, 312, 399, 443
Unemployment 159, 161, 166, 180, 189, 193, 227-8
Enlightenment, *The* 5, 16-7, 41, 45, 97, 99, 127, 131, 229, 258, 353, 361, 464
'New' 6, 17, 25, 31-2, 203, 240, 353, 412, 438, 442, **445-7**, 450, 458, 460, 465
'old', 'European', 'original' 6, 16, 24, 31, 97, 101, 127, 229-31, 271, 273, 294, 304, 309, 369, 414-5, 437
and Religion 14-5, 32-3, 325, 343, 363, 453
and Science 17, 363, 368-9
Entanglement (Theory) 94, 409, 448
Ethics 13, 116, 140, 144, 149, 179, 181, 202, 205, 267, 296-7, 320, 331, 364, 380-1, 384-5, 392, 405, 432-3, 439, 454-5, 457, 463
European Union / EU 114, 154, 199, 243-4, 296, 301, 305, 311-2, 323, 389

INDEX

Fossil fuel 178, 252, 275, 278, 296, 371, 407
    Coal 178, 278
    Gas 178, 275, 278, 283, 289, 303
    Oil 154, 178, 188, 247, 253, 275, 289, 291, 303, 371
France 54, 99-100, 278-9, 325, 444
    French Revolution 17, 24, 262, 414
Free speech 26, 28, 30, 41, 80, 85, 103, 112, 148, 236, 362, 388
Free Trade 24, 27, 155-8, 285, 288, 290, 294, 301-2

Gender 17-8, 55, 142-3, 209, 221, 417, 442
    Choice / Redefinition 49, 54, 345-6, 362, 454
    Discrimination 3-4, 6, 150, 162, 165, 172, 206, 226, 229, **231-4**, 240-1, 273, 326, 360, 438, **441-3**
    Equality 15, 61, 236, 282, 291, 300, 338, 345, 351
Germany 31, 54, 131, 170, 199, 229, 245, 278, 278, 283, 304, 308
    Nazi Germany 31, 41
    Population / Immigration 282, 312-3
Global Dialogue 29, 32, 34-7, 50, 69, 74, 78, 80, 83, 97, 92, 150, **316-22**, 324, 331, 347, 349, 355, 363-4, 389-90, 408, 421, 428, 434-5, 438-9, 445, 453, 457, 460
Governance 6, 17, 19, 37, 85-6, 88, 105, 107, 148-9, 166, 200, 202-3, 227, 266, 288, 291-3, 300, 302, 320, 437, 459
    Civil Service 93, 270, 292, 306
Gross Domestic Product (GDP) 159-60, 166, 174, 190, 199, 284, 286-7, 287, 293-4, 299, 422

Healthcare 38, 154, 161-2, 164, **166-9**, 174, 275, 281-2, 322, 380-1, 420
Hindu / ism 9, 35, 242, 306, 331, 334, 353, 364
    Beliefs and Challenges 15, 35, 328, 338, 344, 347, 359,
    Caste 11, 35, 53, 93, 225-6, 233, 307, 318, 334, 359
    and Government 51, 114, 307, 358-9, 364
HIV / AIDS 169, 300, 370
Hobbes, Thomas 16, 22, 99, 207-8, 230
Holocaust 9, 31, 37, 211, 232, 258, 357

WHERE ARE WE GOING?

Homo Sapien 3, 11, 71, 84, 369, **374-6**, 408, 425

Housing 54, 78, 87, 112, 122, 166, 183, 198, 212, 218, 219-20, 220, 293, 314-5, 317, 354, 444, 452

    Property 22, 63-4, 78, 81, 101, 109-10, 157-8, 161, 170, 177, 200, 207, 292

Hungary 228, 282-3, 312

Identity Politics 110-2, 124, 237, 441, 449

India 35, 51, 225, 236, 267, 313, 318, 324, 342-3, 364, 372, 378, 411, 417, 458-9

    Economy 110, 195, 289, 299-301
    Family, Population, Women 54-5, 221, 226, 280-1, 307
    Government 52, 114, 319, 357-9, 364
    History 244, 248, 270, 272, 306, 336
    Rabindranath Tagore 75, 271-2, 305, 411-2

Indigenous Peoples 82, 115, 231, 235, 246, 249, 270-1, 294

    Beliefs (Animistic, Totemic, Spirit) 82, 93, 95, 327-8, 330-4, 337, 415, 425-6, 442, 444

Indonesia 104, 267, 287, 289, 301, 332-3, 355, 374, 418

Industrial / Industry 24, 34, 45, 59, 62, 64, 130, 139, 159, 174, 180, 182, 188, 201, 283-4, 297, 322, 369, 371-2, 391, 396, 401, 408, 417-9, 421, 423, 443, 451-3

    Industrialisation 22-3, 36, 59, 82, 100, 130, 157, 164, 207, 246, 270-1, 293, 409, 411
    Industrial Revolution 180, 293, 437

Infrastructure - Civic 30, 34, 87, 123, 136, 161-2, 165, 173-4, 189-90, 198, 271, 288, 436

Infrastructure - Physical 136, 156, 158, 161, 181, 187, 198-9, 202, 251, 256, 279, 281, 283, 288-9, 292, 298, 300, 313, 394, 398, 415

Inheritance (of wealth) 50, 63-4, 79, 87, 139, 157, 160-1, 170-1, 177, 200, 237, 239, -421, 435

Internet 49, 133-4, 149, 180-1, 222, 241, 267, 299, 303, 363, **387-90**

Iran 51, 252-3, 356-7

    Family, Women and Hijab protests 49, 54, 56, 280, 291, 343-4
    Government 31, 129, 251, 263, 337, 342-3, 355-6, 358-9, 458
    Revolutionary Guards 128-9

INDEX

Islam 9, 106, 115, 251-2, 291, 304, 307, 336, 338, 349, 356-7, 360, 364
    Beliefs 14-5, 19, 33, 224-5, 337, 341, 343, 352
    and Government 103, 129, 258, 272, 334, 342-3, 354-6
    Origins, Historic Changes 337, 341-4, 364
    Shia / Sunni 251, 337-8, 342, 355, 360
    Wahhabism 307, 337, 342-3, 356
    Women, Family 54, 221, 226, 233
Islamic State (ISIS, Daesh) 211, 309, 364
Israel 154, 249, **257-9**, 306, 357-9

Jamal al-din al-Afghani 272, 342
Japan 75, 114, 299, 307, 359, 373
    Beliefs / Philosophy 14, 83, 333-4
    Economy 190, 295, 407
    History 41, 104, 130, 272-3
    Population, Family, Women 54, 181, 226, 282, 291, 306, 312, 315
Judaism 70, 258-9, 336
    Anti-Semitism 119, 231, 258, 348
    Divisions 224, 335, 357-8
    and Government 357-8
    Origins and Beliefs 14, 33, 206, 224, 335, 337, 340-1, 354, 357, 414

Kant, Immanuel 5, 99, 429

Liang Qichao 272
Liberalism 27-31, **36-8**, 51, 81, 115, 123, 138, 348
Libertarian 41, 81, 88, 100, 175, 464
Life Expectancy 23, 51, 60, 167, 198, 227-8, 227, 274, 286-7, 301, 364, 384-5, 419-21, 427, 430, 456
Luddite 49, 128, 406

Machiavellian 10, 75, 96, 125, 139, 232
Machine Learning 52, 87, 363, 379, 383, **390-7**, 401, 403-4, 447-8, 456
    (also see Algorithms, Artificial Intelligence)
Materialism 21, 23-4, 80, 82, 85, 101, 121, 157-8, 200, 202, 266, 270,

WHERE ARE WE GOING?

        294, 307, 321, 354-6, 411, 444, 449, 465

Media 3, 26, 92, 184, 211, 221, 226, 250, 267, 280, 298, 459
    Independent, in society 101, 104-7, 119, 132, 139, 144, 149, 265, 321, 359, 436, 440-1, 463
    'Social media' 26, 33, 46, 53, 86,104, 118, 122, 133, 221-2, 233, 269, 296, 363, 391-3, 437, 463

#Metoo 111, 137, 221

Meritocracy 124, 126, 149, 177, 237-9

Mexico 54, 105, 267, 289, 313, 333, 340, 359

Middle East incl. Israel-Palestine *(see individual nations separately)* 56, 211, 291
    'Arab Spring' 49, 104, 263, 318
    Conflict 249, 252-3, **257-9**, 258, 265, 357-8
    Government 103, 115, 258
    Religion 251, 335-7, 342-3

Migration 62, 105, 239-40, 253, 294, 286, 309, **311-16**
    Global nature, flow 4, 11, 98, 178, 201, 233, 267, 319, 364, 402, 457
    Emigration 258, 300, 304, 308, 316
    Immigration Concern, Rejection 127, 234, 283, 300, 304, 320
    Immigration and Multiculturalism 306, 311, 345, 348
    Migrant Labour 2, 313-4

More, Thomas 21, 24, 75, 206, 223, 321

Multi-cultural 55, 236, 244, 268, 306-7, 309, 311, 348, 363

Nationalism 4, 110, 115, 271-2, 303-4, **304-9**, 312-3, 353, 367, 464
    and the State 107, 131, 137, 211, 320, 342, 358, 360, 408,

NATO 252, 305

New Zealand 115, 117, 245, 265, 270, 273, 290
    Maori 19, 117, 332-3

Nigeria 106, 227, 248, 281, 290

North, Douglass 10, 73, 203, 291, 320

North Korea 114, 129, 246

Norway 214, 217, 289

Nuclear Energy / Power **278-80**, 284, 410, 449

Nuclear Weapons 260, 262, 265, 322, 449, 455, 459

INDEX

Obama, President Barack 87, 269, 317
Occupy Movement 154-5, 161, 287, 318

Pinker, Steven 72-3, 206, 465
Population
    Ageing 167, 181, 247
    Birth Rate 280-3, 290, 306, 311-2, 316
    Control / Family Planning 274, **280-4**
    Demography 48-9, 163, 166, 254, 270, 287, 314, 378, 456
Populism 26, 122, 124-6, 128, 146, 155, 161, 243, 258, 269, 286, 305, 358, 390, 406,
Propaganda 18-19, 41, 47, 65-6, 68, 119, 131, 133, 136, 236, 261, 319, 346, 359, 389, 463
    Censorship 65-6, 121, 131-3, 319, 463

Race 17, 24, 26, 29, 49, 137, 150, 229, 304-5, 337
    Affirmative action 236-7
    Racial Discrimination 4, 6, 119-20, 133, 206, **231-9**, 240-1, 249-50, 268, 360, 391, 338, 441, 455 *(also see Slavery)*
    Roma and Traveller Prejudice 228-9
    in the USA 107, 225, 227, 246, 308
Rawls, John 37-8, 80, 464
Reformation 28, 38, 205, 304, 353, 369
Religion *(see specific religions separately)* 3, 13-14, 23, 33-4, 71, 123, 222, 322, **325-365**, 420, 437, 445, **452-4**
    and Conflict 247-8, 258,
    and the 'Golden Rule' 14, 79,
Leadership and Government 92, 95-6, 163, 207,
    and Science 368, 370, 404, 407,
    and Women, Family, Equality, Individualism 15, 19, 55-6, 58, 233, 240,
Renaissance 16, 304, 353, 369, 447
Revolution
    Economic and Scientific 180, 294, 386, 437, 453, 461
    Political 16, 24, 99-100, 104, 262, 342, 414, 464
    Social, Religious, Cultural Revolution (in China) 1, 3, 36, 129-

32, 344, 359
    Rights Revolutions 24-5, 48-9, 441-2
    Civil Rights 229, 318
    Human Rights 11, 28, 44, 101, 200, 208, 221, 229, 248, 253-4, 256, 322, 389, 395, **404-8**
    Universal Rights or Values 6, 58, 132, 136
Russia 72, 115, 128, 211, 289, 305, 319, 324, 422
    Early history, Soviet Union / USSR 130, 132, 154, 244, 246, 250-1, 272, 286, 305, 378, 410
    Putin 30, 129, 249, 251, 324
    Ukraine, and Values 29, 137, 178, 186, 247-9, 251-2

Sanctions (international) 247, 252, 288, 356

Saudi Arabia 54, 103, 252, 295, 313, 322, 343, 355-8, 458

Secularism 14, **23-8**, 29, 32, 36, 40, 52, 76, 96, 114, 271, 326-7, 342-3, 360, 364

Sikhism 15, 335, 348, 352

Singer, Peter 4, 413, 414-6, 419

Slavery 15-16, 24, 31, 73, 75, 98, 211-2, 229, 234, 249, 272, 308, 333, 336, 340, 342, 409, 412, 437

Socialism 100, 131, 159-60, 251, 272

Social Care 2, 50, 64, 167, 171, 181, 211, 405

Social Contract 83, 100, 157, 161, **162-77**, 178, 192, 197, 200-2, 207, 209, 213, 256, 304, 461
    Jean-Jacques Rousseau 99, 153, 157, 207

South Korea 92, 104, 114, 122, 180, 281, 289, 295, 440

Spirituality 1, 24, 32-3, 82-3, 266, 272, 326, 330, 350, 352, 360, 409, 411

Stoicism 12, 76, 98

Taiwan 104, 136, 138, 244-5, 251, 307

Taliban 44, 103, 307, 355, 364

Transport 92, 134, 176, 183, 193, 275, 276, 281, 333, 452
    Car 39, 135, 181, 237, 281, 404, 407
    (Aero)Plane 281, 284, 398

INDEX

Ukraine 29, 137, 186, 247-9, 251-2, 278, 286, 319-20, 324, 335

United Kingdom (UK) (incl. Great Britain) 27, 33, 100, 281, 304, 322, 370, 372, 444

    Economy / Science, Foreign Policy, Government 27, 108, 111, 114, 173-4, 188, 190-1, 253, 290, 299-300, 381, 386

    Society 2, 51, 54-5, 166, 206, 211-4, 219-20, 225, 227-8, 231, 310, 312-3, 326, 354, 416-7

United Nations (UN) 28, 41, 200, 208, 229, 242, 248-9, 252-3, **254-7**, 280-1, 290-1, 299-300, 322-3, 357, 426, 458-9

    General Assembly (GA) 252, 255-6, 299, 322, 459

United States of America (USA) 29, 53-5, 59, 206, 211, 214, 217-8, 276, 291, 308, 313, 333, 422-5

    Discrimination and Inequality 194, 212, 215, 225, 227, 236, 246, 388

    Economy 56, 155, 160, 173-4, 176, 181, 192-3, 199, 289-90, 295-6, 401

    Foreign Policy / Relations, incl. Aid 250, 285, 299, 324, 378

    Government and Politics 27, 81, 114, 167, 173, 175, 192-3, 243, 308, 309, 381, 449

    Urbanisation 35, 53, 59, 94, 100, 115, 124, 164, 207, 238, 209, 354, 368, 418, **451-2**

Utilitarianism 24, 30, 38, 100

Wealth 21, 23, 110, 147, 172, 175, 192, 310, 451, 465

    Inherited wealth, Generational wealth, and Inequality 50, 63-4, 79, 87, 100, 113, 155-6, 161-2, 170-1, 177, 200, 237-8, 274, 318, 421, 435-6

    of Nations, and Global Wealth 56, 62, 128-9, 160, 182, 184, **286-95**, 303, 306-9, 323, 418

    Meaning of, and Wealth Creation 42-3, 111, 121, 153-4, 156-60, 188, 190, 198-9, 207, 256, 270, 284, 303, 409, 418, 446, 461

Welfare 62, 154, 162, 165, 174, **192-8**, 315

    Attitudes to 70, 74, 216-8, 222, 348, 352, 362, 455

    Development of 50, 61-2, 73, 100, 158, 164, 212-8, 222-3, 281, 300

    Welfare Net / Dependency / Support 60, 161-2, 168, 189, 192, 213, 280

Author Bio

Paul Hodson was born in Lincoln, where he now lives and works as a writer and researcher. He has worked as a secondary school History teacher in a range of schools and locations including Lincolnshire, Kent, inner and outer London and the Middle East. This is his second published book.

Previous Works by the Author

English and British History in 100 Bite-size Chunks,
2020

www.ingramcontent.com/pod-product-compliance
Lightning Source LLC
Chambersburg PA
CBHW011750220426
43670CB00020B/2935